Units 11–13

Management accounting

Study Pack

Technician (NVQ Level 4)

Published May 1996 by Financial Training, 10–14 White Lion Street, London N1 9PE

ISBN 1 85179 704 1

This text has been published by Financial Training, one of the leading providers of training in accountancy and finance. Although it is aimed at students on the Education and Training Scheme of the Association of Accounting Technicians (AAT) it is not published or approved directly by the AAT. Any queries on the Education and Training Scheme and AAT Administration should be addressed to Student Services at AAT, 154 Clerkenwell Road, London EC1R 5AD (0171 837 8600).

We are grateful to the Association of Accounting Technicians for their kind permission to reproduce tasks from the central assessments.

All business entities referred to in this publication are fictitious. Any resemblance to any actual organisation, past or present, is purely coincidental.

Contents

Introduction

Units 11, 12 and 13 are each assessed by a two hour central assessment which can be taken in June or December. Although we have combined them into one study pack, they can be studied separately if required. However, there is quite a lot of overlap between these units and it does make sense to study the units together.

Listed below are the performance criteria for each unit with references to which session in this pack covers those criteria.

PERFORMANCE CRITERIA

Each unit is divided into three or four elements which are in turn divided into performance criteria, as follows:

Unit 11: Preparing information for cost analysis and control

Element 1 Prepare and present standard cost reports   *Sessions*

■ Standard cost reports with variances clearly identified are presented in an intelligible form   4, 11

■ Unusual or unexpected results are identified and brought to the attention of managers   4

■ Any reasons for significant variances from standard are discovered and the explanations presented to management   4, 5

■ More detailed analysis and explanation of specific variances is produced for management, on request   5

■ Staff working in operational departments are consulted to resolve any queries in the data   5

Element 2 Analyse accounting information

■ Relevant data are identified and analysed in accordance with defined criteria   6, 8

■ Relevant ratio calculations highlight significant relationships in the data   6

■ Significant trends are identified and brought to the attention of management   6, 9

■ Timely information is presented to managers in a clear and appropriate form   1, 3, 6, 8

Element 3 Collect, analyse and disseminate information about external costs

■ Reports highlighting significant trends are presented to management in an appropriate form   1, 6, 9

■ Valid, relevant information is identified from internal and external sources   6, 9

■ Trends in prices are monitored and analysed on a regular basis   6, 9

■ Forecasts of trends and changes in factor prices and market conditions are reasonably consistent with actual experience — 6, 9

■ Staff in the organisation who can contribute towards the analysis of external trends are consulted — 1, 9

Element 4 Contribute to the reduction of costs and the enhancement of value

■ Specific contributions towards the objectives of cost reduction, quality improvement and value enhancement are made after full discussion with relevant specialists — 7

■ Routine cost reports are assessed, compared with other sources of information and findings recommended to management in a clear and appropriate form — 1, 6, 7

■ Relevant performance indicators are monitored and assessed — 7, 8

■ Special reports to follow up matters which require further investigation are prepared — 7, 8

Unit 12: Operating a budgetary control system

Element 1 Prepare forecasts of income and expenditure

■ Forecasts are made available to operational departments in a clear, easily understood, format, with explanations of assumptions, projections and adjustments — 10

■ Relevant data for projecting forecasts of income and expenditure are identified — 9, 10

■ Appropriate adjustments are made for changing price levels and seasonal trends — 9, 10

■ Forecasts take account of significant anticipated changes in circumstances which would affect the validity of the statistically derived calculations — 9, 10

■ Personnel who might contribute towards making realistic forecasts of trends are consulted — 9, 10

Element 2 Produce draft budget proposals

■ Draft budget proposals, agreed with budget-holders, are consistent with organisational objectives, realistic and potentially achievable — 10

■ Draft budget proposals agreed with budget-holders are consistent with organisational objectives, realistic and potentially achievable — 10

■ Annual budgets are broken down into periods in accordance with anticipated seasonal trends — 10

- Discussions with budget-holders are conducted in a manner which maintains goodwill   10

Element 3 Monitor the actual performance of responsibility centres against budgets

- Variances are clearly identified and reported to management in routine reports   4, 5, 11

- Actual cost and revenue data are correctly coded and allocated to responsibility centres   2, 4, 5

- Budget figures are checked and reconciled on an ongoing basis   10, 11

- Significant actual requested or potential over-/under-spends are discussed with managers and assistance given in taking remedial action   5, 11

Unit 13: Preparing information for the appraisal of activities

Element 1 Prepare cost estimates

- Estimates are prepared in an approved form and presented to the appropriate recipient(s) within an agreed timescale   12, 14

- Appropriate staff are consulted about technical aspects and any special features of projects   12, 14

- Current material, labour and other variable costs are identified and future trends assessed   2, 9, 13

- Estimates account for the effect of possible variations in capacity on fixed overhead rates   2, 12

- Cost estimates are monitored and checked against actual costs incurred and significant discrepancies investigated   11, 12

Element 2 Evaluate proposed current activities

- Recommendations are logically derived and clearly reported   12, 13

- Internal and external information relevant to making a decision is identified and used   13, 14

- Costs relevant to the decision to be made are identified and only those are used in making a recommendation   13

- Alternative solutions are assessed and tested using relevant accounting concepts   13

- Technical, marketing and other relevant specialists are consulted when conducting an evaluation   13

Element 3 Contribute to the appraisal of long-term projects

- Recommendations which optimise the long-term benefits to the organisation are clearly reported   14, 15

■ Internal and external information relevant in estimating future costs and revenues are used   13, 14, 15

■ Technical, marketing and other relevant specialists are consulted when conducting a project appraisal   14

CENTRAL ASSESSMENT

Management accounting

There will be three separate central assessments for Units 11–13:

Unit 11 *Preparing information for cost analysis and control* (2 hours)
Unit 12 *Operating a budgetary control system* (2 hours)
Unit 13 *Preparing information for the appraisal of activities and projects* (2 hours)

For each central assessment, you will be provided with a question booklet and a separate answer booklet into which you should write your answers.

What will be covered?

The central assessments will test a selection of performance criteria plus the related aspects of knowledge and understanding. Typical formats and contents have emerged from past sittings and assessor's statements as follows. Please note that all tasks must be completed.

Unit 11 *Preparing information for cost analysis and control* (2 hours)

The assessment is likely to be divided into two parts, each with a number of tasks. It may be in a case study format, with some initial data given concerning a particular organisation to which some or all of the tasks will be related.

The tasks will assess the student's ability to apply basic management accounting techniques in simple business situations. Examples of such tasks would include:

●   Preparation and presentation of standard costing reports

●   Calculation of materials, labour and overhead variances, and discussion of possible causes and/or responsibility

●   Analysis of accounting information, including graphical presentation, index numbers, general price changes and the analysis of trends

●   Accounting ratios and performance indicators (calculation and interpretation)

●   Use of published statistics and other sources of information about external costs and revenue trends

●   Cost reduction, quality improvement and value enhancement

Relevant underpinning knowledge as defined in the standards will also be tested including a basic understanding of such topics as:

●   Activity-based costing
●   Time series analysis
●   Total quality management

- Value, SWOT and cost benefit analysis

Unit 12 *Operating a budgetary control system* (2 hours)

The assessment is likely to be divided into two parts, each with a number of tasks. It may again be in case study format, as for the Unit 11 assessment.

The tasks will assess the student's ability to apply basic management accounting techniques in simple business situations. Examples of such tasks would include the following:

- Preparation and presentation of forecasts of income and expenditure, including allowance for price changes

- Preparation of budgets

- Flexible budgeting

- Co-ordination of the budgeting system

- Reporting to budget-holders, including budgetary control statements incorporating basic variances

Relevant underpinning knowledge as defined in the standards will also be tested including a basic understanding of such topics as:

- Types of budget
- Sources of data for budget forecasts
- Time series analysis
- The effect of capacity levels on budgets
- Key factors
- The effect of budgetary control systems on the motivation of managers

Unit 13 *Preparing information for the appraisal of activities and projects* (2 hours)

The assessment is likely to be divided into two parts, each with a number of tasks. It may again be in case study format, as for the Unit 11 assessment.

The tasks will assess the student's ability to apply basic management accounting techniques in simple business situations. Examples of such tasks would include:

- Preparation of cost estimates

- Submission of tenders and quotations

- Presentation of information to guide short-term decisions of the 'make or buy' type

- Pricing decisions

- Appraisal of long-term projects using payback and DCF techniques

- Marginal cost presentations to aid production decisions, such as the discontinuance of products

- Break-even analysis

- Identification of relevant costs, including opportunity costs

Relevant underpinning knowledge as defined in the standards will also be tested including a basic understanding of such topics as:

- Cost behaviour, including the identification of fixed, variable and semi-variable costs
- Basic principles of risk analysis (expected monetary return)
- Marginal costing
- Identification of limiting factors
- Economic basis of pricing policies

Common problems with central assessments for Units 11–13

The assessor has made the following comments on the performance of candidates in past central assessments of these units:

General comments (applicable to all units)

- There was some improvement in the students' ability to carry out computations but students were rarely able to interpret the results of their calculations. Inadequate skills in these areas were still the most common reason for failing to demonstrate competence.

Comments on particular tasks

- Unit 11 *Preparing information for cost analysis and control* (2 hours)

    - Several candidates were unable to prepare an appropriate reconciliation statement (*of total standard direct cost of production to the actual direct cost, using variances calculated*).

    - Some very vague answers were given of the meaning of the variances.

    - A significant number of candidates had no idea of what was meant by interdependence of variances.

    - Few candidates suggested more than one or two items of information which might be needed (*to determine the standard price per kg of material*) and they were very vague about where this information might be found. Many wasted time discussing at length how the standard material usage might be determined.

    - A few candidates were able to provide a reasonable interpretation of the accounting ratios but most could not explain them clearly and did not comment on their limitations.

- Unit 12 *Operating a budgetary control system* (2 hours)

    - Several answers (to a question on principal budget factors and budget co-ordination) gave detailed descriptions of participative budgeting which was only partly relevant to this assessment task and few marks could be awarded.

    - Most candidates did not use the data, as requested, to illustrate their explanations (of seasonal variations and of a trend line).

    - The most common error was to forecast the trend data correctly but then to omit to adjust for the seasonal variations.

    - The most common error (in preparing a flexible budget) was to treat indirect labour as a variable cost, despite the description of the fixed element given in the assessment data.

    - The standard of presentation (of a budgetary control statement) was often disappointing.

- Unit 13 *Preparing information for the appraisal of activities and projects* (2 hours)

  – The most common problem (in a break-even analysis question) was failing to note the problems associated with forecasting the costs and revenues for an activity level outside the relevant range.

  – Very few candidates correctly identified all the relevant costs but many made logical assumptions for which full credit was given.

  – It is disappointing to note that a large number of candidates still do not know how to deal with opportunity costs.

  – Many candidates were able to calculate the payback period correctly but did not provide an adequate explanation of the advantages and disadvantages of the payback method.

What the assessor is looking for

From the above comments on past candidates' performances, it can be seen that the assessor places importance upon the following factors.

A high level of basic costing knowledge

Before addressing the more advanced topics, such as activity-based costing or value analysis, you must ensure that your knowledge of basic costing topics studied in earlier units is sound.

Relevant answers

If you do not know the answer to the question being asked, do not give an answer to a question you do know about! It will not earn you marks and will waste time.

Ability to explain

At Technician level, it is not enough simply to get the calculations correct. You need to be able to demonstrate a clear understanding of the principles, assumptions and limitations of the techniques upon which the calculations are based.

Ability to interpret results

Once you have calculated your answers, you need to be able to make sensible comments on what they show and their relevance to the particular management function being addressed.

You must make your comments specific to the particular situation rather than list out all possible interpretations whether they are likely to apply or not.

Answering all the requirements

No matter how good your answer is to pat (a) of the task, if you ignore part (b) you cannot expect to earn full marks. Watch out for several requirements being included in one sentence.

Good presentation

You should aim to present your work as if it were to be submitted to management. However, if you do make mistakes, do not use correcting fluid, but cross them out neatly.

If you are required to prepare a statement or schedule, think about its layout before starting work. Put any detailed computational workings on a separate page and cross-reference them to the main answer.

How to tackle the central assessment

Always read all the instructions before starting

Although it is likely that you will be required to complete all tasks in the assessment, always check that this is the case.

Ensure you note the advised amount of time to spend on each section, given at the start of the assessment.

Allocate your time sensibly between sections and tasks

The timings given at the start of the paper indicate the relative importance placed upon them by the assessor. Do not overrun these times significantly – leave unfinished tasks at the end of the time and move on, but do allow yourself some time at the end to return to them and complete them as far as possible.

Work through the paper in the order set

Although each section will be largely self-contained, it is quite likely that there will be some link (for example, they may all involve the same organisation). Some of the tasks in later sections may relate to information given or computations from earlier ones.

Read the data and requirements for each task carefully and fully before starting work

Note all details given of the business you are dealing with to ensure your answers are tailored to its particular business and circumstances.

Ensure that all parts of the requirements are addressed in the required format (schedule, table, statement, memorandum, etc.) and comply with the requirement to explain, discuss, comment, suggest, etc.

Consider using examples from previous tasks to illustrate explanations; you must, of course, do this if it is specifically required.

If asked for *four* causes/actions/examples, etc. comply with this exactly – extra ones will not earn you extra credit; they will just be ignored.

THE ROLE OF STUDY

Studying for different reasons

Finally, we need to consider the role of study within the scheme. Whatever your previous experience, you will inevitably need to devote a considerable amount of time to studying, even if it is only to familiarise yourself with the coverage and likely content and format of the central assessment. This Study Pack contains study and practice material covering all the performance criteria and knowledge and understanding required for this unit.

The objective of this Study Pack is to provide you with:

● guidance on completing the central assessment for this unit

● study material and practice materials to prepare you for the central assessment

Using this Study Pack

Whatever your previous experience, you are therefore encouraged to work through the Study Pack, paying attention to the areas which are most relevant to you. Here is a short explanation of the aim of each aspect of this Study Pack and the areas in which they are relevant. This will help you decide.

Sessions 1–7

Study material and examples on particular topics to help you learn the required techniques. The relevant performance criteria are identified at the start of each session. In addition, the knowledge and understanding required for that topic are included within that session.

The questions at the end of each session are designed to enable you to consolidate your knowledge as you progress through the Study Pack.

Practice central assessment

A practice central assessment in the style of the real Central Assessment. Try to sit it under exam conditions, giving yourself a clear three hours of uninterrupted time to complete the task.

How sessions relate to Units 11–13

The following table indicates the sessions of this Study Pack that you should study for each of the units. Note that some sessions are common to two or three units.

	Relevant to Unit		
Study Pack Session	*11*	*12*	*13*
1	√	√	√
2	√	√	√
3	√	√	
4	√	√	
5	√	√	
6	√		
7	√		
8	√		
9	√	√	
10		√	
11		√	
12			√
13			√
14			√
15			√

Further study material

The Financial Training Company also publishes a *Central Assessment Pack* designed to give you additional practice towards the Central Assessment for this unit. As well as containing new exercises of the sort featured in the real central assessments, it also contains brief revision notes on all major topics and a mock central assessment *in the style of the real central assessment*. The Central Assessment Packs are available from your usual supplier of Financial Training Company study materials.

PUBLISHER'S NOTE

Financial Training study materials are distributed in the UK and overseas by Stanley Thornes (Publishers) Limited. They are another company within the Wolters Kluwer group. They can be contacted at: Stanley Thornes, Ellenborough House, Wellington Street, Cheltenham GL50 1YD. Telephone: (01242) 228888. Fax: (01242) 221914.

Your chances of success in the AAT assessments will be greatly improved by additional tuition, either at one of Financial Training's centres or by home study. For details of our open learning programmes please contact us at:

The Financial Training Company

1st Floor, Centre City Tower, 7 Hill Street, BIRMINGHAM B5 4UA
Tel: 0121- 625 1296/Fax:0121-625 1297

5th Floor, Market Chambers, 5-7 St Mary Street, CARDIFF CF1 2AT
Tel: 01222-388 067/Fax: 01222-327 408

49 St Pauls Street, LEEDS LS1 2TE
Tel: 0113-245 7455/Fax: 0113-242 8889

3rd Floor, Beckville House, 66 London Road, LEICESTER LE2 0QD
Tel: 0116-285 6767/Fax: 0116-285 6787

3rd Floor, Coopers Building, Church Street, LIVERPOOL L1 3AA
Tel: 0151-708 8839/Fax: 0151-709 4264

10 – 14 White Lion Street, LONDON N1 9PE
Tel: 0171-837 1898/Fax: 0171-278 1693

3rd Floor, Excalibur Building, 77 Whitworth Street, MANCHESTER M1 6EZ
Tel: 0161-236 9646/Fax: 0161-2369047

Provincial House, Northumberland Street, NEWCASTLE-UPON-TYNE NE1 7DQ
Tel: 0191-232 9365/Fax: 0191-232 2115

1st Floor, Victoria House, 76 Milton Street, NOTTINGHAM NG1 3QZ
Tel: 0115-950 8088/Fax: 0115-950 5104

Pegasus House, 463a Glossop Road, SHEFFIELD S10 2QD
Tel: 0114-266 9265/Fax: 0114-268 4084

32 Castle Way, SOUTHAMPTON SO14 2AW
Tel: 01708-220852/Fax: 01708-634379

Swift House, Market Place, WOKINGHAM RG11 1AP
Tel: 01734-774922/Fax: 01734-894029

Mathematical tables

PRESENT VALUE TABLES

Present value of 1, ie. $\dfrac{1}{(1+r)^n}$

where r = discount rate

n = number of periods until payment

Discount rates (r)

Periods (n)	1%	2%	3%	4%	5%	6%	7%	8%	9%	10%	
1	0.990	0.980	0.971	0.962	0.952	0.943	0.935	0.926	0.917	0.909	1
2	0.980	0.961	0.943	0.925	0.907	0.890	0.873	0.857	0.842	0.826	2
3	0.971	0.942	0.915	0.889	0.864	0.840	0.816	0.794	0.772	0.751	3
4	0.961	0.924	0.888	0.855	0.823	0.792	0.763	0.735	0.708	0.683	4
5	0.951	0.906	0.863	0.822	0.784	0.747	0.713	0.681	0.650	0.621	5
6	0.942	0.888	0.837	0.790	0.746	0.705	0.666	0.630	0.596	0.564	6
7	0.933	0.871	0.813	0.760	0.711	0.665	0.623	0.583	0.547	0.513	7
8	0.923	0.853	0.789	0.731	0.677	0.627	0.582	0.540	0.502	0.467	8
9	0.914	0.837	0.766	0.703	0.645	0.592	0.544	0.500	0.460	0.424	9
10	0.905	0.820	0.744	0.676	0.614	0.558	0.508	0.463	0.422	0.386	10
11	0.896	0.804	0.722	0.650	0.585	0.527	0.475	0.429	0.388	0.350	11
12	0.887	0.788	0.701	0.625	0.557	0.497	0.444	0.397	0.356	0.319	12
13	0.879	0.773	0.681	0.601	0.530	0.469	0.415	0.368	0.326	0.290	13
14	0.870	0.758	0.661	0.577	0.505	0.442	0.388	0.340	0.299	0.263	14
15	0.861	0.743	0.642	0.555	0.481	0.417	0.362	0.315	0.275	0.239	15

	11%	12%	13%	14%	15%	16%	17%	18%	19%	20%	
1	0.901	0.893	0.885	0.877	0.870	0.862	0.855	0.847	0.840	0.833	1
2	0.812	0.797	0.783	0.769	0.756	0.743	0.731	0.718	0.706	0.694	2
3	0.731	0.712	0.693	0.675	0.658	0.641	0.624	0.609	0.593	0.579	3
4	0.659	0.636	0.613	0.592	0.572	0.552	0.534	0.516	0.499	0.482	4
5	0.593	0.567	0.543	0.519	0.497	0.476	0.456	0.437	0.419	0.402	5
6	0.535	0.507	0.480	0.456	0.432	0.410	0.390	0.370	0.352	0.335	6
7	0.482	0.452	0.425	0.400	0.376	0.354	0.333	0.314	0.296	0.279	7
8	0.434	0.404	0.376	0.351	0.327	0.305	0.285	0.266	0.249	0.233	8
9	0.391	0.361	0.333	0.308	0.284	0.263	0.243	0.225	0.209	0.194	9
10	0.352	0.322	0.295	0.270	0.247	0.227	0.208	0.191	0.176	0.162	10
11	0.317	0.287	0.261	0.237	0.215	0.195	0.178	0.162	0.148	0.135	11
12	0.286	0.257	0.231	0.208	0.187	0.168	0.152	0.137	0.124	0.112	12
13	0.258	0.229	0.204	0.182	0.163	0.145	0.130	0.116	0.104	0.093	13
14	0.232	0.205	0.181	0.160	0.141	0.125	0.111	0.099	0.088	0.078	14
15	0.209	0.183	0.160	0.140	0.123	0.108	0.095	0.084	0.074	0.065	15

ANNUITY TABLES

Present value of an annuity of 1, ie. $\dfrac{1}{r}\left(1 - \dfrac{1}{(1+r)^n}\right)$

where r = interest rate

n = number of periods

Interest rates (r)

Years (n)	1%	2%	3%	4%	5%	6%	7%	8%	9%	10%	
1	0.990	0.980	0.971	0.962	0.952	0.943	0.935	0.926	0.917	0.909	1
2	1.970	1.942	1.913	1.886	1.859	1.833	1.808	1.783	1.759	1.736	2
3	2.941	2.884	2.829	2.775	2.723	2.673	2.624	2.577	2.531	2.487	3
4	3.902	3.808	3.717	3.630	3.546	3.465	3.387	3.312	3.240	3.170	4
5	4.853	4.713	4.580	4.452	4.329	4.212	4.100	3.993	3.890	3.791	5
6	5.795	5.601	5.417	5.242	5.076	4.917	4.767	4.623	4.486	4.355	6
7	6.728	6.472	6.230	6.002	5.786	5.582	5.389	5.206	5.033	4.868	7
8	7.652	7.325	7.020	6.733	6.463	6.210	5.971	5.747	5.535	5.335	8
9	8.566	8.162	7.786	7.435	7.108	6.802	6.515	6.247	5.995	5.759	9
10	9.471	8.983	8.530	8.111	7.722	7.360	7.024	6.710	6.418	6.145	10
11	10.370	9.787	9.253	8.760	8.306	7.887	7.499	7.139	6.805	6.495	11
12	11.260	10.580	9.954	9.385	8.863	8.384	7.943	7.536	7.161	6.814	12
13	12.130	11.350	10.630	9.986	9.394	8.853	8.358	7.904	7.487	7.103	13
14	13.000	12.110	11.300	10.560	9.899	9.295	8.745	8.244	7.786	7.367	14
15	13.870	12.850	11.940	11.120	10.380	9.712	9.108	8.559	8.061	7.606	15

	11%	12%	13%	14%	15%	16%	17%	18%	19%	20%	
1	0.901	0.893	0.885	0.877	0.870	0.862	0.855	0.847	0.840	0.833	1
2	1.713	1.690	1.668	1.647	1.626	1.605	1.585	1.566	1.547	1.528	2
3	2.444	2.402	2.361	2.322	2.283	2.246	2.210	2.174	2.140	2.106	3
4	3.102	3.037	2.974	2.914	2.855	2.798	2.743	2.690	2.639	2.589	4
5	3.696	3.605	3.517	3.433	3.352	3.274	3.199	3.127	3.058	2.991	5
6	4.231	4.111	3.998	3.889	3.784	3.685	3.589	3.498	3.410	3.326	6
7	4.712	4.564	4.423	4.288	4.160	4.039	3.922	3.812	3.706	3.605	7
8	5.146	4.968	4.799	4.639	4.487	4.344	4.207	4.078	3.954	3.837	8
9	5.537	5.328	5.132	4.946	4.772	4.607	4.451	4.303	4.163	4.031	9
10	5.889	5.560	5.426	5.216	5.019	4.833	4.659	4.494	4.339	4.192	10
11	6.207	5.938	5.687	5.453	5.234	5.029	4.836	4.656	4.586	4.327	11
12	6.492	6.194	5.918	5.660	5.421	5.197	4.988	4.793	4.611	4.439	12
13	6.750	6.424	6.122	5.842	5.583	5.342	5.118	4.910	4.715	4.533	13
14	6.982	6.628	6.302	6.002	5.724	5.468	5.229	5.008	4.802	4.611	14
15	7.191	6.811	6.462	6.142	5.847	5.575	5.324	5.092	4.876	4.675	15

Management accounting and information

OBJECTIVES

This is the first of two introductory sessions that are common to Units 11, 12 and 13. Units 11 and 13 are concerned with the preparation of information for control and planning, whilst Unit 12 considers the budgetary control system in more depth. These are all areas that come under the general heading of *Cost accounting*, which in turn forms part of the management accounting function.

This session outlines how the cost and management accounting functions contribute towards the planning and control of an organisation's activities.

The performance criteria addressed by this session are as follows:

■   Timely information is presented to managers in a clear and appropriate form.

Reports highlighting significant trends are presented to management in an appropriate form.

■   Staff in the organisation who can contribute towards the analysis of external trends are consulted.

■   Routine cost reports are assessed, compared with other sources of information and findings recommended to management in a clear and appropriate form.

THE PURPOSE AND NATURE OF COST AND MANAGEMENT ACCOUNTING

Management accounting vs financial accounting

Accountants have to provide information to very diverse groups. The specific needs of each determine whether these can best be served by the financial accounting or the management accounting function of the business organisation. The main differences between financial accounting and management accounting are as follows:

●   Financial accounting provides information to users who are external to the business, whereas management accounting is usually concerned with internal users of accounting information such as the managers of the business.

●   Financial accounting draws up financial statements, the formats of which are governed by law and accounting standards for limited companies, whereas management accounting reports can be in any format which suits the user and may differ considerably from one company to another.

●   Financial accounting reports on past transactions, but management accounting records historic transactions, compares actual figures to budget figures and hence makes predictions for the future.

Cost accounting

This function is normally a large part of the management accounting role. As its name suggests, it is primarily concerned with ascertainment of costs and it was developed to a great extent within a manufacturing context where costs are most difficult to isolate and analyse. In such a business there are two things which the financial accountant's profit and loss accounting will not disclose:

- the amount of profit attributable to each unit of a product or service;
- the amount of cost and/or revenue attributable to each manager.

The provision of this product line and departmental information is one aspect of cost accounting.

Although cost accounts are drawn up on established double-entry principles, they nevertheless differ from financial accounts in several important respects, as shall become apparent as you work through these units.

The information provided by the cost accountant will be part of the management information system of the business (often the major part). We shall first consider the nature of the MIS overall.

MANAGEMENT INFORMATION SYSTEMS (MIS)

A management information system (MIS) is a system using formalised procedures to provide managers at all levels with appropriate information from all relevant sources (internal and external to the business) for the purposes of planning and controlling the activities for which they are responsible.

A MIS has been defined as 'a system in which defined data are collected, processed and communicated to assist those responsible for the use of resources'.

The study of MIS cannot be undertaken in a vacuum and will be determined by the type of organisation or business; the products or services offered; the principal markets, the principal objectives; the organisation structure and reporting relationships; the principal users of information and the use to which the information is put.

The information systems will operate within different levels, from the board of directors down to shop-floor supervisors, and within different functions (for example, production, marketing and finance).

MANAGEMENT INFORMATION

Why information is needed

There are a number of reasons why information will be needed by the management of an organisation. The key considerations are:

- to assist management in **planning** the most effective use of resources, such as labour and materials;

- to assist management in **decision-making** (ie. choosing between alternative courses of action), for example whether to make a product or purchase it from an outside supplier;

- to aid management in **controlling** day-to-day operations, for example by comparing actual results with those planned.

The functions – such as planning and controlling – involved in managing an organisation therefore require knowledge that is relevant to the particular situation. How often is it said, 'If only I had known that at the time'? Managers' judgements will be greatly enhanced by receiving the appropriate information on which to base their decisions.

A manager will use resources in the light of the information available to him. Furthermore, the whole complex process of management can be broken down into manageable sections or problems. The problem facing the chairman of a large group might be to decide how much funds to allocate to a particular activity, whereas a foreman in the machine shop might be deciding which machine to use and which operators should be asked to operate it to turn out a particular job. Information is necessary at each level to guide decisions and, in due course, to measure the effectiveness of the action taken.

Information flows

Normally, most organisations develop around major functional areas, for example, the functions of production, finance, distribution etc., and within each area there are additional sub-divisions. In the past managers were usually held responsible for obtaining the information they needed and such information was prescribed by the manager at the top and his accounts influenced reports at all levels. In addition, statutory requirements such as annual accounts provided the other main source of information. As organisations grew, more data was required than individual managers could handle and systems and data-processing departments began to develop in order to collect, route and manipulate data. The information flowed up the channels of management largely by summarisations from varying levels of detail.

With the gradual introduction of company-wide systems, many organisations began to recognise the information systems function as separate from the normal lines of responsibility/authority. This can often be seen where basic data gathered (eg. by the sales representatives) could well be of value to the manufacturing staff when they consider the volume of production. Furthermore, improved efficiency often requires departmental co-ordination within functions, geographical areas and divisions and the cost of collecting data could also force management to consider improved methods and flows. The information flows, if traced from one responsibility unit to another, present an information network which reflects horizontal and vertical flows of data.

Requirements of management information

A successful business needs management capable of making decisions. In turn, a successful business manager has the responsibility and authority to make those decisions. Irrespective of whether these decisions may dictate the future long-term policy or conduct of the business or simply the day to day routine operation of the business, management must be equipped with adequate and timely information.

Management information may be of two types:

- information about the past results of the type of action envisaged – historical information; or
- information about the future effects of decisions – forecast information.

Three basic types of information have been identified:

(a) *Scorekeeping* – The accumulation of data to enable both internal and external parties to evaluate organisational performance and position. This embraces internal reporting for use in planning and controlling non-routine operations. To some extent this also embraces external reporting to shareholders, government and other external parties.

(b)   *Attention-directing* – The reporting and the interpretation of information which helps managers to focus on operation problems, imperfections, inefficiencies and opportunities. This aspect of accounting assists managers with the provision of important data about the operations enabling timely decision making, whether on a long-term or a short-term basis. Attention directing is frequently associated with current planning and control and with the analysis and investigation of recurring, routine and non-routine internal accounting reports.

(c)   *Problem-solving* – This *ad hoc* aspect of accounting involves the concise quantification of the relative merits of possible courses of action, often with recommendations as to the best procedure. In this it is seen that the cost accountant is a very vital part of the management team.

Attributes of information

Since management at all levels must perform a certain amount of planning, decision-making and control, it is vital that the manager has the necessary information to perform his tasks. There are four fundamental attributes of information, namely that it should be:

(a)   *Relevant to the scope of responsibility.* A production manager will primarily be concerned with information about stocks, production levels, production performance and machine loads within his department. He will not be interested in the shortcomings of other departments unless they specifically affect his area. Indeed, he may well only be interested in one part of the manufacturing environment, for example, the manager of the machine shop will not be concerned with an assembly shop in another part of the plant.

(b)   *Relevant to any particular decision.* This is a difficult one. Management have to be able to identify the decisions that need to be made. This requires information that directs attention to specific problems. However, having identified the decisions, the information that enables the right decisions to be made needs to be acquired.

(c)   *Produced in time.* This is an area of great conflict for manager and accountant. Two of the most desirable attributes of the accountant's work are accuracy and timeliness. Of course, information to satisfy the requirements already outlined, must be accurate, but to be of use in the business it must be presented quickly. The demand for information in business is like the demand for news, and it is about as perishable. A beautiful, well written, superbly accurate report, covering and analysing all the facets of a particular problem and all the possible solutions and their consequences is useless if it cannot be prepared in time for the decision to be taken, or is delivered after the problem has been resolved.

(d)   *Valuable.* This value may be assessed by the resulting change in the planned course of action. If no change takes place then the information had no real value; if a change takes place then the value is represented by the benefit in changing. The information also has a cost and the cost of obtaining information must be compared with the potential benefit arising from it. Even cost accounting must be cost-effective!

The accounting information system

The major objective of most commercial organisations is to make profits. Consequently, the accounting system is the most important information system, providing the basis for the process of budgetary planning and control and linking together the other information systems within the organisation created by the functions of research and development, production, personnel, etc.

The purpose of a MIS is to determine, and to provide as efficiently, effectively and economically as possible, what management need to know. Since most of the information within any business is handled by the accounts department, the accountant, and particularly the cost accountant, is thus in a very important position.

THE ROLE OF THE MANAGEMENT ACCOUNTANT

The accountant's skills

The chief role of the accountant was traditionally 'stewardship'. He began as the custodian of the firm's assets and the faithful recorder of their movement. He developed the role of the company profit calculator because profit is the net increase in asset values.

However, stewardship involves the careful, effective and efficient use of assets, and so the management accountant is concerned with the pursuit of efficiency and of productivity in the use of the firm's resources.

The tool of the management accountant is figures. He must be able to collate them according to logic, fully understand what they tell him, and to know how to help management to understand the significance of his information. In other words, he collects all the available data; records, collates, and analyses it, and then reports his findings to the company's management.

The functions of a management accountant

The management accountant assists management in the following areas:

- *Planning* – Primarily through preparation of a short-term annual budget, but also through long range strategic planning.

- *Organising* – Planning enables all departments involved to be organised and avoids lack of goal congruence, ie. individual managers seeking good results for their department but with a bad overall effect on the company.

- *Controlling* – Comparing actual results with the budget helps to identify where operations are not running according to plan. Investigation of the causes and subsequent action achieves effective control of the business.

- *Communicating* – Liaising with departments and reporting relevant information on a timely basis.

- *Motivating* – A tight but attainable budget communicated effectively should motivate staff and improve their performance. If the target is too difficult, however, it is likely to demotivate and is unlikely to be achieved.

Management accounts will therefore serve a variety of purposes; it is no surprise then that they take a variety of forms. There is no set format; the accounts should include information relevant to their purpose.

COMMUNICATION ISSUES

We have already looked at some key requirements of management information and at an appropriate format for presenting such documentation as a profit and loss account. More generally, a management accountant needs to be aware of the use and layout of memos, reports and letters. These issues were dealt with in depth in Unit 7. In summary, attention needs to be given first to preparation.

Follow the three basic stages:

- Collect ideas and facts.
- Select what is needed.
- Plan how to set it out.

Once you know what you want to say, assess the essential information you may need to include, using the following list:

- the name of the person requesting the copy of the report;
- the name and position within the company of the writer;
- the date;
- the title.

In the text and the end of session questions, you will need to be aware of and decide on an appropriate presentation of information to others.

Finally, you should also consider, where appropriate, the use of visual material such as graphs and bar charts to present information, using the knowledge gained from Unit 7.

COST ACCOUNTING AND MIS

The scope of cost accounting

It will become evident that the role of the cost accountant is intimately involved with the business information systems. Originally, traditional cost accounting referred to the ways of accumulating and assigning historical costs to units of product and departments, primarily for the purposes of stock valuation and profit determination.

Nowadays, cost accounting embraces a much wider function. Cost accounting is used as a means of gathering and providing information as a basis for making all kinds of decisions, ranging from the management of resources within an operation to the formulation of non-recurring strategic decisions and major organisational policies.

Definition of cost accounting

Cost accounting may be defined as the application of accounting and cost accounting principles, methods and techniques in the ascertainment of costs and the analysis of savings and/or excesses as compared with previous experience or with standards. The key factor is the **ascertainment of costs**. Meaningful comparisons cannot be made or analysed until costs have first been ascertained by applying certain accepted principles, methods and techniques.

Cost accounting is primarily directed at providing the required information for management, whether on a routine basis, or on an *ad hoc* basis to enable management to perform the functions of planning, control and decision making. To that end, cost accounting is concerned with:

(a)   the determination of costs and profit during a control period;

(b)   the value of stocks of raw materials, work in progress and finished goods and control stock levels;

(c)   preparation of budgets, forecasts and other control data for a forthcoming control period;

(d)   the creation of a reporting system which enables managers to take corrective action where necessary to control costs;

(e)   the provision of information for decision-making.

Items (a) and (b) are traditional cost accounting roles; (c) to (e) extend into management accounting.

Cost accounting is thus an integral part of the MIS of a business.

Students should also recognise that cost accounting is no longer confined to the environment of manufacturing, although it is in this area that it is most fully developed. Service industries, central and local government, and even accountancy and legal practices make profitable use of cost accounting information. Furthermore, it is not restricted purely to manufacturing and operating costs, but also to administration, selling and distribution and research and development.

The cost accountant's role

Since cost accounting is a vital element of the MIS, the cost accountant has a vital role within the management team, generating the essential information required. In his relationship with the various levels of management the cost accountant is required to provide information on:

(a)   past performance and the results of past decisions;

(b)   implications of current and future decisions through forecast information;

(c)   information relating to current decisions regarding choice of methods and expected results – what systems analysts call *feedback*.

A later session will examine the focus and organisation of cost accounting in more detail.

BEHAVIOURAL AND ORGANISATIONAL ASPECTS

Since management accounting is concerned with the provision of information to management as well as the technical aspects of such areas as cost control, decision-making and investment appraisal, it is also important to take account of the impact of any decision or action on the behavioural and organisational aspects of the business.

Decision-making impacts on people involved in the organisation at all levels. The method of generating information on which those decisions are to be based will therefore impact on those people and may consequently influence their behaviour patterns. Therefore the management accountant must always bear in mind how employees may react to different policies.

This aspect will be examined further in a later session, in the context of budgetary control.

The management accountant must also be aware of the impact of his role on the organisational structure of the firm. A suitable organisational structure must be implemented to allow effective delegation of information-gathering roles and decision-making responsibility. This must allow for a chain of authority and information flow, and also to enable responsibility to rest at the appropriate level in the corporate hierarchy.

QUESTION

Attributes of MI

Management accounting information should comply with a number of criteria including verifiability, objectivity, timeliness, comparability, reliability, understandability and relevance if it is to be useful in planning, control and decision-making.

(a)   Explain the meaning of each of the criteria named above and give a specific example to illustrate each.

(b)   Give a brief explanation of how the criteria detailed in (a) might be in conflict with each other giving examples to illustrate where such conflict might arise.

SUMMARY

The cost accountant is mainly concerned with the proper recording and analysis of costs incurred in a business in a manner that will enable management to control current operations and plan for the future.

Information for decision-making is a key aspect of the cost accountant's function.

The management accountant's role is essentially that of internal planning and control. Effective communication with the workforce and management is vital and will be achieved via:

(a)   a suitable organisational structure; and

(b)   a variety of forms and reports together with accounting statements produced on a timely basis; these will form part of the MIS.

In many smaller organisations, these two overlapping roles will be performed by the same person.

You should now be aware of:

•   the need for management accounting as well as financial accounting information within a business

•   the nature of a MIS and the functions of a management accountant

•   the cost accountant's role within the MIS.

The principles and techniques of cost accounting

OBJECTIVES

This session is also common to all three units and is largely a revision of relevant areas covered in your earlier studies – in particular for Unit 6, *Recording cost information.*

It concentrates on the work of the cost accounting department.

The following areas will be revised in this session:

■　　the functions of the cost accounting department and the characteristics and benefits of the information it produces

■　　definitions of cost units and cost centres, and the different types of cost classification

■　　cost behaviour

■　　treatment of overheads (including ABC)

■　　introduction to standard costing and variance analysis

The performance criteria addressed by this session are as follows:

■　　Actual cost and revenue data are correctly coded and allocated to responsibility centres.

■　　Current material, labour and other variable costs are identified and future trends assessed.

■　　Estimates account for the effect of possible variations in capacity on fixed overhead rates.

COST ACCOUNTING

The need for cost accounting

Historically, financial accounts have reflected the transactions of a business entity in its relationships with the outside world: customers, suppliers, employees, shareholders and other investors. To this end, financial accounting has been geared up to the preparation of annual and other periodic accounts, with the emphasis upon statutory requirements.

A typical profit and loss account statement follows the following general layout (in summary):

Profit and loss account for period ended . . .

	£
Turnover	500,000
Cost of sales	(370,000)
Gross profit	130,000
Expenses	(80,000)
Profit on ordinary activities before taxation	50,000

Typically the profit and loss account will include a subjective analysis of expense according to category either by function (distribution/administrative) or by nature (materials/staff costs/depreciation). Despite some recent changes, financial accounts do not readily disclose:

(a)   profit performance by individual products, services or activity; but more important

(b)   the responsibility of individual managers for performance.

Thus they can only provide 'scorekeeping' statistical information, rather than information that will form the basis of decision-making or control. The provision of this additional detail is one of the functions of cost accounting: **cost-finding**.

Cost-finding means taking the transactions which make up the financial accounts and analysing them to turn data into information which will be more helpful to the managers of the business. This will be an 'objective' analysis, matching the expenses to the purposes for which they were incurred.   This analysis may be done on a purely memorandum basis, the results being reconciled with the financial records, or it may be sometimes incorporated into the general bookkeeping system of the company.

Whichever procedure is adopted, cost accounting has two important effects on business documentation:

(a)   Additional internal documents will be needed to identify which products or departments are affected by various transactions (covered in detail in Unit 6).

(b)   Additional data regarding transactions will be needed to assist accurate classification and analysis.

As an example of product cost analysis, assume that the profit and loss account illustrated above related to a company marketing four different products.

From his analysis of the source documents (purchase invoices, payrolls, petty cash vouchers and so on), the cost accountant is able to provide the following detailed report:

	Product A	Product B	Product C	Product D	Total
Sales					
Quantity	315,000	32,500	80,500	28,100	–
Price per unit	£0.50	£2.50	£1.50	£5.00	–
Amount	£157,500	£81,250	£120,750	£140,500	£500,000
Costs	£	£	£	£	£
Materials	50,000	40,000	75,000	85,000	250,000
Wages	40,000	30,000	20,000	30,000	120,000
Expenses	22,000	25,500	17,500	15,000	80,000
Total	112,000	95,500	112,500	130,000	450,000
Net profit/(loss) before tax	45,500	(14,250)	8,250	10,500	50,000

From this 'product profit and loss account', the managers of the business can see that the total profit of £50,000 resulted from profits on products A, C and D, offset by a loss on product B, and that product A alone yielded 91% of the company total. We do not know at this stage whether the information will lead them to take any decision to change things for the future, because we do not know whether the above result is in accordance with a deliberate plan or not. Nor can we be sure without further information whether it would be a good thing to discontinue product B since such a decision might involve some further analysis of the costs incurred, and some forecasts of future developments.

Both comparisons against plan and the preparation of special analyses for decision purposes fall within the scope of the cost accounting function.

The cost accounting department

Data required for reports

A review of a company's requirements for historical information shows that they include three main types of data:

(a)   Data from the normal financial accounts of the business: the balance sheet and profit and loss account with their supporting notes and schedules, and the cash flow statement.

(b)   Data obtained by analysing the accounts of the business, identifying items with cost units and cost centres: in other words the work of the cost accounting department (details of stockholdings would come from this source).

(c)   Data derived immediately from source documents without evaluation, such as statistics on labour efficiency, material usage, sickness, absenteeism and machine breakdowns.

In addition, most reports will include comparisons with budgets, standards, targets or estimates, and the explanations of variances based on detailed investigation and close knowledge of the data used in budget preparation.

Organisation

The accounts department, therefore, will comprise a financial accounting segment, a costing segment and a budgetary control segment, though the extent to which these will be separate departments within the accounting organisation will depend on the number and diversity of the transactions to be handled and on the management organisation of the business, including the extent of divisional autonomy, all of which will affect the required number of accounting staff and the consequent need for specialisation of effort.

Cost accounting record-keeping

The cost department is responsible for maintaining the cost accounting records. To be effective these records should:

(a)   analyse production, administration and marketing costs to facilitate cost and profit computations, stock valuations, forecast and budget data and decision-making data;

(b)   enable the production of periodic performance statements which are necessary for management control purposes;

(c)   permit analysis of:

      (i)   past costs for profit measurement and stock valuation;
      (ii)   present costs for control purposes;
      (iii)   future costs – forecasts, targets, budgets and decision-making.

The cost accountant, because his job is to interpret physical facts into money values, is in an excellent position to ensure that all types of report are integrated and are prepared on a consistent basis. Although inevitably other departments will wish to report on their own activities, the cost accountant should maintain close liaison and build a good relationship with them so that:

(a)   the information he provides can assist them in interpreting the results of their own activities;

(b)   there is no conflict on questions of fact between reports prepared by, for example, the sales manager or the production manager and the information emerging from the costing system.

Such data may be held as manual or computer-based records. The more data that can be stored on computer media such as floppy disks, the easier report preparation will be.

Computer-based data concerning sales and production quantities, stock levels, costs, etc. will assist the cost accounting function in the following ways:

(a)   reports and cost accounts can be prepared quickly;

(b)   information for decision-making will be more plentiful and be available more speedily than would be the case with manual data;

(c)   large volumes of data can be stored and manipulated with ease.

If companies cannot afford to have their own in-house computing department it will be possible to have computer software designed to meet their specific needs by an external software supplier.

The benefits of cost accounting

A cost department will always be enthusiastic about cost control and cost effectiveness. The student will, however, be conscious of a very expensive team being drawn together. Not surprisingly, therefore, consideration needs to be given to the benefits of cost accounting.

These can be identified as:

(a)   disclosure of profitable and non-profitable activities (as might appear in the product profit and loss account already illustrated). This data would also be modified to identify locations which are unprofitable;

(b)   identification of waste and inefficiency, particularly in relation to usage of materials and labour;

(c)   analysis of movements in profit;

(d)   assistance in the determination of selling prices;

(e)   valuation of stocks (there are auditing and taxation implications here);

(f)   development of planning and control information;

(g)   evaluation of the cost effect of policy decisions.

COST UNITS

Explanation

It will be helpful to an understanding of this term to revert to the costing profit and loss account illustrated earlier. This showed the sales quantity of various products (A–D) and the total cost of those sales under the headings materials, wages and expenses.

The following additional calculations could be made from that example:

Calculation of cost per unit for month ended .... 19....

	Product A £	Product B £	Product C £	Product D £
Materials	0.16	1.23	0.93	3.02
Wages	0.13	0.92	0.25	1.07
Expenses	0.07	0.78	0.22	0.53
Total cost per unit	0.36	2.93	1.40	4.62

We have taken the total costs attributable to each product in a month (any other period could have been used) and arrived at the average cost per unit of each product, rounded to the nearest penny, by dividing the totals by the numbers of units involved. The 'cost unit' in this instance is the unit of product sold.

The unit might have been a piece, a pack, a kilogram, a litre or any other measure appropriate to what was being produced.

Averaging of costs

It should be noted that in practice the business would probably have produced more units that it sold in the period, the unsold quantity being taken into stock. In such a case, the costs of production would have been collected and divided by the number of units *produced* to give the average unit cost. This would have been applied to the number of units sold to give the cost of sales, and to the number of units remaining to give the costs of the residual stock.

This average unit cost approach is used whenever production is continuous and leads to uniform product units, as in the case of many chemical plants, food processors or extractive operations such as mining and quarrying.

Job costs

Some businesses, however, undertake special jobs for their customers. A workshop making tools and jigs does this; and so on a much larger scale does the contractor building bridges or putting up a factory. In such cases, costs are first analysed between the various jobs or contracts, and then the costs of the jobs invoiced will be gathered together into the periodic summary profit and loss account. For such businesses, in other words, the 'cost unit' is the job or contract.

Batch costs

A third situation may be exemplified in the manufacture of mechanical or electrical components or products, which are customarily made in batches of say 1,000 or 10,000 items, according to the circumstances of the case. In this type of business, the cost of each batch is determined and the batch is the primary 'cost unit'. Thereafter it is possible, if desired, to calculate the average cost per item in the batch.

Non-manufacturing cost units

The above examples have concentrated on cost units for production or manufacturing processes. Examples of cost units for service industries, or non-manufacturing activities within a business are as follows:

Service industry/activity	*Cost unit*
Accountants	Chargeable hour
College	Student enrolled
Hotel	Bed-night
Hospital	Patient-day
Transport department	kg-mile
Credit control department	Customer account
Selling	Calls made
Maintenance department	Man-hours

Note that some of these are in fact composite cost units, where a cost is considered to be dependent upon two main factors.

For example, if the manager of a chain of hotels wanted to compare costs between two of the hotels, calculating costs per bed would not take account of the differing levels of occupation of the beds of the two hotels. Thus the cost can be calculated per bed-night (ie. the cost of one bed per night of occupation).

Definition

A cost unit is a quantitative unit of product or service in relation to which costs are associated; the purpose of product costing is to arrive at the cost of the cost unit appropriate to the business concerned.

COST CENTRES

Definition

A cost centre is a location, function or item(s) of equipment in respect of which costs may be ascertained and related to cost units for control purposes.

Explanation

A cost centre therefore is used as an initial collection point for costs; once the total cost of operating the cost centre for a period has been ascertained, it can be related to the cost units that have passed through the cost centre.

The location, function or item of equipment referred to in the definition can be directly related to production, to a service department or to a business.

Examples

Production	Assembly line
	Packing machine
Service dept	Stores
	Canteen
	Quality control
Service	Tax department (accountants)
	Ward (hospital)
	Faculty (college)

Responsibility

Control can only be exercised by people, and for every cost somebody must be responsible; so whether a cost centre is impersonal or personal there must always be a manager in whose sphere of responsibility that cost centre is included.

Overhead costs, therefore, will always be identified with cost centres; and because cost centres are the responsibility of particular functional managers one will find overheads classified according to the main functional divisions of the business.

Profit centres

Definition

> A location, function or item(s) of equipment in respect of which costs and revenues may be ascertained for the purposes of control of the resulting profit.

COST CLASSIFICATION

Types of cost classification

Costs can be classified (collected into logical groups) in many ways. The particular classification selected will depend upon the purpose for which the resulting analysed data will be used.

Purpose	*Classification*
Cost control	By nature – materials, labour, overheads, etc.
Cost accounts	By relationship to cost units – direct/indirect costs, etc.
Budgeting, contribution analysis	By behaviour – fixed/variable costs
Decision-making	Relevant and non-relevant
Responsibility accounting	Controllable and uncontrollable

You will come across these classifications in more detail as you work through the Study Pack. At this stage, we will revise the basic classification terms used in cost accounting.

Direct and indirect costs

For cost accounting purposes, the costs of the business will be classified in quite a different way from the analysis required by a financial accountant for the published accounts.

The basic classification of costs may be illustrated as follows:

	£	£
Direct costs		
Direct materials		250,000
Direct labour		120,000
Direct expenses		10,000
Prime cost (= Total of direct costs)		380,000
Indirect factory costs		25,000
Production cost		405,000
Administration overhead	20,000	
Selling and distribution overhead	25,000	
		45,000
Total cost		450,000

Direct costs

These are costs which can be related directly to one cost unit.

Example: Considering a cost unit of a chair, direct costs will include the cost of wood and screws used (direct material cost) and the cost of manufacturing labour hours per chair (direct labour costs).

In a non-manufacturing context, the direct costs relating to, say, a student enrolled at a college would include the costs of books provided, individual tuition and marking costs.

Indirect costs

These cannot be identified directly with a cost unit and are often referred to as *overheads*. Distinction needs to be made for stock valuation purposes between overheads incurred in the production process (factory costs, eg. factory rent and rates, power etc.) and non-production costs.

Non-production costs are indirect costs involved in converting finished goods into revenue, comprising:

(a)   administrative overhead costs (eg. executive salaries and office costs); and
(b)   marketing, selling and distribution, overhead costs.

These costs are *not* included in stock valuation since they are not costs of making a product, but costs of selling it. Stock on hand at the end of a period is valued at total *production* cost only.

With the same cost unit of a chair, the salaries of the salesmen who promote and sell the chairs to retail outlets would be a selling overhead.

Indirect costs associated with a college would include premises' running costs, lecturers' salaries and administrative staff costs.

COST BEHAVIOUR

The nature of costs

We mentioned earlier the need for cost classification by behaviour for budgeting purposes. In order to make predictions of future cost levels, we must determine the basis of the charge.

As an example, consider the cost of direct materials expected next month. The charge would depend on the amount used and the cost per unit. The amount used would depend, in turn, on the production anticipated for the period.

In order to estimate this cost therefore we must estimate the following:

(a)	Production levels	10,000 units
(b)	Usage of materials per unit	
	material A	2 kg
	material B	1 kg
	material C	0.2 kg
(c)	Costs per unit	
	material A	30 pence per kg
	material B	25 pence per kg
	material C	50 pence per kg

Estimate

		£
Material A	20,000 kg	6,000
Material B	10,000 kg	2,500
Material C	2,000 kg	1,000
Total estimated material cost		9,500

Mathematical modelling

What have we done? We have set up a simple mathematical model which will, for any level of production, usage and unit cost, enable the level of cost in a future period to be predicted. The direct materials example was perhaps the easiest to use and, in practice, we may wish to deal with other variables which affect the cost such as wastage rates thus producing a slightly more complex model.

Direct labour costs may tend to vary due to changes in productivity and other factors in addition to the more obvious variables such as grade and rate of payment. A certain amount of estimation will still be required; if payment is on a production related basis we would expect a cost which, like materials, will vary in line with the volume of production.

At this stage, therefore, we have come to the rule-of-thumb guide that direct material, labour and expenses will probably vary roughly in line with anticipated production levels or the level of activity (**variable costs**).

This will not be the case with all costs. If we take the cost of rent and rates, for example, the charge is not determined on the basis of the intensity of usage of the premises but rather on the basis of time used (**fixed costs**). Labour paid on a time basis would also fall under this heading. How then can we predict the cost of such expenses for next month? Well, there is no difficulty in doing this as all we have to do is consult our rental agreement and the rates notice and we can forecast with complete certainty what these costs will be for the month.

Once budgeted or standard costs have been prepared for next month they can be used for control purposes by comparing the actual costs incurred during next month with those set as the target.

Differences between actual and budgeted costs can be investigated to determine the cause(s) and responsibility can be assigned to managers to improve future control.

Classification of costs by behaviour

The above example illustrates the need for cost behaviour classification. For cost prediction purposes, we must make a distinction between costs which vary with production or activity levels (**variable costs**) and those which do not (**fixed costs**). There also exists a type of cost which moves in sympathy with production levels but contains an element which does not, such as an electricity charge which contains a minimum standing charge plus an element which relates to the usage of the period. Such a cost would be described as **semi-variable** or **mixed**.

Definitions

> **Variable costs** are those that vary (usually assumed in direct proportion) with changes in level of activity of the cost centre to which they relate (eg. output volume). Example: the raw material used in a product.

It should be noted that the variable cost per unit may not remain constant over a wide range. It may be possible, for example, to obtain discounts for large purchases of material, reducing the cost per unit.

> **Fixed costs** are those that accrue with the passage of time and are not affected by changes in activity level; they are therefore also known as *period* costs. Example: rent of premises.

> **Stepped costs** are fixed over a range of output and then suddenly increase in one big jump. Example: a staffing level of up to 20 people may only require one foreman but, if the staff level is more than 20, an extra foreman will be needed.

> **Semi-variable (mixed) costs** contain both a fixed and a variable element. When output is nil, the fixed element is incurred, but they also increase, like variable costs, as output increases. Example: telephone charges where there is a fixed rental to which is added the charge for calls made.

Graphical illustrations

Various cost behaviour patterns are illustrated graphically by way of the example following.

(a) **Fixed cost**: rent of factory payable under a long-term lease (Figure 1)

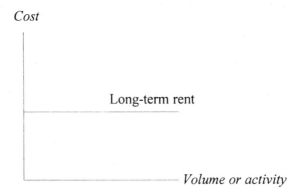

Figure 1

(b) **Variable cost**: direct materials, the purchase price per unit being constant (Figure 2)

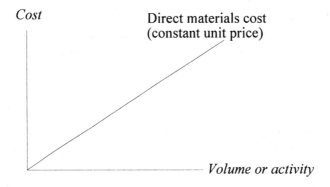

Figure 2

(c) **Semi-variable costs**

    (i)   Direct materials cost (trade discount at higher levels of activity)
    (ii)   Salesmen's remuneration with added commission from a certain level of activity
    (iii)   Electricity charges comprising fixed standing charge and variable unit charge

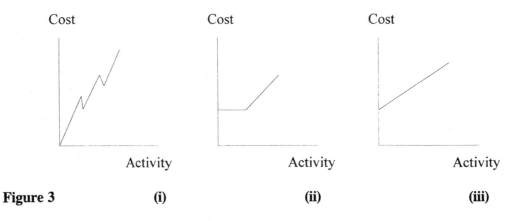

Figure 3   **(i)**   **(ii)**   **(iii)**

(d)   **Step functions**

In practice, many costs will increase by jumps when certain levels of activity are reached. These are known as **step functions** or **stepped costs**.

Two examples are shown in Figure 4:

(i)   Canteen cost where additional assistants are required as increases in activity result in larger numbers of factory personnel

(ii)   Rent of premises, additional accommodation eventually being required.

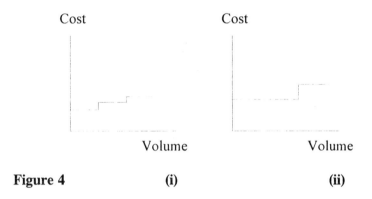

Figure 4   **(i)**   **(ii)**

Conclusion

The common solution is as follows:

(a)   Treat as variable those costs which change by regular steps.

(b)   Treat as fixed those costs which only change at wide intervals of activity; this recognises that review will be required if there is a permanent change in the normal level of activity.

COST ESTIMATION

As mentioned above, some costs may have both fixed and variable elements. These will need to be identified for budgeting and contribution analysis purposes.

If it is not easy to do this directly (as it is in the case of the telephone cost, where the bill clearly shows the fixed charge and rate per unit), then an analysis of past cost and volume data will need to be carried out.

It is assumed that there is a linear relationship, ie:

Total cost = Fixed cost + Variable cost per unit × Units produced

and that the total fixed cost and the variable cost per unit are constant at all levels of production unless told otherwise.

Possible techniques include the *high-low method* and *regression analysis*.

THE HIGH-LOW METHOD

Introduction

This is a simple method of estimating future costs from past results. It takes the costs for the highest and lowest activity levels, and assumes that a linear relationship covers the range in between.

Example

Widgets are produced by a process that incurs both fixed and variable costs.

Total costs have been recorded for the process for each of the last six months as follows:

Month	Output (units)	Total cost £
1	4,500	33,750
2	3,500	30,500
3	5,100	34,130
4	6,200	38,600
5	5,700	38,000
6	4,100	31,900

Required

(a)   Formulate an equation that relates cost to output.
(b)   Plot output against total cost on a graph.
(c)   Predict total cost at the budgeted activity level for month 7 of 6,000 units.

Solution

Select the months with the highest and lowest output levels as follows:

	Output	Total cost £
Lowest output	3,500	30,500
Highest output	6,200	38,600
Increase	2,700	8,100

For an increase of 2,700 units, cost has increased by £8,100. If we assume that the fixed cost element remains constant, this cost increase must represent a change in variable costs only.

Assuming a straight-line relationship, then the variable cost per unit $\dfrac{£8,100}{2,700} = £3$ per unit

Note that the factor determining which values to choose is the total cost at the highest output level and the total cost at the lowest output level. These are not necessarily the highest and lowest costs. The high/low observations are always based on the independent variable (in this case, output).

We can now substitute back into either of the two output levels to obtain the fixed cost.

At the 3,500 units level:

	£
Total cost	30,500
Variable cost (3,500 × £3)	(10,500)
Fixed costs	20,000

As a check on the accuracy of the calculations, at the 6,200 unit level:

	£
Total costs	38,600
Variable costs (6,200 × £3)	18,600
Fixed costs	20,000

Now answering the questions set

(a) If we let x = Production level in units
y = Total cost in £

Then Total cost = Fixed cost + Variable cost per unit × Production level

ie. y = 20,000 + 3x

(b) We can now plot the original data on a graph of cost against output, along with the line given by the equation in (a):

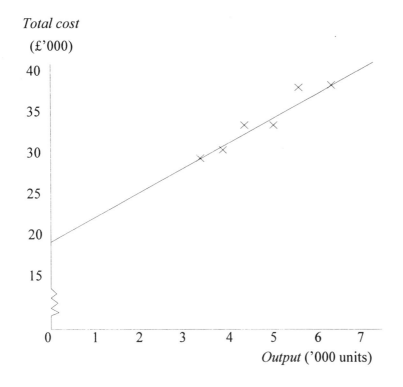

(c)   At an output level of 6,000 units, the equation would predict costs of:

$$y = 20,000 + (3 \times 6,000) = \text{£}38,000$$

Advantages

* Simple to operate
* Easy to understand

Disadvantages

The problem with the high-low method is that it could give a completely inaccurate result. This is because we are only considering two sets of data, and ignoring all of the others. It is possible that the points we have chosen are completely unrepresentative of the rest of the data. This is a distinct possibility since we have chosen the two points at the extreme ends of the activity range. At these levels it is more likely that operating conditions will be atypical compared with more normal output. One way around this problem is to choose the 'next to highest' and 'next to lowest' figures, but this destroys some of the simplicity of the model.

LINEAR REGRESSION

Introduction

Repeated below are the data from the initial widgets example above, which we will now use to illustrate the technique of linear regression.

Output (Units)	Total cost (£)
4,500	33,750
3,500	30,500
5,100	34,130
6,200	38,600
5,700	38,000
4,100	31,900

The technique of regression requires a particular choice of variables for the x and y axes.

The rule is:

x axis – the *independent* variable
y axis – the *dependent* variable

Thus we must designate output as x and total cost as y, since it is cost which is dependent upon output.

The previous graph of cost against output shows that the points lie more or less on a straight line. Such a graph is called a **scatter diagram**, for obvious reasons.

Onc could draw a straight line through the points by eye, but there is an equation for the line which statistically fits the points most closely – the **regression line**.

The regression line

The **regression line** (the *line of best fit* or *least squares line*) is the line which minimises the sum of the squares of the *vertical* distances of the scatter points from the line. In other words, if you take each scatter point, measure how far above or below the line it lies, square each of the distances and then add them up, the regression line is designed to give you the smallest possible total.

This somewhat peculiar procedure for getting to the line is not important, as you are given formulae for working out what the line looks like. However, it is important to note that the *vertical* distances are used in the definition. This is why you must get the correct variable on each axis.

The equation of the regression line is:

$$y = bx + a$$

and the constants 'a' and 'b' are given by:

$$b = \frac{\Sigma(x - \bar{x})(y - \bar{y})}{\Sigma(x - \bar{x})^2} \qquad a = \bar{y} - b\bar{x}$$

where a   represents the point where the regression line crosses the *y* (vertical) axis, and

   b   represents the slope (gradient) of the regression line

   $\bar{x}$ and $\bar{y}$ are the average values of the *x* and *y* variables respectively and can be calculated from the general expression:

$$\bar{x} = \frac{\Sigma x}{n} \qquad \text{and} \qquad \bar{y} = \frac{\Sigma y}{n}$$

Σ is the Greek letter sigma and stands for 'the sum of ….'. So in the context of $\bar{x}$ the expression $\dfrac{\Sigma x}{n}$ means 'sum together all the *x* values and divide this result by *n* (the number of *x* values)'.

Applying this to the figures in the example:

x	y	$(x - \bar{x})$	$(y - \bar{y})$	$(x - \bar{x})^2$	$(x - \bar{x})(y - \bar{y})$
4,500	33,750	(350)	(730)	122,500	255,500
3,500	30,500	(1,350)	(3,980)	1,822,500	5,373,000
5,100	34,130	250	(350)	62,500	(87,500)
6,200	38,600	1,350	4,120	1,822,500	5,562,000
5,700	38,000	850	3,520	722,500	2,992,000
4,100	31,900	(750)	(2,580)	562,500	1,935,000

$\Sigma x = 29,100 \qquad \Sigma y = 206,880 \qquad\qquad\qquad 5,115,000 \qquad 16,030,000$

$$\uparrow \qquad\qquad \uparrow$$

$$\bar{x} = \frac{29,100}{6} \qquad \bar{y} = \frac{206,880}{6} \qquad\qquad \Sigma(x - \bar{x})^2 \quad \Sigma(x - \bar{x})(y - \bar{y})$$

$$= 4,850 \qquad\qquad = 34,480$$

Thus $\quad b \quad = \quad \dfrac{16,030,000}{5,115,000} = 3.13$ (this represents the variable cost per unit)

$\quad a \quad = \quad 34,480 - (3.13 \times 4,850) = 19,300$ (the fixed cost for a month)

The equation of the line is therefore:

$$y \quad = \quad 19,300 + 3.13x$$

Interpolation and extrapolation

Now using the regression line to estimate costs for different output levels. For example:

- What is the expected cost for output of 4,900 units?

$$y \quad = \quad 19,300 + (3.13 \times 4,900) = £34,637$$

- What is the expected cost for output of 8,200 units?

$$y \quad = \quad 19,300 + (3.13 \times 8,200) = £44,966$$

At first glance there may seem to be little difference between the two computations we have just performed. Look more carefully at the value of x (output).

For the first example, the activity level is within the range covered by the data. This is known as **interpolation**.

For the second example, the output level is above the range of data. What happens if the production capacity is limited to, say, 7,500 units? In order to produce 8,200 units additional machinery would need to be purchased and extra workers engaged, which would make the cost far higher. It is for this sort of reason that extending beyond the data (**extrapolation**) can be very misleading.

Just because a linear relationship has been established within the range of data examined, it does not follow that the same relationship will persist beyond that range.

Measurement problems

In determining the values for use in regression or for plotting on a scatter diagram, we would generally use historic cost analysis obtained from the accounting records of the firm. This gives rise to a number of potential problems such as:

- Timing differences – The relationship between output levels and costs could be obscured if costs are recorded after the output levels. For example, we would expect maintenance costs to increase as machinery is used more, but the increased costs may not be recorded in the same period as the output, if the maintenance work is deferred until after the peak period is past.

- The accounting treatment of some costs may obscure true cost behaviour. A common example here would be the allocation of fixed overhead costs to production departments. If the objective is to determine the cost behaviour pattern in a single department, then only those costs incurred within the department should be included.

- It is too simplistic to assume that it is only output level that affects costs.

  Other factors that will affect costs will be:

  (i)   technological changes;

  (ii)   the impact of learning effects;

  (iii)   inflationary effects (we can compensate for this by discounting all costs to a common time period); and

  (iv)   extraordinary circumstances in any given period(s).

The assumptions of regression analysis

The regression analysis is based on sample data and if we selected a different sample it is probable that a different regression line would be constructed. For this reason, regression analysis is most suited to conditions where there is a relatively stable relationship between cost and activity level.

Assumptions we are making:
- The relationship is a linear one.
- The data used is representative of future trends.

Linearity

In the majority of cases, management will rely on linear models to relate costs to output levels. This in itself makes certain assumptions:
- Each unit of output uses the same physical quantity of inputs.
- Unit prices of inputs remain constant regardless of the quantity used or purchased.

Management must carefully assess a range of output levels over which such assumptions are likely to hold good. Preliminary assessments as to linearity can be made by considering a scatter diagram.

Representativeness of observations

Where the data includes one unusual observation, then the least-squares criterion gives a great deal of weight to that individual observation. For example results for a single period could have been distorted by a strike or material shortage, keeping costs artificially high compared with output level. In such circumstances we may be justified in eliminating such an outlying observation from our analysis, since it is wholly unrepresentative of our normal operating conditions.

Consider the diagram below:

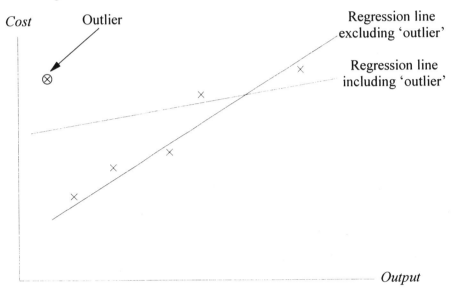

$\otimes$ = *outlying observation that could be validly excluded from regression analysis*

It should be noted that we must not simply exclude observations just to get a line of good fit! There must be a valid reason for exclusion of any given data.

ACCOUNTING FOR OVERHEADS

Introduction

We have discussed the idea of the collection of costs: initially in cost centres and then attributing them to the cost units passing through those cost centres.

Do all costs eventually get attributed to (absorbed by) cost units?

Two points to note regarding the absorption of costs into cost units:

Production/selling costs – In a manufacturing context, stocks of finished goods will *never* include an element of selling costs. The stocks will be valued at production costs only (including overheads). However, for pricing or profitability purposes, the cost of units sold may well include a selling cost element.

Fixed/variable costs – Whether or not all production costs will be absorbed into cost units for stock valuation will depend upon the particular system being used.

A **total absorption costing (TAC)** system will absorb all production costs (direct or indirect, fixed or variable) into cost units.

A **marginal costing (MC)** system will only absorb variable costs (direct and indirect) into cost units. Fixed costs will be treated as period costs, and treated as a 'lump sum' against the profits of the period concerned.

We shall compare and contrast these two systems in detail in a later session.

For the remainder of this session, it is assumed that a TAC system is in operation and we shall consider how, in particular, all production overheads are allocated, apportioned and absorbed into cost units.

Allocation, apportionment and absorption

We have already identified two types of costs that make up the full production cost of a unit:

(a)   **Direct costs** are those that can be uniquely identified with an individual cost unit (eg. direct materials, direct labour, direct expenses).

(b)   **Indirect costs** (overheads) are costs incurred in production, not easily 'traced' to individual units, eg. machine power (variable), factory rent (fixed), heat and light (semi-variable).

The problem we are considering here is how to divide indirect costs between cost units, in order to prepare a 'standard' cost card for budgeting stock valuation and pricing purposes.

Standard cost card

	£
Direct materials	X
Direct labour	X
Direct expenses	X
Prime cost	X
Variable production overhead	X
Marginal cost	X
Fixed production overhead	X
Total production cost per unit	X

The method used to divide overheads between production units is made up of three processes: *allocation*, *apportionment* and *absorption*. Before commencing these processes, it is necessary to split the factory up into separate cost centres, because the first step in the process is to collect these indirect costs via cost centres.

Cost allocation

Certain cost items will be incurred entirely by one cost centre. Allocation deals with this type of cost and simply allots it to the cost centre which has incurred the cost.

Illustration

Cost centre	*Allocated cost*
Canteen	Tea bags
	Spaghetti
	Chef's wages
Packing department	Cardboard
	String

Cost apportionment (primary)

More frequently, however, the benefit of an item of cost will be shared by a number of cost centres. The overhead will be split or apportioned between the relevant cost centres on an 'equitable' basis.

The rent of buildings, for example, can relate to the total floor space occupied by a number of different departments and it is usual to allot the rental charge to those departments in proportion to the floor space they occupy.

Examples of bases of apportioning overheads

Nature of cost	*Possible bases of apportionment*
Rent and rates	Floor area occupied by various departments
Lighting and heating	Cubic capacity of locations or metered usage
Insurance of stocks	Value of stockholdings in various locations

Apportionment (secondary)

After completing the allocation and primary apportionment stages, you should have assigned all costs to cost centres.

Some cost centres, however, will not have production units passing through them; these cost centres are called *service departments* (eg. quality control department, works canteen). Before the final stage of absorption into cost units can be carried out, it is necessary to perform a further type of apportionment whereby the total costs of the service cost centres are reassigned to production cost centres. This is known as **secondary apportionment**. This should be done on a fair basis to reflect the benefit derived from the service centre.

Absorption

Having collected all indirect costs in the production cost centres via overhead allocation and apportionment, the cost has to be spread over the output of the production cost centre.

The allotment of accumulated overhead costs to cost units is called **overhead absorption**. The absorption rate is normally calculated at the start of the period and therefore based on budgeted quantities. Various methods of absorption exist and the one most fitting should be chosen.

The following are the most common methods you will encounter:

Rate per unit

The simple unit rate is obtained by dividing total overheads by the number of units produced. However, where more than one product is produced, this is an unsatisfactory basis for absorbing overheads as it will not reflect the relative demands of each product on the production departments through which they pass.

Alternative bases of absorption

There are a number of bases commonly used as an alternative to the simple unit rate:

(a)   rate per direct labour hour;
(b)   rate per machine hour;
(c)   percentage of material cost;
(d)   percentage of wage cost;
(e)   percentage of prime cost.

It is important to appreciate, however, that whichever method or combination of methods is used, the result will only be an approximate estimate of what that product actually costs.

Comments

In practice, many businesses use a 'direct labour hour rate' or 'machine hour rate' in preference to a rate based on a percentage of direct materials cost, direct wages or prime cost, as it may be possible to associate some overheads either with labour time or with machine time.

Notes

(1)   It may be possible to analyse the total overhead apportioned to each production department into fixed and variable elements. In this case a variable overhead rate per unit and a fixed overhead rate per unit can be calculated.

(2)   The absorption rates will normally be calculated at the beginning of a period and hence be based on budgeted costs and production levels. This can lead to problems when actual costs and volumes are not the same as budgeted (see over- and under-absorption in a later session).

Worked illustration

The following illustration covers all stages of overhead allocation, apportionment and absorption summarised above. Work through it carefully to ensure you have fully revised this area.

Squareplant Ltd manufactures confectionery which they sell to the retail market. At present, it makes two products: the Dig-Dog and the Floater. Each product is sold in boxes of 500. Variable cost per 500 for each of the two lines is as follows:

	Dig-Dog £	Floater £
Chocolate	6	7
Biscuit	4	8
Wrapping	7	7
Labour	7	8
Variable production overheads	8	10
	32	40

A fixed overhead rate per unit has not yet been established, but the following information is relevant.

Fixed overhead budget

	£
Rent and rates	160,000
Plant and machinery depreciation and maintenance	250,000
Supervisors' salaries	80,000
Heat and light	120,000
Insurance of fixed assets	30,000
Sundry fixed costs	35,000
Sundry canteen costs	50,000
Sundry quality control costs	75,000

The products are made in two departments, Mixing and Packaging. The time taken in each department per box of 500 of each product is as follows:

	Mixing (hours)	Packaging (hours)
Dig-Dog	2	0.50
Floater	1.5	0.775

The two production departments are serviced by the Canteen and the Quality Control Department. You ascertain the following information regarding the four departments.

(a)   Staff numbers

Canteen	4
Quality control	10
Packaging	30
Mixing	65

(b)   The Quality Control Department members spend, on average, five times as long working on the Mixing Department compared with the Packaging Department.

(c)   There are ten supervisors included in the staff members above: one each in the Canteen and Quality Control, three in Packaging and the remainder in Mixing.

(d)   The net book value of fixed assets in the Quality Control Department is £80,000, none of which is plant and machinery. The other departments have fixed assets as follows:

Canteen	£80,000
Packaging	£640,000
Mixing	£400,000

These include plant and machinery of £40,000, £600,000 and £360,000 respectively.

(e)   The factory occupies 12,800 square metres. The Mixing Department accounts for 4,800 square metres and the Packaging Department accounts for 5,600 square metres. The remaining area is split in the ratio 2 (Canteen): 1 (Quality Control).

(f)   Sundry fixed costs should be split £10,000 (Mixing), £17,500 (Packaging) and £7,500 (Quality Control).

(g)   The budgeted production levels (in boxes of 500) for the forthcoming period are 90,000 Dig-Dogs and 40,000 Floaters.

Required

Calculate, using suitable bases of apportionment of fixed overheads, a total absorption cost for each product if the overheads are to be absorbed on a labour hours basis.

Solution

The requirement is for a total absorption cost for each product. Since the variable costs per unit are given , the main task is to calculate a fixed overhead cost per unit.

Allocation and primary apportionment

We are told that there are four cost centres: two production (Mixing and Packaging) and two service [Canteen and Quality Control (QC)]. Thus we will first need to allocate and apportion the costs shown in the fixed overhead budget between these four centres.

The first task is to draw up a table, with the fixed costs as listed in the question shown on the left-hand side. Five more columns are needed – one to indicate the basis of apportionment and one for each of the cost centres. Now start to allocate and apportion costs:

Sundry canteen and QC costs – These can be directly allocated to the respective departments.

Rent and rates – The most common basis for apportionment is floor area. The necessary information is given in paragraph (e).

The calculations are as follows:

The Mixing and Packaging departments occupy a total of 4,800 + 5,600 = 10,400 square metres. This leaves 12,800 – 10,400 = 2,400 for canteen and QC. This is split in the ratio 2:1, ie. 2/3 (1,600) to canteen and 1/3 (800) to QC.

Thus the final split is as follows:

Cost centre	Floor area (sq. m)					Apportioned cost £
Mixing	4,800	£160,000	×	4,800/12,800	=	60,000
Packaging	5,600	£160,000	×	5,600/12,800	=	70,000
Canteen	1,600	£160,000	×	1,600/12,800	=	20,000
QC	800	£160,000	×	800/12,800	=	10,000
	12,800					160,000

These costs can be entered into your table.

Plant and machinery depreciation and maintenance – Look for some information about numbers or values of machines used in each department. This is given in paragraph (d). Note that QC has no plant and machinery, and the cost will therefore only be apportioned between the other three departments, using the values of their plant and machinery as a basis:

Cost centre	P&M NBV £					Apportioned cost £
Mixing	360,000	£250,000	×	360,000/1m	=	90,000
Packaging	600,000	£250,000	×	600,000/1m	=	150,000
Canteen	40,000	£250,000	×	40,000/1m	=	10,000
	1,000,000					250,000

The remaining costs will be apportioned in the same way, using the bases and with the results shown below. Make sure you are happy with the amounts computed.

Overhead	Total £	Basis of apportionment	Mixing £	Packaging £	Canteen £	Quality control £
Sundry canteen costs	50,000	Direct allocation	–	–	50,000	–
Sundry quality control costs	75,000	Direct allocation	–	–	–	75,000
Supervisors' salaries	80,000	Number of supervisors 5:3:1:1	40,000	24,000	8,000	8,000
Heat and light	120,000	Floor space 6:7:2:1	45,000	52,500	15,000	7,500
Rent and rates	160,000	Floor space 6:7:2:1	60,000	70,000	20,000	10,000
Machine depreciation and maintenance	250,000	NBV of plant 9:15:1	90,000	150,000	10,000	–
Fixed asset insurance	30,000	NBV of fixed assets 5:8:1:1	10,000	16,000	2,000	2,000
Sundry fixed costs	35,000	As specified	10,000	17,500	–	7,500
	800,000		255,000	330,000	105,000	110,000

Secondary apportionment

All costs have eventually to end up apportioned between the two production departments. Therefore we have to use suitable bases for reapportioning the total costs currently in the two service departments (£105,000 – canteen and £110,000 – QC).

Apportioning of canteen costs is commonly done on the basis of the number of staff in each department. This information is given in paragraph (a). Because we want to empty the canteen of all costs, we will ignore the number of staff in the canteen itself. Thus the canteen's cost will be re apportioned between Mixing, Packaging and QC in the ratio 65:30:10.

Note that this will add an extra £105,000 × 10/105 = £10,000 to the costs of QC. Thus we now have a total of £120,000 to reapportion from QC. This only serves the two production departments, and paragraph (b) gives the necessary information to split it in the ratio 5:1 (Mixing : Packaging).

The final apportionments are thus as follows (this would normally follow straight on in the statement from the initial apportionment and absorption):

Allocated/ apportioned costs	255,000	330,000	105,000	110,000
Reapportion canteen (65:30:10)	65,000	30,000	(105,000)	10,000
				120,000
Reapportion QC (5:1)	100,000	20,000		(120,000)
	420,000	380,000		

Note that the order in which you choose to reapportion the service departments' costs is important if you are to be as efficient as possible. Consider what would have happened if QC's costs had been cleared out first – splitting the original £110,000 in the ratio 5:1. The canteen would have been reapportioned, as above, and so put £10,000 back into QC. This would then have had to have been reapportioned out again (5:1). The same results would be derived, but it would have taken more work – and even more so had there been more than two service departments.

Thus the general rule is to reapportion the service department that does not receive service from elsewhere first; the canteen does not receive service from QC.

You may wonder what happens if the canteen had indeed received service from QC, as well as vice versa. This is known as **reciprocal service** and is dealt with after this example.

Absorption

The overhead costs have now been attributed entirely to production departments and can now be absorbed into cost units (which in this case are boxes of 500 of each product).

This is to be done via a labour hour absorption rate. First, a cost per labour hour for each production department, based upon budgeted production [paragraph (g) and hours per unit (given after the fixed overhead budget figures)] needs to be worked out:

For each department, absorption rate per labour hour $= \dfrac{\text{Overheads}}{\text{Hours worked}}$

For Mixing

Hours worked	$90,000 \times 2$	180,000
	$40,000 \times 1.5$	60,000
		240,000

$$\therefore \quad \text{Rate} = \frac{420,000}{240,000} = \text{£1.75 per hour}$$

For Packaging

Hours worked	$90,000 \times 0.5$	45,000
	$40,000 \times 0.775$	31,000
		76,000

$$\therefore \quad \text{Rate} = \frac{380,000}{76,000} = \text{£5.00 per hour}$$

Now each product is to be charged with the appropriate number of hours' worth of overheads from each department – so a Dig-Dog gets charged with 2 hours of Mixing overheads (at £1.75 per hour) and 0.5 hours of Packaging overheads (at £5 per hour). Combining these charges with the variable costs already given in the question gives the TAC per unit for each product as follows:

TAC per unit

Fixed overhead per unit:

Dig-Dog	(1.75×2)	+	(5×0.5)	=	£6 per unit
Floater	(1.75×1.5)	+	(5×0.775)	=	£6.50 per unit

$\therefore$ Cost per unit:

	Dig-Dog £	*Floater* £
Marginal cost	32.00	40.00
Fixed overhead	6.00	6.50
	38.00	46.50

Over-/under-absorption of fixed overheads

The TAC requires all production costs, fixed and variable, to be identified with individual cost units. Thus the above example shows a standard cost of a Dig-Dog as £38, £32 variable and £6 fixed. Similarly, the cost of a Floater, £46.50, included a fixed element of £6.50.

The original budget for the production of these products was 90,000 units and 40,000 units respectively. Thus the budgeted total costs were as follows:

Variable:	$90,000 \times$ £32 $+ 40,000 \times$ £40	= £4,480,000
Fixed:	$90,000 \times$ £6 $+ 40,000 \times$ £6.50	= £800,000

Suppose in the period the actual levels of production were 120,000 Dig-Dogs and 40,000 Floaters, and that all material, labour and variable overhead costs per unit and fixed costs for the period were as budgeted.

The TAC system would account for total costs as follows:

Variable: $120,000 \times £32 + 40,000 \times £40 = £5,440,000$
Fixed: $120,000 \times £6 + 40,000 \times £6.50 = £980,000$

Are these correct? Variable costs, by definition, are expected to rise with increased production, but why should £980,000 fixed overheads be accounted for when only £800,000 were actually incurred?

The problem arises from the calculation of the fixed overhead rate per unit. This was calculated via absorption rates for each production cost centre, where a fixed total cost (which is not expected to vary with production levels) was divided by a budgeted activity level – in this case, direct labour hours.

If it had been known that a higher number of Dig-Dogs would be produced, then different (lower) hourly absorption rates and thus costs per unit would have been calculated.

However, actual production levels are not known until the end of the period, by which time each product has been charged with the standard fixed costs per unit.

So an adjustment for the over-absorption of overheads needs to be made at the end of the period. The over-absorption has arisen from a surplus production (over budget) of 30,000 Dig-Dogs, which have each absorbed £6 per unit in fixed costs. The adjustment would thus be made as follows:

	£
Standard fixed cost absorbed into production	980,000
Less: Over-absorption, due to surplus production of Dig-Dogs (30,000 × £6)	(180,000)
Actual (= budget) fixed overhead incurred	800,000

Had there been a deficit in production or a change of mix of products, an adjustment for under-absorption may have to have been made.

ACTIVITY-BASED COSTING (ABC)

Criticisms of traditional approach to overhead absorption

In the worked example above, a direct labour hour rate was used for absorption of all fixed overheads. This has historically been a very common method, as production tended to be highly labour-intensive in the past. Thus it was reasonable to assume that the more labour time spent on a product, the more production resources in general were being used. Thus the product should be charged with a higher share of the overheads.

However, nowadays, production is far more mechanised. This has two impacts:

(a)   A higher proportion of the overheads is accounted for by machine-related costs (power, depreciation, maintenance, etc.).

(b)   The amount of labour time spent upon a unit is far less representative of its final significance in the use of production resources.

To take a simple example, Product A may use 9 machine hours and 1 labour hour, whilst Product B requires 4 labour hours and 1 machine hour. The traditional approach would charge B with four times as much production overhead (including machine costs) as A, even though it takes half the time overall.

In this example, one solution would be to use machine hours as a basis. However, this still tries to relate all overhead costs, whatever their nature, to usage of machines. This would not necessarily be appropriate for, say, costs of receiving and checking materials going into the production process. This will be more likely to depend upon the number of times an order of material is received into stores for a particular product.

Activity-based costing (ABC) approach

Professors Robin Cooper and Robert Kaplan at the Harvard Business School have developed a costing system called **activity-based costing** (ABC) which avoids the problems experienced by traditional costing methods. If management are keen to control costs, then it is vital that they should know the activities that cause costs to arise. Those activities that are the significant determinants of cost are known as **cost-drivers**. For example, if production-scheduling cost is driven by the number of production set-ups, then that number is the cost-driver for the cost of production–scheduling. The cost-drivers represent the bases for charging costs in the ABC system, with a separate cost centre established for each cost-driver.

The following example contrasts a traditional product costing system with an ABC system and shows that an ABC system produces much more accurate product costs.

Illustration

Mayes plc has a single production centre and has provided the following information for the period just ended.

	Product A	*Product B*	*Product C*	*Total*
Production and sales (units)	40,000	25,000	10,000	75,000
Direct material cost	£25	£20	£18	£1,680,000
Direct labour hours	3	4	2	240,000
Machine hours	2	4	3	210,000
Number of production runs	5	10	25	40
Number of component receipts	15	25	120	160
Number of production orders	15	10	25	50

Direct labour is paid £8 per hour.

Overhead costs in the period have been as follows:

	£
Set-up	140,000
Machine	900,000
Goods inwards	280,000
Packing	200,000
Engineering	180,000
	1,700,000

A traditional costing approach would cost each product as follows:

	Product A £	Product B £	Product C £
Direct materials	25.0	20.0	18.0
Direct labour (@ £8 per hour)	24.0	32.0	16.0
Over head(@ £7.08 per hour)	21.24	28.32	14.16
	70.24	80.32	48.16

$$\text{Overhead recovery rate} = \frac{£1,700,00}{240,000} = £7.08 \text{ per direct labour hour}$$

An ABC system needs to investigate the cost determinants for the indirect overheads not driven by production volume. Assume that these are as follows:

Cost	Cost-driver
Set-up	Number of set-ups
Goods inward	Number of receipts
Packing	Number of production orders
Engineering	Number of production orders

The machine overhead of £900,000 is likely to be related primarily to production volume, so it will be recovered on the basis of machine hours used.

The cost per activity for each of the cost centres is as follows.

$$\text{Set-up cost} \quad \frac{£140,000}{40} = £3,500 \text{ per set-up}$$

$$\text{Goods inward} \quad \frac{£280,000}{160} = £1,750 \text{ per receipt}$$

$$\text{Packing} \quad \frac{£200,000}{50} = £4,000 \text{ per order}$$

$$\text{Engineering} \quad \frac{£180,000}{50} = £3,600 \text{ per order}$$

An ABC approach would cost each product as follows:

	Product A £	Product B £	Product C £
Direct materials	25.0	20.0	18.0
Direct labour	24.0	32.0	16.0
Set-up	0.44	1.40	8.75
Machine	8.57	17.14	12.86
Goods inwards	0.66	1.75	21.00
Packing	1.50	1.60	10.00
Engineering	1.35	1.44	9.00
	61.52	75.33	95.61

It can be seen that product C is significantly under-costed under the traditional system, while products A and B are over-costed. This situation arises because the large proportion of costs driven by product C is not picked up under the traditional costing system. Since it is the cost-drivers identified in the ABC system which generate the costs in the first place, the ABC system must produce a more accurate final analysis.

STANDARD COSTING AND VARIANCE ANALYSIS

Standard cost card

Whilst dealing with overheads, we referred to the standard cost card for a product (see page 30).

You will recall from your earlier studies that this sets out a predetermined cost per unit for the product, based on management's estimation of prices and rates prevalent through the budget period and reasonably efficient levels of efficiency and usage of resources.

This may be used as a basis for setting prices, for valuing stock and for providing control over actual costs through the process of variance analysis.

The setting and use of standard costs is an important part of your studies for Units 11–13, and will be revised in depth in the following session.

Variance analysis

Variance analysis is the comparison of expected results with actual results. Expected results will be derived from the budgets, which will incorporate forecasts (often of demand), planned production levels and product unit standards (costs and prices).

Periodically throughout the budget period, variances from budget will be isolated, analysed by cause wherever possible and any necessary corrective action taken.

Variance analysis and investigation form part of the required knowledge for Units 11 and 12 in particular; the topic is covered in detail in the following two sessions.

QUESTIONS

1   AB Ltd   **(AAT CA J94)**

You have been asked to give a short talk to new employees who are attending your company's trainee induction programme.   The talk will be entitled *The importance of understanding cost behaviour*.

You are now in the process of preparing materials for your talk.

Assessment tasks

(a)   You have decided that you will use sketch graphs to demonstrate cost behaviour patterns. In preparation for your talk, produce sketch graphs which will demonstrate the way in which the following costs behave in relation to the level of activity:

  (i)   fixed costs
  (ii)   variable costs
  (iii)   semi-variable costs
  (iv)   fixed cost per unit
  (v)   variable cost per unit

  Note: You do not need to use graph paper because only sketches will be necessary. However, it is important that you should draw clear diagrams with correctly labelled axes. For ease of explanation, you decide to assume that all costs are linear.

(b)   For each of the graphs in Task 1, prepare brief notes for your talk which explain the shape of the graph. Also note down **two** examples of **each** of costs (1), (2) and (3) above so that you can give them to your audience if requested.

(c)   Prepare a further brief set of notes for your talk which explains why an understanding of cost behaviour patterns is necessary for effective planning and control in an organisation.

2   Linear costs

(a)   Give three examples of pairs of variables which are linearly correlated over a certain range but where the linear relationship breaks down outside the range.

(b)   Calculate the regression line of total cost on output from the figures given below and hence estimate the fixed and variable costs of production:

Output (thousands of units)	Cost of production (£'000)
5	11.8
7	14.7
9	18.5
11	24.0
13	26.2
15	30.1

3 Luda Ltd

Luda Ltd manufactures three products: P, Q and R. Each product is started in the machining area and completed in the finishing shop. The direct unit costs associated with each product forecast for the next trading period are as follows:

	P	*Q*	*R*
	£	£	£
Materials	18.50	15.00	22.50
Wages:			
Machining area @ £5 per hour	10.00	5.00	10.00
Finishing shop @ £4 per hour	6.00	4.00	8.00
	34.50	24.00	40.50

There are machines in both departments and machine hours required to complete one of each product are:

	P	*Q*	*R*
Machine area	4	1.5	3
Finishing shop	0.5	0.5	1
Budget output in units	6,000	8,000	2,000

Fixed overheads

Machine area	£100,800
Finishing shop	£94,500

Required

(a) Calculate the overhead absorption rate for fixed overheads using:

(i) a labour hour rate for each department;
(ii) a machine hour rate for each department.

(b) Calculate the total cost of each product using:

(i) the labour hour rate;
(ii) the machine hour rate, as calculated in (a) above.

(c) Set out your comments to the factory manager who has suggested that one overhead rate for both departments would simplify matters.

4 Lorus Ltd

Lorus Ltd makes cupboards. This involves three production departments (Sawing, Assembly and Finishing) together with two service departments (Maintenance and Materials Handling).

Last year 4,000 cupboards were made.

Costs incurred:

	Sawing	*Assembly*	*Finishing*
	£	£	£
Materials	120,000	80,000	20,000
Wages	50,000	25,000	40,000
Overheads	75,000	50,000	20,000

Materials Handling wages: £9,000

Maintenance wages: £15,000

Consumable stores: £5,000 (Maintenance)

The benefits derived from the service departments are estimated to be as follows:

	Sawing *%*	*Assembly* *%*	*Finishing* *%*	*Materials Handling* *%*
Maintenance	30	40	20	10
Materials Handling	50	20	30	

Required

(a)   Prepare a memorandum to the managing director, copied to each production head, showing the overheads allotted to each production department.

(b)   Calculate the unit cost of a cupboard.

5   Bennick Ltd

Bennick Ltd has two departments (A and B) engaged in manufacturing operations and they are serviced by a Stores, Maintenance Department and Tool Room.

The following has been budgeted for the next financial period:

				Overheads		
	Total *£'000*	*A* *£'000*	*B* *£'000*	*Stores* *£'000*	*Maintenance* *£'000*	*Tool Room* *£'000*
Indirect labour	1,837	620	846	149	115	107
Supervision	140					
Power	160					
Rent	280					
Rates	112					
Plant insurance	40					
Plant depreciation	20					
	2,589					

Additional information available includes the following:

	A	*B*	*Stores*	*Maintenance*	*Tool Room*
Floor area (square metres)	1,000	2,500	1,100	600	400
Number of employees	30	50	10	20	30
Power (kilowatt hours)	60,000	30,000	3,000	15,000	12,000
Number of material requisitions	5,000	6,000	–	2,000	3,000
Maintenance hours	8,000	9,000	–	–	6,000
Plant valuation (£)	50,000	40,000	–	5,000	5,000
Tool room hours estimated	7,000	10,000	–	–	–
Machine hours estimated	55,200	99,000	–	–	–

Required

Calculate appropriate machine hour overhead absorption rates for both manufacturing departments in which all overheads will be recovered, and to show clearly the method of overhead allocation.

6   Costing methods

The traditional methods of cost allocation, cost apportionment and absorption into products are being challenged by some writers who claim that much information given to management is misleading when these methods of dealing with fixed overheads are used to determine product costs.

Required

Explain what is meant by **cost allocation**, **cost apportionment** and **absorption** and describe briefly the alternative approach of **activity-based costing** in order to ascertain total product costs.

SUMMARY

This session has revised several fundamental cost accounting topics from your earlier studies. You will need to be prepared to use any of the techniques and ideas covered in any of the Units' examinations.

In particular, ensure you are confident on:

- the derivation and use of cost units for different types of activities and businesses

- the techniques for splitting semi-variable costs

- the treatment of overheads, including:

    – allocation/apportionment/absorption
    – service departments
    – over-/under-absorption
    – activity-based costing approach

Presentation of reports

OBJECTIVES

Unit 11, in particular, requires a knowledge of methods of presenting reports, including tables, diagrams and graphs.

This represents revision of your earlier studies for Unit 7, *Reports and Returns*. Relevant parts of study material for Unit 7 have been reproduced here, covering

- report preparation and writing
- tables
- charts and diagrams
- graphs

The performance criteria addressed by this session is as follows:

- Timely information is presented to managers in a clear and appropriate form.

INTRODUCTION

A report could be defined as an orderly and objective *communication* of factual *information* which serves some business aim. Its purpose is to convey information to particular readers or to answer a question.

Report is a general term. A letter containing specific information or a memo drawing someone's attention to certain details could be classified as a report.

Reports do not even have to be written; people are often requested to, or offer to, make oral reports.

Its object is **communication**, not to show how much knowledge the writer possesses. Reports vary in length and status from simple printed forms (such as *accident reports*) to the major investigative reports commissioned by governments.

The prime reason for producing a report is to save time (and thus money). The further people rise up the promotional ladder within a firm or an organisation, the more money they receive and the more precious their time becomes. They have no time to do the research and investigation necessary before producing a report. Generally, someone else produces the report for their use. Furthermore, successful report-writers package the document in such a form that it can be quickly and easily read to ensure no more time is spent in reading the report than is absolutely necessary.

Another reason for producing written reports is to provide a permanent source of reference.

Even a number of years after being produced, a report might need to be consulted to solve a problem, to find out the details of an accident or to determine who recommended a certain course of action.

DATA COLLECTION

The difficulty of this exercise will depend upon the nature of the report.

A lot of management reports will consist of the analysis of sales, costs and other internal data that will already be available from the financial and cost accounting systems, and thus will be easy to ascertain.

Other reports may involve information that is external either to the monetary accounting systems (eg. customer preferences, satisfaction, etc.) or to the business (eg. information concerning market or industry volumes, trends, averages, etc.).

In these latter cases, information will need to be collected by survey or from external sources, often by use of sampling from an appropriate population.

Population and sample

Before setting out on an exercise involving collection of data, we must decide what data or figures we wish to collect. This may seem rather obvious but take the following situation: *You are required to determine average annual turnover of companies in the engineering sector.*

Firstly, does this mean all companies in the world, only the EC or can we assume we are only concerned with the UK? Secondly, are we to consider all types of engineering or a specific type of engineering? Do we want all companies with any interest in the engineering sector or only those whose interest is in this sector alone? How are we to describe turnover? Should it be in numbers of individual products or services sold, or in overall money terms or some other description?

As you can see, care must be taken at this stage. The first step is to decide what the aim is in collecting the data. When we have decided exactly what we are trying to establish we can determine what people or companies or other sources we need to collect data from. The whole group of items or people we are concerned with is called the **population**. As we have already mentioned it is unlikely that we would collect data from all the members of a population, but rather from a selection of the population. The group of members of a population is called the **sample**.

Suppose we wish to establish average earnings per month of college lecturers, we might go to one or two colleges and ask those lecturers we meet what their monthly earnings are. In this situation the population would be all college lecturers and the sample would be those college lecturers who actually told us their monthly salary.

The word population does not only refer to people. Consider a situation where we wish to find the average contents of bottles stored in a warehouse. As there are several thousand crates of bottles within the warehouse we decide to measure the contents of a few bottles chosen at random from some of the crates. In this instance the population is every bottle in the warehouse and the sample is the group of bottles whose contents we actually measure.

Sampling methods

If we decide that collecting data from a whole population is inappropriate, then we need to choose a sample. But how do we select our sample? There are many methods of sampling used. Our aim is to obtain as fair and representative a sample as we can manage within the limitations of cost, time and required accuracy. Suppose we wish to determine the average annual earnings of adult employees in the UK. Before we can consider the sample we are going to use, we need a list of the population to be investigated. This list is called the **sampling frame**. This is not always easy to establish but, if we assume such a list is available, how do we decide which members of the population to sample?

Simple random sampling

This is a method in which every member of a population has an equal chance of being chosen in the sample. One way this can be achieved is by *numbering* every member of a population, putting their numbers into a hat, mixing the numbers up and drawing out numbers of those to be used in the sample. In practice, this exercise would generally be carried out by use of a computer. If a sample is to be fair, it is necessary for some sort of random sampling to be used. In our example above, if we selected a random sample then those people chosen would be spread all round the UK and it might turn out to be very costly and time-consuming to collect the data. However, if this were acceptable, we might wish to improve the accuracy of our results.

Stratified random sampling

If our population consists of a collection of different groupings, then we can extend the idea of random sampling so that our population is split into these sub-groups and a random sample taken from the different sub-groups. If a population has sub-groups within it, then this is the most reliable method of sampling. It is usual for the sample size for each sub-group to be in the same *proportion* as the size of the sub-group to the population.

Multi-stage sampling

If the expense and/or time involved in carrying out simple or stratified random sampling is excessive, then a possible alternative is to use multi-stage sampling. This involves the selection of a few areas at random from the population as a whole (say a few counties picked at random). We then take a random sample of boroughs from each county. Finally we pick a random sample of people from each borough (from each sub-group). It is hoped that this will reduce the time and cost involved in collecting the data required but we lose some of the reliability of our results as a consequence.

Cluster sampling

We can take multi-stage sampling a step further and say that certain areas are representative of the population as a whole and we will sample everyone in these areas, rather than take a random sample.

Quota sampling

In this method, you specify how many people or items within a certain group you want to sample (ie. set a quota) and then collect your data from anyone or anything that fits the required category until the quota is filled. This method is widely used by interviewers encountered in town centres; it is also the least accurate of sampling methods.

Systematic sampling

This method (also called 'interval sampling') picks the first item or person at random then subsequently samples each 10th or 100th or 834th (or any other *interval* you want to use). This is a method widely used in *quality control* of items produced.

Survey design

We now consider how to obtain the information we require from those items or people we have chosen to form our sample. There are basically two approaches we can use: direct measurement or questioning.

Direct measurement

Where the information we require can be measured or counted we can arrange for ourselves or someone else to take the necessary measurements directly. This method has the distinct advantage that accurate measurements can be obtained.

Questioning

This method is usually based on a formal questionnaire and it is important that it is designed properly. A questionnaire can be administered in several different ways but the three methods used are personally, by post or by telephone.

- *Personal questionnaires*. An interviewer has a set of questions that he or she asks selected individuals. It has the advantage that the results can be obtained quickly and reliably.

- *Postal questionnaires*. This involves sending the respondent a questionnaire which he or she then completes and returns. This method, although cheaper than using personal interviews, has a problem in that the response rate is usually quite low. Also, there can be problems if the respondent fails to understand the questions or simply does not answer some of the questions.

- *Telephone questionnaires*. This method, if used at off peak rates, can be cheaper than the postal questionnaire and usually gives a higher response rate. There is, however, one major consideration with this method which should not be overlooked. Not everyone has a telephone, so the population you are trying to reach should be those who have telephones, otherwise the sample can be unrepresentative.

Questionnaire design

Great care must be taken in the design of questionnaire. The following points should be noted:

- Ask as few questions as you can while still obtaining the information you require.

- Make the questions themselves as short as possible.

- Make the questions as simple as possible.

- Avoid ambiguous questions.

- Do not ask questions leading to a certain answer.

- Do not use questions which use emotive language.

- Do not ask personal questions.

- Make sure the questions being asked are relevant to and can be understood by the person answering them.

- Whenever possible give people a set of answers to choose from. This will minimise the problems you will encounter when categorising answers. You should, however, allow people the opportunity to give an answer other than those you specify, should they wish to.

- Make the questionnaire look simple and interesting so people will want to answer the questions.

PLANNING THE REPORT

Once you have gathered all the facts and data that may be relevant to the report, there are two further steps to be carried out before you start actually writing it:

- select what is needed
- plan how to set it out

Select what is needed

Resist the temptation to put all you know into the report. Knowing what to leave out is as important as knowing what to put in. Ask yourself the following questions.

- What is the purpose of this report?
- What do I want to tell my readers?
- What do they need to know?
- Who is going to read it?
- What do they know already?
- When are they going to read it?

The answers to these questions will determine such matters as:

- how much information is included;
- how technical or simple the report should be;
- how much background material is required;
- whether some of the material will be irrelevant when the report is read.

Plan how to set it out

The aim at this stage is to get a logical sequence of what you are going to write.

Check that your main headings are in the right order and that sections most closely connected in ideas stand next to each other physically (as far as possible) and that they follow in logical sequence.

Within these sections, you might want to write in subheadings; if so, make sure that these too are in a logical order.

The report should be clearly structured into sections under relevant headings, so that the main topic of the report is clearly set out, developed and explained, and the subsequent conclusions fully supported.

Paragraphs should be more than one sentence long and each should revolve around a common theme or sub-topic. Paragraphs usually consist of a key sentence making a point, with examples or evidence in support of the point.

Sections should consist of one or more paragraphs, dealing with different aspects of the same subtopic, if necessary divided into sub-sections each with an appropriate heading. All headings should appear in the table of contents.

The conclusions should not come as a surprise, due to inadequate preparation of the reader in the main body of the report. You should be clear what your conclusions are before you write the report.

Summary

Collecting and organising the content of a report are vital steps in report writing. However well written a report, it will fail if the basic facts and figures upon which it is based are incorrect, inadequate, biased or irrelevant.

THE STRUCTURE OF THE REPORT

Five different functions that reports can serve can be established as follows:

- informing
- analysing
- evaluating
- recommending
- describing

Reports can take many forms and can vary in length and status. Management reports may take one of the following forms:

(a)   simple reports in short report, letter or memo format
(b)   reports on internal matters within a company which may be formal or informal

Simple reports in short report, letter or memo form

Most written reports in industry are short informal types, concerning day-to-day problems. As such they have a short life. They are not likely to be kept on file for posterity to read, but are intended for only a few readers who know the problem and its background. The reader's interests are generally in the findings of the report and any action it will lead to.

The situation that gives rise to a short informal report usually involves more personal relationships. Such reports tend to be from and to people who address each other informally when they meet and talk. In addition, the shorter reports by their nature are apt to involve a personal investigation. The finished work represents the personal observations, evaluations and analyses of the writers. The writers are expected to report their work as their own and, as such, the writing style tends to be more personal, using I, we, you, rather than a third party approach.

Of the conventional short forms of informal report, three in particular deserve special attention: the short report, the letter report and the memorandum report. Varying widely in form and arrangement, they make up the bulk of the reports written in industry and commerce.

The short informal report

This is generally only a two or three section report. The main areas are:

- the name of the person requesting the report;
- the title;
- an introduction, which may also give the background;
- the procedure, information, findings and 'overview' of the problem;
- the conclusion;
- the name and position within the company of the writer; and
- the date.

The following example shows the basic structure but may be adapted to suit different requirements.

To: D Fagen

Accounts Department reaction to proposed hot drinks vending machine installation

Introduction

This report describes the reaction of staff in the Accounts Department of the Kenilworth branch office of Teck Bros. to a proposal to replace existing tea and coffee-making arrangements with a hot drinks vending machine. The report was prepared on the instructions of D Fagen, Branch Manager and written by J Ely, Office Junior, Accounts Department. Instructions to prepare the report were received on 24 July 1996 and it was submitted on 29 July 1996.

Procedure

It was decided to interview personally all twelve members of staff in the Accounts Department. All staff were notified in advance. Questions were devised, three to establish staff reactions and a fourth inviting comments. All staff were then interviewed and the results noted. (A copy is appended to this report.)

Findings

(a)   In response to the question 'Would you be happy to see a vending machine installed?' EIGHT people said Yes, THREE said No and ONE was uncertain.

(b)   In response to the question 'Are you happy with the present arrangements?' THREE people said Yes, EIGHT people said No and ONE appeared unconcerned.

(c)   In response to the question 'Would you like to have a wider range of hot drinks available to you?' EIGHT people said Yes, THREE people said No and ONE was uncertain.

(d)   Amongst the comments made when staff were invited to comment on the proposal were 'Will fixed times for coffee and tea breaks disappear?' 'What about the tea ladies?' and 'I would prefer to obtain drinks at my own convenience'.

Conclusion

A clear majority of the staff (two-thirds) are in favour of this proposal.

J Ely
Office Junior
Accounts Department

The letter report

As the name implies this is a report written in letter form. Primarily it is used to present information to someone outside the company. For example, an outside consultant may write his analysis and recommendations in the form of a letter, signing the letter as normal.

Memorandum reports

Memorandum reports are used primarily for routine reporting within an organisation, although some companies use them for external communicating. Because they are internal communications, often they are informally written on standardised inter-office memorandum stationery.

Following the company's identification, if there is one, the words From, To and Subject appear at the page top. Sometimes the date is also part of the heading. Like letters the memorandum may carry a signature or the writer may merely initial the heading.

Illustration

The business supplies buyer of Datewise has asked one of his clerks to investigate the costs and supply of 108mm × 219mm white envelopes, with a view to finding a cheaper source.

Solution

Memorandum

To: Mr Hopkins
From: A Clerk Date: 4 January 1997

Supply of envelopes

As requested I have investigated the local suppliers of the 108mm × 219mm white envelopes and compared the costs.

There are three main office suppliers to choose from: Paper Products, Office Treasures and Bestbuy.

Our current supplier, Bestbuy has free delivery and offers us a 25% discount on orders over £100.

Paper Products offer boxes of 1,000 envelopes £3 cheaper than Bestbuy on orders of six or more boxes. They offer the same discount and have a free delivery once a fortnight in this area. Special deliveries carry a charge of £20.

Office Treasures are the same price as Paper Products but, as we would be new customers, they will not discuss discounts.

Paper Products would be most suitable for us as we always order more than six boxes and rarely need special delivery. I would recommend them for future supplies of envelopes.

Reports on internal matters within a company which may be formal or informal

The length and style of reports produced and internally circulated will vary because of the subject matter. Some examples of this type of report are as follows:

(a)   *Employee reports* – Produced by managing directors or chief executives to inform employees, usually on an annual basis, of the events and progress of that particular business, to help employees feel part of a greater whole and to get an overview of an organisation of which they form a very small but not insignificant part.

(b)   *Shareholder reports* – Managing directors or chief executives produce reports to inform shareholders on the current state of their investment in a given year.

(c)   *Progress reports* – Where a job of work is being undertaken (for example, the transferring of records from papers stored in filing cabinets to microfiches stored in wallets or where a department is in the process of restructuring) then progress reports will be periodically commissioned and produced to ensure that a formal communication exercise takes place to establish the extent of the progress.

(d)   *Completion reports* – Where jobs of work such as those mentioned above have been completed, or rather when those persons who have been instructed to perform jobs of work say that they are completed, it is often the case that requests will be made for the production of completion reports. In their most simple form these consist of the results of a survey to compare the stated goals in a particular job of work with the end result.

The short formal report

This type of report is suitable for more complex and important investigations that are to be reported to senior management.

As illustrated below, the most common plan begins with a quick **summary** of the report, including and emphasising conclusions and recommendations. There usually follows a single paragraph covering the facts of **authorisation** and a brief statement of the **problem and its scope**. After the **introductory words** come the **findings** of the investigation. From all this comes a final **conclusion** and, if needed, a **recommendation**.

Where detailed tables of figures or computations are to be supplied to support the findings of the report, these will often be included at the end of the main text, as **appendices**.

Example of the formal report

**Recommendations for depreciating delivery trucks
based on an analysis of three plans proposed for the
XYZ Company**

Submitted to:

        Mr Big
        XYZ Company
        41 London Road
        Bedford

Prepared by:

        N McClellan
        Tubbes Systems

Recommendations for depreciating delivery vans based on an analysis of three plans proposed for the XYZ Company

Recommendations and summary of analysis

The reducing charge method seems to be the best method to depreciate the XYZ Company delivery vans. The relative equality of cost allocation for depreciation and maintenance over the useful life of the vans is the prime advantage under this method. Computation of depreciation charges is relatively simple by the reducing charge plan but not quite so simple as computation under the second best method considered.

The second best method considered is the straight-line depreciation plan. It is the simplest to compute of the plans considered, but it results in yearly charges different from those under the reducing charge plan. The unequal cost allocation resulting from increasing maintenance costs in successive years, however, is a disadvantage.

Third among the plans considered is the service hours. This plan is not satisfactory for depreciating delivery vans mainly because of the complexity and cost of computing yearly charges under the plan. Also significant is the likelihood of poor cost allocation under this plan. An additional drawback is the possibility of variations in the estimates of the service life of company vans.

Background of the problem

Authorisation of the study

This report on depreciation methods for delivery vans of the XYZ is submitted on 8 January 19X6 to Mr Big, Managing Director of the XYZ Company.

Statement of the problem

Having decided to purchase a fleet of delivery vans, the problem is to select the most suitable method to depreciate them.

The vans have an original cost of £8,000, an estimated five-year life and a trade-in value of £2,500.

Method of solving the problem

Study of company records and a review by the authoritative writings on the subject have been used in seeking a reliable solution to the XYZ company's problem. Alternative methods of depreciation have been selected through the experience and study of the writer. Conclusions are based on generally accepted business principles as set forth by experts in the field of depreciation.

Steps in analysing the problem

The depreciation methods evaluated in this report are discussed in order of their rank as a solution to the problem. No attempt has been made to isolate the factors discussed under each method. Since each method contains fixed factors, a comparison of them directly would be meaningless, because they cannot be manipulated. The method of computation, amount of depreciation each year and effect of maintenance costs are the factors to be considered. 'The reducing charge method will be discussed first.

Marked advantages of the reducing charge method

The reducing charge method, in this case that version known as the sum-of-the-digits method, is an application of a series of diminishing fractions to be applied over the life of the vans.

The depreciation charge in the penultimate year is planned to be twice that in the final year, in the pre-penultimate year it is three times that in the final year. With an asset having a five-year life, annual depreciation charge will be in the ratio 5:4:3:2: 1. Since the sum of 5, 4, 3, 2 and 1 is 15, the total amount to be written off (£8,000 – £2,500 = £5,500), must be split into 5/15, 4/15 etc. as shown below.

This method results in larger depreciation in the earlier years with subsequent decreases in the latter years. Since maintenance and repair costs can be expected to be higher in later years this method provides a relatively stable charge for each year as shown in Table 1.

Table 1

Depreciation and maintenance costs for delivery vans of XYZ for 19X6–19Y0 using reducing charge depreciation

Year	Depreciation		£	Maintenance £	Sum £
1	5/15 (£5,500)	=	1,833	50	1,883
2	4/15 (£5,500)	=	1,467	250	1,717
3	3/15 (£5,500)	=	1,100	450	1,550
4	2/15 (£5,500)	=	733	650	1,383
5	1/15 (£5,500)	=	367	850	1,217
			5,500	2,250	7,750

The reducing charge depreciation using the sum-of-the-digits method combines the most desirable combination of factors to depreciate the vans. The equalisation of periodic charges is considered to be the prime factor. Although computation of this method is relatively easy, it is slightly more complicated than the straight-line depreciation which is the next method discussed.

Runner-up position of the straight-line method

Compared to the reducing charge method, straight line depreciation is easy to compute. The depreciable value of each van (£5,500) is divided by the five-year life of the van to arrive at an equal annual depreciation charge each year of £1,100.

Since the maintenance cost of operating the van will increase in later years this method will result in much greater periodic charges in the last years. As illustrated in Table 2 the inequality of the charges is the major disadvantage of this method.

Straight-line depreciation is widely used. It has the advantage of simplicity and under normal conditions offers a satisfactory method of cost allocation. For normal conditions to prevail, two factors must exist: (i) accumulation of assets over a period of years so that the total of depreciation and maintenance costs will be comparatively even, and (ii) a relatively stable amount of earnings each year so that depreciation as a percentage of net income does not fluctuate widely.

Table 2

Year	Depreciation			Maintenance	Sum
		£		£	£
1	£5,500 / 5	=	1,100	50	1,150
2	£5,500 / 5	=	1,100	250	1,350
3	£5,500 / 5	=	1,100	450	1,550
4	£5,500 / 5	=	1,100	650	1,750
5	£5,500 / 5	=	1,100	850	1,950
			5,500	2,250	7,750

However, the vans considered in this report have not been purchased over a period of years. Consequently the straight-line method of depreciation will not result in equal periodic charges for maintenance and depreciation over a period of years.

Poor rank of service hours' depreciation

The service hours method of depreciation combines the major disadvantages of the other ways discussed. It is based on the principle that a van is bought for the direct hours of service that it will give. The estimated hours that a delivery van can be used efficiently according to the motor engineers is 100,000 miles. The depreciable cost £5,500 for each van is allocated pro rata according to the number of service hours used, so that in the first year (when the van would be driven 30,000 miles) the calculation would be $30,000/100,000 = 0.3$ which is then multiplied by the depreciable value of £5,500 to give £1,650.

The difficulty and expense of maintaining additional records of service hours is a major disadvantage of this method. The depreciation cost for the vans under this method will fluctuate widely between first and last years. It is reasonable to assume that as the vans get older more time will be spent on maintenance. Consequently it is convenient for the larger depreciation costs to occur in the initial years.

Another difficulty encountered is the possibility of a variance between estimated service hours and the actual service hours. The wide fluctuations possible make it impractical to use this method. Since it combines the major disadvantages of both the reducing charge and straight-line methods, it is not satisfactory for depreciating the delivery vans.

Table 3

Year	Estimated service (hours)	Depreciation £	Maintenance £	Sum £
1	30,000	1,650	50	1,700
2	25,000	1,375	250	1,625
3	20,000	1,100	450	1,550
4	15,000	825	650	1,475
5	10,000	550	850	1,400
	100,000	5,500	2,250	7,750

Summary

The structure of the report should reflect the function. The questions that need to be answered are:

- Is there a specific aim?
- Is it just a presentation of facts?
- Does it need a demonstration of analysis used?

All reports, whether short or long, formal of informal, need the basic structure of beginning, middle and end.

The **beginning** should determine:

- what the document is about;
- the relevance for the reader.

The **middle** should contain:

- the main analysis;
- the detailed argument supporting your conclusions, recommendations or proposed action.

The **end** should tell the reader:

- what will happen or what you want them to do;
- conclusions and recommendations.

TABLES

The purposes of tabulation

Any method of data collection will often result in large amounts of data being available. This is the case when an organisation's own internal sources are used or when the data collection is by either a survey, abstraction from secondary sources or other sampling methods. These large amounts of data will need to be examined to obtain relevant information. This means we must discard any irrelevant details, usually leaving us with a number of categories and sub-categories from which we wish to obtain some overall impression. The data remaining from the elimination of irrelevant details can be summarised using either narrative or by use of tables.

As will be seen in the following paragraph, a major drawback of the narrative approach is that the information required is not clearly presented and only a limited amount of data can be presented. A properly constructed tabular presentation, however, gives the required information immediately and clearly.

The narrative approach

Example

A major bank is interested in the types of accounts held by its customers. The information below has recently been collected:

A sample of 5,000 accounts was taken, each account belonging to a different customer. 729 accounts were held by customers aged under 25 of whom 522 held current accounts, the remainder holding ordinary deposit accounts. 1,383 of the accounts were held by customers aged between 25 and 44, 1,020 being current accounts, 271 were ordinary deposit accounts and the remainder were high-interest deposit accounts. There were 1,621 accounts belonging to customers aged between 45 and 59, of these 61% were current accounts, 29% were ordinary deposit accounts and 10% high interest deposit accounts. Of customers aged 60 and over, 628 held current accounts, 410 held ordinary deposit accounts and the remainder held high interest deposit accounts.

Here the data on the 5,000 accounts has already been examined and irrelevant details on, for example, sex of customer or length of time the account has been held for have been eliminated. We are thus left with a reasonable amount of data and, by reading the narrative a few times, we are able to gain some useful information. The main drawbacks, however, in using this approach to present the data are as follows:

(i)   What if the two eliminated variables, sex of customer and age of account, are considered relevant? This would make the narrative much longer and more cumbersome.

(ii)   What if other categories were included? For example, an investment account. This would have a similar effect to (i).

(iii)   Perhaps we might like to make comparisons with another major bank or a similar sample of customers. We would then have two pieces of narrative to consider.

These points highlight the problems of using solely a narrative approach and hence point us to the benefits of tabulation.

Using tables

Reconsidering the above example we will work through the process of constructing a single table to summarise all the information contained in the narrative.

A simple one-way table

A major point of interest in the given data is obviously the age breakdown of account holders. Working through the narrative, this could be presented as follows:

Ages of customers

Age	*Number of customers*
Under 25	729
25–44	1,383
45–59	1,621
60 and over	1,267
Total	5,000

The figure for the 60 and over group is given by $5,000 - (729 + 1,383 + 1,621)$ since there are a total of 5,000 accounts each held by different customers.

Note that for clarity, you should label both columns clearly and tell the reader what the subject of the table is. It is also useful to show relevant totals (ie. in this case the total number of accounts).

A two-way table

Another major point of interest in the data is the number of accounts held of each type. A table of this information is more difficult to extract from the narrative and some steps of working may be helpful. Once this information has been extracted, we can combine it with the previous table to show both ages and types of account held.

Types of account

There are three types of account: current accounts, ordinary deposit accounts and high interest deposit accounts.

(i)   Current accounts:

       522 (age under 25);

       1,020 (aged 25 – 44);

       989 (aged 45 – 59; 61% of 1,621 accounts $= 0.61 \times 1,621 = 988.81$ or 989 accounts by rounding to nearest whole number of accounts);

       628 (aged 60 and over).

(ii)   Ordinary deposit accounts:

207 (aged under 25; ie. 729 minus the number of current accounts = 729 – 522);

271 (aged 25 – 44);

470 (aged 45 – 59; 29% of 1,621 accounts = $0.29 \times 1,621 = 470$);

410 (aged 60 and over).

(iii)   High interest deposit account:

0 (aged under 25; we must assume this since no other detail is given);

92 (aged 25 – 44; 1,383 minus the number of current and ordinary deposit accounts = $1,383 - (1,020 + 271) = 1,383 - 1,291$);

162 (aged 45 – 59; 10% of 1,621 accounts = $0.10 \times 1,621 = 162.1$ or 162);

229 (aged 60 and over; total aged 60 and over minus number of current and ordinary deposit accounts = 1,267 (from (a)) – (628 + 410) = 229).

Our objective at the start of this paragraph was to construct a single table to summarise all the information contained in the narrative. Having carried out the simple calculations above, this is now easily done by employing a two-way table (sometimes called a **cross-tabulation**). In this example, the two 'variables' are obviously age of customers and type of account held. These become the headings for the following required two-way table:

Ages and types of account held by sample of 5,000 customers

Type of account	Age				
	under 25	*25–44*	*45–59*	*60 and over*	*Total*
Current	522	1,020	989	628	3,159
Ordinary deposit	207	271	470	410	1,358
High interest deposit	0	92	162	229	483
Total	729	1,383	1,621	1,267	5,000

Guidelines for constructing tables

There are no set rules for constructing tables since tables often vary markedly in content and format. The following guidelines should however be adhered to:

(a)   Always give the table a title and suitable headings.

(b)   If the data contains a number of categories or sub-categories, use a two-way table.

(c)   Give column and row sub-totals where appropriate.

(d)   If the draft table contains too much detail, it will fail in its objective of summarising the data. Further simplified tables should then be constructed, each dealing with different aspects of the data.

(e)   It is important to state the source of the data. This may be included in the title or given beneath the table.

(f)   The units in the table should be 'manageable'. This can be accomplished by, for example, dividing particular column entries by 1,000 and including this fact in the column heading.

(g)   It is sometimes useful to show *percentages* in the table in addition to the actual figures.

In analysing large amounts of data, tables similar to those already considered prove very useful. However, it is often the case that the data is in such a basic form (*raw data*) that using tables of this type is not easy. However an example of producing such a two-way table from raw data was illustrated in the previous session.

The following example illustrates an alternative type of question – that of interpretation of information already presented in tabular form.

Illustration – Interpretation of a table

The following table is an extract from the *Monthly digest of statistics* and gives detail on consumer expenditure between 19X0 and 19X4. Study this table and then answer the following questions:

(a)   Calculate the percentage change in consumer expenditure between 19X0 and 19X4 for the following categories:

(i)   total consumers' expenditure
(ii)   cars, etc.
(iii)   food
(iv)   beer

What do these figures suggest?

(b)   What do the 'revalued at 19X0 prices' figures indicate? Make reference to the categories listed in (a).

	Durable				Other goods								Services	
Total consumer expenditure	Total	Cars, motor cycles and other vehicles	Furniture and floor coverings	Other durable goods	Food (household expenditure)	Beer	Other alcoholic drink	Tobacco	Clothing other than footwear	Foot-wear	Energy products	Other goods	Rent, rates and water charges	Other services
At current prices														
19X0 136 789	13 320	6 307	3 429	3,584	22 873	5 320	4 634	4 822	8 103	1 760	10 957	14 369	16 044	34 587
19X1 152 125	13 885	6 511	3 513	3,861	24 170	5 970	5 183	5 515	8 406	1 853	13 367	15 538	19 465	38 773
19X2 166 538	15 165	7 064	3 698	4,403	25 590	6 453	5 554	5 882	8 854	2 067	14 954	16 809	22 399	42 811
19X3 182 420	18 310	9 142	4 150	5,018	27 148	7 140	6 232	6 208	9 804	2 310	16 212	18 292	23 576	47 188
19X4 194 654	18 858	9 088	4 398	5,372	28 151	7 734	6 585	6 631	10 637	2 536	16 958	19 873	25 250	51 441
Revalued at 19X0 prices														
19X0 136 789	13 320	6 307	3 429	3,584	22 873	5 320	4 634	4 822	8 103	1 760	10 957	14 369	16 044	34 587
19X1 136 429	13 486	6 366	3 354	3,766	22 676	5 000	4 612	4 470	8 189	1 696	10 992	14 420	16 279	34 609
19X2 137 581	14 193	6 510	3 424	4,259	22 587	4 838	4 545	4 128	8 329	1 810	11 038	14 624	16 530	34 959
19X3 143 011	16 459	7 909	3 724	4,826	22 858	4 914	4 816	4 082	8 892	1 948	11 129	14 968	16 764	36 181
19X4 145 192	16 298	7 302	3 754	5,242	22 468	4 943	4 962	3 948	9 392	2 051	11 254	15 541	16 978	37 357

Solution

In questions of this type, data from a government publication is presented. Because of the volume of information in the table, questions asking for a general interpretation of the data are quite difficult. In this question (as is often the case) well-defined questions are asked making the task easier.

(a)   The percentage changes in consumer expenditure between 19X0 and 19X4 are as follows:

$$\text{Total consumers' expenditure \% change} = \frac{194,654 - 136,789}{136,789} \times 100$$

$$= 42.3\%$$

$$\text{Cars, etc. \% change} = \frac{9,088 - 6,307}{6,307} \times 100$$

$$= 44.1\%$$

$$\text{Food \% change} = \frac{28,151 - 22,873}{22,873} \times 100$$

$$= 23.1\%$$

$$\text{Beer \% change} = \frac{7,734 - 5,320}{5,320} \times 100$$

$$= 45.4\%$$

$$\text{Energy products \% change} = \frac{16,958 - 10,957}{10,957} \times 100$$

$$= 54.8\%$$

$$\text{Rent, etc. \% change} = \frac{25,250 - 16,044}{16,044} \times 100$$

$$= 57.4\%$$

The figures indicate that the increase in consumer expenditure has been greater in some categories than others. If total consumers' expenditure is taken as the 'average' then, for the categories listed, food is the only category where the increase in expenditure is less than this average. On the other hand the increase in expenditure on cars, beer, energy and rent is higher than the average increase.

These figures highlight a trend that has actually been taking place over a number of years. In general, the public has been spending less money on food items and more money on other goods and services.

(b)   The figures entitled 'revalued at 19X0 prices' are presented to remove the effect of inflation from the unadjusted data. In other words, these indicate 'real' changes.

Reconsidering the categories listing in (i) and calculating the percentage changes between 19X0 and 19X4 for this data, we have the following:

Total consumers' expenditure % change   =   6.1% increase

Cars, etc. % change   =   15.8% increase

Food % change   =   1.8% decrease

Beer % change   =   7.1% decrease

Energy products   =   2.7% increase

Rent, etc.   =   5.8% increase

These percentage change figures are very revealing. If we take into account the effect of inflation, then the amounts spent on both food and beer have decreased. Additionally, expenditure on cars, etc. has seen a large increase in expenditure between 19X0 and 19X4. These facts are not revealed by using the data considered in part (i).

Note that the use of indices to revalue data to a given year's prices is studied in a later session.

CHARTS AND DIAGRAMS

Basic charts

Charts and diagrams are frequently used to present data in a clear and eye-catching way. Large masses of complicated data can be presented in such a way as to be readily understood. There are many different charts and diagrams which can be used. The choice depends on:

(a)   the type of data;
(b)   the amount of data;
(c)   what factors should be emphasised, if any.

You should always ensure that the end result is a chart or diagram which is clear and intelligible. Also, remember that charts and diagrams give visual information for comparing relative size. As such, they are unsuitable for conveying precise numerical information. Where precision is required, tables of data should be used.

Pictograms

A pictogram is a simple diagram which uses pictures to represent numbers. Suppose we have the number of letters received by mail-order firms in the following table:

Firm	*Annual number of letters*
Grand Galaxy	3,475,000
Commonwealth	8,122,000
Largeforests	5,108,000
Ells	4,427,000
Berties	6,381,000

We could use a picture of a letter to represent a number of actual letters. In this case if we use a picture of a letter to represent 1,000,000 letters received, we obtain the following pictogram:

Annual number of letters

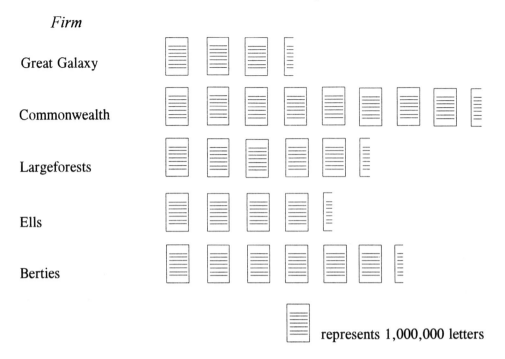

Firm

Great Galaxy

Commonwealth

Largeforests

Ells

Berties

represents 1,000,000 letters

Always remember to include the key on your diagram.

As can be seen fractions in the pictogram are difficult to show accurately, but that is not the purpose of these diagrams. They are to give us a quick, rough idea of relative size and as such are fairly successful.

An alternative approach sometimes adopted is to magnify the picture so that its size represents the figure being illustrated. The preceding pictogram might look like this:

Great Galaxy

Commonwealth

Largeforests

Ells

Berties

represents 1,000,000 letters

This diagram uses area of the pictured letter to represent size; for example, the figure for Commonwealth represents almost double the figure for Ells. However, if we had increased each dimension in proportion to the relative size of the figures, it would be very misleading. Just taking the figures for Commonwealth and Ells, these would be represented by:

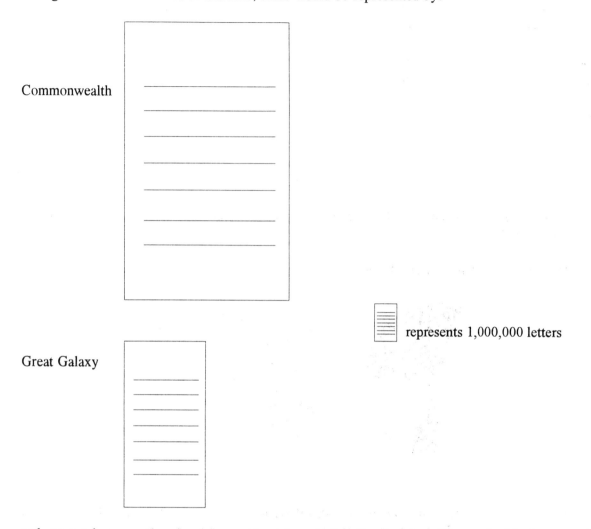

and, as can be seen, the visual impression given is that the first is well over double the second. If magnification is to be used, the earlier method should be used and not this method!!

Pie charts

A pie chart consists of a circle split into *segments*. The circle represents a total and the segments represent the parts which go to make up the total. The 360° of the circle is divided in *proportion* to the figures making the total. Suppose a family's income in 19X5 is £1,000 per month.

There now follows the split of their expenditure, along with the proportion each category represents of the whole and the angle this will represent on a pie chart:

	Amount £	*Proportion* %	*Angle* (degrees) – see note
Mortgage and insurance	300	30	108
Electricity and gas	50	5	18
Food and drink	200	20	72
Clothes	40	4	14
Car and petrol	150	15	54
Telephone	10	1	4
Savings	70	7	25
Fares	60	6	22
Miscellaneous	120	12	43
	1,000	100	360

Note: The degrees are calculated as the percentage proportion 360° (eg. the first category will be represented by 30% × 360 = 108°).

The corresponding pie chart is shown below:

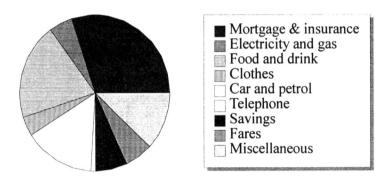

You can replace the names in the segments with different colours or shadings provided a key is given. Again, we do not obtain a precise idea of expenditure on certain items or services, just an idea of their relative proportions.

Simple bar charts

In a simple bar chart the figures we wish to compare are represented by bars. These can either be drawn vertically or horizontally. The height or length of a bar is proportional to the size of the figure being illustrated. Suppose we know that production figures of different car companies are as follows:

Firm	*Number of cars produced*
Ausota	180,000
Vauxsun	145,000
Moruar	165,000
Trihall	160,000
Fortin	170,000

The vertical bar chart for these figures is as follows:

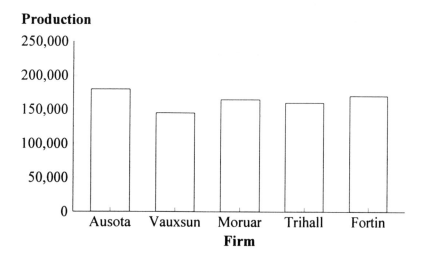

The horizontal bar chart for the same figures is as follows.

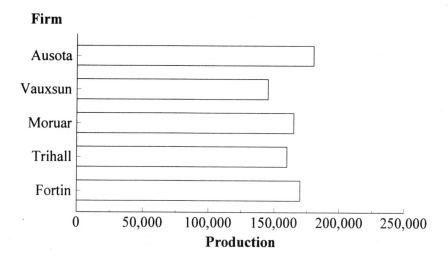

We can put the appropriate identification either in the bar itself, immediately adjacent to the bar, or use a key for shadings or colours. There is no need to draw 3-dimensional bars, 2-dimensional are perfectly adequate and often less confusing. When drawing these charts it is very important to start the scale from zero. A very misleading picture may be shown otherwise. This is, in fact, a very common way in which readers are misled. Look out for the trick in your newspaper!

Component bar charts

When we draw bar charts the totals we wish to illustrate can often be broken down into sub-divisions or components. Suppose we have the following table of wine consumption by type and year:

Consumption figures
(10,000 litres)

	White	Red	Rosé	Total
19X2	59.3	46.5	14.2	120.0
19X3	63.6	47.0	14.4	125.0
19X4	72.3	48.2	14.5	135.0

We start by drawing a simple bar chart of the total figures. The columns or bars are then split up into the component parts. Remember to put the key on the diagram otherwise it is useless. This chart can still be drawn either vertically or horizontally.

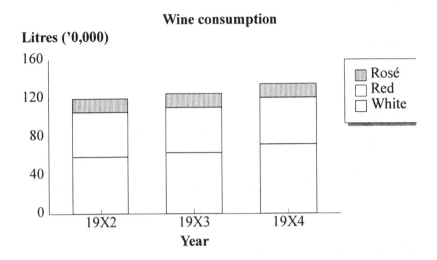

Here, different colours for the different components would be especially effective.

Percentage component bar chart

If we wish to know what *proportion* of a total each component represents, we can use a percentage component bar chart in place of a pie chart. All the columns of the bar chart are the same height or length representing 100%. These are then divided in the appropriate proportions.

The proportions for the wine consumption example are calculated as follows:

	White	*Red*	*Rosé*
19X2	$\dfrac{59.3}{120.0} \times 100 = 49.4\%$	$\dfrac{46.5}{120.0} \times 100 = 38.8\%$	$\dfrac{14.2}{120.0} \times 100 = 11.8\%$
19X3	$\dfrac{63.6}{125.0} \times 100 = 50.9\%$	$\dfrac{47.0}{125.0} \times 100 = 37.6\%$	$\dfrac{14.4}{125.0} \times 100 = 11.5\%$
19X4	$\dfrac{72.3}{135.0} \times 100 = 53.6\%$	$\dfrac{48.2}{135.0} \times 100 = 35.7\%$	$\dfrac{14.5}{135.0} \times 100 = 10.7\%$

and the chart is drawn as follows:

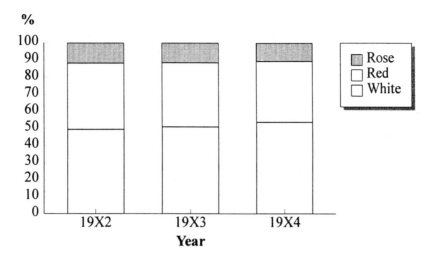

Compound bar charts

Our concern may not be with proportional comparisons but rather with comparisons of the component figures themselves. If this is the case we can use a compound bar chart. The wine consumption data could be illustrated as follows:

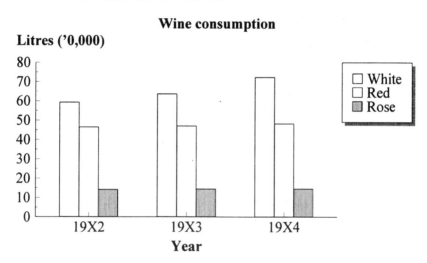

This type of chart allows us to follow trends of each individual component as well as make comparisons between the components. It does not, however, give any direct indication of total consumption.

Conclusion

When drawing diagrams and charts, there are several points to consider:

(a)   Try to make the diagrams neat and uncluttered. Use a ruler.

(b)   If graph paper is available, use it.

(c)   The diagram should have a title.

(d)   The variables and scales should be shown on each *axis*.

(e)   Set the scale so that you use as much of the paper as you can for the diagram; this will keep the diagram neater and assist accuracy.

(f)   Units must be indicated on both axes.

(g)   Where diagrams are combined or superimposed ensure that each is recognisable separately and suitably labelled.

(h)   Too much detail on a diagram makes it confusing rather than enlightening.

(i)   Remember the key where appropriate.

(j)   Remember to start scales at zero on bar charts.

(k)   Remember that component and compound bar charts become less and less effective the more sub-divisions you use. It is often worth considering a pie chart as an alternative.

Gantt charts

These are a special type of bar chart where the bars are drawn horizontally and scaled in units of time. They are particularly popular as progress charts in manufacturing organisations and are often drawn to a scale large enough to occupy a wall of the office of, for example, the works manager or chief cost accountant.

To construct a Gantt chart for use as a progress chart, actual performance is compared with planned performance. Suppose we have the following monthly production figures for a particular product, together with the monthly forecasted production.

Month	Forecast	Actual	Actual as a % of forecast
1	600	480	80
2	500	500	100
3	700	910	130
4	400	270	67.5

To draw a Gantt chart for this data we also need to express the actual figures as a percentage of the forecasted figures. These are shown above. The Gantt chart for these production figures is shown below and explanation of its construction follows the chart.

Month 1		Month 2		Month 3		Month 4	
Monthly Forecast 600	Cum. Forecast 600	Monthly Forecast 500	Cum. Forecast 1,100	Monthly Forecast 700	Cum. Forecast 1,800	Monthly Forecast 400	Cum. Forecast 2,200

Actual monthly production (% of forecast)　　　Cumulative production (% of forecast)

For each period, the actual production figures as a percentage of the forecast figures are plotted as a solid line on the chart. The forecast is represented by the full width of the columns, consequently the actual performance line will occupy the available width only if actual performance is 100% of forecast performance. In other cases, the line will either be shorter than the target line (for performance less than 100%) or it will be necessary to draw an additional actual line to account for the excess (see month 3).

In addition, the chart contains a shaded line showing cumulative production. This line illustrates to what extent the business is keeping up to, beating or failing to achieve its target as the year progresses. It should be noted that the individual columns are not separate charts drawn each month. They are the same chart which is gradually built up over the months as the figures become available.

Other charts

Up to now in this session we have considered various charts which are used to illustrate data. If, however, the data is contained in a *frequency distribution* then bar charts, pie charts and pictograms are limited in the amount of data they can illustrate.

When frequency tables or distributions are drawn up the intention is that the tables should tell us what sort of data and spread of data we have. Some people find it easy enough to spot these characteristics from a table but for many people it is still a mass of numbers so an alternative simpler method of presentation is required. As we are trying to picture what our data is like we use pictures or pictorial representations of frequency tables. The three common methods used are by:

(a)　　histograms;
(b)　　frequency polygons (and frequency curves);
(c)　　ogives (or cumulative frequency polygons).

Histograms

The usual diagram used to illustrate a frequency distribution is a histogram. The horizontal scale is used for the variable or measurement of importance and the vertical scale to indicate frequency.

Consider the following data for the weights of sweets in a particular box of assorted sweets.

Weight of package (grams)	*Frequency* (number of sweet boxes)
≥ 485 but < 490	1
≥ 490 but < 495	3
≥ 495 but < 500	12
≥ 500 but < 505	22
≥ 505 but < 510	8
≥ 510 but < 515	2
	48

The histogram for this frequency distribution would be drawn as shown below.

Distribution of sweet box weights

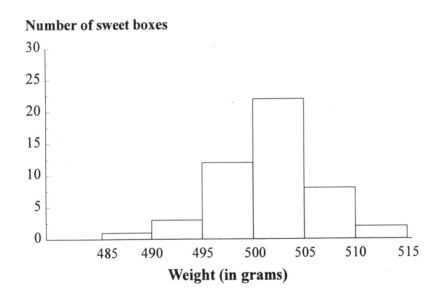

The columns are drawn up from the horizontal axis and, because the intervals we have are of equal width, are drawn to a height on the vertical scale representing frequency. Because the horizontal scale represents a (continuous) variable, the bars touch each other.

Difficulties with discrete data

If our data is discrete, then there are difficulties in specifying the values on the horizontal axis since it is a continuous scale. The way round the problem is to treat each integer as if it represented all values which would round to it. In other words, 6 would be treated as 5.5 to 6.5 and so on.

Alternatively, discrete intervals of 0–4, 5–9 could be re-expressed as 0 to <5, ≥ 5 to < 10, etc.

The following example deals with two further problems commonly encountered when drawing a histogram.

Example

A firm has recorded the time it takes to serve 55 individual customers, to the nearest $^1/_{10}$ minute.

For the service time frequency table given below, draw the appropriate histogram.

Service time (in minutes)	Frequency
< 5	1
≥ 5 but < 10	15
≥ 10 but < 15	18
≥ 15 but < 20	12
≥ 20 but < 30	7
≥ 30	2
	55

Unequal class intervals

In all the histograms seen so far, the class intervals used have had equal widths. The data given does not use equal intervals, so how do we draw the histogram? Strictly speaking the vertical scale on a histogram represents relative frequency (frequency density). In histograms, it is the area of the columns which represents frequency, not the column heights. This being the case, if an interval is four times as wide as another interval, its column height would be drawn to a height one quarter of frequency so that the columns are comparable. If the heights obtained involve fractions, they should be drawn in at that height, not rounded.

Open-ended class intervals

The first and last classes are open-ended – that is, there are no lower/upper limits. The accepted convention is to treat the open-ended interval as if it were the same width as the adjacent interval. This allows us to draw in the height of the column. On the scale for the horizontal axis, we remove the scale under the interval's column and replace it with a description of what interval the column represents.

Solution

As can be seen from the figure that follows the interval ' < 5' is treated as if it had the same width as its adjacent interval. The next interval is '≥ 5 but < 10', so draw the open-ended interval as if from zero to 5 (we could write in ' < 5' on the scale). As five units is the width of most intervals we draw in the open-ended interval height equal to its frequency (ie. a height of one).

At the other end the adjacent interval is '≥ 20 but < 30', so draw in '≥ 30' from 30 to 40 (possibly writing on the scale '30 or over'). As both these intervals are drawn in as double width intervals their columns are drawn in with height as half the frequency, ie. 3½ and 1 respectively.

(**Note:** The use of a vertical scale becomes somewhat ambiguous when class intervals are of varying width. It is wise to try and avoid the problem.)

Histogram for service times

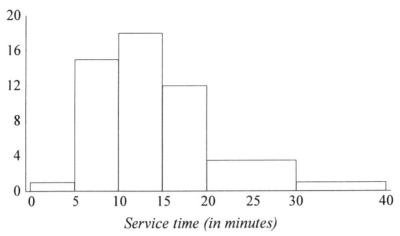

Frequency density

Service time (in minutes)

Frequency polygons

As an alternative to histograms, we may use **frequency polygons**. The diagram that follows attempts to emphasise the 'shape' of our data. The easiest way to illustrate the frequency polygon is to assume we have already drawn a histogram. To obtain the frequency polygon mark the mid-point of the top of each histogram column, then join them up. (This could be said to treat each interval as if all its frequency were at the mid-point of the interval.)

The polygon is usually neatened up at the ends of the distribution by bringing it down to meet the horizontal axis at what would have been the mid-point of the adjacent class interval if it had existed. If you do not have a histogram to work from then follow the same rules as were used in the construction of the histogram as regards treatment of unequal class intervals and open-ended class intervals.

Illustration

The histogram for the service time example is shown, together with a frequency polygon superimposed.

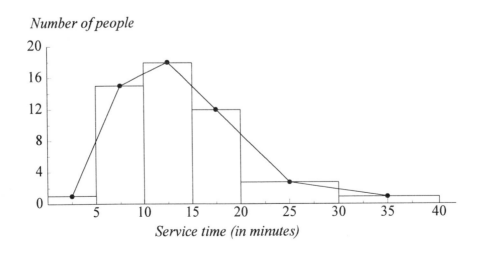

Number of people

Service time (in minutes)

Frequency curves

The frequency polygons we have obtained were rather jagged figures. If we had a histogram with very small *class intervals*, and therefore with very many columns, then points of the frequency polygon would be close together. This has a smoothing effect on the polygon and, if we continued the process, we should eventually arrive at a smooth curve (a **frequency curve**).

Cumulative frequency curves (ogives)

We sometimes wish to be able to answer questions like 'how many people earn less than £200 per week?', 'how many machine breakdowns last longer than 35 minutes?', etc. If we have a frequency distribution or histogram we would need to do some calculations before we could answer such questions. An alternative is to draw an *ogive* and read off the answers directly.

The **ogive** (or cumulative frequency curve) is drawn with the cumulative frequency total plotted against the **upper limit** of the corresponding interval. Hence, the curve gives numbers less than a specified value. This diagram is sometimes called a 'less than' ogive. For the sweet boxes weight example, we have the following cumulative totals appended to the frequency table:

Sweet box package weights

Weight of packages (in grams)	Frequency	Cumulative frequency			
≥ 485 but < 490	1	1			
≥ 490 but < 495	3	4	(1	+	3)
≥ 495 but < 500	12	16	(4	+	12)
≥ 500 but < 505	22	38	(16	+	22)
≥ 505 but < 510	8	46	(38	+	8)
≥ 510 but < 515	2	48	(46	+	2)
	48				

The final cumulative frequency figure should always be the same as the total of frequencies. The cumulative frequency can be seen in the diagram that follows.

The points are joined with straight lines. Open-ended intervals are treated in the same way as when drawing a histogram.

Ogive

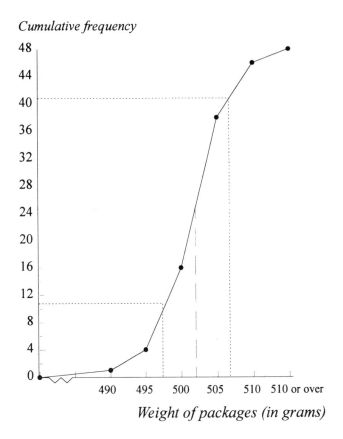

Cumulative frequency

Weight of packages (in grams)

This curve can now be used to read off 'less than' figures. For example, to find the number of packages weighing under 507 grams, we look up 507 grams on the horizontal scale and read off the corresponding value on the vertical scale. In this case we obtain about 41, so we can say approximately 41 packages were below 507 grams in weight. To obtain the exact answer, we would need to go back to the original raw data.

Medians

A common use of the ogive is to help find the *median*, the middle item from a series of values arranged in ascending or descending order.

In the case of the weights of packages we have 48 observations. Strictly speaking, the median is the $\frac{1}{2} (n + 1)^{th}$ item (here the $\frac{1}{2} \times 49^{th} = 24\frac{1}{2}^{th}$ item). However, we said earlier that for large amounts of data we might simply choose the $\frac{1}{2} n^{th}$ item (here the 24th).

By moving up the vertical (cumulative frequency) axis till we reach 24 and drawing a horizontal line that just touches the ogive, the median can be found. Dropping down from the point where the construction line just touches the ogive, the median is the point that we reach on the horizontal axis.

From a carefully constructed ogive this would be seen to be 501.8 grammes. In our case, the best we can see is:

Median = 502 grams

Example

(a)   For the service times table draw a cumulative frequency curve.

Service time (in minutes)	Frequency	Part of solution: Cumulative frequency
< 5	1	1
≥ 5 but < 10	15	16
≥ 10 but < 15	18	34
≥ 15 but < 20	12	46
≥ 20 but < 30	7	53
≥ 30	2	55
	55	

(b)   Determine from the curve the number of service times:

(i)   under 18 minutes
(ii)   under 7½ minutes
(iii)   over 12 minutes

(c)   Find the median service time.

Solution

(a)   The first step is to include an extra column of cumulative frequencies in the given table – see above. The ogive can then be drawn as follows:

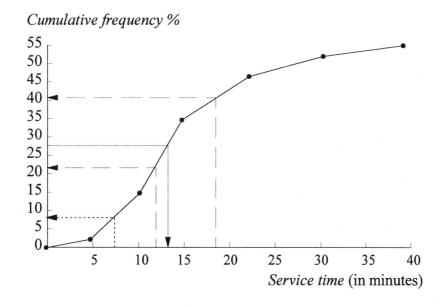

Cumulative frequency %

Service time (in minutes)

The dotted and solid lines drawn onto the diagram are to help in answering parts (b) and (c).

(b) (i) Looking up 18 minutes on the graph, we obtain 41 from the vertical axis so 41 customers had service times of under 18 minutes.

  (ii) Looking up 7½ minutes on the graph, we obtain 8 from the vertical axis so 8 customers had service times of under 7½ minutes.

  (iii) Looking up 12 minutes on the graph, we obtain 22 from the vertical axis so 22 customers had service times of under 12 minutes. This means 33 customers had service times of over 12 minutes.

(c) The median, the middle item, is the 28th item. From the ogive this appears to correspond to a service time of about 13½ minutes.

GRAPHS

Graphs and charts are very useful as a means of presenting and interpreting data. In this section we introduce graphs of simple relationships. Graphs are also very important in economics for illustrating, for example, cost and profit functions. Further, in more complicated statistical techniques, graphs are often used as a starting point in the analysis.

Examples of graphs

Straight-line graphs

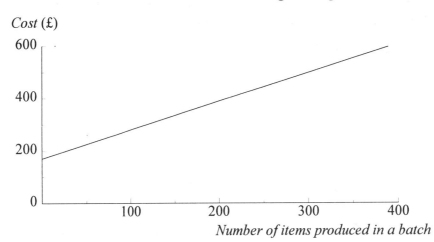

Production line costs for AM Engineering Ltd

This is a simple straight-line graph showing the cost of producing a number of items on a production line. It shows that, even if no items are produced, there is a cost of about £170 to 'set up' the production line. After that, costs increase as production increases at a direct rate.

Time series

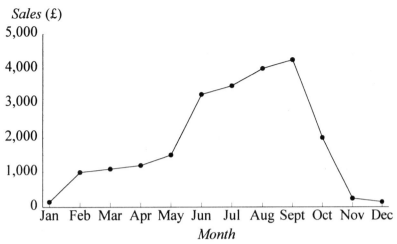

Sales of Rocco Ice-cream

This graph illustrates the sales of Rocco Ice-cream for the 12 months of a particular year. It shows that, as expected, sales increase over the summer months. The data in such a graph is called a **time series** and is considered in detail later.

The two graphs shown here are significantly different. The first has a clear, direct relationship from which it would be fairly easy to obtain an expression explaining how costs and number of items produced were related. The pattern shown in the second graph is more complicated and it would be very difficult to obtain a relationship in this case.

How to draw a graph

In many graphs we wish to draw we will have two variables, x and y, which are related. The major points to be remembered when drawing such graphs are given below.

(a)   Since there are two variables we require two axes. The vertical axis is used to represent y, the **dependent variable** in the relationship. The x variable is represented on the horizontal axis, this being the **independent variable**.

(b)   The horizontal and vertical axes are used to represent both positive and negative values. This is done by dividing the graph into four quadrants.

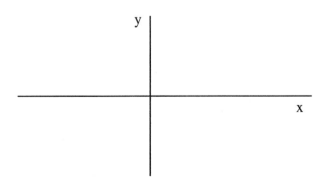

Financial Training

The point where the axes intersect is called the **origin** and is where x = 0 and y = 0. The four quadrants are used for the following values of x and y:

	y	
Second quadrant x negative y positive		First quadrant x positive y positive
		x
Third quadrant x negative y negative		Fourth quadrant x positive y negative

For example, the point	x = 2,	y = 3	falls in the first quadrant
" "	x = -2,	y = 3	falls in the second quadrant
" "	x = -2,	y = -3	falls in the third quadrant
" "	x = 2,	y = -3	falls in the fourth quadrant

(c)   Choosing suitable scales for the axes is very important. When using graph paper, the squares are divided up in multiples of ten and it is therefore logical to use multiples of ten for the intervals on the scale. It is not practical to use intervals of, say, three or seven on an axis.

(d)   The intervals for the scales need not be the same for both the x and y axes. For example, an interval of five units on the x-axis and 100 units on the y-axis is permissible. Care should, however, be taken to examine the scales of the x and y axes when interpreting a graph.

(e)   Always remember to label the axes on a graph. The minimum requirement is to label them x and y (or some other letters). If the graph has a practical meaning, then label the axes the actual title of the variable.

Example

Draw a graph of the following values:

x	*5*	*–10*	*–5*	*–2*	*10*	*15*
y	*50*	*–100*	*–50*	*20*	*75*	*25*

Solution

In this data, the x values range from –10 to +15, while the y values range from –100 to +75. Our scales, logically based on intervals of a multiple of 10, must therefore cover these ranges. It would not be sensible in this example to use the same scale for both the x and y axes because of the very different ranges.

A suitable graph is as follows:

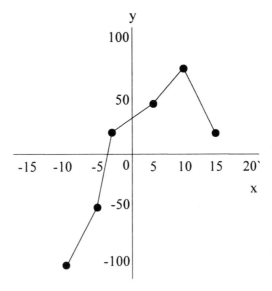

The equation of a straight line

If, when we plot values of x and y on a graph, we obtain a straight line this is called a straight line or linear relationship.

Suppose x and y are two variables related by the equation:

$$y = 2x + 3$$

then we can work out values of y from values of x. Using a table we have:

x	0	1	2	3	4	5	6
$2x$	0	2	4	6	8	10	12
$+3$	3	3	3	3	3	3	3
$y = 2x+3$	3	5	7	9	11	13	15

If we now draw this on a graph, we obtain the straight line that follows.

A straight line has two characteristics: it has a slope (a gradient) and it cuts the y-axis at a certain value, called the intersect. In this example we see the intersect is $y = 3$ and the slope is 2.

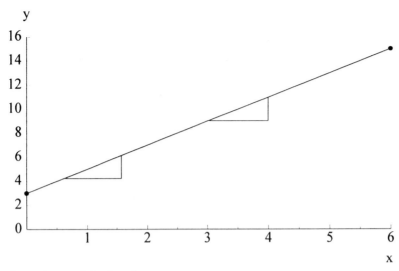

The general equation of a straight line is:

$$y = mx + c$$

(m is used for slope and c is used for the intersect)

Any equation which has this form is a straight-line equation, so the following are examples of straight lines.

(a)	y	=	x + 5	m	=	1	c	=	5
(b)	y	=	–2x + 10	m	=	–2	c	=	10
(c)	y	=	8	m	=	0	c	=	8
(d)	y	=	3x – 7	m	=	3	c	=	–7
(e)	y	=	–x – 1	m	=	–1	c	=	–1

Such equations are also called 'linear' equations.

One easy way to recognise them is that they can never contain powers of x or y. An equation that contains a term of x^2 is called a quadratic equation.

To draw a straight line on a graph, we only need two points on the graph and we can then join them with a ruler. It is common practice to make one of these points the intercept, ie. value corresponding to x = 0) and the other the value corresponding to a suitable value of x.

For example, to draw the first two lines above, use the following points:

(a)   When x = 0, y = 5
        When x = 6, y = 6 + 5 = 11

(b)   When x = 0, y = 10
        When x = 6, y = –12 + 10 = –2

Example

> *Draw the following straight lines on the same graph:*
>
> *(a)   y = 4x + 2*
> *(b)   y = 5x*
> *(c)   y = –3x + 25*
> *(d)   x = 5*

Solution

(a) When x = 0, y = 2
     When x = 6, y = 26

(b) When x = 0, y = 0
     When x = 6, y = 30

(c) When x = 0, y = 25
     When x = 6, y = 7

(d) x = 5 all the time

These are shown on the following graph:

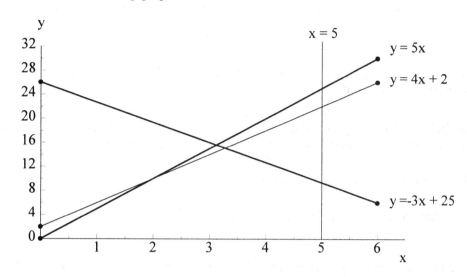

Practical example – Cost functions

The idea of a straight-line relationship occurs in the calculation of costs or in some depreciation calculations. Suppose a company produces just one product. If the fixed costs are £20,000 and the unit variable cost of one item of each product is £10, the costs of producing x items of the product are

Total cost   =   Fixed costs + Unit variable cost × Number of items produced
              =   20,000 + 10x

Note that fixed costs are defined as those costs that do not vary with the level of output. Thus rent and rates are examples of fixed costs.

Unit variable costs are costs that vary with the level of output. An example would be the material that makes up each product. The more products we make, the more material is used and hence the greater the cost.

A graph of total costs against the number of items produced is shown below

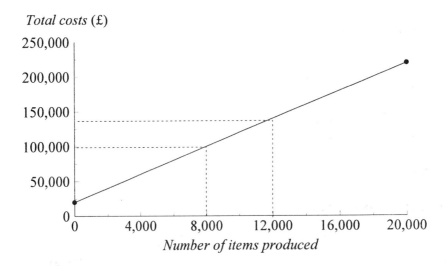

When no items are produced, costs equal £20,000;   when 20,000 items are produced, costs equal £20,000 + £200,000 = £220,000

If we want to find the costs for producing a number of items, we simply read them off the graph or substitute in the equation. For production of 8,000 items, the costs are:

$$\text{Costs} = 20,000 + 10 \times 8,000 = £100,000$$

This is also the value if we read the value from the graph. (The value vertically at the 8,000 point is 100,000.)

If we know the total cost, we can work backwards to find the number of items produced either from the graph or by solving an equation. Suppose total cost is £140,000 and we wish to know the number of items, we have:

$$140,000 = 20,000 + 10x$$
$$120,000 = 10x$$
$$12,000 = x$$

so, if 12,000 items are produced, the total cost is £140,000. (Again, using the graph we obtain 12,000 items.)

QUESTIONS

1   ICI profits

Interpret the following diagram.

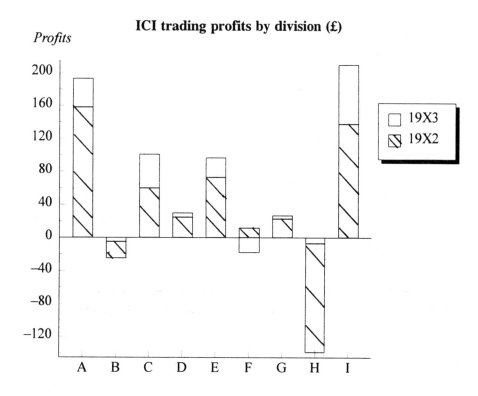

ICI trading profits by division (£)

Profits

Key

A = Agriculture
B = Fibres
C = General chemicals
D = Explosives
E = Oil

F = Organics
G = Paints
H = Petrochemicals and plastics
I = Pharmaceuticals

2   Pydec

Pydec Ltd is a British company manufacturing television sets and audio equipment. The attached is a section from their company report for 19X1/X2.

Pydec Ltd – Difficult times ahead?

As you all know this has been a very difficult year for the company. The following diagrams illustrate this all too clearly.

Profits tumble

From the following graph, you can see just how badly we have done in respect of profits. There are two main reasons for this fall in profits (down by almost 20%). Firstly, and most importantly, we have had sold fewer of our products. Secondly, we have to contend with inflation which has greatly increased both our overheads and our costs of production (not least of which has been the increase in wages – see later).

Total profits

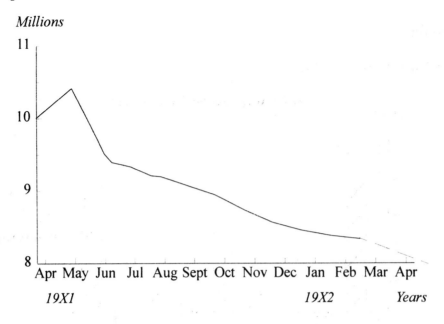

Production falls

As you know, we have three factories, at Dundee, London and here at Leicester (Head office). The following bar chart gives a breakdown of the production of TV sets at the three factories.

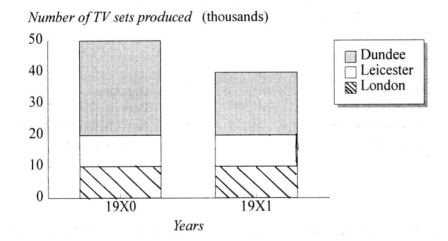

From this one can clearly see that production has fallen significantly over the last year. This is disturbing, especially since some of our competitors have been doing much better.

Wages up

In the past we have always rewarded our employees well; last year was no different. In fact, the average wage of all employees rose by £7.23 per week from 19X0 to 19X1.

In fact, if we compare average wages between 19W5 and 19X0 we can see the following:

19X1

19W6

£43.65

£84.06

Prospects for the future are not good and any wage increases must be earned by increasing our efficiency.

The future

The above diagrams give a gloomy forecast for the coming years. To remain competitive we may have to reduce our workforce significantly. However, in some respects we can help ourselves quite a lot.

Our main cost is employees' wages. If wage increases are kept to a minimum this can only do us good and may help us retain staff.

Our aim for the coming year must be to try and become more competitive.

I look forward to your support.

James Telly
Chairman

Assessment task

You have been asked by the co-ordinating committee of a trade union at the Leicester factory of Pydec to comment critically on this report.

3   **Data presentation**

Which of the following methods is unlikely to be suitable for presenting data concerning the numbers of audit, tax, investigation and other clients of a firm of accountants for each of the last five years?

(a)   A series of pie charts
(b)   Percentage component bar chart
(c)   Compound bar chart
(d)   Gantt chart

4   Not at all obvious

Look at the following extract from a written report:

> Ten newsagent shops in the Bristol area were selected to test the effectiveness of two different display stands in generating sales. For the purposes of the survey the shops were designated with the letters A–J (see Appendix for the address of each shop).
>
> During the period 15 March to 20 March, the total sales for the three items were recorded. Two different stands were used to display those items for sale. Five of the stands were the traditional sloping top 5 ft wide stand made of formica with perspex divisions while the other five were the metal revolving type, 2 ft in diameter. Shops A, C, D, G, I, used the traditional stand and shops B, E, F, H, J, used the revolving stand.
>
> Total sales of the items during the six day test period (Monday to Saturday inclusive) were as follows: Shops E, F, G, H showed sales of 435, 475, 286 and 575 cards and Shop I 275 with Shop J at 525.
>
> There is an obvious correlation between sales and type of display stand. This correlation is reflected in similar studies carried out in Manchester and Aberdeen.

This material is taken from a survey report. How well have you been able to assimilate the information? Was the correlation between the sales and the type of display stand quite as 'obvious' as the author suggests?

Assessment tasks

(a)   Your immediate superior, Mrs Jenkins, has asked you to rewrite this report in the short report format illustrated in an earlier section, presenting the facts in a more understandable manner.

(b)   Write a memo to the author, Jo Bloggs, raising any further queries you may have about the survey report.

SUMMARY

This session has revised the main principles to be followed in preparing a report and the various ways in which data may be presented – by tabulation or diagrammatically, including charts and graphs.

Many of the questions in your exam will either require you to present the answer in report format or to interpret information presented in a table or diagrammatic form.

Standard costing and variance analysis

OBJECTIVES

This session is relevant to Units 11 and 12 in particular, although the use of standards will also arise in Unit 13.

It is again largely revision of your earlier studies, but needs careful consideration as the subject matter is key to these Level 4 units.

This session aims to:

- examine the purposes of a standard cost reporting system
- consider how suitable standard costs may be set
- revise the nature and computation of traditional cost variances
- consider how these would be presented to management

The performance criteria addressed by this session are as follows:

- Unusual or unexpected results are identified and brought to the attention of managers.

- Any reasons for significant variances from standard are discovered and the explanations presented to management.

- Variances are clearly identified and reported to management in routine reports.

- Actual cost and revenue data are correctly coded and allocated to responsibility centres.

OBJECTIVES

Cost accounting is frequently carried out on an historical basis: a budget is prepared for the period in question, costs are accumulated and analysed after they have been incurred, and a comparison of budget and actual cost is subsequently made.

This approach suffers from two basic problems:

(a)   any information obtained from the comparison may be too late to be effective; and

(b)   the cost headings are frequently too general to enable management to pinpoint reasons for the deviations from budget.

Standard costing provides us with a system that provides more immediate and detailed information to management as to why budgeted performance differs from actual performance.

Standard costing systems are widely used because they provide cost data which can be used for many different purposes, including the following:

(a)   to assist in budget setting and evaluating performance;

(b)   to act as a control device by highlighting those activities that do not conform to plan and thus alerting managers to those situations which may be 'out of control' and hence in need of corrective action;

(c)   to provide a prediction of future costs to be used in decision-making;

(d)   to simplify the task of tracing costs to products for stock valuation;

(e)   to provide a challenging target that individuals are motivated to achieve.

An effective standard costing system relies on standard cost reports, with variances clearly identified, to be presented in an intelligible form to management as part of the overall cost reporting cycle.

DEFINITIONS

Standard cost

A predetermined cost which is calculated from management's standards of efficient operation and the relevant necessary expenditure. It may be used as a basis for fixing selling prices, for valuing stock and work in progress, and to provide control over actual costs through the process of variance analysis.

Standard costing

The preparation and use of standard costs, their comparison with actual costs, and the analysis of variances to their causes and points of incidence.

METHODS OF DEVELOPING STANDARDS

The nature of standards

Whenever identical operations are performed or identical products are manufactured time and time again, it should be possible to decide in advance not only what they are likely to cost but also what they *ought* to cost. In other words, it is possible to set a standard cost for each operation or product unit, comprising:

(a)   technical standards for the quantities of material to be used and the working time required;
(b)   cost standards for the material prices and hourly rates that should be paid.

Standards from past records

Past data can be used to predict future costs if operating conditions are fairly constant between past and future time periods. This method may not be appropriate for newly introduced operations due to learning curve effects (see later).

The main disadvantage with this method is that past data may contain inefficiencies which would then be built into the standards.

Engineering standards

This involves engineers developing standards for materials, direct labour and variable overheads by studying the product and the production process, possibly with the help of time and motion studies. This method is particularly useful when managers are evaluating new products as the historical records are only of value where they can be related to operations needed to make the new product.

The main disadvantage is that engineering standards may be too tight as they may not allow for the behaviour of the workers.

SETTING TECHNICAL (USAGE) STANDARDS

Standard material usage

In setting material usage standards, the first stage is to define what quantity of material input is theoretically required to achieve one unit of measured output.

In most manufacturing operations the quantity or volume of product emerging will be less than the quantity of materials introduced. This type of waste is normal to the type of operation and the usage figure would be increased by an allowance for this normal waste.

Standard time allowed

The standard or allowed time for an operation is a realistic estimate of the amount of productive time required to perform that operation based on work study methods. It is normally expressed in standard hours.

Various allowances may be added to the theoretical operating time, to take account of operator fatigue and personal needs and periodical activities such as machine setting, clearing up, regrinding tools and on-line quality inspection. An allowance may also be made for spoilt work as indicated under material usage above, or for rectification of defects appearing in the course of processing.

SETTING COST STANDARDS

Basic approach

When setting cost standards at a point in time, there are two basic approaches:

(a)   To use the prices or rates which are *current* at the time the standards are set.

This has the advantage that each standard is clearly identifiable with a known fact. On the other hand, if prices are likely to change then the standards based on them will have a limited value for planning purposes.

The standards would have to be revised in detail from time to time to ensure that they are up to date. If this is not done, then any differences between standard and actual costs are likely to be largely due to invalid standards.

(b)   To use a *forecast* of average prices or rates over the period for which the standard is to be used.

This can postpone the need for revision, but has the disadvantages that the standard may never correspond with observed fact (so there will be a price variance on all transactions) and that the forecast may be subject to significant error.

Neither method, therefore, will be ideal for all purposes and in deciding between them it will be necessary to consider whether the cost standards are being set principally to put a consistent value on technical variances, or as a help in budgeting, or as a means of exercising cost control, or merely to simplify bookkeeping.

Material price standards

In setting material price standards, it will often be found that a particular item of material is purchased from several suppliers at slightly different prices and the question arises which price shall be adopted as standard. There are three possible approaches:

(a)   *To identify the major supplier and to use his price as the standard*

This is particularly appropriate where there is no intention of buying large quantities from the alternative suppliers, but merely to use them as a means of ensuring continuity of supply should there be any delay or failure by the principal supplier.

(b)   *To use the lower quoted price as the standard*

This method can be used if it is desirable to put pressure on the buyer to obtain price reductions from other suppliers.

(c)   *To forecast the proportion of supplies to be bought from each supplier and to calculate a weighted average price as the costing standard*

This is the most satisfactory method for control purposes if the required forecast can be made with reasonable accuracy.

Another question in relation to material price standards is whether to include the cost of carriage inwards and other costs such as non-returnable packing and transit insurance. The object always will be to price incoming goods at their total delivered cost, so the costs such as those instanced above should be included in the standards.

Standard labour rates

A decision to be made when setting standard labour rates, is whether to use basic pay rates only, or to incorporate overtime premiums. The answer will depend on the nature of the overtime work and the approach to cost control adopted by management.

(a)   If a normal level of overtime work can be identified and is accepted as necessary, or if overtime is planned for the company's convenience, then the relative overtime premium payments will normally be included in the standard labour rate.

(b)   If it is a management objective to reduce or eliminate overtime working, the standard rate may be restricted to basic pay.

(c)   Where overtime is worked at the request of particular customers, then the related premium payments are a direct cost of the work done and would not be included in a standard rate which was applied generally to other work.

(d)   Where part of employee remuneration takes the form of incentive bonuses, then it will be necessary to forecast the level of efficiency to be achieved and the bonus payments appropriate to that performance. These bonuses will then be included in the calculation of the standard rate.

LEARNING CURVES

The concept

There are certain types of industry where the unit of production changes at regular intervals rather than a standard unit of production being manufactured for a very long period of time. Examples of such industries are clothing manufacture, where patterns change with the season and current fashion, and light engineering where many production runs are to a customer's particular specification.

In such industries it is known that the time taken to produce a unit in the early stages of a new product is significantly longer than the time per unit once the item has been manufactured for some time. The successive reduction in the time taken for each unit is caused by a learning process affecting the labour force.

Wright's law

When an operator is given a new task to carry out, it will initially take a long time, but as the operator becomes familiar with the routine, the time will diminish progressively until a steady state is reached.

The first observations of this phenomenon were made by TP Wright in the US aircraft industry and his findings were formalised as Wright's law which states:

'For any operation which is repeated, the overall average time for the operation will decrease by a fixed percentage as the number of repetitions is doubled'.

Wright found that the reduction percentage for aircraft manufacture was 20%, so that an operation obeying Wright's law would have the following time characteristics:

Time for first unit   = 100 hrs
Overall average time per unit for 2 units   = $100 \times 0.8 = 80$ hrs (ie. 100 hrs – 20% × 100 hrs)
Overall average time per unit for 4 units   = $80 \times 0.8 = 64$ hrs
Overall average time per unit for 8 units   = $64 \times 0.8 = 51.2$ hrs
Overall average time per unit for 16 units   = $51.2 \times 0.8 = 40.96$ hrs

This situation is said to follow an 80% learning curve. Note that the 20% reduction in time is not quoted as the learning factor. The total time taken at each stage would be:

		Total time (hrs)
1st unit		100
2 units	(2 × 80 hrs)	160
4 units	(4 × 64)	256
8 units	(8 × 51.2)	409.6
16 units	(16 × 40.96)	655.36

Graphical presentation

Plotting these figures on a graph with the number of units on the horizontal axis and the overall average time on the vertical axis, as shown below, demonstrates the tendency to move towards a steady state as the curve flattens out.

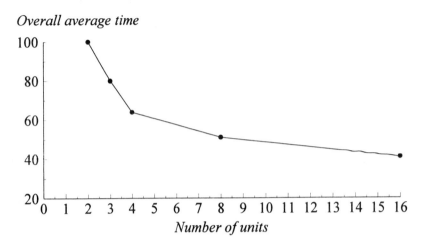

Overall average time

Number of units

Note that the times recorded on this graph are overall average times, covering all units produced up to a particular point. Thus, referring back to the figures above, the time taken for the first unit is 100 but the overall average time for the first two units is 80. Therefore the total time taken for the first two units is 160. From which it can be deduced that the actual time taken to produce the second unit was 60.

Illustration

The distinction between overall average time per unit and time to produce the latest unit is demonstrated more fully in the following example of a firm experiencing a learning factor of 80% (or 0.8).

A trial batch of 100 units of a new product is produced in an average time of 20 minutes per unit. Production times based on continually doubling the batch size would be as follows:

Batch quantity (units)	*Cumulative quantity (units)*	*Overall average time per unit (minutes)*	*Total time (minutes)*	*Batch time (minutes)*
100	100	20.00	2,000	2,000
100	200	20 × 0.8 = 16.00	3,200	1,200
200	400	16 × 0.8 = 12.80	5,120	1,920
400	800	12.8 × 0.8 = 10.24	8,192	3,072

If the planned production of this item for the coming month was, say, 300 (over and above the initial 100 and making cumulative production 400), the total time and average time per unit for this 300 would be:

Total time for 300 units = 5,120 – 2,000 = 3,120 minutes
Average time for these units = 3,120 300 = 10.4 minutes

Effect on budgeting

From this example, it can be seen that the total estimated time to complete the total of 800 units is 8,192 minutes. This is considerably less than we would expect if there were no learning effect and each unit required 20 minutes, as in the first batch. In this case the total time required would be 800 × 20 = 16,000 minutes.

Obviously this would make a considerable difference to production planning, delivery dates and costing for this product and therefore, if it is known that a learning effect is likely to occur, it should be taken into account when preparing budgets.

When preparing cost budgets it must be remembered that costs other than the direct labour cost will be affected by the learning process. Variable overhead costs (typically machine power) are normally dependent on direct labour hours. A saving in labour hours will therefore result in cost savings on both labour and variable overhead.

Effect on standard setting

A further area affected by the learning process will be that of standard setting. When setting a standard for labour time, particularly at the onset of a new product's life, we must take into account the possibility of any learning.

Why not, then, set a standard at the steady state level? The drawback here is that this will initially cause very high adverse variances, and so may lead to demotivation of the workforce as a consequence.

Perhaps we may try to eliminate both of the preceding problems by continuously resetting the standard period on period to reflect the reduction in anticipated time that the learning effect causes. But this has two effects:

(a)   we lose the benefits that predetermined standards give; and

(b)   the workforce may become disillusioned if they feel the standard is following the actual result and not vice versa.

In the real world the practical solution may well be:

(a)   Set standards that management are aware of to compare to actual performance.

(b)   Ensure that workers do achieve maximum efficiency by linking actual performance to rewards – perhaps by some form of piece-rate working.

Research into the learning effect

Research has shown that, for a particular workforce and type of operation the learning effect is measurable from historic data and would normally be of approximately the same magnitude in future. Thus Wright found an 80% learning factor appropriate for the US aircraft industry, but this might not be the correct figure for a company manufacturing clothing in the UK. Commonly learning factors range from 60% to 85%.

It must also be borne in mind that the learning effect is not an automatic natural phenomenon. Not all production processes will show increased efficiency.

In general, the higher the labour content the more opportunity for learning. Highly automated processes offer relatively little opportunity for improvement.

Another most important factor is motivation, which arises from the belief that something can be learnt and that it is desirable that it should be learnt. An organisation which believes that it has no need or no room to improve is unlikely to demonstrate any marked learning.

TYPES OF STANDARD

The way in which control is exercised and the interpretation and use of variances from standards will depend on the manner in which those standards are set.

Ideal standards

In some cases standards are established on the assumption that machines and employees will work with optimal efficiency at all times, and that there will be no stoppages and no losses of material or services.

Such standards would represent an ideal state of affairs and therefore the objectives they set are never achieved.

Managers who are responsible for the costs can hardly approve of targets which they can never reach and which, therefore, result in large adverse variances from the standards.

Attainable (expected) standards

In other cases the standards set will be those which are reasonably attainable, consideration being given to the state of efficiency which can be achieved from the existing facilities. There is no question of assuming, as for ideal standard costs, that production resources will be used at maximum efficiency.

A positive effort is still made to achieve a high level of efficiency, but there is no question of going beyond what is attainable.

Basic standards

A basic standard is one which, having been fixed, is not generally revised with changing conditions, but remains in force for a long period of time. It may be set originally having regard to either ideal or expected conditions. Under circumstances of rapid technological change or of significant price changes, basic standards are of limited value in relation to the achievement of the benefits outlined above.

There may be variations on these methods, but the aim should be to select the standard cost which is likely to be the most realistic for the business concerned. It should be remembered that standards are the yardstick against which efficiency is measured and therefore, if they are unrealistic then the variances will be of little meaning.

ADVANTAGES AND DISADVANTAGES OF STANDARD COSTING

Advantages

The advantages of standard costing fall into two broad categories: planning and control.

Planning

Predetermined standards make the preparation of forecasts and budgets much easier. If the standards are to be used for these operational decisions then they must obviously be as accurate as possible. This again means that standards should be revised on a frequent basis.

Control

Control is primarily exercised through the comparison of standard and actual results, and the isolation of variances. This will highlight areas of apparent efficiency and inefficiency, and as necessary investigations as to the causes of the variance can be made. If these investigations discover the causes of the variances, then corrective action can be taken to improve efficiency in the future.

In addition to the above, there are subsidiary advantages such as:

(a)   If the standards are perceived to be attainable, then they will serve to motivate the employees concerned.

(b)   A standard costing bookkeeping system can be set up that will fulfil all requirements, for both internal and external reporting.

(c)   Recording of stock issues is simplified, as it is done at the standard price.

Disadvantages

These relate primarily to the costs incurred in setting up and maintaining the system. As indicated, standards must be revised on a regular basis to retain effectiveness. It is for this reason that standard costing is most effective for well-established and repetitive processes, so that the revisions of standards are kept to a minimum.

VARIANCE ANALYSIS: INTRODUCTION

We have seen how management will develop standard costs in advance of the period under review. During the course of that period, actual costs will be compared with standard costs and any differences isolated for investigation as to their cause, enabling corrective action to be taken as soon as possible.

Management will wish to see a clear and succinct summary of the results for the period and in particular will want any unusual or unexpected items to be brought to their attention. They will also rely on the reasons for significant variances being discovered and the explanations being presented to them to enable them to decide the appropriate response. In general, this will take the form of a reconciliation between budgeted and actual profits which highlights the differences between them. To be useful as a management tool, the reconciliation should be part of an overall report to management.

TRADITIONAL VARIANCE ANALYSIS: A REVIEW EXAMPLE

You will have already covered in Unit 6 *Recording cost information* the calculation of basic or 'traditional' cost variances.

The following budgeted and actual data for TJB Ltd for 19X1 will be used to revise the principles and computations.

TJB Ltd

Budgeted profit and loss statement for the year ending 31 December 19X1

Production   10,000 units

Production cost	£/unit	£
Direct materials – 10,000 tons @ £1 per ton (1 ton per unit)	1.00	10,000
Direct labour – 20,000 hours @ 50p per hour (2 hours per unit)	1.00	10,000
Variable production overhead – 20,000 hours @ 25p per hour	0.50	5,000
Fixed production overhead – 20,000 hours @ 75p per hour	1.50	15,000
Total budgeted production cost	4.00	40,000

During the year to 31 December 19X1, the following actual results were obtained.

TJB Ltd

Actual cost statement for the year ending 31 December 19X1

Production   8,000 units
            15,500 hours worked on actual production

Production cost	£
Direct materials – 7,750 tons purchased and used (£1.096)	8,500
Direct labour – 16,500 hours paid (£0.4545 per hour)	7,500
Variable production overhead incurred (15,500 hours @ £0.3548)	5,500
Fixed production overhead incurred	15,500
Total budgeted production cost	37,000

The purpose of the analysis is to explain the difference between the budgeted cost of £40,000 and the actual cost of £37,000.

Total cost variances – budgetary control statement

A possible initial step would be to compare the budget with actual costs and compute the total variances for each item, marking F for favourable if they lead to decreased cost and A for adverse if they lead to an increase in costs.

However, this can quickly be shown to be unhelpful, if not misleading, to management, in the circumstances of this question.

Consider the cost of direct materials. The above analysis would indicate a favourable cost saving of £1,500 (£10,000 – £8,500). Bearing in mind however that the budgeted cost of £10,000 relates to the budgeted production of 10,000 units, whereas the actual cost of £8,500 relates to the actual production of 8,000 units, it is clearly questionable whether it is useful to produce an analysis that indicates a cost saving of £1,500.

A more useful reconciliation of the budgeted profit and actual profit is one that will evaluate cost savings by comparing the actual costs of producing a certain actual level of output with the standard cost of producing the **same actual level of output**. Thus, ideally, the analysis will compare, for example, the actual direct materials cost of producing 8,000 units (£8,500) with the standard direct materials cost of producing 8,000 units (8,000 units at a standard material cost of £1 per unit = £8,000), ie. an unfavourable **overspending** on materials of £500 rather than any favourable cost saving.

So far, of course, we have only discussed the cost of direct materials. Naturally, similar considerations will apply to the other items of cost, and one can draw up a table showing the difference between the actual cost of producing 8,000 units and the standard cost of producing that level of output (8,000 units) – the latter being referred to as a **flexed budget**.

	Flexed budget cost of producing 8,000 units	*Actual cost of producing 8,000 units*	*Difference (variance)*
	£	£	£
Direct materials	8,000	8,500	500 A
Direct labour	8,000	7,500	500 F
Variable production overhead	4,000	5,500	1,500 A
Fixed production overhead	12,000	15,500	3,500 A
Total	32,000	37,000	5,000 A

Such a reconciliation, between actual costs and flexed budgeted costs is often known as a **budgetary control statement** or **budgetary control report**.

Variance analysis

The total variances illustrated in the above statement are simply the differences between:

(a)   the actual costs; and
(b)   the standard costs for actual production.

If you think about this you will see that, in general, only two things could have caused the actual cost to be different from the standard cost: firstly, the actual price or rate (per kg, hour etc.) was different from the standard price or rate and, secondly, the actual amount used per unit was different from the standard.

Hence each of these total variances can be analysed into two types of variances:

(a)   a price variance;
(b)   a usage or utilisation variance.

Materials

The total materials cost variance may be analysed into a price variance and a usage variance.

Total direct material cost variance

The total variance is the difference between the amount that the materials did cost and the amount that they should have cost to produce the actual output achieved. It is the difference between:

		£
(a)	the **actual** amount of material used at the actual price	8,500
(b)	the **standard** amount of material that should have been used at the standard price 8,000 kg × £1	8,000
		500 A

Direct materials price variance

The part of the total variance that is caused by the actual price per ton being different from the standard price (ie. the difference between what you actually paid and what you should have paid for the amount **actually purchased**).

	Tons	£
Actual materials purchased, at actual price per ton	7,750	8,500
Actual materials purchased, at standard price per ton (£1)	7,750	7,750
Materials price variance	–	750 A

Direct materials usage variance

The part of the total variance that is caused by the actual amount used per unit being different from the standard amount. It is the difference between the cost (at standard) of the amount of material you did use and the amount you should have used for the output achieved.

	Tons	
Actual materials used	7,750	
Standard materials allowed for production achieved	8,000	
Materials usage variance (@ £1 per ton)	250	£250 F

Labour

Total direct labour cost variance

The total direct labour cost (or rate) variance is the difference between the actual amount paid for labour and the amount that should have been paid to produce the actual output achieved.

It is the difference between:

		£
(a)	the **actual** hours paid at the **actual** rate per hour	7,500
(b)	the **standard** time allowed to **produce the output**, priced at the **standard** rate per hour (16,000 × £0.50)	8,000
		500 F

The total variance can be analysed into *price* and *usage* variances as normal, but the usage variance is itself sub-analysed further into an *idle time* and a *utilisation* or *efficiency variance*, if idle time is present.

Remember that the usage variance, for any element of cost, measures the difference between the amount actually purchased/used and the amount that should have been purchased/used to produce the output achieved (priced at standard price). In the case of labour, there are two reasons why the actual amount of labour paid for might be different from the standard amount allowed for that output:

(a) *Idle time*

   The labour may be idle for part of the time it is being paid. There may be many reasons for this (eg. machine breakdown, shortage of materials, power failure etc.).

(b) *Utilisation or efficiency*

   When the labour is actually working it may actually produce more (or less) than the standard number of units per hour.

The idle time and efficiency variances in TJB are calculated as follows.

Calculation of direct labour cost variances

Rate of pay (price) variance

The part of the total variance that is caused by paying a lower (or higher) rate than the standard for the actual number of hours paid. Notice that again the rate variance (price variance) is calculated on the amount of the input that is actually purchased.

It is the difference between what you did pay and what you should have paid for the actual number of hours 'bought'.

	Hours	£
Actual hours paid at actual rate per hour	16,500	7,500
Actual hours paid at standard rate per hour	16,500	8,250
Direct labour rate variance	–	750 F

Idle time variance

The part of the total variance that is caused by labour not working for all the hours paid (16,500 hours paid – 15,500 hours worked).

	Hours	£
Actual hours paid at standard rate per hour	16,500	8,250
Actual hours worked at standard rate per hour	15,500	7,750
Direct labour rate variance	1,000	500 A

Utilisation of efficiency variance

That part of the total variance that is caused by labour producing more or less output than the standard allows when it is actually working (15,500 hours worked – 16,000 hours worth of output produced).

	Hours	
Actual hours worked	15,500	
Standard hours allowed for production achieved	16,000	
Direct labour efficiency variance (@ £0.50 per hr)	500	£250 F

Make sure that you understand the labour cost variances.

The rate of pay variance (price) performs the usual role of accounting for that part of the total variance caused by the actual price being different from the standard price.

The idle time and efficiency variances simply explain (at the standard rate) why a certain number of hours of labour was paid for and a different amount of output (measured in labour hours) was produced.

Their net effect is to explain how 16,500 hours were paid for and only 16,000 hours worth of output was achieved. They explain by showing that 1,000 hours were lost through 'idle time' but that 500 hours were gained through efficient working (net loss: 500 hours).

Variable production overhead

Variable production overheads are such costs as the electricity or oil used to power the machines that produce the output. The normal treatment of these overheads is to assume that they are only **incurred** when the labour force is working. Thus, if labour is idle, for whatever reason, it is assumed that the machinery is turned off and the overhead cost not incurred.

Because of this assumption, that the overhead is incurred with the labour hours worked, the basis for the computation of the variances is the **hours worked**. Thus, in TJB Ltd, the budgeted cost of the overhead (£5,000) was computed by taking the budgeted hours worked and multiplying by the budgeted (standard) cost of the overhead per hour.

The total variance is the difference between the amount TJB did pay and the amount TJB should have paid for the overhead. This is divided into a price and usage variance.

Total variable overhead variance

The difference between what the variable overhead did cost and what it should have cost for the output actually achieved (ie. for the production of 8,000 units).

It is calculated as follows:

	Hours	£
Actual hours worked at actual cost per hour	15,500	5,500
Standard cost, ie. the amount that the overhead should have cost (8,000 units × 2 hours × £0.25)	16,000	4,000
Total variance	500 A	1,500 A

Price variance

The difference between what the overhead did cost during the actual hours actually worked, and the cost that should have been incurred during the hours actually worked. (**Note:** The expenditure variance is again calculated on the actual amount of the input that was 'purchased'.)

	Hours	£
Actual cost – actual hours worked at actual cost per hour	15,500	5,500
Standard cost of hours worked	15,500	3,875
Price variance		1,625 A

Usage (or efficiency) variance

That part of the total variable overhead variance that is caused by the actual hours worked to produce the output, being different from the standard hours allowed to produce that output (all valued at standard cost £0.25 per hour).

	Hours	
Actual hours worked	15,500	
Standard hours allowed for actual production achieved	16,000	
Variable production overhead usage (efficiency) variance (@ 25p/hr)	500	£125 F

Note: In our example, we have recovered variable overheads at the standard rate of 25p per labour hour. This infers that the incurring of variable overheads is related to labour hours worked. It is possible that variable overheads might depend on some other activity base, such as machine hours. Another alternative might be to compute a variable overhead rate per unit, in which case there would be no usage variance and the price variance will be equal to the total cost variance.

Fixed production overheads

At the beginning of this section on variance analysis, we stated that the original budget is always flexed to the actual production level achieved. This was to eliminate the cost difference simply due to the fact that more, or less, units than budget were in fact produced.

This causes problems with regard to fixed overheads which, by definition, are not expected to change with the level of production.

Remember that, in order to set a fixed overhead absorption rate, we have to make an estimate of the level of activity in hours or in units, as well as of the fixed cost itself. Thus, for TJB, we will have obtained the standard fixed overhead absorption rate as follows:

$$\frac{\text{Budgeted cost}}{\text{Budgeted activity}} = \frac{\pounds 15,000}{(10,000 \times 2\text{hrs})} = \pounds 0.75 \text{ per hour or } \pounds 1.50 \text{ per unit}$$

This means that as units are produced, we will absorb £1.50 per unit. This will lead to the correct total of £15,000 to be absorbed only as long as actual production = budgeted production = 10,000 units. If more or less than this is produced, there will be an adjustment due to over or under-absorption at the end of the period. The fixed overhead variance analysis therefore recognises the 'true' price variance by comparing actual cost with **original** budgeted cost, and the need for the under-/over-absorption adjustment by the volume variance. The calculations are as follows:

Fixed overhead total cost variance

The difference between the actual fixed overhead cost and the standard (flexed) cost for actual production (ie. the amount that will be absorbed into production):

	£
Actual fixed overhead cost	15,500
Standard cost absorbed into actual production (8,000 × £1.50)	12,000
Total cost variance	3,500 A

Fixed overhead price variance

This *expenditure* variance is simply the difference between budgeted and actual expenditure.

	£
Actual expenditure	15,500
Budgeted expenditure	15,000
Expenditure variance	500 A

Thus, we have actually incurred £500 more fixed overhead than expected.

Fixed overhead volume variance

This is the under-absorption (at standard rates) due to the lower actual production level than that budgeted.

	Units
Actual production	8,000
Budgeted production	10,000
Volume variance (in units)	2,000 units (A)
Valued at standard absorption rate per unit (£1.50)	£3,000 A

The variance is adverse because we have under-absorbed fixed overhead by 2,000 units' worth. We thus require an extra charge to the cost account to compensate for this under-absorption.

Sub-division of the volume variance

Because the original fixed overhead absorption rate was based on labour hours (50p per hour), the volume variance as computed above can be subdivided further to explain why the level of activity was different from budget. Management will want to know why a shortfall of 2,000 units of production occurred. How did this happen?

Usage (efficiency)

Were the workforce inefficient, producing each unit in more than the standard number of hours? We already know from previous work on labour variances that in fact the workforce was efficient to the tune of 500 hours. This would, on its own, lead to **extra** production and **over-absorption** of fixed overheads. Thus this will in fact be a **favourable** element of the volume variance.

Capacity

Another reason for producing fewer units would be if, instead of being inefficient, the workforce simply worked shorter hours in total during the period. The capacity variance compares the actual number of hours worked with the number of hours budgeted for the period. Here we have a shortfall of 4,500 hours, which will restrict production and thus absorption of fixed overheads.

Computations are shown below.

(a)   Usage variance

	Hours		
Actual hours worked for actual production	15,500		
Standard hours allowed for actual production achieved	16,000		
Efficiency variance (@£0.75 per hr)	500	=	£375 F

(b)   Capacity variance

	Hours		
Actual hours worked	15,500		
Budgeted hours for the period	20,000		
Capacity variance (@£0.75 per hr)	4,500	=	£3,375 A

We can see that these two variances reconcile to the volume variance (£3,000 A) and show that the principal reason for our under production was a failure (by 4,500 hours) to devote sufficient hours to production during the period. The efficiency of the workforce was not sufficient to make up for this.

COMPARISON OF BUDGETED WITH ACTUAL RESULTS

Having computed all the variances, we can now reconcile budgeted with actual cost. This is a more detailed version of the budgetary control statement in a slightly different format.

		£	£	£
Flexed budgeted cost				32,000
Cost variances		*Adverse*	*Favourable*	
Materials	Price	750		
	Usage		250	
Labour	Price		750	
	Idle time	500		
	Utilisation		250	
Variable overheads	Price	1,625		
	Usage		125	
Fixed overheads	Price	500		
	Capacity	3,375		
	Efficiency		375	
Total / net variances		6,750	1,750	5,000
Actual cost				37,000

STOCKS OF FINISHED GOODS

Not all of the production in any period may be sold; some will be left in closing stock.

The stock can be valued at two different amounts: actual cost or standard cost.

Referring to the previous example, let us assume only 7,500 of the 8,000 units produced were sold. The standard cost is £4 per unit. Total costs incurred were £37,000 and total net variances were £5,000 adverse.

Stock at standard cost

We simply carry forward the balance of 500 units at the standard cost of £4 each (total £2,000), whilst transferring the remainder to cost of sales.

Under this method, the variances would be written off in full against profits for the period (as occurs automatically under traditional variance analysis as presented in the example above).

Stock at actual cost

If it is desired to carry forward closing stock at actual cost, then we must convert the stock value back to actual cost. This is done by transferring a proportion of the net cost variance back to finished goods stock, rather than writing it all off against profits.

The proportion would be $500/8,000$ since of 8,000 units produced 500 are in stock and 7,500 have been sold.

The actual cost incurred in total was £37,000 to produce 8,000 items.

Thus, at actual cost, finished goods stock will be valued at $500/8,000 \times £37,000 = £2,312.50$. This is £312.50 higher than when valued at standard, representing stocks share of the total adverse variance: $500/8,000 \times £5,000 = £312.50$

Interpretation of results

We have seen that valuing stock at standard or actual cost will give two different results. The impact of this is that, since closing stock is valued differently, then under the two methods cost of sales would be different and so reported profit would also be different.

Thus:

	£	£
Stock at standard cost		
Actual cost of production	37,000.00	
Less: Closing stock	(2,000.00)	
Cost of sales		35,000.00
Stock at actual cost		
Actual cost of production	37,000.00	
Less: Closing stock	(2,312.50)	
Cost of sales		(34,687.50)
Net effect on profit		312.50

In this case, because the cost variances are adverse, then stock at actual cost has a higher value than stock at standard cost. Consequently, valuing stock at actual cost gives the following:

- a higher closing stock figure
- a lower cost of sales figure
- a higher profit figure

Points to note from the above:

- The result will only be a timing difference – after all, this period's closing stock will form next period's opening stock.

- Both alternatives are used in practice.

- What we are effectively doing is deciding whether or not to capitalise part of the variances and carry them forward. There is an argument that says, if cost variances arise from factors peculiar to a particular period, then they should be written off in full in that period, since the profit figure will be distorted if this is not done. Thus we are really considering whether the cause of the variances is a normal business occurrence and, if it is, then we may well decide to pro-rate them over the cost of goods sold and closing stock.

- Note that, if the net production variance were favourable, then actual cost would be lower than standard cost. Thus valuing stocks at standard cost would lead to a higher reported profit figure.

In the absence of instructions to the contrary, always value stocks at standard cost in examination questions, since this avoids the need to pro-rate the variances.

QUESTIONS

1   Standard revision

A company operates a system of 'rolling budgets' with quarterly reviews. What guidelines would you lay down for the revision of technical and cost standards?

2   Standards come unstuck?

A company manufactures a standard range of petroleum-based adhesives which are packaged to meet the requirements of particular distributors or industrial users. There are no catalogue prices, each batch being made for a particular customer and being priced by negotiation. Would a standard costing system be helpful to this company?

3   WH Ltd I   (AAT CA D94)

WH Ltd uses a standard costing system which produces monthly control statements to monitor and control costs. One of their products is product M.

To manufacture product M, a perishable, high quality raw material is carefully weighed by direct employees. Some wastage and quality control rejects occur at this stage. The employees then compress the material to change its shape and create product M.

All direct employees are paid a basic hourly rate appropriate to their individual skill level and a bonus scheme is in operation. Bonuses are paid according to the daily rate of output achieved by each individual.

A standard allowance for all of the above operational factors is included in the standard cost of product M. Standard cost data for one unit of product M is as follows:

		Standard cost £ per unit
Direct material X:	4.5 kg × £4.90 per kg	22.05
Direct labour:	10.3 hours × £3.50 per hour	36.05
Standard direct cost		58.10

The production manager has approached you for further explanations concerning the standard costing control system. He is particularly interested in understanding how the standard price is set per kg of material used.

Assessment task

Write a memo to the production manager, explaining:

(a)   what information would be needed to determine the standard price per kg of material X;

(b)   the possible sources from which this information might be obtained.

4 Attainable and ideal standard

(a) Explain the terms *attainable standard* and *ideal standard*, and explain briefly why attainable standards tend to be used in preference to ideal standards.

(b) The budget for product A for a period is as follows:

Production	2,000	units
Sales	2,000	units: £15 per unit
Direct material cost 6,000		kg of XYZ: £2 per kg
Direct labour cost 4,000		hours: £2 per hour

Actual results for the period were:

Production	2,500	units
Sales	2,250	units: £15 per unit
Direct materials	5,000	kg purchased and consumed at a total cost of £12,000
Direct labour	6,000	hours at a total cost of £9,000

There were no opening stocks. It is company policy to value stocks at standard cost.

(i) Prepare a statement of actual profit for the period.

(ii) Calculate the following:

- material price variance;
- material usage variance;
- labour rate variance;
- labour efficiency variance.

5 Product XY

The following data relate to actual output, costs and variances for the four-weekly accounting period number 4 of a company which makes only one product. Opening and closing work-in-progress figures were the same.

Actual production of product XY	18,000 units

Actual costs incurred

	£'000
Direct materials purchased and used 150,000 kg	210
Direct wages for 32,000 hours	136
Variable production overhead	38

Variances

	£'000
Direct materials price	15 favourable
Direct materials usage	9 adverse
Direct labour rate	8 adverse
Direct labour efficiency	16 favourable
Variable production overhead expenditure	6 adverse
Variable production overhead efficiency	4 favourable

Variable production overhead varies with labour hours worked.

A standard marginal costing system is operated.

Required

(a) Present a standard product cost sheet for one unit of product XY.

(b) Describe briefly *three* types of standard that can be used for a standard costing system, stating which is usually preferred in practice and why.

6   AB Ltd   (AAT CA D94)

You work as assistant accountant for AB Ltd. The company manufactures a single product and uses a standard costing system to monitor and control costs.

Standard and actual cost data for direct costs for the month of June are shown below:

Standard costs	£ per unit
Direct material: 4.3 kg × £8 per kg	34.40
Direct labour: 1.5 hours × £4 per hour	6.00
Total direct costs	40.40

Actual results

Direct material purchased and used	=	19,500 kg at £8.50 per kg
Direct labour costs incurred	=	£26,286 paid for 6,740 hours

4,500 units were produced in June.

Assessment tasks

(a) Calculate the direct cost variances for June.

(b) Present the variances in a statement which reconciles the standard direct cost of production with the actual direct cost for June, using the following format.

Reconciliation of standard direct cost of production
with actual direct cost for June

	£	£
Standard direct cost of production = 4,500 × £40.40		181,800
Direct cost variances:	9750 (A)	
Direct material price	1200 (A)	
Direct material usage	10950 (A)	
	674 (F)	
Direct labour rate	40 (F)	
Direct labour utilisation	714 (F	
		10236 (A)
Actual direct cost of production		192036

7　WH Ltd II　　　　　　　　　　　　　　　　　　　　(AAT CA D94)

WH Ltd uses a standard costing system which produces monthly control statements to monitor and control costs. One of their products is product M.

To manufacture product M, a perishable, high quality raw material is carefully weighed by direct employees. Some wastage and quality control rejects occur at this stage. The employees then compress the material to change its shape and create product M.

All direct employees are paid a basic hourly rate appropriate to their individual skill level and a bonus scheme is in operation. Bonuses are paid according to the daily rate of output achieved by each individual.

A standard allowance for all of the above operational factors is included in the standard cost of product M. Standard cost data for one unit of product M is as follows:

		Standard cost *£ per unit*
Direct material X:	4.5 kg × £4.90 per kg	22.05
Direct labour:	10.3 hours × £3.50 per hour	36.05
		————
Standard direct cost		58.10
		————

During November, the following costs were incurred producing 400 units of product M:

			Actual costs *£*
Direct material X:	2,100 kg	£4.60.	9,660
Direct labour:	4,000 hrs	£4	16,000
			————
Actual direct cost			25,660
			————

Assessment tasks

(a)   Calculate the following direct cost variances for product M for November:

      (i)   direct material price
      (ii)   direct material usage
      (iii)   direct labour rate
      (iv)   direct labour utilisation or efficiency

(b)   Present the variances in a statement which reconciles the total standard direct cost of production with the actual direct cost for product M in November.

SUMMARY

In this session, we have looked at the various ways of establishing standard costs within a standard cost reporting system.

We have also revised the computation and interpretations of variances; in particular, fixed overhead variances which are a little more taxing.

Remember that the expenditure variance simply compares the budgeted cost with the actual cost. The volume variance compares budgeted activity level with the standard activity level and can be split further into a capacity and efficiency variance.

The important differences between possible stock valuations and their impacts on profit have also been examined.

Investigation of variances

OBJECTIVES

In the previous session, we revised the computation of cost variances. This session examines what might happen as a result of these variances being identified. It looks at the following:

- the factors to take into account when deciding on the significance of a variance
- how variance trends can enhance management information
- the analysis of variances by cause and responsibility
- costs and benefits of variance investigation

The ideas and techniques of this session can be examined in either Unit 11 or Unit 12.

The performance criteria addressed by this session are as follows:

- Any reasons for significant variances from standard are discovered and the explanations presented to management.

- More detailed analysis and explanation of specific variances is produced for management, on request.

- Staff working in operational departments are consulted to resolve any queries in the data.

- Variances are clearly identified and reported to management in routine reports.

- Actual cost and revenue data are correctly coded and allocated to responsibility centres.

- Significant actual requested or potential over/under-spends are discussed with managers and assistance given in taking remedial action.

MEASURING THE SIGNIFICANCE OF VARIANCES

Introduction

As we have seen, the key tool for management control within a standard costing system is some form of *variance analysis report*. The aim is to prepare a report to management on a routine basis in which variances are clearly identified and can be acted upon as appropriate.

In exercising control, it is generally impracticable to review every variance in detail at each accounting period and attention will usually be concentrated on those variances which have the greatest impact on the achievement of the budget plan.

One method of identifying significant variances is to express each variance as a *percentage of the related budget allowance or standard value*. Those showing the highest percentage deviation would then be given the most urgent attention.

This method, however, could result in lack of attention to variances which, although representing a small percentage of the standard value, nevertheless involve significant sums of money. Both percentages and money should be looked at in deciding where the priorities for control actually lie.

It is important that both favourable and unfavourable variances be reviewed, since both represent deviations from a predetermined plan.

In practice, management will review the variance report presented to them and decide which variances should be investigated on the basis of whether the *costs of investigation are outweighed by the benefits*. Management will often request a more detailed analysis and explanation of specific variances to be produced as the decision as to whether or not a variance merits investigation may need more information than is provided in the original variance report.

Fluctuating variances – looking at trends

It will sometimes happen that the variances of a particular period are not representative of a general trend. Items like stationery costs can fluctuate widely from month to month, dependent on the amount of stationery that has been invoiced. Sometimes the accountant will make estimated adjustments to either the budget or the actual figures in an attempt to give a better picture of the underlying trend but this is not a completely satisfactory way of dealing with the matter. The simplest way of getting the month's figures into context is to show also the *accumulated cost for the year to date*. High cost and low cost periods will then be revealed but will balance out in the cumulative figures.

A development of the above idea is also to report each period the manager's *latest forecast compared with the annual budget*. It will then be possible to see whether variances from budget currently being reported are likely to continue to accumulate during the remainder of the year, or whether they will be offset by later opposite variances. Although this technique of forecasting is dependent on managers' subjective assessments, it is a good way of ensuring that the correct control action gets taken on the current figures.

Illustration

An example of a report incorporating forecast figures for the year as a whole is given overleaf.

You might like to spend a few minutes considering what this report tells you about the business. For example:

(a)   Sales, which had obviously been below budget on the first six periods of the year, are significantly in excess of budget on period 7 (reducing the cumulative shortfall to £80,000), and are now expected to exceed the budget for the year as a whole.

(b)   Direct costs are naturally higher when sales are higher. The percentage of direct costs to sales value is not consistent, however, as the following calculations show:

	Budget	*Actual*
Period 7	56.0%	53.6%
Cumulative	56.0%	57.0%
Forecast	58.3%	62.1%

For the seven periods as a whole, direct costs have been in excess of the budgeted percentage and even though the budget for the twelve months provides for an increase in that percentage the forecast actual increase is still higher. Period 7 in isolation shows an anomalous result, perhaps due to some peculiarity in sales mix.

(c)   The variance on factory overhead, which is favourable over the seven periods as a whole, has become adverse in period 7 and is forecast as adverse for the year as a whole (though not at the rate experienced in period 7). Failure to budget adequately for inflationary increases is one possibility.

(d)   Administration and selling costs have a cumulative favourable variance of £40,000 against a budget of £840,000, ie. 4.8%. By the end of the year a favourable variance of £173,000 (13.1% on budget) is expected. It would appear that considerable economies are planned, and have already commenced. The fact that period 7 above shows a small adverse variance is obviously not significant. Such results can emerge in administration costs, which can be influenced by random occurrences like a large purchase of stationery or a major visit overseas by the managing director.

Profit and loss account

7 Periods cumulative to.....................19........ (£'000)

	Budget	*Period 7 Actual*	*Variances F or (A)*	*Budget*	*Cumulative Actual*	*Variances F or (A)*	*Budget*	*Whole year Latest forecast*
Sales	500	600	100	3,500	3,420	(80)	6,000	6,200
Direct cost of sales	280	322	(42)	1,960	1,951	9	3,500	3,850
Factory overhead	58	69	(11)	420	400	20	700	750
Administration and selling costs	122	123	(1)	840	800	40	1,320	1,147
Total costs	460	514	(54)	3,220	3,151	69	5,520	5,747
Operating profit	40	86	46	280	269	(11)	480	453
Profit: Sales %	8%	14.3%	–	8%	7.9%	–	8%	7.3%

Comparing against forecasts

Some large organisations in the UK have taken the idea of comparing against forecasts a step further. Many companies employ the following comparisons:

Comparison	*Information*
1 Budget v Actual	What progress have we made towards achieving objectives?

2	Budget v Forecast	Will we continue to progress towards achievement of objectives?
3	Budget v Revised forecast	Will suggested corrective actions lead us back to achievement of objectives?
4	Latest forecast v Previous	Why are the forecasts different and are circumstances getting better or worse?
5	Actual v Past forecast	Why were forecasts incorrect and can they be improved?

It may not be necessary to perform each of these control comparisons every month or quarter. The actual versus past forecast may only be necessary annually or less frequently.

It must be remembered that managers will need to be motivated to produce these forecasts and use them. They must be educated to recognise why and how they can use them to enable them to do a better job and not feel that they are just another means for higher level management to check on them and apply pressure.

Finally, this year's results are sometimes compared with those for the corresponding period last year. In some cases this may be helpful in establishing a trend, but it must never be forgotten that the budget is this year's plan, and it is against that plan that performance must be controlled.

INVESTIGATION OF VARIANCES

Introduction

Variance analysis, if properly carried out, can be a useful cost-controlling and cost-saving tool. However, the traditional variance analysis seen so far is only a step towards the final goal of controlling and saving costs.

Generalised reasons for variances

It has been suggested that the causes of variances can be classified under four headings:

- planning errors
- measurement errors
- random factors
- operational factors

Planning errors lead to the setting of inappropriate standards or budgets. This may be due to carelessness on the part of the standard setter (not taking account of known changes in the production process or expected price rises, for example) or due to unexpected external changes (a market shortage of a resource leading to increased price or technological advancements by competitors, leading to loss of sales). These need to be isolated from hindsight information and a revision of the standard considered for future budgets.

Under the second heading would come errors caused by inaccurate completion of timesheets or job cards, inaccurate measurement of quantities issued from stores, etc. The rectification of such errors or errors caused by random factors will probably not give rise to any cost savings (though this is a generalisation).

Thus, it is the specific operational causes of variances to which we will devote our attention and consider rectifying.

Specific reasons for variances

Examples of more specific reasons for individual variances are shown below.

Variance		*Possible causes*
Materials:	Price	Bulk discounts
		Different suppliers
		Different materials
		Unexpected delivery costs
		Different buying procedures
	Usage	Different quality material
		Theft, obsolescence, deterioration
		Different quality of staff
		Different mix of material
		Different batch sizes and trim loss
Labour:	Price	Different class of labour
		Excessive overtime
		Productivity bonuses
		National wage negotiations
		Union action
	Utilisation	Different levels of skill
		Different working conditions
		The learning effect
		Lack of supervision
		Works to rule
	Idle time	Machine breakdowns
		Lack of material
		Lack of orders
		Strikes (if paid)
		Too long over coffee breaks
Overhead:	Price	Change in nature of overhead
		Incorrect split of semi-variable costs
	Usage	Excessive idle time
		Increase in workforce

The variance report presented to management may not always identify or explain variances adequately enough to pinpoint their cause. It will often be useful to consult staff working in operational departments to resolve any queries in the data as they will have 'local' knowledge of the day-to-day operations.

As we have seen, if a responsibility accounting system is to be motivational, the budget-holders must be given the opportunity to offer an explanation for variances before he is judged by them.

Example

An adverse materials usage variance of £50,000 arose in a month as follows:

Standard cost per kg	£10
Actual cost per kg	£12
Units produced	2,000
Standard quantity per unit	25 kg
Actual quantity used	55,000 kg

	£
Standard cost of actual usage (55,000 kg × £10)	550,000
Standard cost of standard usage (2,000 × 25 kg × £10)	500,000
Adverse usage variance	£50,000

On further investigation, the following is ascertained:

(1)   The actual quantity used was based on estimated stock figures. A stocktake showed that 53,000 kg were in fact used.

(2)   3,000 kg is the best estimate for what might politely be called 'shrinkage' but, in less polite circles, theft.

(3)   2,000 kg of stock were damaged by hoodlums who broke into the stores through some of the shaky panelling.

(4)   The foreman feels that existing machinery is outmoded and more efficient machinery could save 1,000 kg a month.

Additional considerations

(1)   A security guard would cost £9,000 a year to employ and would stop 20% of all theft. Resultant dissatisfaction amongst works staff might cost £20,000 per annum.

(2)   Given the easy access to stores, vandals might be expected to break in every other month; £10,000 would make the stores vandal-proof.

(3)   New machinery would cost £720,000.

Required

Analyse the usage variance in the light of this information and comment on your results.

Solution

The original £50,000 usage variance could be analysed as follows:

Adverse/(favourable)
variance
£

(a)	Bad measurement (53,000 – 55,000) × £10	20,000
(b)	Theft (3,000 × £10)	30,000
(c)	Damage (2,000 × £10)	20,000
(d)	Obsolete machinery (1,000 × £10)	10,000
(e)	Other operational factors (balance)	(30,000)
		50,000

In each case, the variances should be studied and compared with the cost of rectification.

(a)   *Bad measurement* – Assuming no costly decisions were made, or are likely to be made in the future, such as over-stocking, the component is of no consequence.

(b)   *Theft* – Annual cost due to theft is 12 × £30,000 or £360,000; 20% of this saved would amount to £72,000 at a cost of £9,000 + £20,000, thus the security guard is worth employing.

(c)   *Damage* – Annual cost due to vandalism is 6 × £20,000 or £120,000; this would presumably be avoided by spending £10,000 now; again worthwhile.

(d)   *Obsolete machinery* – Annual cost of using old machines is 12 × £10,000 or £120,000; the cost of making this saving (the saving would increase as purchase prices increased or if production increased) is £720,000; the decision over this investment would require further consideration such as discounted cash flow analysis. This technique is considered in a later session.

(e)   *Other factors* – We now see a favourable usage variance once all known factors above have been accounted for. This may need further investigation, particularly if it affects the quality of goods produced.

Fixed overhead variances

These are worth a special note, due to the particular nature of the fixed overhead volume variance.

In the previous session, we saw that the volume variance was a product of the TAC system, and represented the adjustment for over-/under-absorption of fixed costs due to actual production being higher or lower than budgeted. Unlike the other variances, it does not actually represent a cost saving or overspend.

If this is the case, is it worth spending any time on the investigation of fixed overhead volume variances? Does it really matter if overheads are under-/over-absorbed, since it will all be adjusted for in the end?

The problem with having an inappropriate absorption rate is that decisions may have been taken on a unit cost that is too high or too low – for example, in setting the price of a product. If this is too high, sales may have been unnecessarily lost; if it is too low, profit margins may have been significantly eroded.

To minimise such effects of over-/under-absorption, regular reviews should be conducted of expenditure and activity levels arising throughout the period. The absorption rate can then be adjusted if it is felt necessary to reflect more recent estimates of expenditure and activity levels.

THE COST OF VARIANCE ANALYSIS

The provision of any information involves the costs of collecting the basic data, processing it, and reporting the results. Variance analysis is no exception and, as with other forms of management information, the benefits to which it gives rise must be commensurate with the costs incurred.

Four general points may be made:

(a)   Variance analysis allows 'management by exception' and it is presumably for this purpose that a standard costing system has been introduced.

(b)   When variances are known to exist, failure to make adequate investigations, even on a random basis, will weaken the control system and thus the motivation of managers.

(c)   The amount of analysis required can sometimes be reduced by defining levels of significance below which detailed investigation is not required.

(d)   The costs of clerical work can be over-estimated. In most working days there will be some spare capacity that can be utilised without extra cost.

What has to be considered, therefore, is the amount of detail that can be incorporated usefully in variance analysis. This will fall into two categories:

(a)   Extension of formal analysis procedures by the incorporation into source documents of more detailed codings indicating causes and responsibilities. Such coding is likely to involve people outside the accounts department, who may be unwilling to give time to the task. How useful the analysis will be, will depend on whether or not it is practicable to identify causes and responsibilities at the time the document is initiated.

(b)   *Ex post* investigations and re-analysis of variances (possibly incorporating the distinction between planning and operational variances outlined earlier). This can involve the time of quite senior people, but the process of investigation may well be more useful from the point of view of the management of the business than any quantity of formal variance calculations.

One is concerned, as always, with costs and benefits. The benefits to be sought from the analysis of variances are:

*   better planning and forecasting;
*   correction of inefficiencies;
*   positive action to improve the profitability of the business.

RESPONSIBILITY ACCOUNTING AND THE INTERDEPENDENCE OF VARIANCES

It is part of any system aimed at improving the performance of a business or any part of the business, that actions shall be traced to the person responsible. This may give the impression of 'laying the blame', but it is equally possible to award praise.

We have already seen that the general title for such a system is responsibility accounting; that is, a system which recognises various decision centres within a business and traces costs (and possibly revenues) to the individual managers who are primarily responsible for making decisions about the items in question.

As an example of difficulties in identifying responsibilities for variances from standards one might instance the following situation:

An opportunity arises for the buying department to obtain a consignment of a particular material at an exceptionally low price. The purchase is made; a favourable price variance is recorded and the buying department is duly praised.

Subsequently, when products are being manufactured using this type of material, significant adverse material usage variances and labour efficiency variances are recorded, and are initially regarded as the responsibility of the department where the work is done.

Investigations, however, reveal a number of relevant facts, for example:

- The 'cheap' material was of poor quality, and in consequence much of it was wasted in the process of machining. The resultant material usage and labour efficiency variances should presumably be regarded as the responsibility of the buying department, to offset the favourable price variance.

- Due to an employee leaving it had been necessary to use an operator who was not familiar with the job. At least part of the excess usage of materials could be attributed to this cause; but whether it should be regarded as the responsibility of the operating department or of the personnel department (for failing to recruit a replacement) is still open to question. If the employee who left had been highly paid, his removal might cause a favourable wage rate variance in the period under review – an offset to the adverse efficiency variance.

- The tools used had been badly worn, thus causing excessive time on the job. It would be necessary to consider whether this condition was attributable to the operating department (failing to sharpen tools or to requisition replacements) or to the tools store-keeper or to the buying department (for failing to buy on time or for buying poor quality items again).

The important points to bear in mind are as follows:

- Different types of variance can be inter-linked by a common cause.

- In many cases, the responsibility for variances cannot be identified merely by reference to the cost centre where the variance has been reported. Responsibility may be shared by several managers or may lie completely outside the cost centre in which the variance has arisen.

QUESTIONS

1   AB Ltd   (AAT CA J94)

Refer back to question 6 in Session 4 before attempting this question

A colleague at AB Ltd has prepared the following statement of fixed production overhead variances for June but is finding it difficult to suggest possible reasons for the variances.

Statement of fixed production overhead variances for June

	£
Overhead price variance	(450)
Overhead efficiency variance	65
Overhead volume variance	208
Total overhead variance	(177)

Note: Variances in brackets are adverse.

Assessment task

Write a memo to your colleague, explaining for each overhead variance the significance of the adverse or favourable result, and suggesting one possible reason for each of the overhead variances.

2   Revamp Furniture Ltd

Revamp Furniture Ltd manufacture a lounge chair by subjecting plasticised metal to a moulding process, thereby producing the chair in one piece.

(a)   From the information provided below, you are required to analyse the cost variances and prepare a reconciliation of budgeted with actual cost incorporating the result of your analysis.

Standard/Budget data

Unit variable costs:

Direct material	6lb at 50p per lb
Direct labour	2 hours at 160p per hour
Variable overhead	60p per direct labour hour

Budgeted fixed overhead for the year (240 working days)	£30,000
Budgeted production/sales for the year	60,000 chairs

Actual data for period 1

Number of working days	20
Production/sales	5,200 chairs

Direct material received and used:

Delivery No. 1	12,000 lb	Cost £	5,880
Delivery No. 2	14,000 lb	Cost £	6,790
Delivery No. 3	6,000 lb	Cost £	3,060
Direct labour hours worked	10,080	Cost £	17,540
Variable overhead		£	6,150
Fixed overhead		£	2,550

(b)   'Cost variances are often found, upon investigation of causes, to be interdependent.'

Briefly explain this statement using as illustrations:

(i)   material price and usage variances;
(ii)   labour rates and efficiency variances,

taken from your answer to (a) above and comment briefly on any possible interdependence between material cost variances and labour cost variances.

3   XYZ Manufacturing Company   (AAT CA Pilot)

As the management accountant of the XYZ Manufacturing Company, you have prepared the following variance report for the general manager:

Variance report: July 19X3

	Variance (Adverse) £	Variance (Favourable) £	Total variance £
Materials			−2,000
Usage	5,500		
Price		3,500	
Labour			−1,500
Utilisation	3,000		
Rate		1,500	
Overheads			−500
Price		4,500	
Efficiency	2,000		
Volume	3,000		

Actual costs for July 19X3 were as follows:

	£
Materials	100,000
Labour	80,000
Overheads	75,000
Total	£255,000

The general manager tells you he is quite satisfied with this result because the total adverse variance of £4,000 is only 1.57% of total costs.

Assessment task

Write a brief report to the general manager giving your *own* interpretation of the month's results.

4 WH Ltd (AAT CA D94)

Refer back to question 7 in Session 4 before attempting this question.

The production manager receives a copy of the standard costing control statement for product M every month. However, he has recently confessed to you that he does not really have a clear understanding of the meaning of the variances.

He has also been baffled by the following statement made by the finance director at a recent meeting of senior managers:

'Assigning responsibility for variances can be complicated if the variances are interdependent, for example if an adverse variance in one part of the organisation is caused by a favourable variance elsewhere.'

Assessment task

As assistant accountant for WH Ltd, you are asked to write a memo to the production manager which explains the following:

(a)   The meaning of each of the direct cost variances calculated for product M

(b)   Two possible causes of each of the variances which you have calculated for product M for November

(c)   Two examples of interdependence which may be present in the variances which you have calculated for product M for November. Explain clearly why the variances may be interdependent, so that the manager can better understand the meaning of the finance director's statement.

SUMMARY

In this session, we have examined the causes of variances and outlined techniques which may be used to decide whether to investigate.

We have also considered the possible interaction of variances and the implications for responsibility accounting.

Before you move on to the next session, make sure you can compute all of the variances to date.

Analysis of accounting information

OBJECTIVES

As well as looking at the detailed operations and costs of the organisation, useful information can be gained for planning and control purposes from taking an overall view. The accounts of both the organisation itself and those of its competitors can highlight significant relationships between items and ongoing trends.

This session considers two areas of accounting analysis:

- SWOT analysis
- ratio analysis.

Areas covered in other sessions relevant here would include attributes of good management information (Session 1), presentation of reports (Session 3), trend analysis and index numbers (Session 9).

The performance criteria addressed by this session are as follows:

- Relevant data are identified and analysed in accordance with defined criteria.

- Relevant ratio calculations highlight significant relationships in the data.

- Significant trends are identified and brought to the attention of management.

- Timely information is presented to managers in a clear and appropriate form.

    Reports highlighting significant trends are presented to management in an appropriate form.

- Valid, relevant information is identified from internal and external sources.

- Trends in prices are monitored and analysed on a regular basis.

- Forecasts of trends and changes in factor prices and market conditions are reasonably consistent with actual experience.

- Routine cost reports are assessed, compared with other sources of information and findings recommended to management in a clear and appropriate form.

SWOT ANALYSIS

Introduction

It has been said that before any long-term planning decision can be made, four factors have to be taken into consideration: the organisation's *strengths* and *weaknesses* and the *threats* and *opportunities* presented to the organisation by its environment (**SWOT analysis**). Internal appraisal is the assessment of the strengths and weaknesses of an organisation; external appraisal is the assessment of threats and opportunities.

Note that the strengths and weaknesses defined by an organisation are peculiar to that organisation alone (it cannot be a strength if it is shared equally by other competitors). However, opportunities and threats are open to all participants in the industry concerned.

Internal appraisal – strengths and weaknesses

The object of assessing performance is to ascertain the company's strengths and areas where improvements can be made, and to forecast what the results may be if the company continues as it is, in the light of information at present available to it. The review should be organised and co-ordinated throughout the company and carried out in a way that motivates management to face up to the true issues and think constructively and not defensively.

Such a review should include the following:

(a)   a comprehensive review of the company's results;

(b)   an investigation to ascertain the strengths of the company (the areas in which it has exclusive skills or does well as compared with competitive standards) and areas where significant improvements are needed, the word *improvements* is used instead of 'weaknesses' because people are reluctant to confess to weaknesses and are likely to make a better contribution if they are asked to suggest how they think improvements can be made;

(c)   comparisons with competitors, and other industries where useful. It is this feature which gives the situation appraisal its alternative title of 'competitive audit'.

The way in which such reviews are carried out will vary according to the organisation. When decided upon, they should be carried out quickly. Decisions must be made about the information that is needed, how it is to be collected and assembled and what changes in the organisation are needed to ensure that it is obtained.

The main areas considered in a strengths and weaknesses survey would include the following:

Products

Age, life span and current position in product life cycle
Quality comparisons with competition
Profitability, price sensitivity

Marketing

Market size and share, presence in target segments
Success of promotions and advertising campaigns
Quality of customer service, both actual and perceived

Distribution

Delivery promise performance
Depot location, delivery fleet condition and capacity

Production

Age, condition and capacity of plant and equipment
Valuation of assets
Production scheduling

Research and development

Number of commercially viable products
Costs and benefits of past/current projects
Relevance of current/proposed projects to overall plan

Human resources

Adequacy of manpower plans for future
Skills and utilisation of existing workforce
Strength of management team
Training and recruitment
Level of morale

Finance

Availability of cash, short- and long-term finance
Risk exposure
Contribution levels
ROCE and other accounting ratios

Presentation

A summary should be made of the major strengths and weaknesses revealed by this survey. In some American texts, you will find that strengths relative to competitors are referred to as 'leverage' – the ability to generate higher profits. Weaknesses on the other hand indicate areas of 'vulnerability'; for example, a company could be vulnerable to adverse conditions if:

- its products were becoming obsolete, and could be replaced by competitors' developments;
- it was short of liquid resources;
- particular markets (for example, overseas) ceased to be available;
- the strength of competition was augmented by amalgamations or mergers;
- selling prices were being forced below an economic level.

It is important therefore to identify clearly which are the key areas of strength or weakness at the time of the review.

The form in which the appraisal is summarised will vary according to the complexity of the business, and may in fact be a detailed narrative presentation with supporting tables and charts. A very simple example, confined to purely internal matters, is illustrated in Figure 1.

Strengths

---

(1)   *People* – A high level of expertise (technical) in production departments.

(2)   *Marketing* – Good brand image among consumers (especially for quality and after-sales service). Six established brand names.

(3)   *Finance* – £600,000 available for expansion from internal sources. Up to £3 million capital can be raised without difficulty.

Weaknesses or limiting factors

(1)	*Management*		*Immediate strategic implications*
	(a)	MD aged 65, no obvious successor.	Serious handicap. Recruitment, merger or sale of business.
	(b)	Weak middle management.	Recruitment training, position can be improved – but some weaknesses will exist for five years.
	(c)	Marketing manager incapable of handling any expansion.	Serious block. Solve by organisation change or replacement.
(2)	*Marketing*		
	(a)	85% of profits emanate from product X, with market declining at 6% a year, market share constant.	Reduce dependence. Change market strategy to improve performance. Reduce cost to improve position (introduce value analysis).
	(b)	32 products contribute no profit and have no potential.	Cease production; redeploy resources.

Figure 1: Example of a summary of company strengths and weaknesses

Strengths and weaknesses survey – cautionary notes

Potential

The examination of strengths and weaknesses is not so much concerned with performance, but rather with potential. The examination is supposed to draw to the attention of the planner those points which should be watched not only in one part of the entity, but throughout it. It is therefore crucial that the process concentrates on aspects of the organisation which are likely to be critical in the future rather than aspects that caused problems in the past. It is quite possible to become too immersed in previous performance to realise that demands placed upon organisations change to such an extent that what was once a strength may become a weakness.

Need for continuous reviews

Internal appraisal is a necessity if a useful strategic decision is to be made. The absence of an objective analysis of the organisation's strengths and weaknesses may result in the selection of a strategy which is totally inadequate or inappropriate. Circumstances change rapidly and it is therefore necessary to see the process of internal appraisal as a continuous monitoring of critical aspects of the business. A single snapshot of the organisation is only relevant for one point in time and consequently continual review is essential.

External appraisal – opportunities and threats

Environment

There are three main ways in which an organisation is affected by its environment:

(a)   The organisation *imports* goods and services from the environment. Labour, public services, materials, finished goods, professional services etc. are bought in by the company, and the organisation *exports* goods and services to other groups in the environment.

(b)   Outside groups can make *demands* upon the organisation and can impose *constraints*. Such groups are customers, government, employees, shareholders, general public etc. These constraints can be mandatory (eg. safety requirements imposed by law) or self-imposed (eg. maintaining clean factory areas, restricting noise levels).

(c)   The environment contains *opportunities* and *threats* for the organisation. A change in market may create an opportunity for a new product or it may hasten the demise of an existing product. An oil crisis in the Gulf will affect all companies' transport costs but will have more serious repercussions in a company which uses petroleum products in its manufacturing processes.

Opportunities and threats could be expected to arise in five main areas and will be available to all companies in the industry: economic, Government, social aspects, competitors and technology.

Economic

General economic conditions and trends are critical to the success of an organisation. Wages, price changes by suppliers and competitors, and government policies affect both the costs of producing products or offering services and the market conditions under which they are sold.

Common economic indicators measure national income and product, savings, investment, prices, wages, productivity, employment, government activities, and international transactions. All these factors vary over time, and managers devote much of their organisation's time and resources to forecasting the economy and anticipating changes.

There are two types of economic change: structural and cyclical. Structural changes in the economy are major alterations, whether permanent or temporary, in the relationships between different sectors of the economy and key economic variables; such changes challenge our basic assumptions about how the economy works. The shift from an industrial to a service economy and the rise in energy costs relative to the cost of other raw materials are examples of structural changes.

In contrast, cyclical economic changes are periodic swings in the general activity. Some examples are the rise and fall of interest rates and inflation. Cyclical changes have far different implications for organisational strategies than structural changes, because they are a function of normal economic volatility. The real problem lies in distinguishing cyclical and structural changes from one another.

Government

Environmental legislation, concerning the control of pollution and other health hazards, can affect the future plans of a company. The banning of the use of a particular substance (eg. asbestos) will initially represent a threat to the manufacturers and to suppliers of goods that use it, but it will also present an opportunity for the development of new replacement products.

Full use needs to be made of government grants and tax concessions available in the industry. Plans for the levels and directions of government spending must be monitored carefully for business opportunities and threats.

Social aspects

Changes in demographic variables – such as age, sex, family size, income, occupation, education, nationality and social class – can have major effects upon the organisation.

People's attitudes and values are an important consideration and are reflected in their lifestyles. In recent years, change rather than stability has become the norm for lifestyle in the UK. For example, families account for a shrinking proportion of UK households and fewer of these families include married couples; households consisting of single adults and one-parent families are becoming more numerous.

Other lifestyle changes include a trend towards better education. Smaller cars, diet and paid household help are only a few examples of new consumption patterns. Physical fitness has experienced a big surge in popularity, and other home-centred activities – notably satellite TV and video recorders – are more and more prevalent as households distribute their leisure time.

All these factors will have an affect, favourable or adverse, upon businesses in the consumer sector.

Competitors

It is argued that competition in an industry is rooted in its underlying economics, and competitive forces exist that go well beyond the established combatants in a particular industry.

Competitors will therefore be concerned with the degree of rivalry between themselves in their own industry and the degree of potential rivalry or threat of entry from others.

The degree of rivalry between organisations already operating within the market is likely to be based on:

- whether there is a dominant organisation(s) – generally the most stable markets have dominant organisations;

- whether the market is growing or declining – generally when markets are entering a 'maturity' phase and firms are trying to establish themselves as market leaders, competitive rivalry will be high;

- whether the product or service can be differentiated between competitors – generally if products and services can be clearly differentiated then competitive rivalry will be lower;

- whether the economy is in recession or booming – generally as an economy goes into recession competitive rivalry will intensify in an attempt to 'survive'.

The 'degree' of potential rivalry depends on the extent to which existing firms are making profits and the effectiveness of any barriers to entry. Typical barriers to entry are as follows:

(a) *Financial or capital requirement of entry.* The *amount* of capital required may not be the major barrier to entry but rather the *availability* and *cost* of raising finance.

(b) *The patterns of distribution or access to distribution channels.* The soft drinks industry in the UK for example, is dominated by two companies because brewers such as Bass and Whitbread own the soft drinks companies and the distribution outlets (ie. the public house). This pattern of distribution, however, has been forced to change with recent government legislation restricting the number of public houses that can be owned by brewers.

(c)   *Government legislation* and changes in such legislation obviously have a major affect on *barriers to entry*. Deregulation and privatisation has meant that extensive barriers to entry have now been lowered in an attempt to make markets contestable.

(d)   *The 'learning curve' phenomenon* could put new entrants at a cost disadvantage. Initially, in the early stages of entry, new firms would probably be operating at higher average costs than existing firms until they have 'learnt' from experiences to operate in a more efficient manner.

There are other barriers to entry such as advertising, patents and trade secrets, but it is not possible to state which are the most important. What is important is the recognition that barriers to entry have a major impact on the threat of potential entry.

Technology

The level of technology in a particular industry determines to a large extent what products and services will be produced, what equipment will be used and how operations will be managed.

Technological development begins with basic research, when a scientist discovers some new phenomenon; other researchers then examine the breakthrough for its potential. If further development leads to a workable prototype and engineering refinements make commercial exploitation practical, then the technology is finally put to use and may be widely adopted. Government institutions, independent research establishments, universities, and large corporations all carry out basic research. Independent entrepreneurs, business firms, and some government agencies carry the developments out of the laboratory and into the marketplace.

Businesses must be aware of the research currently being undertaken either to take the opportunity of its exploitation or to prepare for the threat from competitors who do.

Illustration – SWOT analysis

The following scenario involves two companies in the same business, on whom we can perform SWOT analyses.

Bulgary is an East European country which, until recently, operated a centralised economy. Most industries were nationalised, including the telephone system.

Citizens could not buy a phone at all, only rent one from the single state monopoly supplier. There was no choice of what type of phone was installed and it would have come with a dial, not buttons. It could only be installed by a fully trained employee of the supplier and was not 'plugged in', but wired in. For many calls you would have to ask the operator for assistance and the exchange used old electro-mechanical switching equipment that frequently broke down. All calls used conventional land lines.

A poor economy meant that only 50% of private households had a phone; phones were relatively rare even amongst private businesses, which were almost all based in the capital, Budia. Although well behind the Iron Curtain, Bulgary was always more 'capitalist' than other Warsaw pact countries and had a relatively liberal attitude towards private business. Entrepreneurial attitudes are most apparent in Budia where it is planned to establish an international stock exchange. Many foreign banks and other financial institutions have set up offices.

The new government, committed to market economies, has recently announced that the state telephone system is to be privatised and will be known as Bulgary Telecom. So that an element of competition is introduced, permission is also to be given to a new company to offer telecommunications services.

This company, QS, is about to start operating its own network. Regulations allow QS to make use of Bulgary Telecom's local lines. QS and Bulgary Telecom will both be subject to state regulation of prices. In five years' time the government intends to open up the telecommunications market much more and will invite other businesses to set up both terrestrial and cellular radio systems. (It is reckoned that cellular radio technology is advancing so quickly that it will soon be cheaper to install and operate than conventional land lines.) Established foreign businesses will also be able to apply for licences. Once the telecommunications system appears to be sufficiently competitive, state regulation will cease.

Characteristics of a strategic plan

Ansoff specifies that a business should have a basic economic objective (eg. maximise profitability), a variety of other objectives (such as survival) and various social objectives.

Andrews argues that there is a theoretical distinction between strategy formulation (thinking) and implementation (action). In other words, you plan and then you do. Strategy should not be made up on the hoof. Minzberg defines five meanings of strategy. It is a plan, it can be a ploy (eg. to put a competitor off-balance), it can emerge as a pattern, it can be a competitive position in a market or a desired position, and it can be a perspective through which environmental information is filtered.

Strategic management has been defined by Johnson and Scholes as being 'concerned with deciding on a strategy and planning how that strategy is to be put into effect'. Any strategic plan will be a guide for strategic decision-making, or will contain strategic decisions itself. It can include:

(i)   the scope of the organisation's activities;
(ii)   the matching of the organisational capacity with its environment;
(iii)   the allocation of resources;
(iv)   the long-term impact of strategy on the organisation's activities;
(v)   implications for change;
(vi)   the firm's strategy towards attaining competitive advantage.

Strategic decisions are affected by, and have an influence on, the organisation's structure and culture.

A strategic plan is an input to the strategy-making process. It is what Minzberg terms *intended strategy*. Decisions with strategic effect might be taken at operational level and might emerge. Not all intended strategies are actually implemented.

A strategy for business exists at a number of levels. A corporate strategy deals with the overall position and direction of the organisation as a whole.

PEST analysis

There are two obvious strategic business units: domestic and business telecommunications systems. Any analysis should consider both of these separately where necessary.

- *Political*

    Bulgary is embracing western democratic methods and is hoping to turn itself into a modern capitalist state. The government appears dedicated to privatising industries, encouraging competitors and attracting western investment and financial institutions. We have no information as to how stable the government is, but there appears to be optimism and the potential for economic success.

    There will be state regulation initially, presumably to control costs.

- *Economic*

Bulgary appears ripe for an economic boom. The suppressed entrepreneurial spirit of the citizens has been released. Considerable inward investment can be expected as foreign companies set up offices and manufacturing facilities. Most of these will be completely new and the demand for new (business) telecommunications equipment is likely to be great as all of the new enterprises will need to be serviced. The new stock exchange and associated financial institutions will need high quality, high volume communications for voice and data.

Economic prosperity will also affect the domestic market.

Initially competition is limited (and regulated) but, after five years, competition could become intense.

- *Social*

As standards of living rise, there is likely to be increased demand for domestic phones, both in terms of numbers of phones installed and the volume of calls made. Improved quality of connections and ease of dialling long distance will also increase telephone traffic.

- *Technological*

Electro-mechanical switching gear and traditional wire land lines are now old fashioned. Computerised exchanges, optical fibre, microwave links and cellular radio networks now represent standard telephone technology. These systems can offer enormous capacity, great reliability and low running costs. It may not even be necessary to wire up individual homes as radio telephone systems will be inexpensive and reliable.

SWOT analysis – Bulgary Telecom

Strengths	• already in possession of a telephone network and the necessary infrastructure
	• established
Weaknesses	• old equipment
	• state industry structure and mentality
	• poor finance (perhaps)
	• poor management (probably)
Opportunities	• increased domestic demand
	• increased business demand
	• falling costs through new technology
	• additional products and services
	• joint ventures with foreign telecommunications companies
Threats	• price regulation
	• new competition – now and in five years' time
	• new technology that can bypass the fixed network
	• economic recession
	• buyer lobby (user group pressure)

SWOT analysis – QS

Strengths	• new management
	• new ideas
	• profit hungry
	• market-oriented
	• no old network to maintain

Weaknesses	• starting from scratch – unknown quantity
	• dependence on Bulgary Telecom for local lines (a particular weakness in the domestic market)
	• likely to remain small in comparison to Bulgary Telecom for some time
	• no existing infrastructure at all

Opportunities	• increased domestic demand
	• increased business demand
	• cost-efficient high quality installations
	• innovative products and services
	• joint venture with foreign telecommunications companies

Threats	• price regulation
	• new competition five years away
	• unfair trading practice by Bulgary Telecom
	• economic recession
	• buyer lobby

Five forces analysis – Bulgary Telecom

Rivalry	At present, Bulgary Telecom is effectively a monopoly supplier. QS has only just started, but can be expected to compete vigorously. Will it compete in both the business and domestic sectors? It would be much easier for QS to compete in the business market. Most cable laying would be in the capital's business area and perhaps to several other major towns once their economy takes off. In contrast, to wire up domestic users, widely scattered throughout the country, would be a very major undertaking even 'piggybacking' on some of Bulgary Telecom's local networks.
Threat of new entry	No new competitors for five years. Then others could apply for licences but would have to compete against Bulgary Telecom and QS who will have had time to adopt the latest technologies. They may compete for domestic and mobile phone systems if these have not been properly addressed by Bulgary Telecom and QS (see *Threat of substitutes* below).
Threat of substitutes	People want to be able to talk to each other, either by land-line or radio telephone systems. It is only the ownership of the final piece of wire connecting the customers' phones to the network that gives telephone companies unique privileges. So far, establishing the wiring infrastructure has constituted the key barrier to entry. New technology, in particular cellular phones, eliminates the need for expensive and time-consuming hard-wiring as a network of transmitters is all that is required. This could represent a considerable threat to conventional communication companies.

The power of buyers	In the domestic sector, buyers are unlikely to be co-ordinated. No doubt in time, user groups will form but this is probably not an immediate problem.
	The business sector is likely to be quite different. Large, knowledgeable and influential institutions who will be powerful buyers are establishing themselves. It is likely that they will ask both Bulgary Telecom and QS to submit tenders for phone services. No doubt they will expect significant discounts in return for a large volume of business.
The power of suppliers	Many international electronic and communication companies will be eager to compete for telecommunication business in Bulgary. There is no great threat from suppliers.

Five forces analysis – QS

Rivalry	Presently the market is dominated by Bulgary Telecom which already has wiring and exchanges in place, although these are old. Because of this, it will be difficult to compete in the domestic market. In the business market it will be easier to compete as new high quality systems will be demanded, so Bulgary Telecom and QS will be in similar positions. However, Bulgary Telecom will undoubtedly find it difficult to change culture from that of state enterprise to a customer-oriented service business. QS will have no such problems and is likely to be more convincing to business customers.
Threat of new entry	No new competitors for five years. Then others could apply for licences but they would have to compete against Bulgary Telecom and QS who will have had time to adopt the latest technologies. They may compete for domestic and mobile phone systems if these have not been properly addressed by Bulgary Telecom and QS (see *Threat of substitutes* below).
Threat of substitutes	QS has to think carefully about which technology to adopt. This company is starting with a clean slate and has no vested interest in already installed systems. QS could start with the most advanced technology available: fibre optics in and between the business areas of cities; cellular phone systems for domestic users. This would bypass dependence on Bulgary Telecom and the need for extensive cable laying to domestic premises.
The power of buyers	In the domestic sector, buyers are unlikely to be co-ordinated. No doubt, in time, user groups will form but this is probably not an immediate problem.
	The business sector is likely to be quite different. Large, knowledgeable and influential institutions, who will be powerful buyers are establishing themselves. It is likely that they will ask both Bulgary Telecom and QS to submit tenders for phone services. No doubt they will expect significant discounts in return for a large volume of business.
The power of suppliers	Many international electronic and communication companies will be eager to compete for telecommunication business in Bulgary. There is no great threat from suppliers.

Advice to QS

It will be much easier to enter the business sector and QS should target there first as it will be a rapidly-growing, lucrative market. Business users are concentrated in cities and this will make cable-laying easier; those users will distrust the ability of Bulgary Telecom to deliver the goods.

Domestic customers should be targeted after the business market has been successfully attacked. At that time QS will have to consider the type of technology to use – conventional lines or cellular radio. The latter would completely bypass Bulgary's system and would also offer users mobile communications.

Advice to Bulgary Telecom

The company has a major credibility problem which will be a serious impediment in succeeding in the business market. The company's image must be changed quickly if it is to have any chance of success but it is doubtful if there is sufficient time to do so.

The company does have the advantage of existing infrastructure (although old) which allows it to reach customers that QS is unable to reach, both domestic and small business consumers. This part of the market must be protected by a programme of modernisation and expansion. Cellular radio technology should be considered.

RATIO ANALYSIS

Introduction

Ratio analysis is one of the main tools utilised in appraising the performance of a company, the main advantage being that the magnitude of the individual figures is eliminated allowing the appraiser to concentrate on relative movements.

Ratio analysis is generally utilised in two ways:

(a)   comparison of performance year to year; and
(b)   comparison with other companies.

The techniques covered here occur in many branches of accountancy and it is important that you can calculate and interpret appropriate ratios.

The main types of ratio used are:

(a)   profitability ratios;
(b)   liquidity ratios;
(c)   gearing ratios; and
(d)   investment ratios.

Of these, profitability and liquidity ratios are perhaps of the greatest significance to the management accountant and it is those we shall examine in more detail.

Ratios are not only used for internal appraisal but also for assessment of potential targets. They are therefore often based on published accounts. This also raises some problems.

Illustration – Knotty plc

In order to illustrate the most common ratios, there now follow calculations based on the summarised accounts of Knotty plc:

Profit and loss account year ended 31 July 19X9

	19X9		19X8	
	£'000	£'000	£'000	£'000
Turnover		37,589		30,209
Cost of sales		(28,380)		(22,808)
Gross profit		9,209		7,401
Distribution costs	(3,755)		(3,098)	
Administrative expenses	(2,291)		(2,030)	
		(6,046)		(5,128)
		3,163		2,273
Other operating income		108		279
Operating profit		3,271		2,552
Interest receivable		7		28
		3,278		2,580
Interest payable		(442)		(471)
Profit on ordinary activities before taxation		2,836		2,109
Tax on profit on ordinary activities		(1,038)		(650)
Profit on ordinary activities after taxation		1,798		1,459
Preference dividend		(6)		(6)
		1,792		1,453
Ordinary dividends		(606)		(441)
Retained profit for the year		1,186		1,012

Balance sheet as at 31 July 19X9

	Notes	19X9 £'000	19X9 £'000	19X8 £'000	19X8 £'000
Fixed assets					
Tangible assets			8,687		5,669
Investments			15		15
			8,702		5,684
Current assets					
Stocks		8,486		6,519	
Debtors	1	8,836		6,261	
Cash at bank and in hand		479		250	
		17,801		13,030	
Creditors: Amounts falling due within one year:					
Bank loans and overdrafts		(929)		(511)	
Other amounts falling due within one year		(9,178)		(6,645)	
		(10,107)		(7,156)	
Net current assets			7,694		5,874
Total assets less current liabilities			16,396		11,558
Creditors: Amounts falling due after more than one year:					
Debentures			(2,840)		(2,853)
Net assets			13,556		8,705
Capital and reserves					
Called-up share capital					
Ordinary shares of 20p each	2		2,003		1,762
4.2% cumulative preference shares of £1 each			150		150
			2,153		1,912
Share premium account			123		123
Other reserves			2,576		–
Profit and loss account			8,704		6,670
			13,556		8,705

Notes

(1) Debtors at 31 July 19X9 include trade debtors of £8,233,000 (19X8 £5,735,000).

(2) The number of ordinary shares in issue at 31 July 19X9 was 10,014,514 (19X8 8,808,214).

PROFITABILITY

Interlocking ratios

Return on capital employed (ROCE) expresses profit as a percentage of the assets in use/capital employed in the business and can be further sub-divided into *profit margin* and *asset turnover* (use of assets):

Profit margin $\times$ Asset turnover = Return on capital employed (ROCE)

$$\frac{\text{Profit}}{\text{Turnover}} \times \frac{\text{Turnover}}{\text{Assets}} = \frac{\text{Profit}}{\text{Assets}}$$

The equation helps to demonstrate how management can influence the rate of return on capital employed:

(a)   By increasing profit margins:

      (i)   increase prices; and
      (ii)   reduce costs.

(b)   By increasing asset turnover (use of assets):

      (i)   increase sales; and
      (ii)   reduce assets (capital employed).

Return on capital employed (ROCE)

Year-end or average capital employed

Ideally, the profits for the year ended 31 July 19X9 should be related to the assets in use/capital employed throughout the year (average capital employed). In practice, the ratio is usually computed using the assets/capital employed at the year-end (year-end capital employed). Using year-end figures of capital employed can distort trends and inter-company comparison; if new investment has been undertaken near to the year-end and financed (for example) by the issue of new shares, the capital employed will have risen by the total finance raised, whereas the profits will only have a month or two of the new investment's contribution.

A range of different acceptable measures of assets in use/capital employed is available; the matter of principle should be that the profit figure which is related to the capital employed should include all types of return on those assets/capital before charging any remuneration for the providers of that capital.

For Knotty plc, a suitable calculation would be:

	19X9	*19X8*
	£'000	£'000
Capital and reserves	13,556	8,705
Add: Debentures	2,840	2,853
Year-end capital employed	16,396	11,558

	19X9 £'000	19X8 £'000
Operating profit	3,271	2,552
Interest receivable	7	28
Profit before interest payable and tax	3,278	2,580

Thus the return on capital employed is calculated as:

$$\frac{\text{Profit before interest and tax}}{\text{Capital and reserves and long-term debt}} \times 100$$

19X9 $\dfrac{3,278}{16,396} \times 100 = 20.0\%$

19X8 $\dfrac{2,580}{11,558} \times 100 = 22.3\%$

The rate of return on year-end capital employed has fallen compared with 19X8, and might indicate less effective management. To comment further, we need to sub-analyse the ratio into profit margin and asset turnover.

Profit margin

If the profitability ratios are to interlock perfectly, the profit margin will be calculated expressing the same profit before interest payable and tax as a percentage of turnover:

$$\frac{\text{Profit before interest and tax}}{\text{Turnover}} \times 100$$

A small problem with the approach in this example is that the profit includes interest receivable which is not represented in turnover; however, as the amount is small, this can be ignored.

(In order that the profit can be related more fairly to turnover, profit margin is sometimes calculated using operating profit.)

For Knotty plc: 19X9 $\dfrac{3,278}{37,589} \times 100 = 8.7\%$

19X8 $\dfrac{2,580}{30,209} \times 100 = 8.5\%$

Profit margins have improved slightly over the last year, possibly due to better cost control.

Sectors which have traditionally generated relatively high margins include publishing, electronics manufacturing, distillers and brewers, whereas food retailing and motor vehicle distribution are examples of low margin businesses.

Low margins within a sector may arise from a policy designed to increase market share by cutting selling prices, or may be due to high development costs associated with new products, both of which may be positive factors for the future. However, low margins are often associated with inefficiency and poor quality management.

Conversely, high margins relative to competitors, or improving margins, are usually taken as indicators of efficiency and good management. High margins achieved by dominating a particular market may, however, attract competitors into that market and imply lower margins in the longer term.

Asset turnover

Another aspect of efficient management is to 'make the assets work'. This may involve disposing of those 'underperforming' assets which cannot be made to generate sales, as well as developing and marketing the company's products or services.

Once again, the simplest method of computing the ratio is to relate turnover to the same figure of year-end capital employed used in calculating return on capital employed:

$$\frac{\text{Turnover}}{\text{Capital employed}} \times 100$$

19X9 $\dfrac{37,589}{16,396} \times 100 = 2.3$

19X8 $\dfrac{30,209}{11,558} \times 100 = 2.6$

However, as with profit margins, certain assets represented by capital employed have no turnover implications. One method of avoiding this illogicality is to exclude long and short-term investments from capital employed. For companies with substantial investments this will make a considerable difference.

Asset turnover will tend to be lower in capital-intensive manufacturing industries, which carry substantial stocks and trade debtors, than in service industries where the principal resource is people rather than plant and machinery, and where stocks are low.

There are often trade-offs between asset turnover and profit margins in different sectors. For example, food retailers have relatively low profit margins compared to electronic equipment manufacturers, but asset turnover is higher:

	Profit margin %	×	*Asset turnover*	=	*ROCE* %
Food retailer	3.7	×	6.7	=	24.8
Electronic equipment manufacturer	10.3	×	2.3	=	23.7

Gross profit margin

The profit margin given above used a profit figure that included non-productive overheads and sundry items of income. The gross profit margin looks at the profitability of the pure trading activities of the business:

$$\frac{\text{Gross profit}}{\text{Turnover}} \times 100$$

For Knotty: 19X9 $\dfrac{9,209}{37,589} \times 100 = 24.5\%$

19X8 $\dfrac{7,401}{30,209} \times 100 = 24.5\%$

The company has maintained its gross profit margin; thus the slight rise in net profit margin must be due to overhead costs being better controlled (sundry income has, in fact, gone down).

LIQUIDITY

When analysing a company's balance sheet without access to management information, it is customary to calculate two ratios as indicators of the company's ability to pay its way:

$$\text{Current ratio} = \frac{\text{Current assets}}{\text{Creditors due within one year}}$$

$$\text{Quick ratio (or acid test ratio)} = \frac{\text{Current assets less stocks}}{\text{Creditors due within one year}}$$

For Knotty plc:

(a)   current ratio $\dfrac{17,801}{10,107} = 1.76$ $\dfrac{13,030}{7,156} = 1.82$

(b)   quick ratio $\dfrac{9,315}{10,107} = 0.92$ $\dfrac{6,511}{7,156} = 0.91$

Distortions in the current ratio

Taking one year as the 'current' period, then the current ratio is a reflection of liquidity as demonstrated at that point in time, unless for example:

(a)   the operating cycle is so long that part of the stocks or work in progress will not be converted into sales invoicing until after the end of the year, as might be the case with a public works contractor;

(b)   because spasmodic customer demand is linked to a high level of service from stock, it is necessary to hold some stocks which will not be turned over within the year (eg. a capital equipment spares supply business); or

(c)   the figure of debtors includes contract retention moneys or items under dispute which will not be collected within the year.

If such features exist, then this should be known from the nature of the business and one would expect to see a higher current ratio than in a business with fast-moving stocks and restricted credit terms.   Thus current ratios for a heavy engineering company will be higher than those for a supermarket.

Cash and funds flow analysis

Although current and quick ratios are used to measure liquidity, they are limited insofar as they concentrate on only one area of the balance sheet. If the company needs adequate cash to meet its obligations, there are sources other than the sale of stocks and the collection of amounts owed by debtors.

Analysis of cash and funds flows is a more comprehensive method of assessing liquidity, although significant variations in the liquidity ratios may indicate important changes.

Other working capital ratios

A more detailed analysis of the movement in the elements of working capital can be made with the help of the following ratios.

Stock turnover

Stock turnover ratios can be compared if they relate costs of sales as a measure of activity to stocks which are usually included at cost:

$$\frac{\text{Cost of sales}}{\text{Stocks}}$$

$$19X9 \quad \frac{28,380}{8,486} = 3.34$$

$$19X8 \quad \frac{22,808}{6,519} = 3.5$$

There has been a slight fall in stock turnover, indicating stock is taking longer to sell. A review of stocks may be necessary to determine whether levels of obsolete or damaged stocks are increasing. There may be a deliberate policy to increase stocks.

Average debtors collection period

This calculation is always made using turnover since trade debtors includes the profit element:

$$\frac{\text{Trade debtors}}{\text{Turnover}} \times 365 \text{ days}$$

$$19X9 \quad \frac{8,233}{37,589} \times 365 = 79.9 \text{ days}$$

$$19X8 \quad \frac{5,735}{30,209} \times 365 = 69.3 \text{ days}$$

The company is taking approximately 10 days longer, on average, to collect its debts.

As the year-end figures may be unrepresentative (due perhaps to seasonality of sales), an average debtors figure for the year might be used if this were available.

A similar calculation can be made to determine *creditors payment (settlement) period*:

$$\frac{\text{Trade creditors}}{\text{Purchases or Cost of sales}} \times 365$$

INTER-FIRM AND INTRA-GROUP COMPARISONS

Problems with comparisons using ratio analysis

(a)   *Need for comparison*

      (i)   over time, to observe trends (time series analysis);

      (ii)   with other departments within the company or with other firms (cross-sectional analysis).

(b)   *Use of 'norm' or average*

One should look not only at the average ratio for an industry (or department or division), but also at the ratios for various percentiles, because the norm may be in a 'bad' industry (or department or division).

(c)   *Comparison of different entities*

Not all companies within an industry are of a similar nature, nor are all departments/division within a particular company necessarily similar, so any comparison is meaningless.   For example, in a company which diversifies into different areas, comparison of ratios between the areas is invalid and comparison of ratios for the company as a whole with those of an undiversified firm in the same industry has little point.

(d)   *Size*

Within any industry, there will be a wide range of companies in terms of size, which is a further factor to consider when comparing ratios within an industry.

(e)   *Estimated accounting data*

A lot of accounting data is comprised of estimates rather than absolute measures, eg. bad debt provision.

(f)   *Accounting conventions*

Companies do not all conform to the same accounting conventions and many will have unstandardised data.

(g)   *Time factors*

Different companies have different financial years and some will be in a seasonal business.

(h)   *Inflation*

Comparisons of one year with the next can be distorted by inflation, particularly over a long period. We will see in a later session how data can be adjusted to put on a comparable basis using appropriate indices but, within a set of accounts, there will be many different rates of inflation affecting the figures and this becomes a complex task.

Use of ratio analysis for comparative purposes

The best way to explain how ratio analysis can be used to compare companies' relative financial strengths and weaknesses both within a conglomerate and within an industry, is through a case study.

This case study shows how ratio analysis can be used to assess a company's financial condition by comparing a selection of its ratios (predominantly concerned with liquidity) with the industrial norms over time.

(a)   *Background information on the company and its banking arrangements*

The financial position of Buyafield Company plc has deteriorated and this information has been transmitted to the company's bank, North West, via the bank's newly installed computer loan-analysis programme. The bank requires quarterly financial statements (balance sheets and profit/loss statements) from Buyafield. This information is fed into the computer, which then calculates the key ratios for its customer, charts trends in these ratios over time, and compares the statistics of each customer with the average ratios and trends of other firms in the same industry. If any ratio of any company is significantly poorer than the industry average, the computer output makes note of this fact. If the terms of a loan require that certain ratios be maintained at specified minimum levels and these minimums are not being met by a company, the computer output notes the deficiency.

When an analysis was run on Buyafield three months ago, the bank noticed that some of the company's ratios were showing downward trends, dropping below the averages for its industry. The bank sent a copy of the computer output, together with a note voicing their concern to Winnie Scale, the financial manager of Buyafield. Although Winnie acknowledged receipt of the material, she took no action to correct the situation.

The first financial analysis indicated that some problems were developing, but no ratio was below the level specified in the loan agreement between North West and Buyafield. However, the second analysis, which was based on the data given in Tables 1, 2 and 3, showed that the current ratio was below the two times specified in the loan agreement. According to this agreement, the North West Bank could legally call upon Buyafield for immediate payment of the whole bank loan, and if they did not pay in within ten days, the bank could force Buyafield into liquidation. The bank's loan officer, Rose E Actor, had no intention of actually enforcing the contract to the full extent that she legally could, but she did intend to use the loan agreement provision to prompt Buyafield to take some decisive action to improve its financial picture.

Buyafield is a company which produces both perishable and storable products with longer lives. Seasonal working capital needs have been financed primarily by loans from the North West Bank and the current line of credit permits Buyafield to borrow up to £240,000. In accordance with standard banking practices however, the loan agreement requires that the bank loan be repaid in full at some time during the year, in this case by February 19X5. A limitation on Buyafield's prices, coupled with higher costs, caused a decline in its profit margin and net income during the last half of 19X3 as well as during most of 19X4. However sales increased during both of these years due to an aggressive marketing programme.

Table 1: Balance sheets for Buyafield as at 31 December

	19X0 £	19X2 £	19X3 £	19X4 £
Cash	34,000	51,000	23,800	17,000
Debtors	136,000	204,000	231,200	323,000
Stock	170,000	255,000	425,000	688,500
Total current assets	340,000	510,000	680,000	1,028,500
Land and building	51,000	40,800	108,800	102,000
Machinery	68,000	125,800	98,600	85,000
Other fixed assets	40,800	23,800	6,800	5,100
Total assets	499,800	700,400	894,200	1,220,600

	19X0 £	19X2 £	19X3 £	19X4 £
Creditors (Bank only)	–	–	85,000	238,000
Other creditors	74,800	81,600	129,200	255,000
Accruals	34,000	40,800	47,600	64,600
Total current liabilities	108,800	122,400	261,800	557,600
Mortgage	51,000	37,400	34,000	30,600
Ordinary shares	306,000	306,000	306,000	306,000
Retained earnings	34,000	234,600	292,400	326,400
Total liability and equity	499,800	700,400	894,200	1,220,600

Table 2: Profit and loss accounts for Buyafield plc

	19X2 £	19X3 £	19X4 £
Net sales	2,210,000	2,295,000	2,380,000
Cost of goods sold	1,768,000	1,836,000	1,904,000
Gross operating profit	442,000	459,000	476,000
General administration and selling	170,000	187,000	204,000
Depreciation	68,000	85,000	102,000
Miscellaneous	34,000	71,400	102,000
Net profit before taxes	170,000	115,600	68,000
Taxes (50%)	85,000	57,800	34,000
Net profit	85,000	57,800	34,000

Table 3: Industry ratios for 19X4[a]

Quick ratio	1.0
Current ratio	2.7
Stock turnover[b]	7 times
Average collection period	32 days
Fixed asset turnover[b]	13.0 times
Total asset turnover[b]	2.6 times
Return on total assets	9%
Return on net worth	18%
Debt ratio	50%
Profit margin on sales	3.5%

[a] Industry average ratios – constant for the past three years

[b] Based on year-end balance sheet figures

When Winnie received a copy of Rose's latest computer analysis and the blunt statement that the bank would insist on immediate repayment of the entire loan unless the firm presented a programme showing how the poor current financial picture could be improved, she began trying to determine what could be done. She rapidly concluded that the present level of sales could not be continued without an increase of the bank loan from £240,000 to £340,000, since payments of £100,000 for construction of a new plant would have to be made in January 19X5. Even though Buyafield has been a good customer of North West bank for over 50 years, Winnie began to question whether the bank would continue to supply the present line of credit, let alone increase the loan outstanding. Winnie was especially worried by the fact that the government had recently tightened bank credit, forcing the North West bank to ration credit even to its best customers.

(b)   *Financial analysis of the company*

From the above information, we will now proceed to undertake a financial analysis of Buyafield, ending with a brief critique of comparative ratio analysis.

(i)   *The key financial ratios for Buyafield, showing trends in the ratios against the industry averages*

		19X0	*19X2*	*19X3*	*19X4*	*Industry average (19X2 – 19X4)*
Liquidity ratios						
(1)	Current ratio	3.1	4.2	2.6	1.8	2.7
(2)	Quick ratio	1.6	2.1	1.0	0.6	1.0
(3)	Gearing ratio – total debt to total assets (%)	32	23	33	48	50
Activity ratios						
(4)	Stock turnover	NA	6.9X	4.3X	2.8X	7.0X
(5)	Average collection period (in days)	NA	34	37	50	32
(6)	Fixed asset turnover	NA	11.6X	10.7X	12.4X	13.0X
(7)	Total assets turnover	NA	3.2X	2.6X	1.9X	2.6X

Profitability ratios

(8)	Profit margin on sales %	NA	3.8	2.5	1.4	3.5
(9)	Return on total assets %	NA	12.1	6.5	2.8	9
(10)	Return on net worth %	NA	15.7	9.7	5.4	18

NA = not available

(ii) *Financial strengths and weaknesses of the company identified by the ratio analysis*

The only strength shown by Buyafield's ratios is its debt position, it has a relatively low level of debt. Its weaknesses are a different matter! Among them are the following.

Liquidity – Both the current and quick ratios are below the industry average and show a downward trend.

Stock – The stock turnover ratio is significantly below the average for the industry, and is also showing a downward trend. This suggests that:

– the company has too much stock on hand;
– the actual liquidity may be worse than is indicated by the current ratio;
– some stock may be deteriorated or in fact, be obsolete.

Debtors – Measured by the average collection period, the debtors are above the average for the industry and are again inclined towards an unfavourable trend. Some of the debtors may well be uncollectable.

Asset turnover – The fixed asset turnover is not too far below the industry norm, but the total asset turnover is. This indicates that Buyafield's major problem lies in its management of current assets, rather than its fixed assets.

Profitability – All Buyafield's profitability ratios imply that it is less profitable than the average firm in that industry. The low profit margin on sales could be due to either too low selling prices or too high costs. The low rate of return on total assets and net worth reflects both the low profit margin on sales and the relatively low turnover ratios. The latter, in turn, reflect over-investment in predominantly current assets.

(iii) What amount, if any, is available from internal sources to repay the loan, if the due date were extended from February 1 to June 30 19X5?

There are mainly four sources of internal funds which might be used to pay off the loan:

Net profit and depreciation – In 19X4, cash flows from earnings, plus depreciation amounted to £136,000. If the same rates hold in 19X5, these two sources of funds would provide £68,000 by June 19X5.

Reduction of debtors – If the debtors figure was reduced to that of the industry average, this would provide Buyafield with about £110,000:

$$\text{Sales per day} = \frac{\text{£2,400,000}}{365} = \text{£6,575}$$

$$\text{Average collection period} = \frac{\text{Debtors}}{£6,575} = \text{industry average of 32 days}$$

Therefore debtors should be £210,411

Debtors are actually £323,000

Therefore extra funds provided = £323,000 – £210,411 = £112,589

Stocks – If stocks could be reduced to the average level for the industry, this would provide Buyafield with roughly £417,000.

$$\text{Stock turnover} = \frac{£1,900,000}{\text{Stock}} = \text{industry average of 7 times}$$

Therefore stock should be £271,429

Stocks are actually £688,500

Therefore extra funds provided = £688,500 – £271,429 = £417,071

We can see from the above discussion that Buyafield has the potential for raising about £595,000 by:

–   net profit plus depreciation
–   reduction of debtors
–   reduction of stocks

The stock and debtors reductions could not be achieved immediately, but if stocks are saleable and the debtors collectable, it should be possible for the company to generate a substantial amount of funds from these sources. Of course, it will require some effort on the part of the managers.

(iv)   *Factors causing a fall in Buyafield's profitability*

By comparing Buyafield's figures with its industry averages, we can see that a deficiency exists in all three measures of profitability. To improve profitability to start with, Buyafield would attempt to increase revenue, reduce costs or both. If demand allows for higher selling prices, then through selective price increases, profitability could be improved. Otherwise, Buyafield will have to attempt to reduce costs. The relatively high stock figure might be responsible for high storage costs, larger losses from damage and other factors. Operating expenses might also be cut back.

The low turnover implies that Buyafield is not using its assets efficiently. If increased sales cannot be effected to bring current assets back into line, then the firm should consider reducing its assets, particularly its stock levels, which are almost twice as high as the industry average for the firm's sales level.

(v) *Should the bank grant the additional loan and extend the entire line of credit to 30 June 19X5?*

Buyafield has been a customer of the North West Bank for over 50 years, and furthermore, the firm's debt ratio indicates that in the event of its liquidation, the bank should be able to recover its loan. These factors suggest that the bank should be willing to go along with the company and extend the requested credit. For the sake of its reputation as much as anything, the bank should try to remain loyal to its major customers. Unfortunately though, Buyafield has shown a deteriorating trend in recent years. If this trend goes on, then the company could well go into liquidation, and if the bank lets things go too far, the assets could be dissipated to the point where the bank might actually lose some of its money. Because of this point, the bank should insist that Buyafield instigates a positive programme to correct its problems.

The money situation also has some influence on granting the loan. In view of the credit squeeze and general shortage of funds, the bank could well refuse to extend the line of credit. However, some banks have some flexibility on this point – perhaps North West will insist on a schedule repayment programme based on a reduction in Buyafield's stocks (perhaps by reducing selling prices and increasing advertising) and debtors (for example, by enforcing a 'get tough' policy on the oldest outstanding debtors).

(vi) *What are the alternatives open to the company, if the credit extension is not made?*

Buyafield would most probably go to another potential lender (possibly another bank). It may be granted a loan if it is secured in some way; ie. by stocks, debtors, or a mortgage on its fixed assets. It could also provide a bank with an indication of its credit-worthiness by calculating its 'z-score'.

(vii) *What is the validity of undertaking a comparative ratio analysis for this company?*

This has already been discussed in detail, but the most important factor here is differing accounting practices. If those of Buyafield differed significantly from these in the rest of its industry, the comparison of ratios such as fixed assets turnover could be invalidated. For example, if Buyafield leased its fixed assets rather than owning them, as the other firms in the industry may tend to do, Buyafield's debt ratio would be severely underestimated compared with the industry average, and turnover ratios would be similarly affected.

QUESTIONS

1   Retail ratios   (AAT CA Pilot)

In respect of each of the following ratios calculated for a retail store (a), explain how the ratio is calculated and (b) the use of the ratio as a management tool in retail trading:

–   Rate of stock turnover
–   Gross profit margin
–   Creditors average settlement period (assume that all purchases were on credit)
–   Net profit (before tax) to capital employed

2 WH Ltd (AAT CA D94)

WH Ltd is a member of a trade association which operates an inter-company comparison scheme. The scheme is designed to help its member companies to monitor their own performance against that of other companies in the same industry.

At the end of each year, the member companies submit detailed annual accounts to the scheme organisers. The results are processed and a number of accounting ratios are published and circulated to members. The ratios indicate the average results for all member companies.

Your manager has given you the following extract, which shows the average profitability and asset turnover ratios for the latest year. For comparison purposes, WH Ltd's accounts analyst has added the ratios for your company.

	Results for year 4	
	Trade association average	*WH Ltd*
Return on capital employed	20.5%	18.4%
Net (operating) profit margin	5.4%	6.8%
Asset turnover	3.8 times	2.7 times
Gross margin	14.2%	12.9%

Assessment task

As assistant accountant for WH Ltd, your manager has asked you to prepare a report for the senior management committee. The report should cover the following points:

(a)   an explanation of what each ratio is designed to show;

(b)   an interpretation of WH Ltd's profitability and asset turnover compared with the trade association average;

(c)   comments on any limitations of these ratios and of comparisons made on this basis.

3 XY Builders plc

XY Builders Merchants plc is a major retailer chain serving builders and public solely in the UK. Over the past two years, it has followed a policy of rapid expansion through take-over of locally based retail chains. A dramatic increase in interest rates has increased the cost to XY of its borrowings. In addition, the managing director believes that the rapid expansion has made the group lose its cohesive balance. He cites the following:

(1)   80% of the stores are in the Northern half of the country but yield only 30% of total revenue.

(2)   The company has only four 'C' grade stores (ie. largest and best stocked) in the London area.

(3)   Some towns have both a 'C' and an 'A' grade store.

XY grade their stores into three categories:

'C'   stores in excess of 200,000 square feet and stocking over 12,000 lines

'B'   stores in excess of 100,000 square feet and stocking over 8,000 lines

'A'   stores of less than 100,000 square feet and stocking between 5,000 and 8,000 lines

The board of directors are undertaking a review of group operations prior to formulating a three-year strategic plan. You have been engaged as a management consultant to advise the board.

There are three strategic issues which the board is facing:

(1)   A giant retail chain has offered to purchase all 'C' grade stores on a multiple of 3.5 times gross profit plus property and fixtures and fittings at written down book value.

(2)   The marketing director wishes to introduce ranges of industrial clothing into the 'B' and 'C' grade stores. He anticipates an investment of £1,000,000 stock, £250,000 fixtures and fittings, but expects a stock turnover of three times per annum at a gross profit of 25%. Some existing lines would need to be discontinued.

(3)   Some board members are advocating a 'go for growth' policy in which XY would close or sell off all 'A' grade and probably some 'B' grade stores. Convert the remaining stores to 'value stores' offering a limited choice at lower prices. They would envisage reducing the number of lines by 50%.

These issues are fundamental to the group's future, because although XY is amongst the top ten builders merchants in the UK, it is a small player when compared to the three major groups.

You have been provided with the following operating summary and brief balance sheet.

Operating summary for 12 months ending 30 June 19X4

	'C' grade stores £'000	'B' £'000	'A' £'000	Total £'000
Sales	9,675	5,670	2,415	17,760
Gross profit	4,305	2,369	936	7,610
Direct operating costs	1,281	1,106	988	3,375
Administration costs	703	157	99	959
Interest charges	833	350	110	1,293
	1,488	756	(261)	1,983

Abridged balance sheet of XY plc at 30 June 19X4

	£'000	£'000	£'000
Fixed assets			
Freehold property		9,600	
Leasehold property		1,896	
			11,496
Fixtures and fittings (cost £5,250,000)			3,150
Vehicles, forklifts			465
			15,111
Current assets: retail stock			
'C' shops		1,686	
'B' shops		1,323	
'A' shops		702	
		3,711	
Debtors		6,320	
Cash		400	
		10,431	
Current liabilities			
Trade creditors	1,800		
Overdraft	4,125		
Taxation	450		
Dividend payable	750		
		7,125	
Working capital			3,306
			18,417
Long-term loan: 10% debentures (repayable 19X5)			(1,500)
Net assets			16,917
Financed by:			
Share capital: 50p ordinary shares			15,000
Unappropriated profits			1,917
			16,917

Required

You have been requested, as an independent management consultant, to prepare an interim report for discussion at the forthcoming Strategy Review meeting. In particular you have been asked to comment on the overall performance of the group, identifying areas of weakness that may need further action.

SUMMARY

SWOT analysis

The analysis of a company's strengths, weaknesses, opportunities and threats is an important tool in the planning process.

The following areas are to be considered:

Strengths and weaknesses:	Products
	Marketing
	Distribution
	Production
	Research and development
	Human resources
	Finance
Opportunities and threats:	Economic
	Government
	Social
	Competitors
	Technology

Not all of these areas will be of equal significance to a business at any one time; be prepared to identify four or five from each of the four SWOT categories that are relevant given a particular set of circumstances.

Ratio analysis

The important ratios for you to be able to compute (and interpret) are as follows:

Profitability:	Return on capital employed (ROCE)
	Gross and net profit margins
Liquidity:	Current ratio
	Quick (acid test) ratio
	Stock turnover
	Debtors' collection period
	Creditors' payment (settlement) period

Remember that a ratio on its own is not useful information; it needs to be compared, internally or externally. This gives rise to problems of comparability, which you should be able to discuss.

The worked example at the end of the session (Buyafield Company Ltd) is a very valuable exercise and should be studied carefully. It is unlikely, however, that you will be asked to perform such a detailed analysis.

Cost reduction, quality and value enhancement

OBJECTIVES

This session considers the ways in which the operations and output of a business are analysed and controlled, with the objectives of cost reduction, quality improvement and value enhancement.

The areas covered include the following:

- principles and techniques of cost reduction
- value analysis
- quality control

The performance criteria addressed by this session are as follows:

- Specific contributions towards the objectives of cost reduction, quality improvement and value enhancement are made after full discussion with relevant specialists.

- Routine cost reports are assessed, compared with other sources of information and findings recommended to management in a clear and appropriate form.

- Relevant performance indicators are monitored and assessed.

- Special reports to follow up matters which require further investigation are prepared.

COST REDUCTION

Introduction

Most companies are in business to make profit; non-profit organisations, such as charities and local authorities, are equally expected to keep expenses and costs down to a minimum. In times of inflation, costs are continually rising and it is not always possible to balance this with a rise in sales revenue. Thus improvements to profit may rely heavily upon a cost reduction programme.

Cost reduction has been defined as a process which leads to 'the achievement of real and permanent reductions in the unit costs of goods manufactured or services rendered without impairing their suitability for the use intended'.

This is a useful definition, since it sets the framework for the proper study of cost reduction, while emphasising the importance of maintaining the characteristics and quality of the product. Cost reduction is concerned, therefore, with long-term genuine savings in the cost of manufacture and the administration and service departments; this, incidentally, is why a reduction in tax (or any reduction in 'costs' arising from government backing or intervention) is not a genuine cost reduction.

It is not to be confused with **cost control**, which is based upon the acceptance of target costs and which aims to achieve those costs by preventing or eliminating the causes of variances or excess costs. Cost control accepts the standards which have been set and endeavours to enforce them; by contrast cost reduction actively challenges the agreed standards to find ways of achieving savings of one kind or another. The definition also suggests that there is scope for the use of cost reduction techniques throughout an organisation's activities, from design to production and from distribution and marketing to finance and administration.

Planning cost reduction

The successful application of cost reduction techniques requires the commitment and involvement of senior management. If they are seen to be interested and to have a real conviction of the need for cost reduction, it will be easier to secure the co-operation of other managers, supervisors, employees and their representatives. However committed and enthusiastic the top management is, experiments show that the **gradual** introduction and development of cost reduction techniques is more likely to succeed than a hasty movement. The whole exercise must be thought out first and all stages carefully planned, preferably on a participative basis.

Obviously it is important to determine the overall objective towards which cost reduction should lead. For a manufacturing business, this may be a reduction in the costs of materials or overheads; a service activity will perhaps look at manpower.

It is also important to consider whether cost reduction is being thought of as economic necessity – 'if we do not start doing this, we shall go out of business' – or as a matter of setting realistic targets under a comparison of the firm's prices and margins, against those of competitors. Clearly, a plan for survival will be very different from one aimed at maintaining a relative market position.

Applications of cost reduction – manufacturing

Virtually all areas of both manufacturing and service businesses are open to the use of cost reduction techniques.

To illustrate the principles and techniques, we shall initially look at the particular functions of a manufacturing business. Later we shall consider how these may be applied, in more general form, to activities in the service sector.

The functions to be considered are as follows:

- design
- production and purchasing
- marketing and distribution
- finance
- labour

Design

The area of design often offers the greatest scope for cost reduction initiatives. Management training increasingly emphasises the importance of introducing cost reduction techniques at the earliest possible stage, when the product is still on the drawing board.

The introduction of cost reduction in design activity, however, is fraught with difficulty because design activity has traditionally emphasised the following:

- low cost and functional efficiency
- widest possible application
- quality and durability (or obsolescence threshold)
- appearance

Not all these factors lend themselves to cost reduction considerations.

Cost reduction in design therefore requires a new philosophy or approach under which the potential for cost reduction is investigated throughout the design stage in the following ways:

- Materials specification: use or otherwise of standard parts; suitability of metal in handling and working; yield factor; storage and stock investment

- Labour: effect of design on manufacturing processes – tolerance, performance standards

- Cost of tooling

- Standardisation and simplification

- Compactness: the impact of size and shape on storage and transportation

- Time control: gearing product to possible changes in fashion and to seasonal demands, thus reducing stock obsolescence rates; or developing products that transcend fashion

Many companies have developed cost reduction through design to a fine art – the motor car manufacturers are particularly good at it. The Ford Capri, for example, was an early example of a product design which embodied many of the factors listed above.

When it is not possible to work through a new design philosophy or adopt an approach to design in which cost reduction is an integral part, then for existing designs it is possible for companies to make use of **value analysis** or value engineering. This is considered in its own right later in the session.

Production and purchasing

- **Factory organisation and production methods**

    The production function is rich with potential for cost reduction. It is also one that has already been thoroughly explored and as a result many cost savings have been incorporated into standard procedures. It would also be true to say that cost reduction in this area has pervaded the whole of manufacturing business.

    Cost reduction effort in the factory begins by checking the allocation and distribution of authority and responsibility, for it is surprising how costs can be increased through inefficiencies in organisational arrangements.

    It is often the case that the reality of organisational structure is very different from that described in the organisation chart or operating manual. In particular, channels of communication are not always properly aligned to the authority structure, leading to waste and increased operating costs.

    The effective arrangement of plant and equipment is a key feature of successful production planning. Plant layout is fundamental to efficient and effective production. Good layout will:

(i)   achieve the optimal use of space

(ii)   allow for the most efficient flow of work

(iii)   facilitate effective control

(iv)   reduce materials handling to a minimum

(v)   minimise waste

(vi)   promote employee satisfaction and motivation

(vii)   allow for change and development

(viii) maximise productivity

- **Purchasing**

  Material cost may be controlled and reduced in two ways: (i) by price, through purchasing policy and (ii) by quality organisation through stock control and material handling, usage and yield. The first route is the easier to follow and can lead to immediate gains. The second way is more difficult and more long-term, although the gains can be considerable.

  Purchasing policy, of course, goes beyond the acquisition of supplies of materials to investment in capital equipment and much else. Everywhere there are opportunities for cost reduction.

  That is why the purchasing function has become so important in most organisations. Purchasing makes full use of value analysis to identify materials that match specification cost. Purchasing also employs equipment analysis to establish levels of relative cost-effectiveness for investing in new, as compared to reconditioning old equipment.

  For firms new to cost reduction, the prospect of reductions in the price of material does not always look promising in the face of the tendency for commodity prices to rise. It is, however, undoubtedly worthwhile to any firm to attempt to obtain from existing suppliers either a price reduction or a discount of some kind. Many businessmen have been pleasantly surprised at the ease with which a variation in contractual conditions or arrangements for supplies can be secured through sensitive negotiation with suppliers. If negotiations do not succeed, then it is always possible to investigate the likelihood of achieving better deals with other suppliers. It may be necessary to buy off or see out present suppliers, but the acquisition of more keenly priced suppliers will normally make the cost of the wait worthwhile. It is one of the functions of the purchasing department to keep prices under constant review in these ways.

  Obtaining a quantity discount in order to obtain a lower price is a common method of achieving reductions in cost. Firms have to be careful, however, not to increase storage cost and interest charges to the point at which the advantages of the quantity discount are lost.

  Nevertheless it is essential to evaluate the effect of discounts on the economic order quantity. Purchasing should also ensure that the delivery of materials is geared to production needs and a defined level of short-term capital investment in stocks.

- **Stock control**

  It is often worthwhile to look at ways of increasing the efficiency with which materials are handled by improving stock control. Among the candidates for cost reduction in this area are the following:

  (i)   storage location and its associated costs;

  (ii)   indirect services to stock control, such as stores administration, and their costs;

  (iii) amount and causes of stock losses and write-offs – pilfering, deterioration, obsolescence;

  (iv) arrangements for inspections and stocktaking;

  (v)   insurance of stock.

- **Materials handling**

  Reductions may also be made in the costs of materials handling, usage and yield. Developments in technology have reduced considerably the costs of handling material through computerised information systems and more advanced material handling techniques.

- **Economies in usage**

  Finding ways of using less material to obtain existing or improved output is often the means of obtaining spectacular cost reductions. In some industries the yield of saleable product from raw materials is high, but in others the waste may be at 10 to 50 percent of the materials purchased. It is therefore important for firms to know what their existing yield is and to see if it can be improved. Analysis may reveal waste through the use of too much material or through the loss of material – unusable off-cuts etc.; it may also reveal opportunities for reworking scrap.

- **Overhead control**

  Unit costs can be inflated by unnecessarily high production and other overheads. These overheads may be effectively controlled and monitored through budgetary control and by the use of standard costing.

  Close inspection of works services often reveal room for further reductions; the cost of maintenance and of things like steam raising have been shown on many occasions to be open to reduction.

Marketing and distribution

Marketing covers selling and distribution: the former entails representatives, advertising, market research, sales, office support and administration and after-sales servicing, while the latter takes in packing, transportation and merchandising. It has been said that marketing does not lend itself so readily to cost reduction as the other business functions. However, experience shows that there is scope for cost reduction in each of the functions of marketing.

- **Representatives**

  When looking at the costs of representatives it is worthwhile asking: is the organisation of territories and consequential arrangement of routes and calls, the most cost-effective way of achieving representation? Some reorganisation and replanning aimed at reduction in travelling time and associated costs may be possible. It may also be found that it is more economical to use agents, rather than representatives, especially in remote areas.

- **Advertising**

  The tendency in recent times has been to place more emphasis on analysing the effectiveness of advertising and to exercise more control over it. For example, an examination of expenditure on advertising as a percentage of sales and, if possible, a comparison of the figure with that of competitors may reveal that particular advertisements are ineffective and produce significant oncosts.

- **Market research**

  The usefulness of market research is obvious. It leads to the provision of information about market size, the source of business, customer preferences and much else that aids management in policy formation, planning, strategy determination and decision making.

Market research can, however, be used directly to investigate opportunities for cost reduction in the analysis of customer and proportion of market and sales, the analysis of order size, particularly in relation to the unit cost of selling per order and so forth. In these effects, the technique of value analysis is especially helpful.

- **Sales office**

  The setting of sales targets makes possible the analysis and assessment of individual performance on either a personal or group basis or both. The advantage of this type of investigation is that it throws light on the inefficiencies and deficiencies that lie behind a substandard performance.

  A salesman may perform poorly, not because he is inherently a bad salesman, or lacks interest and commitment, but because he has not received adequate training in sales techniques. Similarly a sales force may be missing sales targets, not as a result of a lack of effort, but because it does not have sufficient knowledge about the products it is pressing on potential customers, or about competing products. It may be that the sales force lacks leadership, incentive and motivation but this too can be exposed by analysing actual performance against sales targets.

  Something useful may come out of an examination of the type of support that is given to the sales force. The effectiveness of the sales office staff and the procedures that they use may be well below the standards attained in other areas and improvements could mean significant reduction in the sales element of unit costs.

- **After-sales service**

  There are essentially three ways of reducing costs here: firstly, by minimising the amount of after-sales service needed; secondly, by employing local agents to service faulty products; and thirdly, by offering maintenance deals.

  The first method looks either to high quality standards or to after-sales servicing by the purchaser. The provision of guidance to purchasers can be cost-effective: Russell Hobbs, for example, found that by explaining on a label costing 1p how to adjust the screw controlling the cut-out mechanism, they could reduce the number of electric appliances returned by a massive 99%. By employing local agents who are properly trained and who have the resources of the manufacturer available to them, companies have discovered that costs can be reduced. This is not a clear-cut matter – some firms still prefer to service their own goods. But organisations like Zanussi have found that, by offering extensive support and incentives to agents and their staff, suggestions for improvement in design are obtained and these can lead to substantial reductions in unit costs.

  In offering maintenance deals to customers, firms are off-setting and hence reducing after-sales costs. These deals can be very attractive and for those who subsequently make heavy calls on after-sales service extremely cost-beneficial.

- **Packing**

  The scope for cost reduction in packing is considerable. The question of packing and package must be considered at the design stage. But beyond that stage packing might take account of pilfering by developing and using packages less attractive for pilferage – plastic crates instead of wooden ones, for example. The avoidance of damage must always be an important factor in packaging. This is not always simply a matter of strength; damages may be avoided by the disposition of the product in the package. For some drinks, chemicals and gases, attention to efficient ways of returning empty bottles and containers may bring about important savings.

In all of these aspects of packing, the supplier and the purchaser have an interest. The purchaser, however, will have a special interest in the variety of pack sizes available with respect to efficient storage and any discounts offered for bulk.

●   **Transport**

Carriage charges are usually a variable in overhead costs, moving up and down with changes in the volume of business. Cost reductions may be achieved by securing lower haulage costs by, for example, switching from road to rail, minimising premium charges for urgent deliveries and so forth. They may also be reduced by, for example, dispensing with company transport and using someone else's transport by leasing, contract hire, casual hire or by whatever arrangement is calculated to be most cost-beneficial. Furthermore, reductions can flow from bulk despatch which gives lower costs per unit despatched. Some caution is necessary in this area, however, since savings in carriage charges may have to be set against the increased costs of improved packing and storage. In general, three points must always be looked at in cost reduction exercises affecting transport:

(i)   Is the existing method of transport entirely suitable and can it be adapted for higher volumes if required?

(ii)   Is the type of transport cost-effective, best suited to distances covered, satisfactory to the customer and sufficiently protective?

(iii)   Is the matter of transportation currently employed efficient and effective from the standpoint of distribution and sales?

Finance

Every company should seek to achieve the most effective use of its capital. Capital should be employed in ways that produce the maximum possible return. Capital is frequently tied up unproductively in stocks, idle fixed assets and uncooperative debtors.

One way of releasing this unproductive capital is to introduce more effective control systems. In the case of debtors, it may be beneficial for a company to make a contract with a factoring company, rather than introduce an improved system of credit control of its own. Idle fixed assets may be capable of redeployment in a proposed extension of production, or they may be adopted for new products. If no use can be found for them within the organisation, there is the alternative of selling them or, for some types of plant, leasing them.

New capital investment and capital expenditure must always be carefully appraised beforehand. It is important also to consider the additional working capital requirements when contemplating any new capital investment.

Capital investment in improved or new equipment can lead to substantial cost savings by reducing manpower costs per unit of output, or increasing material yield.

Capital replacement and refurbishment programmes should be devised with an eye on both profit forecasts and likely changes in price levels. They should be implemented systematically according to some order of need. The cost-effectiveness of the different methods of funding capital expenditure should be examined to enable the selection of the best method of funding.

Labour

Although rising unemployment and recession have led in the UK to the resuscitation of ideas that were long thought to be dead – such as the notion of reducing labour costs by cutting wage rates or the idea that wages ought to be determined by market forces – the best hope for reduction in labour costs would still seem to be with increased efficiency and productivity. Indeed, many businessmen believe that improved productivity is the only practical way of reducing labour costs.

Productivity is the ratio of output to input and improvements in this ratio can be achieved by reducing the average time required to make a product or provide a service. Such a reduction may be sought in many ways:

(a)   by controlling withdrawal (eg. absenteeism, labour turnover) and the incidence of accidents and industrial diseases;

(b)   through the use of appropriate financial and non-financial incentives, like bonus payments for regular attendance or offering opportunities for advancement;

(c)   by improving the working environment, operating conditions and general facilities;

(d)   by the use of piecework or bonus schemes;

(e)   productivity agreements and perks of various kinds;

(f)   by the careful selection and training of employees.

The most dramatic improvements in productivity, however, usually follow the introduction of either better and faster machines or improved methods of working, or both. These developments often provide additional bonuses by reducing indirect labour costs on maintenance and repairs and by making possible savings in the costs of other items, such as materials (better usage and yield) and fuel.

The service sector

The above detailed analysis concentrated upon the functions of a product-based business. Such a business will also inevitably incorporate service departments to which cost reduction programmes can be applied and, of course, some businesses will be entirely service-based, including those in the public sector.

Due to the wide divergence in the nature of the services provided by such departments or businesses, it is not possible to be very specific about the techniques to be used. Many of the ideas discussed for the manufacturing business will apply, with perhaps a little modification, to the service sector, in particular those regarding marketing, finance and labour. Thus we shall consider the general approach to cost reduction programmes that can be applied in a wide context.

The starting point will often be the examination of existing activities, to determine whether the use of resources by those activities is excessive. Over-consumption of resources may arise from one or a combination of:

–   over-resourced activities
–   inefficiently managed activities
–   unnecessary activities

Over-resourced activities

An activity is over-resourced when the same objective could be achieved with the use of less resource. For example, in a library, the number of counter staff employed may have remained relatively constant for a number of years, despite increasing sophistication of computerised check-out systems.

Individual offices of a firm of accountants may each employ a computer audit specialist, when the same level of service could be achieved at lower cost by employing one specialist per region and requiring him/her to travel to offices as required.

Inefficiently managed activities

Activities are inefficiently managed when current standards of achievement are not being attained. For example, excessive overtime may be incurred by staff in the accounts department at the accounting year-end, which could have been avoided by better planning of schedules and other information-gathering exercises that could be partially completed in advance of the year-end.

Excessive travel time may be incurred by maintenance engineers where their activities have not been properly co-ordinated.

Such deficiencies will usually be highlighted in normal variance reports.

Unnecessary activities

These will normally be activities of service or overhead departments within a business, or activities that are supplementary to the main service activity of the business.

To control the resources consumed by overhead departments effectively, it is necessary to understand:

–   why such departments exist
–   the services they provide
–   their relationship to other areas of the business

It may be decided that costs can best be reduced by curtailing the activities of the department, or, in extreme cases, closing it down altogether. For example, it may be that some or all of the routine computer processing currently carried out by the DP department could be cost-effectively sub-contracted out to an agency, without affecting the level or quality of the service provided to the other areas of the business.

Such a decision may come from the zero-based approach to budgeting, which is covered in Session 11.

Activities that are offered to the customer of a business as an addition to the main service provided should be assessed from a 'value-added' perspective – that is whether the cost spent on the activity is perceived to result in something of extra value to the customer, for which they are willing to pay. If not, the activity should be eliminated.

For example, a college may offer an out-of-hours student help service, for which it has to employ staff on overtime. If, however, this does not influence the students in their choice of college and thus the level of funding (private or public) attracted, it is a non-value added activity and should be stopped.

The techniques of value analysis are important in their own right, not just as part of a cost reduction exercise, and are now discussed further.

VALUE ANALYSIS

Value analysis (VA) was developed by HL Erlichter at General Electric of America in 1947 and has been adopted worldwide. Major British companies who have used VA extensively include Vickers, Ford (UK) and Rolls Royce.

VA is a technique that seeks to find an alternative way to provide a function at a lower cost. Its greatest application occurs in high-volume industries where fractional savings on product costs can be multiplied many times and so produce substantial savings. VA has been of great importance in emphasising the importance of the cost factor in the design function.

Application

Value analysis is not planned obsolescence nor is it cost-cutting. The purpose of VA is to provide the same value at a lower price – the essential element is the safeguarding of the quality involved.

In practice, a team, drawn from various disciplines or a trained quality control team, takes a product, breaks it into its component parts and systematically studies each part in turn.

In analysing each part, the team will initially decide the use value and esteem value of that part.

(a)   *Use value* is the term given to the properties and qualities that accomplish a particular use, purpose or service.

(b)   *Esteem value* is the term given to the properties and qualities needed to be added to protect sales appeal. For example, a pen top for a ballpoint might have a use value since it:

   (i)   protects owner's pocket/clothes
   (ii)   protects ink application
   (iii)   provides clip for storage
   (iv)   denotes colour of ink

and an esteem value since it:

   (i)   promotes manufacturer's name
   (ii)   could bestow sense of luxury/pride

The group would analyse each part by asking the following sequence of questions:

(a)   What is it? Detailed statement of size, material, etc.
(b)   What does it cost?
(c)   What does it do? (Use and esteem value.)
(d)   How many do we use?
(e)   What is its primary function?
(f)   What else will do?
(g)   What would these alternatives cost?
(h)   Can we identify a cheaper alternative whilst maintaining use and esteem values?

An example of VA

One of the most frequently quoted examples is Bic biro for which a fractional saving in design is multiplied by many thousands of times per day during manufacture. Similarly, the substitution of plastic for metal in ball points has maintained the same use value, not damaged esteem value and greatly reduced costs.

Application of value analysis – a short case study

A classic value analysis (VA) success story is provided by the Philips Industries. In 1981, the outlook was bleak – a declining economy, depressed housing and construction markets, and a price-sensitive market.

A corporate VA program was introduced company-wide, with total support of top management. In the first year, resulting savings were $2m, but had risen to $20m by the end of 1988.

The VA concept is now incorporated into the company's annual business plan by:

–   the setting of a savings target for each factory and division, as a percentage of projected sales
–   the adding of this target to the base factory/ division income to set its target profit
–   the linking of managers' bonuses to the level of attainment of their VA target

When applying VA to specific projects, Philips uses teams, including individuals from all areas of the business, with a trained VA specialist as co-ordinator. Sometimes, a non-management employee is included – a secretary or truck-driver, for example – who will often ask questions that reveal that some processes or materials are used simply because its 'always been done that way'.

A particular success stories from Philips involved a ceiling diffuser. Through VA, the number of parts in the product dropped from 31 to 8, material cost was cut by 24%, overhead cost dropped 26%, direct labour was cut 82% and there was a 30% improvement in the unit's performance.

Value analysis has the essential element of the safeguarding of the quality of the product or service involved. We shall now consider the subject of quality control further.

QUALITY CONTROL

Quality control function

Quality control is concerned with maintaining quality standards. There are usually procedures to check quality of bought-in materials, work in progress and finished goods. Sometimes one or all of these functions is the responsibility of the research and development department on the premise that production should not self-regulate its own quality.

Statistical quality control through sampling techniques is commonly used to reduce costs and production interruptions. On some occasions, customers have the contractual right to visit a manufacturer unannounced and carry out quality checks. This is normal practice with Sainsbury's and Tesco's contracts with manufacturers producing 'own label' goods (eg. Tesco Baked Beans).

In the past, failure to screen quality successfully has resulted in rejections, re-work and scrap, all of which add to manufacturing costs. Modern trends in industry of competition, mass production and increasing standards of quality requirements have resulted in a thorough reappraisal of the problem and two important points have emerged:

(a)   It is necessary to single out and remove the causes for poor quality goods before production instead of waiting for the end result. Many companies have instigated 'zero defects' programmes following the Japanese practice of eradicating poor quality as early in the chain as possible and insisting on strict quality adherence at every stage – as Crosby points out in his book *Quality is Free*, this is cost-effective since customer complaints, etc. reduce dramatically.

(b)   The co-ordination of all activities from the preparation of the specification, through the purchasing and inspection functions, right up to the function of delivery of the finished product is essential.

It is accepted that it is not possible to achieve perfection in products because of the variations in raw material quality, operating skills, different types of machines used, wear and tear, etc. but quality control attempts to ascertain the amount of variation from perfect that can be expected in any operation. If this variation is acceptable according to engineering requirements, then production must be established within controlled limits and, if the variation is more than the acceptable one, then corrective action must be taken to bring the variation within acceptable limits.

Overall quality control may be looked at under the following five headings:

(a)   *Setting standards* – Sometimes called 'new design control' this function involves the preparatory work necessary before production commences. It includes the location of possible sources of manufacturing troubles from trial runs, preparing inspection specifications after sampling, and planning the production and inspection functions, based on the results of these preliminary activities.

(b)   *Incoming material control* – This ensures the availability of the necessary material of the required quality standards during production. Close quality contacts must be made with the supplier to establish quality control at the source. The first deliveries received are subjected to 100% inspection to establish the supplier's level of quality. Information is given to the supplier to allow him to take remedial action if necessary. When the required quality level has been reached, other deliveries are subjected to sampling tests only.

(c)   *Product control* – This involves the control of processed parts at the production sources so that most differences from quality specifications that may have arisen are put right before any defective parts are produced. The three aspects of product control are as follows:

    (i)   Quality mindedness of the operatives and, to this end, extensive training programmes in quality control are arranged.

    (ii)   Inspectors and testers with good training and experience help foremen to pinpoint potential causes of defects by showing them how to apply control techniques.

    (iii)   Applying sampling checks to the finished product before delivery.

(d)   *Special purpose studies* – This is the investigation of the causes of defective products and looking for ways of improving elements of production quality.

(e)   *Appraisal* – This is critical appraisal of the overall results obtained from the programme and consideration of ways to deal with changing conditions.

Quality itself must be regarded as relative to other factors such as price, consistency and utility. The market for a product or service will accommodate itself to various degrees of quality.

A concept met today is that of a quality and reliability system, including the following elements:

- A study of customer requirements, particularly as they relate to performance and price.

- The design of the product or service.

- Full specification of the requirements of the design, clearly understood by everybody concerned with production.

- Assurance that operational processes can meet the requirements of the design.

- Acceptance by everybody of responsibility for meeting standards. Many people share in this responsibility. The manager plays a part by declaring what quality standards are to be. Design engineers must work within the parameters which give satisfaction to the customer. Production controllers make sure that output of the right quality is produced on time. Purchasing officers must find reliable suppliers. Operatives must be trained to achieve standards.

- Checking that the product or service conforms to the specification.

- Instructions on the use, application and limitation of the product or service.

- Study of consumer experience of the product, feedback to the departments concerned and immediate remedial action, if necessary, otherwise praise all round.

The quality control function looks at the process as a continuous operation, a series of trends and rejection rates. Reports from the quality control department to management include:

(a)   analysis of defects by cause;
(b)   comparisons between processes and departments;
(c)   comparison of defect levels with previous levels and standard levels;
(d)   longer-term trends in quality;
(e)   reports on customer's complaints.
(f)   developments in quality control practice;
(g)   special reports.

Advantages of quality control

The responsibility for quality control cannot be isolated as we have seen and can only be effective when it is the result of joint effort. The advantages lie in the fact that quality control points out why faulty work is being produced and the extent of it. Action taken as a result can reduce scrap and the amount of necessary re-work. It shows where a design modification could raise efficiency in manufacture. It minimises the chances of poor materials being processed.

The important factor is that quality control must be applied during processing and not after. This can be illustrated by the takeover of Motorola's TV production unit in the USA by the Japanese company Matsushita. As a result of training and emphasis on quality, with virtually the same labour force, the Japanese manager cut the warranty bill from $22 million to $3.5 million, cut defects from 140 per 100 sets to 6 and cut customer complaints from 80% to 7%.

The most effective areas where control can be usefully applied in most enterprises are:

(a)   goods inwards;
(b)   inspection at the supplier's business to see the type of plant and the methods used;
(c)   inspection of all new tools and plant;
(d)   inspection of the first part completed at each stage;
(e)   inspection between processes;
(f)   a final check at the end of the production line with any minor adjustments being made.

It is as much a fault to produce goods of too high a quality as goods of poor quality.

The requirements of the customers must be borne in mind and the sales department and market research can advise on this. They will be aware of competitors' prices and qualities and a decision must be taken whether or not to increase quality. To increase quality means increasing costs and establishing the point at which the customer will decide that the quality is more than he can afford.

Definition of quality is 'a degree of excellence'. It is the correct degree of excellence compatible with costs that management must agree on. If they can arrive at this and maintain it, they will have overcome one of the most difficult factors of production.

Crosby in *Quality is Free* points out that the responsibility for quality control cannot be isolated and can only be effective when it is the result of joint effort.

Both Crosby and Japanese companies emphasise the money-saving value of 'getting it right first time'.

Supplier quality assurance (SQA)

Mention has already been made of the position of supplier quality assurance. Obviously, the student will appreciate that it is necessary to control the quality of components delivered into the organisation, be it factory, health authority or service industry.

This is usually done through supplier quality assurance officers, who control the specification of the goods supplied.

However, some companies follow Japanese practice and use supervisors, work people or quality circles to control suppliers' quality. These representatives or the SQA officer may enter the supplier's plant, to verify that production is to the correct specification, working tolerances, material and labour standards. For example, the Ministry of Defence would reserve the right to ensure that defence contractors produce to specification, since defective work would mean the failure of a multi-million pound aircraft, loss of trained pilots and possibly ground crew as well as damage to civilian life and property. Likewise, a weapons system failure could have disastrous consequences. Students connected with the health service will be concerned about drug production being carried out in acceptable conditions, since impurities in drugs could have far reaching and disastrous consequences.

One great advantage of SQA is that it may render possible reduction of the in-house quality control headcount, since there will be no need to check incoming materials or sub-assemblies or components.

QUALITY CONTROL AND QUALITY ASSURANCE

As we have seen, the quality control function is responsible for ensuring that quality standards are satisfied in terms of the materials bought in, work in progress and finished goods. To fulfil this role, it is necessary for quality control to be independent of purchasing and production. Appleby quotes a survey where 44% of quality control managers interviewed reported direct to the board. This is especially relevant when customers have a clear understanding of their quality expectations.

In *Quality is Free,* Crosby emphasises that quality is the crux of any production operation because if the finished product cannot be used due to failure in specified standards during production, then the whole process has been a waste of effort, time and money.

McDonald's is a company which has consistently emphasised the dimension of quality. For years the motto of McDonald's has been QSC & V – quality, service, cost and value. Peters and Waterman point to the exacting quality standards laid down by the top management team at McDonald's who regularly inspect outlets (there are over 7,000!) throughout the world. The same high quality standards are insisted upon in terms of bought-in materials and in-store operation in all parts of the world. Thus there is consistency of quality standards throughout.

Total quality management (TQM)

In many manufacturing industries, quality standards can be necessary at four levels.

(a)   At *policy levels*, it is necessary to determine the desired market level of quality. An interesting example is the food supermarket chains. Typically, as an industry becomes more mature, so customers respond to higher quality rather than a cheap pricing policy. Tesco, in the last five years, has actively pursued a policy of higher quality of goods and higher standards in stores and service – this supersedes the previous Cohen philosophy of 'pile it high and sell it cheap'. So Tesco are reading the market demand for quality differently from Aldi, the German supermarket chain, which recently opened in the UK. Aldi's policy is a limited choice of brands and a narrow range of goods at a cheap price.

(b)   Quality standards must be determined and specified at the *design stage* to meet the market level of quality. This is an area in which Japanese companies concentrate a great deal of quality effort. Japanese companies are rarely trail-blazers in introducing new products. They prefer to wait until the design is perfected so that quality can be guaranteed. Japan has not been a major inventor in compact disc equipment, video recorders or camera/photography industries, yet Japanese companies dominate all these areas.

(c)   The third area is the *production stage* at which application of quality standards over incoming materials and production operations is necessary to implement the policies and design specifications. This is the traditional quality control area in which quality circles have made an important contribution.

(d)   The fourth area is the *use stage* in the field where installation can affect final quality and where the guarantee of quality and performance must be made effective. This stage would include training of client's staff, format of instruction manuals, availability of after sales service, etc.

The concept of TQM embraces all four of these levels. It is an integrated view of the quality function that emphasises the need for high quality and nil defects in all areas.

Total quality management seeks to define the best available practice and quality in every aspect of the company's operations and creates an employee philosophy that expects high quality throughout.

ITT (USA) is one of the pioneering companies in this field. Although some leading authors reject the term *total quality management* (eg. Crosby in *Quality is Free*), no-one disputes the wisdom of the approach and its increasing relevance in modern industry.

Quality circles

Quality circles started as an American management technique, first developed by IBM, but the framework may well have been pioneered by Hewlett Packard as early as 1937. However, it has been taken up by the Japanese with a high degree of success. This success has led to the re-adoption of quality circles in the USA and Europe.

Wherever it is employed, QC requires both the individual and the organisation to be motivated to improve quality by error reduction, material utilisation, machine operation, productivity etc. The procedure is designed to supplement the conventional quality control procedures.

Installation of quality circles

The decision to install a QC must come from top management, who will allocate finance to it, consider the cost of installing the system, train people to make an adequate contribution, launch the scheme and appoint leaders, etc.

The objectives extend beyond the essential problems of quality. General productivity is considered as well as methods to reduce frustration and grievances, reduce labour turnover and push power down the echelons of the organisation (albeit within the parameters of Japanese traditions of responsibility).

A quality circle usually consists of five to eight employees who meet on a regular basis to discuss any problems related to quality in their area and to make suggestions for improvement. There is a leader who is usually appointed by the organisation initially but can be elected by the group when established.

All members of the circle are voluntary and receive no extra pay for their involvement. The success of quality circles in Japan has been an important contributing factor towards raising standards of quality in Japanese industries. In Japan, there are instances of joint quality circles between manufacturer and supplier seeking to improve the quality of the bought-in components.

Normally, the QC comprises a supervisor and workers who meet within a single area of an organisation. Everyone is trained in identifying quality problems and in problem-solving techniques. Once established, the circle either looks at problems sent down by management or identifies the problem needing consideration for itself. Either way, it will have established financial targets to meet, thus justifying its existence. One important aspect of the QC is that both the financing and the eventual meetings happen in company time, although this often develops into a voluntary meeting in the employees' time.

During the discussions within the group, all members are encouraged to contribute, the subject matter is thoroughly aired, all possible solutions are considered and a written report (the *ringi* in Japan) submitted to management. After agreement, the implementation of the chosen solution often involves the members of the QC.

PW Betts, in his *Supervisory Studies*, advocates the following structured approach to the successful implementation of QC in a western organisation:

(a)   Allow members to select the problem, possibly using a brain-storming technique.

(b)   Draw up a list and vote on the priorities for selecting the problem.

(c)   Gather data and analyse.

(d)   Establish solutions and determine the most suitable one, possibly setting a target and a time scale for achievement.

(e)   Obtain the essential agreement from management.

(f)   Implement the proposal.
(g)   Check periodically and revise if necessary.

In addition, Crosby (an American advocate of QC) suggests the team should exclude specialist problem-solvers and that the member should be of similar status. He sees the leader role as being a quiet co-ordinator.

It is worth reiterating the general points that must be satisfied to ensure a reasonable prospect of success.

(a)   All members should be volunteers.
(b)   Careful selection of the right leader.
(c)   Management commitment and union support and involvement.
(d)   Adequate training programme for all QC members.
(e)   Receptive workers.
(f)   Implementation by members unless there are exceptional circumstances.

The slow adoption of QC in the west

It becomes pertinent to consider why QC has not worked successfully or gained universal recognition in the west. Wild, in *Production and Operations Management* (1984 edition), suggests that the system lends itself to the Japanese philosophy of life. A system that provides no immediate financial incentive and instead only offers the incentive of improvements in organisational status and performance and the benefits of further training appeals to the cultural tradition of the Japanese.

Given that Wild's view has some validity, consider QC being introduced with financial incentives. Again, it does not seem to work for a variety of different reasons:

(a)   The attitude of some British workers to react against any new management technique, treating it with suspicion. This may be valid and it could be suggested that Laura Ashley, textiles-based retailing, would have an easier task of introducing QC than an older established UK firm.

(b)   The Laura Ashley argument falls down when we consider 21st century working environments in the USA. Even in Silicon Valley, California, where the traditions of bad labour and management would hopefully be non-existent, the reality is that in the majority of firms surveyed by Tom Peters (*A Passion for Excellence*) the average worker would not attend the next QC meeting if it were the last day on earth. They see it for what it is: another way for management to jerk labour's chain.

(c)   Tom Peters has a valid objection to the doctrine advocated by Mohr from Hewlett-Packard in his book *Quality Circles Changing the Images of People at Work* (Addison Wesley, 1983): QC demands a degree of commitment by management to its people and its product stretching over a period of decades and lived with persistence and passion which is virtually unknown in most western organisations today, for often very legitimate reasons. Students think about the most talked-about managerial task of the last ten years. Five years ago, Sir Michael Edwardes was a hero, doyen of the management world. Now he is the target for brickbats and criticism. Would history have been different if he had stayed with BL not just to get it back from the brink, but to guide it back to be leader in UK volume car-producers?

Benefits of quality circles

The benefits arising from the use of quality circles are substantial:

* improved quality leading to greater customer satisfaction;
* greater motivation of employees;
* improved productivity;
* shop floor understand and share management/customers problems;
* a spirit of seeking improvements is generated;
* staff become more aware of opportunities for improvement because of training, in areas outside quality circles.

An example of the benefits of quality control and quality circles is in the production of Jaguar cars. In the early 1980s, when Sir Michael Edwardes was appointed to bring British Leyland back from the brink, 11% of the Jaguar workforce were engaged on inspection. Individual employees were not responsible for the quality of their work and consequently poor quality work was passed on and re-work hours were high. In 1981 the number of inspectors was dramatically reduced and employees made responsible for the quality of their own work through a programme of *Getting it right first time*. The number of re-work hours was used to adjust bonus payments.

Initially, task forces were set up to deal with quality and production problems. These had led to the development of about 180 quality circles. Quality circle suggestions which led to improvements in quality or productivity received financial rewards via the 'company suggestion scheme'.

Early analysis of the quality faults revealed that about two thirds were attributable to suppliers. Thus suppliers were made to sign contracts which resulted in stringent penalties, if the component quality did not reach specified levels. Suppliers were also made aware that, if they were responsible for disrupting production, they would be deprived of business.

Quality is controlled by a number of mechanisms. At the individual plant level, the products are audited on a sample basis and the *quality index* for the week is determined by this method. *Statistical process control* has also been introduced. A follow-up of customers is also undertaken on a regular basis; this provides feedback on product quality and customer service.

Jaguar has attempted to develop the commitment of employees to company objectives by improving communications, increasing employee involvement and developing a positive company image.

QUESTIONS

1   Product design

How does product design create opportunities for reducing costs?

2   Control v Reduction

Distinguish between *cost control* and *cost reduction*.

3   Value analysis

What is value analysis, how does it relate to cost reduction and how does it differ from method analysis?

4   Quality circles

Write brief notes on quality circles.

SUMMARY

Experience shows that there is considerable scope for savings on the cost of much organisational activity. If cost reduction is treated seriously and conducted with a sensitivity for the opinions of the people involved in it, substantial reductions in costs can be achieved without damaging morale or motivation. By making its employees cost conscious and inviting them to aim for reasonable cost reductions, a company can greatly enhance its prospects for continuing profitability at the desired level and its reputation as a responsible and reliable employer.

The need to sustain acceptable profitability cannot be overstated as an objective of cost reduction. This objective could of course be pursued by means of one-shot programmes or by a series of one-shot programmes; cost reduction, value analysis and quality control must be part of a continuous dynamic process if profitability requirements are to be met.

Performance indicators

OBJECTIVES

In the previous session, we considered the ways in which costs can be cut and thereby profit improved, without adversely affecting the quality of the product or service provided.

To monitor the effectiveness of these areas of operational control, management will want to be provided with cost and other related reports. These reports will inevitably incorporate some performance indicators.

The nature and interpretation of these measures will vary according to the activity concerned. This session considers the following aspects:

■   the general categorisation of performance indicators

■   performance indicators for

-    manufacturing businesses
-    service departments
-    businesses in the service sector
-    not-for-profit organisations

The performance criteria addressed by this session are as follows:

■   Relevant data are identified and analysed in accordance with defined criteria.

■   Timely information is presented to managers in a clear and appropriate form.

■   Relevant performance indicators are monitored and assessed.

■   Special reports to follow up matters which require further investigation are prepared.

TYPES OF PERFORMANCE INDICATOR

Performance indicators may be categorised in the following ways: quantitative or qualitative, monetary or non-monetary.

Quantitative or qualitative

Quantitative measures are expressed in numerical terms which include the following:

(a)   Variances
(b)   Profit, sales, costs, etc.
(c)   Ratios and percentages
(d)   Indices

Qualitative indicators are far more subjective and cannot be expressed as an objective, numerical measure. Examples relevant to business and managerial performance would include the following:

(a)   level of customer satisfaction: expressed as a subjective level 'very satisfied' .. to.. 'not at all satisfied'

(b)   staff performance grades: 'excellent', 'average', 'poor', etc.

(c)   company performance: 'steady', 'volatile results', 'disappointing', etc.

A lot of these measures may be turned into quantitative measures, by assigning numbers to the various categories (1 = excellent, 4 = poor), etc. but this does not overcome their fundamental subjective nature, as someone has to judge which category is appropriate in the first place.

Monetary or non-monetary

Monetary measures are necessarily quantitative. They are expressed in financial terms (ie. for UK businesses, in £) and are often referred to as *financial measures*. These would include profits, revenues, costs, cash flows, share price, variances and average wages.

In order to provide a means of measuring performance, monetary measures must be compared with something else. Such comparatives would include budgets, standard costs, previous periods, other departments of the business, other companies within the business sector and the market as a whole.

Non-monetary measures are those that are not expressed in financial terms and can be quantitative or qualitative (indeed the latter are, by necessity, non-monetary). Examples of non-monetary, quantitative measures would be:

(a)   *Ratios* and percentages: return on capital employed (ROCE), contribution to sales, staff to customers, defective to good output, wastage, market share, labour turnover rates, etc.

        (Ratios have been discussed in detail in a previous session.)

(b)   *Indices* – materials price index, retail price index, national wage index

The calculation and use of indices is covered in detail in the next session. They are very often used as a method of expressing a trend.

The above are examples of relative measures. Non-monetary, quantitative measures can also be expressed in absolute terms, in anything other than money (eg. hours, units, production volumes, numbers of customers, etc.).

MANUFACTURING INDUSTRIES

The performance of a manufacturing business and its constituent activities will commonly be measured in quantitative terms, mainly monetary. However, we shall also consider relevant non-monetary and qualitative factors that can be useful.

We shall consider possible measures within the categories specified in the performance criteria for Unit 11.

Productivity

This is a measure of the efficiency of resource usage and expresses the rate of output in relation to resource used.

Examples include the following:

(a)   units per labour or machine hour
(b)   productive hours to total hours paid
(c)   actual output to full capacity output
(d)   sales per salesperson

Productivity is closely linked with both efficiency (which is essentially the productivity of labour) and resource utilisation (which is considered later).

Unit costs

Here, traditional variances will play a major part. Each element of unit cost (materials, labour, overheads) will have a standard against which to compare actual costs. This standard cost will incorporate a technical standard (kg per unit, hours per unit) and a price standard (£ per kg, £ per hour).

Technical standards may be used on their own as non-monetary performance measures, particularly where a full-scale costing system is not in place, or where prices of resources are essentially fixed by external forces.

Resource utilisation

This is a measure of the extent to which resources were used in relation to maximum capacity. Examples of utilisation and related measures for different resources include the following:

Machines   –   utilisation (hours used : potential hours)
            –   down time (machine down hours : total hours)

Materials   –   wastage (normal/abnormal loss percentage)
            –   stock turnover (linked to levels of slow-moving stocks)

Labour   –   utilisation (productive : total hours)
            –   absenteeism, lateness
            –   mix variances (where different grades are used)
            –   idle time variances
            –   labour turnover (leavers replaced : total employed)

Profitability

The most common measures of profitability have been covered in a previous session (ROCE, profit margins). Many of the factors considered under other headings will also effect profitability, including all cost variances. Sales measures will also be relevant, such as volumes, mix between products and market shares, etc.

Product profitability should be measured in terms of contribution per unit or, for a budgeted activity level, contribution less directly attributable fixed costs (ie. excluding costs that are shared by other products).

Quality of service

For a manufacturing business, this can be categorised into quality of service to customers and quality of service from service departments. The latter is covered in the section on the service sector.

Quality of service to customers is essentially a subjective, qualitative measure, although some quantitative measures can be used in connection with it – for example, ratios such as customer returns to total sales and customer complaints per units sold. Speed of service can be measured in retail outlets or numbers waiting per checkout in a supermarket.

The main source of measure of customer satisfaction will generally be through some sort of questionnaire.

Other non-monetary measures

We have included relevant non-monetary and qualitative measures under the above headings where appropriate. Quality is a particular area in which such indicators are required; two others that have been recently been identified as important attributes of world-class manufacturing are *innovation* and *flexibility*.

Innovation is concerned with the business's ability to beat their competitors in developing new products, improvements to existing ones or additional customer services.

Measurement of innovation must concentrate on its effectiveness as well as its existence – counting the number of new products developed is of little help without knowing the extent to which they have been accepted by the market.

Possible measures include the following:

(a)   research and development expenditure related to new sales (in value and timing, ie. payback)
(b)   viable new products to existing products
(c)   percentage of total profits relating to new products/ improvements

Flexibility is concerned with the business's ability to respond to customers' needs, in terms of speed of delivery of existing products, speed of reaction to changes in demand patterns and ability to respond to particular customer requests or specifications.

In a manufacturing context, it is often the case that flexibility is connected with the amounts of products using common parts. If demand for one type of product falls, it is easier to switch stock and processing to another if there is a common base between them.

SERVICE DEPARTMENTS

Introduction

Many of the measures discussed above will be relevant in the assessment of the performance of service departments within a business. Unless an internal charge-out system operates (for example, the charging of user departments per hour of computer department time spent on their work), the emphasis will be on costs rather than profits.

As well as the normal cost variances (with activity levels based on the departments own cost unit, eg. maintenance hours, meals served, data processing hours) other cost ratios will be appropriate, for example:

(a)   meal cost per employee per period (canteen)

(b)   running costs per van-mile (deliveries)

(c)   cost per call-out (maintenance department)

Illustration

We shall consider a transport/distribution department in more detail:

In a transport organisation, vehicle costs fall into two categories:

(a)   Standing costs (ascertained as a rate per day), including:

     (i)   road tax

     (ii)   insurance

     (iii)   garage and administration costs

     (iv)   drivers' wages

     (v)   depreciation

(ii)   Running costs (ascertained as a rate per ton/mile), including:

     (a)   fuel and lubricants

     (b)   tyres

     (c)   repairs

     (d)   maintenance

Standing costs will be incurred for vehicles owned whether or not they are in use and are in the nature of stepped fixed costs. Fixed because, for each vehicle, they do not vary in amount and 'stepped' because for each additional vehicle required, costs, on a graph, will rise by a further step and remain fixed for a further range of activity until another vehicle is required.

In addition to these, there will be depot administration and establishment costs to be absorbed. These should be ascertained in total and related to the activity of the depot. Statistical information such as mileage run, loaded and empty, and tonnages carried should also be collected so that a reasonable method of absorption may be derived.

The analysis of expenditure between fixed and variable costs (standing and running costs) gives potential for the use of marginal costing and the consequent improvements in management information.

With such information available, management will be better equipped to deal with:

(a)   control over costs for each vehicle or group of similar vehicles

(b)   pricing

(c)   choice of most economic vehicle for specific tasks

(d)   acceptability of contracts

(e)   vehicle purchase and replacement decisions

(f)   many other day-to-day decisions

SERVICE SECTORS

Introduction

Service organisations include the following:

(a)   *Professional services*, such as firms of accountants, architects, surveyors, solicitors whose main assets will be their employees and who provide individual, personalised services to their customers.

(b)   *Mass services*, such as transport, which are highly capital asset based and provide a standard range of services to a wide range of customers.

(c)   *Public sector services,* such as health, education and local authorities, which fall under the 'not for profit organisations' section covered later in the session.

Service sector measures can be considered under very similar headings as those for manufacturing organisations, although there will be a different emphasis on their relative importance.

The main difference between the two types of organisation is the nature of their output.

Output from manufacturing businesses comprises tangible, clearly identifiable products, usually of a standard design and quality which can be rejected by a customer if not required or unsuitable, and produced in advance of demand and stored until needed.

Think about a service provided to you – can it be said to have any of these characteristics?

This leads to a different approach needed for performance measurement where costs per product or units per hour are of little relevance or meaning. However, in earlier sessions, we have seen that cost units do not have to be in terms of products and that measures may be activity rather than product based.

So, using similar headings as before, particular areas to be considered about the performance indicators of service organisations are productivity, unit costs, resource utilisation, profitability and quality of service.

Productivity

Productivity can be difficult to measure, because services rarely have a standard unit of output. For example, it would be meaningless to measure a conveyancing solicitor's productivity on the basis of 'property purchase completions per month', as each will have a different degree of complexity and value to the business. Similarly, it would be inappropriate to assess a bus line on the basis of 'journeys per day', as the contribution to the company's profits would depend upon the number of people carried at each stage of the journey and how many buses were operating on the line.

Meaningful measures of productivity or efficiency for a service depend upon a clearly defined measures of activity and resource.

So, for example, the measure of activity for the bus line might be 'passenger miles' and of the resource might be 'driver hours'.

Professional firms, such as accountants and solicitors, will generally use 'chargeable hours' as a measure of activity and employees' productivity will be judged by 'chargeable hours per employee'.

Unit costs

Again, the difficulty here is in defining an appropriate unit for the activity being measured. Once this has been established, appropriate costs need to be attributed to it. So the cost of a professional chargeable hour would mainly consist of employee costs (salaries, NICs, benefits, etc.) but will also include a recovery of general overheads.

The cost of a 'passenger mile' for a transport company will include driver costs, vehicle running costs and overheads.

Resource utilisation

Resource utilisation is the extent to which available resources are used for productive service. Examples of suitable measures for various types of service businesses are as follows:

Professional	Chargeable hours	:	Total hours available
Transport	Passenger miles	:	Train miles available
Hotel	Rooms occupied	:	Rooms available
Car hire	Car-Days hired	:	Car-days available

Profitability

Clearly, for the service business overall, the usual measures can apply – ROCE, profit margins, etc. Unit profitability measures will again depend upon the clear definition of the cost unit or unit of activity. The profit can then determined by comparison of the cost per unit (as discussed above) with the income generated (eg. the charge-out rate for a professional chargeable hour or the average fare per mile on a bus/train route).

Quality of service

This has far more significance than in the manufacturing sector, where it was perhaps subsidiary to the quality of the product. Customers will make their buying decisions on the basis of how well the service is provided.

The factors contributing to quality of service will vary according to the nature of the business. As an illustration, consider the service provided to trainee accountancy students by a private college. Possible factors that would influence a potential student in their choice of college and the ways in which these might be measured are set out overleaf:

Factor	*Possible measures*
Technical expertise	Pass rates
Communication	Clarity of lectures, study material and administrative information
Access	Staff/student ratios
	Availability of tutorial help outside lecture hours
	Ease of finding department/member of staff required
	Location of college
Friendliness	Approachability of staff
Flexibility	Ability to tailor service to individual student's needs
Facilities	Availability and standard of canteen, library, phones, etc.
Aesthetics	Appearance of college Staff presentation
Comfort	Roominess of classrooms Heating/air-conditioning Comfort of seats, size of desks

You can no doubt think of some more factors and different ways in which those given could be measured. For example, it is perhaps a little glib to use pass rates as a measure of the college's technical expertise, as theses are also likely to be significantly influenced by the abilities and commitment of the students themselves.

Having identified what needs to be measured, how can this be achieved? Some are a matter of fact or record – like pass rates or the existence of facilities; most of the rest are qualitative judgement, and would need to be measured by the use of assessment forms completed by students.

An overall measure of the quality of service provided by the college could be the trend in the number of students enrolling for courses, although again this can be affected by other factors, such as the location of the college and students, the policy of the students' employers and the size of the market for trainee accountants.

NOT-FOR-PROFIT ORGANISATIONS

Introduction

Not for profit organisations (NFPOs) are largely operating in the public sector, in areas such as education, policing, housing, health, libraries; perhaps the most common private sector example would be charities. These are also predominantly in the service sector.

It is the role of performance indicators to measure the extent to which the organisation's objectives are being met. In organisations that are run for profit, profitability and competitiveness will be paramount and indicators measuring this and its constituent factors of revenue and costs will be given priority in assessment of performance.

The objectives of NFPOs will be quite different and are likely to be multiple, making the development of a useful set of performance indicators a more difficult and subjective exercise. It is however a necessary one, as these organisations are invariably funded by public money and they should be held accountable for the ways in which it is spent.

The following discussion will concentrate on the evaluation of public sector service organisations, which will account for the majority of NFPOs.

Note that, whilst the text will emphasise the particular problems of, and approaches to NFPO performance assessment, many of the measures discussed above for private sector service organisations can still be applied. Provided a unit of activity can be clearly defined, measures of unit costs and resource utilisation can be developed in the same way.

Public sector service NFPOs

For NFPOs, there is no profit objective or similar target. Their services, which represent the output of each organisation, are vague, abstract and very difficult to quantify in financial terms. There is no mathematical relationship between money spent and the value of the service received and ultimately no method of making decisions about where the funds should be allocated, to increase or decrease the level of service.

This lack of quantification in the service-based sectors can create problems, as stated by Harrison (1985):

'a lack of clear and consistent policies creates problems for local authority ... managers. They do not know whether they are to be accountable in terms of the revenues they produce, the numbers of people they provide for, or the breadth of the programmes they offer. In the next ten years we shall experience continuing tight constraints upon public spending ... we will have to be clearer than we are now as to the objectives of provision, and we will need clear and agreed policies by which these objectives can be attained.'

The policy objectives of public sector organisations tend to be lost in terms which mean all things to all men but in most cases the desired goal is to answer the 'needs of the community'. The stated objectives might be quite clear in their intentions but difficulties will arise when trying to translate these intentions into meaningful units of output.

Illustration

For example, objectives of some local authorities in relation to leisure facilities could be:

'to provide residents with a wide range of leisure opportunities of as high a standard as possible at as low a cost as is practicable'; and

'to ensure appropriate provision of facilities for the whole community to enjoy free time in particular to encourage pursuits which contribute to the development of the individual and family life'.

However there are so many problems inherent in these seemingly clear statements, that the quantification of them in terms of objectives and ultimately in performance measurement is nearly, if not totally, impossible. Such problems being:

(a) How wide a range of leisure opportunities is needed and intended? What should be included in the range?

(b) How high a standard is to be set? How is the standard to be determined?

(c) What is a practical cost? Should it cover running and capital expenses?

(d) What is an appropriate provision? Given appropriate provision, will the whole community be served by it?

(e) What pursuits develop the individual's personality and improve quality of life?

It is only when public authorities realise the problems they are imposing on officers who need to devise strategies to attain objectives, that rectification is likely. Should objectives in future be clarified into statements which are quantifiable, then to assess how well these goals are being achieved some sort of performance measure will be required.

PERFORMANCE MEASUREMENT

Unlike the private sector of the economy where there is a clear objective and motive of making profits or returns on capital employed, the public sector has a multitude of demands and objectives. Primarily, the public sector is concerned with providing services to the general public which would not otherwise be available or provided for adequately within the financial resources of all individual members of the public. As we have seen, the nationalised industries and public corporations are required to meet certain criteria set by the government in the form of a return on capital, but for the service sector industries the problem of performance measurement is not so clearly identifiable. This lack of performance assessment in the service sector is of concern and the preceding sections examine this issue.

Why do we need measurements?

Firstly, to ensure that performance is congruent with the objectives of the local authority, ie. to measure the effectiveness of the policy in fulfilling stated objectives. Secondly, to allow comparisons of performance between services and authorities, thus providing an indicator of efficiency, and to discover where improvements may be made. Finally, to provide a guideline for the decision-maker to help decide the value of increasing the outlay of resources in one area as opposed to another. To free the decision-maker from making subjective judgements, objective measures need to be sought.

There are three stages in the process of performance measurement:

(a) the identification and quantification of inputs and outputs;
(b) the weighting of the different outputs to enable them to be related and counted together;
(c) the division of the weighted output by input to produce a performance indicator.

The input/output relationship

Input and output are clearly definable, since they are two distinct components. Inputs are resources placed into a project to produce a desired result, the objective. Output is the level of achievement in obtaining the objective. The two should never be confused, but they are inter-related. Problems exist in the definition and identification of units, and in the measurement of efficiency and effectiveness.

Input

It would seem that there are relatively few problems related to input as compared with output, which is to be mentioned later in this section. Input is viewed as the resources which are combined to give a unit input. The main problem lies in local authority accounting procedures; consistency with regard to the apportionment of central administrative charges and overheads is required, and the writing off of loan or debt charges can cause considerable distortion. However, once it is agreed what is meant by input, definition of units is easy as resources can be expressed in terms of money, manpower or a combination of the two. The last few years have seen a move towards a greater standardisation of local authority accounts, the aim being to provide a valuable new source of information to ratepayers and to facilitate judgement of performance by comparisons of authorities.

Output – general problems of output measurement

It is the characteristics of output in performance measurement which cause local authorities the most problems. It is a complex and difficult process to assess the level and quality of service provided.

The main problems are as follows:

(a)   It is difficult to define output – Services are more concerned with long-term social improvement definable only in moral or political terms. For example, improving the quality of life may be an objective but how is it defined?

(b)   No single criterion or objective function for analysing proposed alternative courses of action. This contrasts with the private sector which has the profit measure to judge performance.

(c)   No accurate way of estimating the relationship between inputs and outputs (cause and effect relationship) eg. what causes better examination results, is it teachers or equipment?

(d)   Some services contribute to more than one objective; for example, the education service is concerned with all aspects of children's lives.

(e)   Difficulties in the collection of data (eg. unreported crimes do not figure in measurements).

(f)   Difficulty in establishing national and relevant standards.

(g)   Cost of collections may be prohibitive when measured against usefulness of output measures.

(h)   Products and services supplied to the community are often not physical assets. If they are intangible, then how can they be measured?

Use of output indicators

The social, economic and community objectives of most authority operations mean that performance cannot be measured directly and must be measured by indicators of the value of the output being produced and the relationship of the output to the input in terms of costs involved. Thus a major task for local authorities is to identify which performance indicator will best reflect the objectives.

For example, the objective of the education service is acknowledged to be:

'to equip children to take their place as useful citizens and work in the community'.

How would one decide units of output in such a case?

The answer must be that at present there is no concise, absolute solution to the problem, so one must turn to intermediate outputs. Intermediate outputs are indicators of success which are based upon subjective agreements as to the minimum standard of achievement acceptable given the policy objectives; for example, five '0' levels may be taken as an indicator of success in educational sectors. This would, however, presuppose a positive correlation between education standards and useful citizens in a similar way as participation in leisure activities enhances the quality of life and this brings up the question of what is meant by the terms *useful citizens* and the *quality of life*?

Illustrations

In areas such as social services, it is probably impossible to obtain quantitative measures of the absolute value of the output being achieved but such indicators could be:

(a)   *Education*

      (i)   Examination results
      (ii)   Attendance records of schools
      (iii)   Numbers going into higher education
      (iv)   Ability to meet requirements of employers

(b)   *Housing*

      (i)   Age structure of houses in area
      (ii)   Occupancy levels
      (iii)   Number on housing waiting list
      (iv)   Length of time on housing waiting list

(c)   *Libraries*

      (i)   Range of books offered
      (ii)   Total hours open
      (iii)   Numbers of mobile libraries
      (iv)   Lending patterns of books

(d)   *National Health Service*

      (i)   Beds per 1,000 population
      (ii)   Bed occupancy rate
      (iii)   Beds per nurse
      (iv)   Operations per annum

Choice of performance indicators

The choice of performance indicator is likely to be greatly influenced by the ease of measurement, and the choice of indicators can limit the accuracy of the output measurement.

It must be realised that the information sought from output measures will differ according to the user. It is possible that policies concerning the same services may differ between local authority and central government, and what may be a suitable measure for central government purposes may be quite inadequate for others. In addition, objectives for some services may differ fundamentally between individual local authorities. The result being that some output measures will be of doubtful value when used for inter-authority comparisons.

Variations in objectives and final output will complicate the problems of measurement when used for external purposes. The answer would seem to lie in an agreed standard range of intermediate output measures which can be related to services.

Output measurement in practice

There are two stages involved: achievement of policy objectives (ie. targets) and effectiveness of policy.

(a) *Targets* – These are an expression of policy in quantifiable terms, over a set period of time and within a given amount of resources. The technicalities of target setting come within a framework of planning, programming and budgeting systems.

(b) *Effectiveness* – It is in this area that most time is spent in attempting to discover the success of policies in satisfying the needs of the community.

The 'needs' of the community are established, and the reaction to the service may be seen as an indicator of the effectiveness of the service from the viewpoint of both client and professional.

The principal method is by statistical sampling of clients. Impracticalities exist such as lack of resources, money, time and labour; when such projects have been undertaken, the response may be so poor as to make any results inadequate for measurement analysis.

A few examples of indicators follow:

(i)	Libraries	Proportion of population who are borrowers
(ii)	Public transport	Percentage increase or decrease in passengers
(iii)	Further education	Demand for individual courses
(iv)	Welfare clinics	Number of mothers who attend in proportion to total population

In the case of no agreed level of performance, it may be useful to compare present performance with performance during some base period. If satisfactory indicators of performance can be identified then how should the results be analysed?

Standard budgetary control

Often a method of assessing performance in local authorities is by the use of such a standard budgetary control system. Actual performance is measured against budget for income and expenditure week-by-week or month-by-month, and this will reveal variances. In this way, the performance of a centre can be monitored throughout the year. Indeed, if the figures are split into functions or activities, closer control of each sub-division of the centre is facilitated. Whilst fulfilling this function it can also be used to assess the performance of resource allocation.

However, it is often the managers of each cost centre who actually set the level at which the budget is to be set. Their objectives may not be in accordance with the overall objectives. Should the budget be fulfilled, this will not imply that performance is as expected. Economy and efficiency may well not be being achieved, and who knows what the effectiveness of the service is. Likewise, if the budget is not being fulfilled to its optimum level, this does not mean that performance is worse than expectations; it may be that resource allocation has not been as anticipated.

Where budgets exist there is a certain need for several measures of performance. Whilst the functions of this process are important, undue attention to cost controls can tend to diminish the importance of other goals. Evaluation of performance requires both quantitative and qualitative measures of performance. Departmental goals may be in conflict, eg. the need to minimise costs and to maintain service quality. Thus, emphasis on specific goals may mean that other goals may not be achieved. Objectives of performance evaluation, already stated, require a balanced view of performance, covering the various areas of managerial responsibility. If management use only conventional measures of revenue, expenses, cost variances it may well mean that in the short-run only economic gains will be realised at the sacrifice of long-run goals.

Obviously for simplicity's sake, an ideal performance measurement is necessary to cover all aspects of input/output combinations.

QUESTIONS

1	**Transport company**	**(AAT CA J94)**

A transport company is reviewing the way in which it reports vehicle operating costs to the company management. In particular, it is interested in the use of performance ratios which will help to assess the efficiency and effectiveness of the use of its vehicles.

Information on the following items is available for each vehicle for the period:

Costs

Variable costs

Fuel	Tyres
Oil	Other parts
Hydraulic fluid	Repairs and maintenance

Fixed costs

Road fund licence	Cleaning
Insurance	Depreciation
Drivers' wages	

Activity

Miles driven	Number of days available for use
Tonnes carried	Number of days vehicle actually used
Journeys made	

Assessment task

You are asked to indicate *six* suitable performance ratios which could be used to monitor the effectiveness and efficiency of the usage of each vehicle.

Three of your ratios should relate to the efficient control of costs and three should relate to the effective usage of vehicles.

2   Loamshire County Council (I)   (AAT CA Pilot)

The information given below relates to the library services operated by the Leisure Services Committee of Loamshire County Council.

Loamshire County Council – Library Services
Annual budget for the financial year 1993/94

	A	B	C	D	E
		Policy		Inflation	
	Budget	variations	A + B	allowance	Budget
	1992/93	1993/94		1993/94	1993/94
	£'000	£'000	£'000	£'000	£'000
Employees					
Professional	1,200	24	1,224	24	1,248
Clerical	2,100				
Other	305				
Premises	550	–	550	16	566
Supplies and services					
Book fund	1,700				
Cassettes and CDs	160				
Other	70	–	70	2	72
Transport	120	–10	110	3	113
Establishment expenses	210				
Debt charges	550				
	6,965				
Income from fees, charges and trading	400	80	480	–	480
Cash allocated to the Library Service	6,565				6,565

Notes

(1)   The committee has approved the following policy variations on the 1992/93 budget:

- A 2% increase in establishment for all staff
- A reduction of £10,000 in the transport budget
- A reduction of £20,000 in CDs and cassettes
- Debt charges to be increased by £20,000
- See below for the treatment of the Book Fund
- There are no other policy variations

(2)   Inflation allowances for 1993/94 allowed on the base budget (Column A) and the policy variations (Column B) are as follows:

-    2% for all employees

-    4% for the Book Fund, CDs and cassettes

-    3% for all other expenditure except debt charges for which there is no inflation allowance

(3)   Income to rise by 20% in 1993/94 cash terms

(4)   It has been decided that the amount of cash allocated to the Library Service in 1993/94 will be exactly the same as in 1992/93. Any shortfall after allowing for other policy changes will be met by a reduction in the Book Fund.

Assessment tasks

(a)   As assistant accountant, you have been asked to draft a budget for the financial year 1993/94 to give effect to the decisions which have been taken by the Committee by completing the columns in the above table. Work to the nearest £'000. Some entries have been already been given to start you off. (**Hint:** Work out the budgets for all remaining items leaving the calculation of the Book Fund till the last; the 1993/94 Book Fund budget will be the balancing figure in column E.)

(b)   What is the budgeted percentage reduction in the Book Fund in real terms?

(c)   A number of councillors have argued that, if the service continues to purchase books at this rate for a number of years, the stock will soon become out of date and worn out. This has led to a general discussion about the total quality of the Library Service. In addition to the information contained in budgets, statistics are available over a number of years on the following items:

-    number of employees in different categories
-    number of books issued over a period
-    total book stock
-    numbers of books/CDs/cassettes purchased in a year
-    numbers of members of the public using the Library Service
-    total population in the county

You have been asked to suggest performance indicators which might give some guidance to councillors and the public at large on the quality of the service provided.

Suggest:

(i)   one ratio which measures the efficiency of staff in carrying out routine duties

(ii)   two ratios which measure the extent of the service provided for the public

(iii)   one method of measuring the contribution made by income-generating activities

(iv)   two indicators which would provide relevant information about the quality of the stock

3   Armstrong Ltd

The following passage is taken from a paper discussing current developments in the costing of specialty activities (such as pathology or neurology) in National Health Service hospitals.

'Departments or 'cost centres' to which expenditure could be identified directly were categorised into four categories:

(a)   primary cost centres (ie. specialties)

(b)   direct support cost centres (ie. nursing departments, diagnostic and paramedical departments, etc.)

(c)   indirect support cost centres (ie. catering, domestic and estate management departments, etc.)

(d)   central services (ie. administration, finance, etc.)

'Costs were, as far as possible, allocated directly to specialties without any apportionment. Such costs included medical staff salaries and wages, some secretarial salaries and some medical and surgical equipment expenditure. For the remaining costs, measures of workload were obtained, where possible, for each department and these were used to apportion the department's costs to others. First, the costs of indirect support service departments were apportioned to the appropriate direct service departments. Then, the costs of direct service departments, both direct and apportioned costs, were apportioned to specialties, the primary cost centres. Where direct workload measures were not available, substitutes were used; for instance, floor area in the case of work costs, and in-patient days or out-patient attendances in the case of CSSD (Central Sterile Supply Department) costs. Costs of central services departments were apportioned to specialties as a final step in direct proportion to the costs accumulated thus far.'

Required

Evaluate these ideas briefly but critically, having particular regard to the purposes for which these measurements might be used.

SUMMARY

As you have seen, there are numerous possible performance indicators and their relevance will depend upon the type of organisation and the aspect of performance being assessed.

The five categories of indicators used initially (productivity, unit cost, etc.) can be used as a framework for the assessment of most types of organisation, but you need to be able to adapt them as necessary.

Many of the ideas covered in earlier sessions will have relevance here (eg. variance analysis and the use of indices and ratios).

Make sure you are quite clear about the necessary attributes of a cost unit (or unit of activity) in order for it to provide a useful basis for measurement. This is particularly important for service activities. Try to think of services you have had experience of yourself and how the various aspects may be measured.

There will rarely be a right or wrong answer, so do not be afraid to use your imagination.

Forecasts and trends

OBJECTIVES

Units 11 and 12 require you to be familiar with the principles and techniques involved in the analysis of trends, in costs and income, and their projection for use in cost control and budgeting.

This session covers the following:

- environmental forecasting considerations and problems
- sources of information costs and prices (internal and external)
- the use of time series analysis
- index numbers

The performance criteria addressed by this session are as follows:

- Significant trends are identified and brought to the attention of management.

- Reports highlighting significant trends are presented to management in an appropriate form.

- Valid, relevant information is identified from internal and external sources.

- Trends in prices are monitored and analysed on a regular basis.

- Forecasts of trends and changes in factor prices and market conditions are reasonably consistent with actual experience.

- Staff in the organisation who can contribute towards the analysis of external trends are consulted.

- Relevant data for projecting forecasts of income and expenditure are identified.

- Appropriate adjustments are made for changing price levels and seasonal trends.

- Forecasts take account of significant anticipated changes in circumstances which would affect the validity of the statistically derived calculations.

  Personnel who might contribute towards making realistic forecasts of trends are consulted.

  Current material, labour and other variable costs are identified and future trends assessed.

INTRODUCTION

Long-range plans are often based on estimations of the future from extrapolations of the past to find trends, a method which can be fairly accurate in the short term. However, using data and relationships derived from past behaviour is limited in that such data cannot forecast something which has never happened before.

If a company were to rely solely on *forecasting* rather than *long-range planning*, it would need to operate in a very predictable environment. Planning is an attempt to control outcomes whereas forecasting is a more passive attempt to predict outcomes, making educated guesses about the future.

Long-range planning is concerned with deciding which courses of action the organisation should take for the future. It is said that corporate planning does not attempt to minimise risks as, usually, the greater the risk the higher the return, but it helps to ensure that the organisation takes the right kind of risks with the best possible knowledge of the consequences.

Systematic forecasting is now a common aspect of organisational activity; it is usually concerned with the early future – say five years hence. To be useful in this context, a forecast is required to be detailed and to be precise to a high degree of probability; consequently, the methodology which has been developed is sophisticated and extensive.

Technological forecasting is different in that it concerns a much further time horizon; thus it cannot be presumed that the present trends will continue or that current assumptions will remain valid. Technological forecasting attempts to quantify the future changes.

ECONOMIC FORECASTING

Economic forecasting is an area fraught with problems and there are various conflicting views on the appropriate model to use. However, it is still essential for a company to be aware of likely trends in, for example, gross domestic product *per capita*. To this end, many large organisations have their own models or adapt the findings of other models to reflect their requirements. Whatever the applicability of the models for forecasting likely effects on a particular organisation, it would be foolish to ignore trends in consumer incomes and expenditure, and sources of long-term finance.

Sources of information for assessing economic change influencing industries

- Government publications such as the *Monthly Digest of Statistics* and *Trade and Industry*
- Government reports on particular industries
- Reports prepared by international bodies, such as UNO, OECD and EEC
- Commercial publications dealing with economic matters of particular industries
- Publications by trade and professional organisations
- Bank reviews
- Stockbroker reports
- Statistics from advertising agencies
- Special sampling surveys

More detail on both internal and external sources of information is included later in the session.

OTHER ENVIRONMENTAL FORECASTING CONSIDERATIONS

Government action

As a result of government intervention the plans of undertakings laid down some time ago can suffer dramatic changes. The government's task is to keep the economy in balance and this may well result in a stop-go type of policy, particularly towards the end of the life of a parliament. Management must therefore be prepared to rethink drastically and immediately should the situation arise.

The effective businessman can only act in the manner of a detective and by thorough reading of party political publications try to predict likely governmental changes and when they will occur. Remember that policies can change drastically with a change of government, sometimes even going into reverse.

Changing business attitudes

Society is taking a very close interest in business organisations, being of the view that companies have other responsibilities (towards its employees and members of the public) as well as making profits.

Regularly in the media there are examples of companies that are considered to lack social responsibility because they fail to protect the area surrounding their factories from the hazards of their product (eg. the disaster at Flixborough where a massive fire and local damage was caused by the explosions at a chemical factory). Society today is far more socially aware and will not accept hazards which it took for granted in the past. This developing awareness has resulted in change in the attitudes of companies.

Awareness of the activities of pressure groups can be of critical importance to business planning. Often items that start off as aspects of consumer pressure can lead to legislative controls.

Indicators

Indicators of likely change in the environment can be identified. Thus for example problems which are occurring currently may indicate major changes, such as late payment from a customer highlighting possible trading difficulties or potential bankruptcy. Current political changes within a country may indicate future problems for the supply of raw materials and availability of markets. The Iranian revolution caused a considerable disruption to trading conditions which continued for some time.

The degree of influence suppliers, markets etc. have on the organisation will determine the priority which should be given to these indicators in the planning process.

The importance of trends

It is important to be able to identify trends in market competition. Increasing competition can provide the threat of likely takeover or the need to merge with another organisation in order to obtain from larger production units any economies of scale available. It is also important to realise that increasing competition, perhaps even within the context of a diminishing market, may present an opportunity. An efficient organisation should be capable of successfully competing, and where organisations go into liquidation this will free sections of the market previously served by the liquidated enterprises.

SOURCES OF INFORMATION

In putting together a budget, you need to be aware of potential sources of information. The first distinction to make is between internal and external sources. Where possible, a management accountant will want to make the most of information already available within the company. Typical sources of information may be as follows:

(a)   *Production and material control*

      (i)   Forward-loading plans for production cycles
      (ii)   Machine capacity forecasts
      (iii)   Departmental operating statements
      (iv)   Stock and work-in-progress reports
      (v)   Wastage reports
      (vi)   Labour utilisation reports
      (vii)   Productivity reports

(b)   *Marketing including distribution*

      (i)   Market surveys
      (ii)   Sales surveys
      (iii)   Order reports by product and geographical area
      (iv)   Discount trends
      (v)   Transport and warehouse cost statements
      (vi)   Salesman performance and expenditure
      (vii)   Product service and support costs, including advertising and promotion

(c)   *Personnel and administration*

      (i)   Numbers employed by category
      (ii)   Overtime hours
      (iii)   Sickness, absence, lateness
      (iv)   Training requirements
      (v)   Career development plans
      (vi)   Recruitment policy
      (vii)   Job descriptions
      (viii)   Costs of maintenance
      (ix)   Postage costs

(d)   *Financial and management accounting*

      (i)   Annual statutory accounts
      (ii)   Budgets and forecasts
      (iii)   Sales and contribution analyses
      (iv)   Cash, management and working capital evaluation
      (v)   Capital project appraisal
      (vi)   Standard cost and variance analysis reports
      (vii)   Returns to government departments (eg. VAT)
      (viii)   Cash in hand
      (ix)   Bad debts
      (x)   Loans held

External sources are obviously extremely varied. A key distinction is between those generated by central government and those from other sources. Examples of the latter include the following:

(a)   *Trade/professional reports* – reports from trade and professional associations (eg. *CBI News*) on particular industries or groups of industries.

(b)   *Bank of England Quarterly Bulletin* – reports on financial and economic matters.

(c)   *Company reports* (usually annual) – information on performance and accounts of individual 7companies.

(d)   *Labour research* (monthly) – articles on industry, employment, trades unions and political parties.

(e)   *Financial Times* (daily) – share prices and information on business.

Statistics from central government include the following:

(a)   *The Government Statistical Service*

This comprises the statistics divisions of all the major government departments plus the two large collecting agencies, these being the Business Statistics Office and the Office of Population Censuses and Surveys. The service is co-ordinated by the Central Statistical Service and exists primarily to solve the needs of government. However, much of the information compiled is readily usable by business and other organisations. In recent years the service to business has been extended and booklets, such as *Profit from Facts*, have been published to encourage businesses to make more use of government statistics.

The service works in the following way. Each government department (eg. Trade, Industry, Employment, Environment and the Treasury) prepares and publishes its own statistics via Her Majesty's Stationery Offices. If any series of data from these departments is of sufficient interest it is usually included in more general publications like the *Monthly Digest of Statistics*. As mentioned earlier, the Government Statistical Service publishes an extensive range of statistical digests. To help find the publication most suitable to anyone's needs two useful guides are available. *Government Statistics – a brief guide to sources* lists all the main publications and departmental contact points. A more comprehensive list is available in *Guide to Official Statistics*. The following two paragraphs indicate some of the important general and specific digests produced.

(b)   *General digests*

(i)   *Monthly Digest of Statistics* – a collection of the main series of data from all government departments.

(ii)   *Annual Abstract of Statistics* – similar to *Monthly Digest* but containing more series and over longer periods of time.

(iii)   *Social Trends* – a collection of key social and demographic statistics, presentation using colour charts and tables.

(c)   *Specific digests*

(i)   *Economic Trends* – from the Central Statistical Office this provides a broad background to trends in the UK economy, presented via commentary, tables and charts.

(ii)   *British Business* – contains statistics and commentary from the Departments of Trade and Industry. The contents varies (weekly) but includes statistics on, for example, capital expenditure, investment intentions, industrial production, food, chemicals, engineering sales and orders, company liquidity, acquisitions and insolvencies, regional development grants.

(iii)   *National Income and Expenditure 'Blue Book'* – detailed estimates of the national accounts, including consumer expenditure; produced by the Central Statistical Office.

(iv)   *Overseas Trade Statistics of the UK* – gives detailed statistics of exports and imports; produced by the Department of Trade.

(v)   *Employment Gazette* – from the Department of Employment this includes articles, tables and charts on manpower, employment, unemployment, earnings, labour costs and stoppages due to disputes.

(vi) *New Earnings Survey* – again from the Department of Employment this contains statistics relating to earnings from employment by industry, occupation and region.

(vii) *Financial Statistics* – contains key financial and monetary statistics of the UK.

(viii) *Business Monitors* – this is a series of publications from the Business Statistics Office. A wide variety of statistics are produced, examples of which are:

MAZ Annual data relating to cinemas
MM1 Monthly data on road vehicles and new registrations
MQ5 Quarterly data on insurance companies and private pension funds
MA3 Annual analysis of the accounts of listed and unlisted companies
MM1 Monthly list of price indices for current cost accounting

Data from the Census of Production and the Census of Distribution are also included in the *Business Monitor* series, these being broken down giving different publications for each industry.

There are many ways of locating the range of information available: personal contacts, libraries, local chambers of commerce, for example.

The use of secondary data

Most of the above external information (and possibly some of the internal statistics) will be secondary data – that is, it was originally collected for a purpose other than that for which the company is now to use it.

We would naturally prefer to use primary data if this is possible since data collected for specific purposes is likely to be better. Some problems with secondary data are listed below:

- The data has been collected by someone else. We have no control over how it was collected. If a survey was used, was a suitable questionnaire used? Was a large enough sample taken (was enough data collected)? Was it a reputable organisation that carried out the data collection?

- Is the data up to date? Data quickly becomes out of date, for example, people's consumer tastes change and prices may fluctuate wildly.

- The data may be incomplete. Certain groups of people are sometimes omitted from the published data. For example, do you know which groups are included in the unemployment figures?

- Is the information actual, seasonally adjusted, estimated or a projection?

- The reason for collecting the data may be unknown. Statistics published on motor cars may include or exclude three wheeled cars, vans and motor caravans. We need to know which categories are included in the data.

If we are to make use of secondary data we need to have answers to these questions. Sometimes the answers will be published with the data itself or sometimes we may be able to contact the people who collected the data. If not, we must be aware of the limitations of making decisions based on information produced from secondary data.

TIME SERIES ANALYSIS

Introduction

The process of forecasting will inevitably involve some analysis of historic data (sales, costs, share prices etc.) in order that future values may be predicted.

The data may concern the economic market as a whole, the particular industry with which the organisation is involved (or wants to be) or the organisation itself.

Time series analysis takes such data and breaks it down into component parts that are easier to extrapolate (predict future values of). In particular, it will isolate the underlying trend which may, in fact, be all that is needed in long-term planning.

Definition

A time series is a set of values for some variable (eg. monthly production) which varies with time. The set of observations will be taken at specific times, usually at regular intervals. Example of figures which can be plotted as a time series are:

- monthly rainfall in London;
- daily closing price of a share on the Stock Exchange;
- weekly sales in a department store.

The following graph shows the volume of sales by month for a department store.

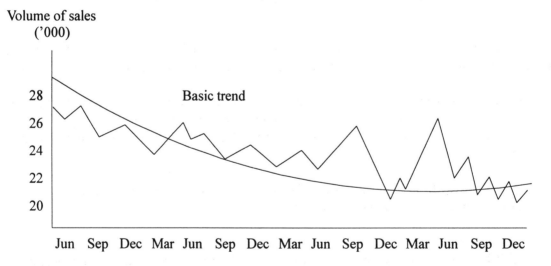

In such a graph each point is joined by a straight line hence the typically 'jagged' appearance. Don't try to draw a smooth curve which will pass through all the points on a time series graph. You will find it practically impossible and, in any case, it is incorrect to do so. The only reason for joining the points at all is to give a clearer picture of the pattern, which would be more difficult to interpret from a series of dots.

Characteristic movements

Analysis of time series has revealed certain characteristic movements or variations. These movements are the components of the time series. Analysis of these components is essential for forecasting purposes.

The four main types of components are:

- long-term movements or basic trends;
- cyclical movements;
- seasonal movements;
- irregular or random movements.

To illustrate these features, the figures below show the graphs of the components of a time series as they are built up into the graph of the complete time series.

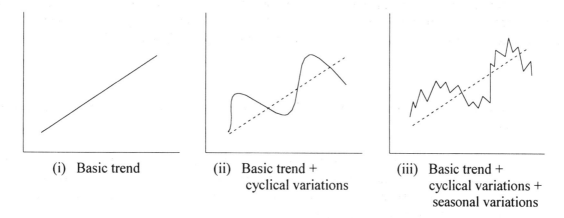

| (i) Basic trend | (ii) Basic trend + cyclical variations | (iii) Basic trend + cyclical variations + seasonal variations |

Basic trend

The basic trend refers to the general direction in which the graph of a time series goes over a long interval of time. This movement can be represented on the graph by a trend curve or line. Three of the most common basic trends are:

- parabolic trend;
- arithmetic trend (linear);
- compound interest trend.

Trend curves for these are illustrated below:

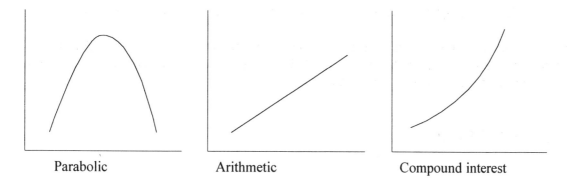

Parabolic Arithmetic Compound interest

Cyclical variations

Cyclical variations refer to long term oscillations or swings about the trend line or curve. These cycles may or may not be periodic; ie. they do not necessarily follow exactly similar patterns after equal intervals of time. In business and economic situations movements are said to be cyclical if they recur after time intervals of more than one year. A good example is the trade cycle, representing intervals of prosperity, recession, depression and recovery.

For cyclical variations to be apparent, data must be available over long periods of time since the periods of oscillation are so long. This is impractical for examination questions and for that reason the calculation of cyclical variations is ignored in this session although you must, of course, realise that they exist.

Seasonal variations

Seasonal fluctuations are the identical, or almost identical, patterns which a time series follows during corresponding intervals of successive periods. Such movements are due to recurring events such as the sudden increase in department store sales before Christmas. Although, in general, seasonal movements refer to a period of one year, this is not always the case and periods of hours, days, weeks, months etc. may also be considered depending on the type of data available.

Random variations

Random variations are the sporadic motions of time series due to chance events such as floods, strikes, elections etc.

By their very nature they are unpredictable and therefore cannot play a large part in any forecasting but it is possible to isolate the random variations by calculating all other types of variation and removing them from the time series data. It is important to extract any significant random variations from the data before using them for forecasting.

Analysis

The analysis of a time series consists of:

- breaking the series down into trend and seasonal variations;
- projecting each characteristic into the future;
- adding together all the individual projections to arrive at one forecast figure.

The analysis which follows concentrates on isolating only the basic trend and seasonal variations. As already stated, random movements are not usually included in analysis and, although cyclical movements may be treated in the same way as seasonal variations, they repeat over such long intervals of time that masses of historical data are required before the pattern becomes evident.

There are many methods of analysing time series, some sophisticated, others simple. The method considered here is known as the additive model. It is the best known and most commonly used although, admittedly, it is not the most sophisticated.

ISOLATING THE TREND

Introduction

You may have noticed that a trend curve was drawn in on the time series graph in the first graph in this session. Indeed one way of isolating the trend, admittedly not very scientific, is simply to draw it in freehand on the graph. Two other common methods are:

- using moving averages; and
- calculating the 'line of best fit' using regression analysis (for a linear trend).

We shall consider the first of these in more detail.

Moving averages

By using moving averages, the effect of any seasonal variation in a time series can be eliminated to show the underlying trend. This elimination process will only work if the moving average is calculated over the correct number of values (being the number of values in one complete cycle). For instance, if a seasonal variation present in a time series is repeated every fourth period, then moving averages with a cycle of 4 should be used.

This may become clearer as you follow through the simple example in the next section.

Illustration

The following time series (column A) shows a set of values which are clearly increasing; at first sight, however, this increase appears to be quite erratic. This is because the time series is in fact made up of two components:

(1)   An underlying trend (column B)

(2)   A seasonal variation which repeats every fourth value (column C)

Time series (A)	=	Arithmetic trend (B)	+	Seasonal variation (C)
3	=	1	+	2
5	=	2	+	3
5	=	3	+	3
5	=	4	+	1
7	=	5	+	2
9	=	6	+	3
9	=	7	+	2
9	=	8	+	1

To determine the underlying trend and seasonal variation within a time series, it is necessary to calculate a number of moving averages for various numbers of values as shown below:

Time series	2 values	Moving averages 3 values	4 values
3			
	4		
5		$4^{1}/_{3}$	
	5		$4^{1}/_{2}$
5		5	
	5		$5^{1}/_{2}$
5		$5^{2}/_{3}$	
	6		$6^{1}/_{2}$
7		7	
	8		$7^{1}/_{2}$
9		$8^{1}/_{3}$	
	9		$8^{1}/_{2}$
9		9	
	9		
9			

The moving average of each four values is the only one which captures the steadily increasing property of the original trend. It is therefore important to **examine** the figures before choosing which order moving average to use. [It will usually be fairly obvious which is the appropriate order in an assessment question due to the way in which the data are presented, eg. in 'quarters' (order 4) or days of working week (order 5).]

Centred averages

You should note the positioning of the moving averages in the above table. Each average has been written exactly opposite the middle of the figures from which it has been calculated. This results in the moving averages for *even* numbers of values being suspended halfway between two of the original figures.

Where this is the case, it is necessary to realign the moving averages so that they fall opposite the original values by calculating a moving average for every *two* values.

Original time series	Moving average (4 values)	Centred moving average Order 4
3		
5		
	$4^1/_2$	
5		5
	$5^1/_2$	
5		6
	$6^1/_2$	
7		7
	$7^1/_2$	
9		8
	$8^1/_2$	
9		9
	$9^1/_2$	
9		

As you can see by the centring process, we have now arrived back at the original trend (although with some data missing). In this case it was rather a circular computation but, since one of the main purposes of time series analysis questions is to identify the trend, it would not normally be known to start with! This illustration is to show that the technique does in fact give us the right answer.

Illustration – TS Ltd

The following data will be used to demonstrate the various techniques in the subsequent paragraphs.

	Quarter			
	1	2	3	4
Year 1	73	99	93	126
Year 2	81	114	108	148
Year 3	91	121	117	154
Year 4	106	131	135	175
Year 5	134	149		

First, the trend could be isolated by moving averages.

Note: An alternative method of finding the centred moving average is shown here. Instead of averaging the four quarter moving totals then taking the average of each adjacent pair as in the previous illustration the averaging is left to the end. The *totals* of each adjacent pair are shown in column (d) and this is then averaged by dividing by eight. Either method gives the same answer.

Year (a)	Qtr	Value (b)	4 quarter moving total (c)	8 quarter moving total (d)	Trend (T) (d)/8 (e)
1	1	73			
	2	99			
			391		
	3	93		790 $\div 8$ =	98.75
			399		
	4	126		813	101.625
			414		
2	1	81		843	105.375
			429		
	2	114		880	110
			451		
	3	108		912	114
			461		
	4	148		929	116.125
			468		
3	1	91		945	118.125
			477		
	2	121		960	120
			483		
	3	117		981	122.625
			498		
	4	154		1,006	125.75
			508		
4	1	106		1,034	129.25
			526		
	2	131		1,073	134.125
			547		
	3	135		1,122	140.25
			575		
	4	175		1,168	146
			593		
5	1	134			
	2	149			
	3				
	4				

Disadvantages of moving averages

- Values at the beginning and end of the series are lost – therefore the moving averages do not cover the complete period.

- The moving averages may generate cycles or other movements that were not present in the original data.

- The averages are strongly affected by extreme values. To overcome this a 'weighted' moving average is sometimes used giving the largest weights to central items and small weights to extreme values.

DETERMINING THE SEASONAL VARIATION – THE ADDITIVE MODEL

Introduction

Having isolated the trend we can consider how to deal with the seasonal variations. The additive model we will use expresses variations in absolute terms with above and below average figures designated by plus and minus signs.

The additive model

The four components of a time series (T = trend; S = seasonal variation; C = cyclic variation; R = random variation) are expressed as absolute values which are simply added together to produce the actual figures:

ie. Actual data (Time series) = T + S + C + R

For unsophisticated analysis over a relatively short period of time C and R are ignored. Random variations are ignored because they are unpredictable and would not normally exhibit any repetitive pattern, whereas cyclic variations (long-term oscillations) are ignored because their effect is negligible over short periods of time. The model therefore simplifies to

Actual data = T + S

The seasonal variation is therefore the difference between the computed trend figure and the original time series figure.

Illustration

Using the same data for TS Ltd from the list table produced in the answer, the seasonal variations can be extracted by subtracting each trend value (using the moving averages method) from its corresponding time series value:

Original time series (b)	*Underlying trend* (e)	*Seasonal variation (S)* (b – e)
93	98.75	–5.75
126	101.625	+24.375
81	105.375	–24.375
114	110	+4
108	114	–6
148	116.125	+31.875
91	118.125	–27.125
121	120	+1
117	122.625	–5.625
154	125.75	+28.25
106	129.25	–23.25
131	134.125	–3.125
135	140.25	–5.25
175	146	+29

Average seasonal variations

One of the purposes of extracting the seasonal variations is to enable forecasts to be made for future time periods. Looking at the result obtained above, we have a problem in deciding which variation to use.

Obviously, if we're making a prediction for a quarter 2 of a year in the future, we'll use a quarter 2 variation, but we have three of these in the above data, all different.

One way to get a representative seasonal variation, if no obvious pattern exists, is to average out the seasonal variations for each quarter:

| | *Quarter* | | | |
	1	*2*	*3*	*4*
Year 1	–	–	–5.75	+24.375
Year 2	–24.375	+4.00	–6.00	+31.875
Year 3	–27.125	+1.00	–5.625	+28.25
Year 4	–23.25	–3.125	–5.25	+29.00
Year 5	–	–	–	–
Sum	–74.75	+1.875	–22.625	+113.5
Average	–24.917	+0.625	–5.656	+28.375

Deseasonalisation of data

Having isolated the seasonal variations, we could now 'deseasonalise' the original data by removing these variations.

Not that, for example, quarter 1 has a generally *below* trend value (negative average seasonal variation) while quarter 4 is generally *above* trend. Thus in adjusting the original data to eliminate effects of seasonal variations, ('deseasonalising'), the quarter 1 data is *increased* by 24.917 whereas quarter 4 data is *reduced* by 28.375.

After data have been deseasonalised they still include trend, cyclical and random movements. The trend has already been found and can now be removed from the deseasonalised data to leave only cyclical and random movements (residual variations).

Year + Qtr		*Original data*	*Average seasonal variations*	*Deseasonalised data*	*Trend*	*Residual variations (cyclical & random)*
1	3	93	–5.656	98.656	98.75	–0.094
	4	126	+28.375	97.625	101.625	–4.0
2	1	81	–24.917	105.917	105.375	+0.542
	2	114	+0.625	113.375	110.0	+3.375
	3	108	–5.656	113.656	114.0	–0.344
	4	148	+28.375	119.625	116.125	+3.5
3	1	91	–24.917	115.917	118.125	–2.208
	2	121	+0.625	120.375	120.0	+0.375
	3	117	–5.656	122.656	122.625	+0.031
	4	154	+28.375	125.625	125.75	–0.125
4	1	106	–24.917	130.917	129.25	+1.667
	2	131	+0.625	130.375	134.125	–3.75
	3	135	–5.656	140.656	140.25	+0.406
	4	175	+28.375	146.625	146.0	+0.625

Forecasting a time series

At the beginning of this section, we noted that the analysis of a time series into its component parts would make extrapolation easier for forecasting future values for planning purposes.

In general, for short-term forecasts, only the trend and seasonal variations will be used; the cyclical variations will only have a significant effect over quite a long period of time and the random variations are, by their very nature, unpredictable.

Thus the approach to forecasting will be to

- project the trend to the appropriate future time
- adjust the projected trend value by the appropriate seasonal variation

We will use the analysis carried out for TS Ltd to illustrate the approach.

Projecting the trend

There is no unique method for projection of the underlying trend, as it will very much depend upon its particular shape (if, indeed, it has a discernible one).

In practice, computers will be of great help in producing various possible equations for the trend, which can be rapidly tested against the data available to determine which fits best. In the examination, you will need to use less sophisticated techniques.

If a linear trend has been isolated using a 'line of best fit' approach, then the equation of that line can easily be used to predict future values.

If the moving averages method has been used, a certain amount of judgement will be necessary. Possible approaches include the following:

- Plot the trend values on a graph and extrapolate by eye. (In fact, an initial sketch graph can be useful anyway to get a visual impression of the trend, before using one of the following methods to predict it.)

- Look at the increments between each trend value for any approximate pattern (eg. roughly equal, which makes the trend approximately linear or steadily increasing) and continue this pattern to the future time required.

- If the increments appear to vary randomly, an average increment for the period may be calculated and used in the forecast.

- If the pattern of the trend appears to change significantly over the period, you may restrict your prediction technique to later data values only, as being more representative of future values.

The trend values obtained by moving averages for TS Ltd (see page 217) have been plotted on a graph (unless specifically required, it is unlikely that you would have time to do this in an exam):

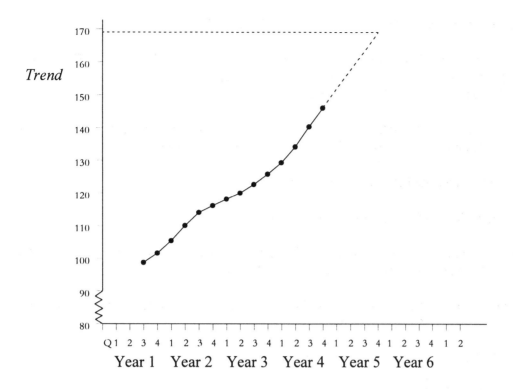

The graph shows an upward sloping trend, very approximately linear, but which shows an increase in gradient over the latter years.

Now suppose we wish to estimate a trend value for year 5, quarter 4.

If we were to use the graphical approach to extrapolation, it is perhaps best to extend linearly using the later, steeper gradient (although it should be noted that the earlier part of the curve shows that this may, in fact, revert to a shallower gradient). This is shown as a dotted line on the graph, and produces a result of approximately 169.

Now consider the increments (the differences between each successive pair of trend values). Note that you do not need to work these out exactly; they will just be used to detect any pattern or change.

From previous quarter to		Approximate
Year	Quarter	increment
1	4	2.9
2	1	3.8
	2	4.6
	3	4.0
	4	2.1
3	1	2.0
	2	1.9
	3	2.6
	4	3.1
4	1	3.5
	2	4.9
	3	6.1
	4	5.8

There is no clear pattern, so some average increment may be used.

The average increment over the whole period is $(146 - 98.75)/13 \cong 3.6$

Note: Divide by the number of increments, not values; we're averaging the 'gaps'. This would result in a forecast trend value for year 5, quarter 4 (which is four increments on from the last trend value) of 146 (the last trend value) $+ 4 \times 3.6 \cong 160$

If we confine ourselves to the latter values, say from year 3, quarter 4, the average increment is now $(146 - 125.75)/4 \cong 5.1$, giving a forecast trend value of $146 + 4 \times 5.1 \cong 166$

So we have a range of predictions between 160 and 169.

Adjusting trend prediction for seasonal variations

This is a lot more straightforward! We already have the average seasonal variations for each quarter (see page 218), the relevant one here being that for quarter 4: $+28.375$

This means that, on average, quarter 4 values are 28.375 above the trend value. Thus, seasonally-adjusted predictions for quarter 4, year 5 would be:

$160, 166$ or $169 + 28.375 = 188.375, 194.375$ or 197.375

depending upon which trend value were used.

In an examination, you should only make one prediction, justifying the approach used. There will rarely be one 'correct' way, so do not spend too long deciding how you are going to do it.

INDEX NUMBERS

Introduction

As part of the forecasting process, an organisation may make use of published indices that indicate the trend in economic/industrial factors, such as inflation.

An index number is a statistic used to reduce a series of data to some common level so that we can make comparisons of variations between items or groups of items. They are used to describe changes in prices, output, income, etc. and can be divided into three types:

- price index numbers, which measure changes in price;
- quantity index numbers, which measure changes in quantity;
- value index numbers, which measure changes in the value of services or activities or goods.

If an index number is constructed from figures for a single item it is known as a simple index or relative. If a combination of figures relating to a group of items is used then the index number is known as a complex index. Many indices are produced by Government departments. The most important in everyday life is the retail price index (RPI), which is used widely as a measure of inflation.

Base period

The base period is the time at which all comparisons are made. It may be a single date, a month or a year. The length of the base period usually depends on the interval at which the index number is to be calculated. The index number for the base period is given the value 100 and this might be allocated to:

(a)   a year – 19X5 = 100
(b)   a month – August 19X5 = 100
(c)   a single date – 16 August 19X5 = 100

For an index number to be a reasonable reflection of change, the base period should be chosen to be as normal a time as possible. It should be a time which is not too far in the past.

One item index numbers or relatives

If we have the price of an item recorded at different times, then an index number can be constructed to show changes in price.

Year	Cost of car service
19X0	£36.50
19X1	£39.20
19X2	£44.70
19X3	£51.40
19X4	£52.50

If we use 19X1 as base year it has index number = 100. The index number for 19X0 is calculated as:

$$\frac{36.50}{39.20} \times 100 = 93.1$$

Similarly, for 19X2 we calculate:

$$\frac{44.70}{39.20} \times 100 = 114.0$$

and if the other years' index numbers are calculated we have:

19X0	$\frac{36.50}{39.20}$	×	100	=	93.1
19X1				=	100.0
19X2	$\frac{44.70}{39.20}$	×	100	=	114.0
19X3	$\frac{51.40}{39.20}$	×	100	=	131.1
19X4	$\frac{52.50}{39.20}$	×	100	=	133.9

The figures obtained are often called **price relatives**. All the figures are calculated as percentages of the figure for 19X1 and so they show percentage changes from 19X1 (eg. the price for 19X3 is 31.1% higher than that in 19X1).

However, you cannot say the percentage rise from 19X3 to 19X4 is:

133.9 – 131.1 = 2.8%

It is in fact:

$$\frac{52.50}{51.40} \times 100 = 102.1$$

so a 2.1% increase. Using the index numbers we work out the ratio of the appropriate index numbers as:

$$\frac{133.9}{131.1} \times 100 = 102.1 \text{ (as before)}$$

The idea of a relative or single item index is not limited to prices. Suppose we know how many cars were serviced at a garage. Then, an index with base year 19X1 is calculated as:

Year	Number of cars serviced				Index number
19X0	2,138	$\frac{2,138}{2,210}$	$\times$	100 =	96.7
19X1	2,210				100.0
19X2	2,356	$\frac{2,356}{2,210}$	$\times$	100 =	106.6
19X3	2,199	$\frac{2,199}{2,210}$	$\times$	100 =	99.5
19X4	2,056	$\frac{2,056}{2,210}$	$\times$	100 =	93.0

This is called a **quantity index**.

Weighted index numbers

The more common situation is where we have several items which we want to combine into a single index number. Suppose a firm's production involves three raw materials, the unit costs of which are as follows:

	Costs (per kg) 19X3	Costs (per kg) 19X4
Steel	£2.00	£2.50
Plastics	£1.50	£1.50
Wood	£0.50	£0.60

To compare costs we would average these costs and then work out an index number comparing those average costs. This, however, does not take account of the quantities required of each raw material. If 3 kg of steel, 2 kg of plastic and 1 kg of wood are used, then a weighted index is found using the quantities as weightings. The formula for a weighted index is:

$$\text{Combined index number} = \frac{\text{Weighted average for given period}}{\text{Weighted average for base period}}$$

and the weighted average is calculated in the usual way as:

Weighted average $= \dfrac{\sum(\text{Weighting} \times \text{Cost})}{\sum \text{Weighting}}$ (where $\sum$ means 'the sum of')

The given period is the period for which we are trying to determine an index number. In this example, the cost index is (base year 19X3 = 100):

Raw material	w	19X3 costs	wx	19X4	wx
Steel	3	2.00	6.00	2.50	7.50
Plastics	2	1.50	3.00	1.50	3.00
Wood	1	0.50	0.50	0.60	0.60
	6		9.50		11.10

Weighted average (19X3) $= \dfrac{9.50}{6} = 1.5833$

Weighted average (19X4) $= \dfrac{11.10}{6} = 1.8500$

The index is then:

Cost index (19X3 = 100)

19X3 $=$ 100.0

19X4 $\dfrac{1.8500}{1.5833} \times 100 = 116.8$

Example

(a) Find an index number for 19X3 and 19X4 with 19X2 as base period for average pay using the figures in the table:

	Average pay (£)		
	19X2 £	19X3 £	19X4 £
Non-skilled	110	115	123
Semi-skilled	128	145	162
Skilled	150	162	180

There are 25 non-skilled, 15 semi-skilled and 10 skilled employees.

(b) What is the percentage rise in average pay from 19X2 to 19X3 and from 19X3 to 19X4?

Solution

(a)   We should use the numbers of employees as weights, so the calculations are:

	w	*Pay (19X2)*	*w × Pay*
		£	£
Non-skilled	25	110	2,750
Semi-skilled	15	128	1,920
Skilled	10	150	1,500
Total employees	50	Total pay	£6,170

19X2 weighted average pay per employee $= \dfrac{6{,}170}{50} = £123.40$

	w	*Pay (19X3)*	*w × Pay*
		£	£
Non-skilled	25	115	2,875
Semi-skilled	15	145	2,175
Skilled	10	162	1,620
Total employees	50	Total pay	£6,670

19X3 weighted average pay per employee $= \dfrac{6{,}670}{50} = £133.40$

	w	*Pay (19X4)*	*w × Pay*
		£	£
Non-skilled	25	123	3,075
Semi-skilled	15	162	2,430
Skilled	10	180	1,800
Total employees	50	Total pay	£7,305

19X4 weighted average pay per employee $= \dfrac{7{,}305}{50} = £146.10$

The index number is then (using 19X2 as base year $= 100$):

Year		*Index*
19X2		100.0
19X3	$\dfrac{133.4}{123.4} \times 100 =$	108.1
19X4	$\dfrac{146.1}{123.4} \times 100 =$	118.4

(b)   To find the percentage increase from 19X2, as it is base year, we simply take the difference in the index number value, For 19X3 then, it is:

% Rise from 19X2 to 19X3 = 108.1 – 100 = 8.1%

However, to find the change from 19X3 to 19X4, as 19X3 is not the base year, we work out the index number ratio and subtract 100, ie:

% Rise from 19X3 to 19X4 $= \dfrac{118.4}{108.1} \times 100 - 100 = 109.5 - 100 = 9.5\%$

Paasche and Laspeyre indexes

In the above examples, only one 'standard' set of weightings was given. Weighting (quantities) can potentially change from one year to the next. The Paasche and Laspeyre indices are two different approaches to this problem.

To illustrate the difference between the Paasche and Laspeyre indices, a simple example using prices and quantities will be used. The data supplied gives prices and quantities consumed by a typical household during the first week of January for 19X0 and 19Y6.

		19X0		19Y6	
Item	*Unit*	*Price*	*Quantity*	*Price*	*Quantity*
Bread	Loaf	12p	2	50p	4
Butter	lb	22p	1	80p	2½
Milk	Pint	4p	7	23p	18

To calculate the general price index, we must use weights to express the relative importance of the items in the index. For the purpose of illustration of the method, we may invent some weights: if one pound of butter is thought to be of exactly the same importance as three loaves of bread and ten pints of milk, then the following weighting system can be used:

Bread – 3   Butter – 1   Milk – 10

The price index will then be calculated as:

$\dfrac{\text{Total of weighted 19Y6 prices}}{\text{Total of weighted 19X0 prices}} \times 100\%$

Thus the price index for 19Y6 with 19X0 as base is:

$\dfrac{(50 \times 3)+(80 \times 1)+(23 \times 10)}{(12 \times 3)+(22 \times 1)+(4 \times 10)} = \dfrac{460}{98} \times 100 = 469\%$

(For most purposes, index numbers are written to the nearest whole number.)

Choice of weights

Should we use the quantities purchased in the *current* year or in the *base* year as the weights? In fact, either could be used they just produce different types of indices. If we use the *current* year quantities we will produce a **Paasche index**, if we use the *base* year quantities we will produce a **Laspeyre index**.

Paasche index

This index indicates how current period costs are related to the cost of buying *current* period quantities at *base* period *prices*. Thus the Paasche index for our example would be:

$$\frac{(50 \times 4) + (80 \times 2\frac{1}{2}) + (23 \times 18)}{(12 \times 4) + (22 \times 2\frac{1}{2}) + (4 \times 18)} = \frac{814}{175} \times 100 = 465\%$$

Laspeyre index

This index indicates how much the cost of buying *base* period quantities at current prices is, compared with base costs. Thus the Laspeyre index for our example would be:

$$\frac{(50 \times 2) + (80 \times 1) + (23 \times 7)}{(12 \times 2) + (22 \times 1) + (4 \times 7)} = \frac{341}{74} \times 100 = 461\%$$

Notice that the Laspeyre and Paasche indices give different results. This does not mean that either of them is wrong – simply that they are expressing the change in prices in slightly different ways.

Laspeyre and Paasche compared

Although both types of index may be used, there are advantages and disadvantages attached to each. Since advantages of one are automatically disadvantages of the other, the two types of index can be compared by listing the advantages of each.

(a)   *Laspeyre index – advantages*

The weights are taken from the base period figures and therefore the only new data to be collected each time a new index is to be produced, will be the new prices. The Paasche index requires new prices and weights each time, resulting in a larger data collection operation.

For the same reason as above, the Laspeyre index requires less re-calculation each time because the denominator remains constant (base period prices weighted according to base period quantities).

Again, because the weights remain constant for a Laspeyre index, it is very easy to make comparisons from year to year, whereas a Paasche index can only be compared with the base year because the weights (and hence the denominator) change for every index.

(b)   *Paasche index – advantages*

Paasche index is though to give a truer result in terms of current consumer patterns because it uses current period weightings. Also, there may be occasions when the quantities (weights) vary so markedly from year to year that it would be unrealistic to use a base year quantity over a number of years as in the Laspeyre index.

For the reasons outlined above, Laspeyre indices are much more common that Paasche indices.

Changing the base period

Index numbers regularly have their base periods changed in order to keep them current. Unfortunately this means that some values of an index number cannot be directly compared to other values of the same index number. Suppose we have an industrial production index worked out with 19W8 as base year to start with, then a change to 19X2 as base year:

Index of industrial production

	(19W8 = 100)	(19X2 = 100)
19W8	100.0	
19W9	105.6	
19X0	104.8	
19X1	103.1	
19X2	105.7	100.0
19X3		99.6
19X4		99.2

If we wish to compare 19W9 with 19X2 then this can be done directly using the index with base year 19W8 but if we wish to compare 19W9 to 19X3 we cannot do it directly. We must first convert the 19X2 base period figures (the second column) so that they have 19W8 as their base period. This conversion can only be done if the indices have an overlap period. Here, the overlap is 19X2. Take the index values with base period 19X2 and multiply them by the ratio of the index numbers for the overlap period.

Converting the 19X3 index to 19W8 base year gives:

$$99.6 \times \frac{105.7}{100} = 105.3$$

Similarly, the 19X4 index converted to 19W8 base year is:

$$99.2 \times \frac{105.7}{100} = 104.9$$

The combined list for the index is now:

Year	Index (19W8 = 100)
19W8	100.0
19W9	105.6
19X0	104.8
19X1	103.1
19X2	105.7
19X3	105.3
19X4	104.9

with base period 19W8. We can now compare 19W9 and 19X3 directly. The index has dropped from 105.6 to 105.3, ie. is at:

$$\frac{105.3}{105.6} \times 100 = 99.7\%$$

of its level in 19X3 that it was in 19W8, a drop of 0.3%.

Example

An index of savings is given as follows:

Year	Index of savings (19W6 = 100)	(19X1 = 100)
19W7	106.7	
19W8	113.9	
19W9	127.2	
19X0	136.7	
19X1	149.2	100.0
19X2		101.6
19X3		103.2
19X4		105.7

(a)   Change all the index values to base year 19W6.
(b)   Create a new set of index numbers for the first five years, using 19X0 as the base year.
(c)   What proportional change in savings occurred from 19X2 to 19X3?

Solution

(a)   To convert the 19X1 base figures to 19W6 base we must multiply by:

$$\frac{149.2}{100}$$

This gives an index as follows:

Year	Index (19W6 = 100)
19W7	106.7
19W8	113.9
19W9	127.2
19X0	136.7
19X1	149.2
19X2	$101.6 \times \dfrac{149.2}{100} = 151.6$
19X3	$103.2 \times \dfrac{149.2}{100} = 154.0$
19X4	$105.7 \times \dfrac{149.2}{100} = 157.7$

(b)   For the figures to have base year 19X0 we must multiply the 19W6 base figures by:

$$\frac{100}{136.7}$$

This gives the following:

Year	Index (19X0 = 100)
19W7	$106.7 \times \dfrac{100}{136.7} = 78.1$
19W8	$113.9 \times \dfrac{100}{136.7} = 83.3$
19W9	$127.2 \times \dfrac{100}{136.7} = 93.1$
19X0	$136.7 \times \dfrac{100}{136.7} = 100.0$
19X1	$149.2 \times \dfrac{100}{136.7} = 109.1$

(c)   The proportional rise from 19X2 to 19X3 was $\dfrac{103.2}{101.6} \times 100$ (using 19X1 base figures) – 100 = 1.6%. Any base can be used to give the same result. This is known as a *chain base index* giving the proportional changes from one year to the next.

Deflating a series using the retail price index (RPI)

If a series of figures is concerned with 'money' value and recorded through time then it will be affected by inflation and so changes can be misleading. To overcome this, 'real prices' or 'money value' are found by deflating the original series. This is effectively changing the money values to values at one point in time, the base time, and so making the figures directly comparable.

Suppose we have the following table of average weekly pay and the RPI, by year:

Year	Average weekly wage (£)	RPI
19X0	69.50	182.0
19X1	78.40	197.1
19X2	90.10	223.5
19X3	108.60	263.7
19X4	120.30	291.8

(Source: *Annual Abstracts of Statistics*)

The 'real' value of earnings in relation to 19X0 would be calculated as:

$$\text{Average wage for year} \times \frac{\text{RPI for } 19X0}{\text{RPI for year}}$$

For 19X1, this gives a deflated figure of:

$$78.40 \times \frac{182.0}{197.1} = 72.39$$

Similarly, for 19X2 the deflated figure is:

$$90.10 \times \frac{182.0}{223.5} = 73.37$$

For 19X3 the deflated figure is:

$$108.60 \times \frac{182.0}{263.7} = 74.95$$

and for 19X4 the deflated figure is:

$$120.30 \times \frac{182.0}{291.8} = 75.03$$

Bringing all this information together in one table, we have:

Year	Average weekly wage (£)	RPI	'Real' weekly wage (19X0)
19X0	69.50	182.0	69.50
19X1	78.40	197.1	72.39
19X2	90.10	223.5	73.37
19X3	108.60	263.7	74.95
19X4	120.30	291.8	75.03

Looking at the change from 19X0 to 19X4 we see the purchasing power of average wages has risen by:

$$\frac{75.03 - 69.50}{69.50} \times 100$$

$$= \frac{5.53}{69.50} \times 100 = 7.96\%$$

QUESTIONS

1   Time series example

Give an example of a time series and explain how the four characteristic movements would be caused in the example that you have chosen.

2 Distribution data

The following table shows capital expenditure by the distributive trades in £million.

	Quarter			
	1	*2*	*3*	*4*
Year 1	173	206	198	218
Year 2	216	223	219	221
Year 3	213	212	225	199

(a) Calculate the trend by the method of moving averages and chart both the original figures and the trend. (State trend values to the nearest £ million.)

(b) Consider the case for using the method of linear regression for deriving the trend for the above data.

3 Ships in time

The following data give the tonnage of shipping entered with cargoes at UK ports (in 100,000 tons).

	1st quarter	*2nd quarter*	*3rd quarter*	*4th quarter*
19X7	134	153	163	151
19X8	135	154	159	155
19X9	132	159	177	159

(a) Compute the seasonal variations (to the nearest 10,000 tons) and apply these as seasonal corrections to the 19X8 figures to deseasonalise them. What factors are now affecting the deseasonalised data?

(b) Forecast a value for 19Y0, quarter 3. Briefly justify the method you use for predicting the trend.

4 Your organisation   (AAT CA D94)

Your organisation is about to commence work on the preparation of the forthcoming year's annual budget.

As assistant management accountant, you have been asked to assist budget-holders and to respond to any queries which they may raise in the course of submitting their budget proposals.

Your organisation's sales analyst had made some progress in preparing the sales forecasts for year 5 when she unexpectedly needed to take a holiday for personal reasons.

She has left you the following memo:

MEMORANDUM

To: Assistant Management Accountant   Date: 12 December 19X4

From: Sales Analyst

Subject: Sales forecasts for year 5

In preparing the sales volume forecasts for year 5, I have got as far as establishing the following trend figures and average seasonal variations.

	Quarter 1 units	Quarter 2 units	Quarter 3 units	Quarter 4 units
Year 3 – Trend figures	3,270	3,313	3,358	3,407
Year 4 – Trend figures	3,452	3,496	3,541	3,587
Average seasonal variation	–50	+22	+60	–32

As a basis for extrapolating the trend line, I forecast that the trend will continue to increase in year 5 at the same average amount per quarter as during year 4.

Sorry to leave you with this unfinished job, but it should be possible to prepare an outline forecast for year 5 with this data.

Assessment tasks

(a)   Briefly explain what is meant by the following:

      (i)   seasonal variations;

      (ii)   extrapolating a trend line.

      Use the data from the memorandum to illustrate your explanations.

(b)   Prepare a forecast of sales volumes for each of the four quarters of year 5, based on the data contained in the analyst's memo.

5   Transport company   (AAT CA J94)

The company directors of a transport company are concerned by the increase in expenditure on fuel over the last few years. Fuel costs have increased although there were no changes in the number of vehicles and negligible changes in the number of miles driven each year.

The company accountant has gathered information on the fuel costs and has also established a price index for fuel as follows:

Year	Expenditure on fuel £	Fuel price index
1	18,000	100
2	19,292	106
3	21,468	120
4	23,010	128

Assessment task

Use the index numbers to express all fuel costs in terms of year 4 prices. All figures should be rounded to the nearest £.

Comment on the results you have obtained.

SUMMARY

This session has been looking at the following types of forecasting: *economic*, *environmental* and *organisation specific*.

You should be prepared to discuss the factors involved in, as well as the potential problems of, forecasting as part of the planning and control process.

Time series analysis and the use of index numbers help with the isolation of trends, although these still may not be easy to extrapolate into the future. Remember you are using historic data which will not reflect future economic and environmental changes.

Make sure you are able to carry out the basic calculations involved and can discuss the four characteristic components of a time series.

Budget preparation

OBJECTIVES

This session aims to cover the important aspects of budget preparation and use the following:

- the planning and administrative framework within which budgets are prepared

- identification of the limiting budget factors and subsequent preparation of functional and master budgets

The performance criteria addressed by this session are as follows:

- Forecasts are made available to operational departments in a clear, easily understood, format, with explanations of assumptions, projections and adjustments.

- Relevant data for projecting forecasts of income and expenditure are identified.

- Appropriate adjustments are made for changing price levels and seasonal trends.

- Forecasts take account of significant anticipated changes in circumstances which would affect the validity of the statistically derived calculations.

- Personnel who might contribute towards making realistic forecasts of trends are consulted.

- Draft budget proposals, agreed with budget-holders, are consistent with organisational objectives, realistic and potentially achievable.

- Annual budgets are broken down into periods in accordance with anticipated seasonal trends.

- Discussions with budget-holders are conducted in a manner which maintains goodwill.

- Budget figures are checked and reconciled on an ongoing basis.

THE APPROACH TO BUDGETARY CONTROL

David Otley, in the *Accountants' Digest on Behavioural aspects of budgeting*, suggested that 'Budgets are a means of attaining organisational control, ie. the achievement of organisational objectives'. Within this context, he then went on to consider the various functions which a budget may fulfil.

- **Authorisation**

    A budget may act as a formal authorisation to a manager to spend a given amount on specified activities. If this is applied to an operating budget, however, it must be appreciated that over-strict enforcement would not be in the best interests of the business.

- **Forecasting**

  Forecasting refers to the prediction of events over which little or no control is exercised. Some parts of all budgets are, therefore, based on forecasts. Budget figures may also be used by one part of an organisation to forecast the likely effect on it of the activities of other parts.

- **Planning**

  Planning is an attempt to shape the future by a conscious effort to influence those factors which are open to control.

- **Communication and co-ordination**

  Budgets communicate plans to managers responsible for carrying them out. They also ensure co-ordination between managers of sub-units so that each is aware of the others' requirements.

- **Motivation**

  Budgets are often intended to motivate managers to perform in line with organisational objectives. The problem in this area is that when budgets are made relevant and designed to act as motivational devices, the attitude of managers using them tends to be negative.

- **Evaluation**

  The performance of managers and organisational units is often evaluated by reference to budgetary standards as these are quite possibly the only quantitative reference points available. The way in which performance is evaluated will be a dominating influence on how a manager behaves in the future and is therefore worthy of separate consideration.

Prerequisites of budgetary control are the definition of objectives and the existence or creation of an organisational structure through which plans may be put into effect. In particular, forecasts on which budgets are based should be made available to operational departments in a clear, easily understood format with explanations of assumptions, projections and adjustments.

The objectives of the business will be defined in the long-term strategic plan and any short-term budget must be framed in such a way as to contribute towards the achievement of these objectives.

The budget, therefore, will incorporate its own short-term objectives, probably expressed in the form that a financial analyst would use when interpreting the final results. ie:

- rate of return on total capital employed
- net profit percentage (ie. net profit: sales)
- the asset turnover ratio (ie. sales: capital employed)
- rate of growth in sales value
- liquidity and asset management ratios supporting the above

THE ADMINISTRATION OF BUDGETARY CONTROL

Budget centres

The organisational structure through which control will be exercised over the achievement of the budget objectives must be based on manager responsibilities.

It is only when the functions to be carried out by each manager have been defined that it becomes possible to define:

- the output he should achieve;
- the resources he can justifiably employ; and
- the costs he is expected to control.

The particular segments of the business for which individuals are allocated budget responsibility are known as **budget centres**.

Some budget centre managers will be responsible for profitability, either profit in relation to output or profit in relation to capital employed under their control. These centres are known as **profit centres** or **investment centres**, depending upon the amount of autonomy given.

Issue of budget instructions

The information which must be available to enable budgets to be prepared by all managers on a consistent basis and in forms which facilitate consolidation into the master budget includes the following:

- The organisational structure of the business, setting out clearly the responsibilities of each manager and the limits of his authority.

- The classification and coding of the various items of income and expenditure to be covered by the budget.

- A statement of the period to be covered by the budget and of the shorter accounting periods into which it is to be subdivided (or 'phased') for purposes of control.

- Copies of the forms to be used in submitting budgets.

- Instructions on what is to be shown on the various forms, and the manner in which particular items are to be calculated. Examples of practical points to be clarified are:

  (i)   whether 'sales' are to be budgeted initially on the basis of order intake or of invoiced amounts;

  (ii)   when costs are expected to increase, whether uniform percentages for particular items are to be used;

  (iii) what rates of salary increase, if any, are to be budgeted by managers;

  (iv)   what types of cost are to be budgeted centrally and not included in departmental budgets.

- The timetable for the preparation of the budgets. In particular, draft budget proposals, presented in a clear and appropriate format, must be completed and submitted to management on schedule to allow the budget-setting process to proceed in a timely manner.

Instructions which are to be binding on all managers must clearly be issued on the authority of the managing director or chief executive; but somebody must be responsible for drafting them, explaining them when necessary, and ensuring that they are being complied with as the work of budgeting progresses. The term 'budget officer' may be used to describe this person; but his precise status will vary from company to company.

The budget officer

The term *budget officer* is used to describe a role which must be played by somebody in the organisation to get the budget processed to completion. This will involve the following duties:

- the issue of the budget instructions;

- the co-ordination of the budgets;

- checking and reconciling the budget figures on an ongoing basis;

- valuing and consolidating the various departmental budgets;

- the submission of the final company budget to the chief executive or the board.

After the budgets have been approved, he will continue the task of budgetary control.

In a large business all these activities may be brought together under a budget officer or 'controller' having equal or senior status to the chief accountant.

In the smaller company a chief accountant may be responsible directly to the managing director, and have under his control all the functions outlined above, including budgetary control.

To facilitate the budget-setting process, it is important that all discussions with budget-holders are conducted in a manner which maintains goodwill.

Co-ordination of budgets

In order that an acceptable master budget can be prepared, it is necessary to ensure that the various subsidiary budgets are co-ordinated. The most obvious example of this is the need to ensure that the quantities which the sales department are forecasting that they will sell are in line with the quantities which production are budgeting to produce.

Co-ordination of activities may be brought about in setting up a budget committee which can include the main function managers under the chairmanship of the chief executive or of the budget officer.

Approval of budgets

Budgets must be approved ultimately by the board of the company. The management accountant or MD will recommend approval by the board. Before doing so, however, he will need to be satisfied that all budgets have been properly co-ordinated and that the budgets are in line with the company's objectives.

To ensure that this is achieved, it is important to ensure from the outset that the draft budget proposals agreed with budget-holders are consistent with organisational objectives and are potentially achievable.

After being prepared, the individual draft budgets will therefore pass through the following stages before being finally approved by the board:

- approval in principle by the manager of the function to which the budget relates;

- examination by the budget controller who will ensure that the principles laid down for preparation of the budgets have been adhered to;

- consideration of the budget in the light of all the other budgets by the budget committee before it recommends to the managing director that the master budget should be submitted to the board for approval.

BUDGET PREPARATION

Limiting factors on budgets

The level of activity at which a business can operate will very seldom be unlimited. Limitations may be imposed, for example, by:

(a) market demand for its products or services;
(b) the number of skilled employees available;
(c) the availability of material supplies;
(d) the space available either as a working area or for the storage of goods; and
(e) the amount of cash or credit facilities available to finance the business.

Therefore, when a manager starts to prepare a budget he should review the elements in it and identify where *limiting factors* (or *governing factors*) exist.

They will not all be equally significant; but where one particular limitation is of major importance it may be necessary to budget for that item first and to construct the rest of the budget around it. This can happen not merely in one department but for the company as a whole, when the item concerned may be referred to as the *principal budget factor*.

Quite commonly, the rate of growth in sales is the principal budget factor and this would have to be forecast before any other budget plans were made.

It is essential to identify the principal budget factor and any other limiting factors at an early stage in the budgeting process so that management may consider whether:

- it is possible to overcome the limitation which they impose (eg. by finding new markets for sales or by obtaining alternative supplies or substitute raw materials); or

- the limitations imposed must be accepted and the business's budgets must be produced within those limitations.

Types of budget

Once the limiting factors have been ascertained the company can prepare the budgets. For a manufacturing company, these will typically comprise the following:

(a)	sales budgets	⎫
(b)	materials usage budgets	⎬ and other *functional* budgets
(c)	materials purchases budget	⎪
(d)	labour utilisation budget	⎭

(e)	forecast balance sheet	⎫ known as the *master budget*
(f)	budgeted profit and loss account	⎭

Budget preparation – a worked example

The following example illustrates the preparation of the functional budgets, starting with projected sales information, and shows how they combine to give a budgeted profit and loss account.

One of the most important points illustrated by this example is how the budgets are inter-related.

It is a simple example and you should be aware that in practice budgeting can be more than simply an arithmetical exercise. The practical problems are discussed after the following the example.

Example

There is a continuing demand for three sub-assemblies – A, B and C – made and sold by MW Ltd. Sales are in the ratios of A 1, B 2, C 4 and selling prices are A £215, B £250, C £300.

Each sub-assembly consists of a copper frame onto which are fixed the same components but in differing quantities as follows:

Sub-assembly	Frame	Component D	Component E	Component F
A	1	5	1	4
B	1	1	7	5
C	1	3	5	1
Buying-in costs, per unit	£20	£8	£5	£3

Operation times by labour for each sub-assembly are as follows:

Sub-assembly	Skilled hours	Unskilled hours
A	2	2
B	1½	2
C	1½	3

The skilled labour is paid £6 per hour and the unskilled £4.50 per hour. The skilled labour is located in a machining department and the unskilled labour in an assembly department. A five-day week of 37½ hours is worked and each accounting period is for four weeks.

Variable overhead per sub-assembly is A £5, B £4 and C £3.50.

At the end of the current year, stocks are expected to be as shown below but because interest rates have increased and the company utilises a bank overdraft for working capital purposes, it is planned to effect a 10% reduction in all finished sub-assemblies and bought-in stocks during period 1 of the forthcoming year.

Forecast stocks at current year-end:

	Sub-assembly		Copper frames	1,000
	A	300	Component D	4,000
	B	700	Component E	10,000
	C	1,600	Component F	4,000

Work-in-progress stocks are to be ignored.

Overhead for the forthcoming year is budgeted to be production £728,000, selling and distribution £364,000 and administration £338,000. These costs, all fixed, are expected to be incurred evenly throughout the year and are treated as period costs.

It is expected that a total of 45,500 sub-assemblies will be sold in the forthcoming year and that one-thirteenth of this will be sold in period 1.

Required

(a)   *Prepare budgets in respect of period 1 of the forthcoming year for:*

    (i)   *sales, in quantities and value*

    (ii)   *production, in quantities only*

    (iii)   *materials usage, in quantities*

    (iv)   *materials purchases, in quantities and value*

    (v)   *manpower budget (number of people needed in the machining department and the assembly department)*

(b)   *Prepare a detailed budgeted profit and loss account for period 1.*

Solution

(a)   **Functional budgets**

    (i)   *Sales budget*

Strictly, this is not a budget, but a forecast. Once sales quantities of each product have been estimated, production quantities can be budgeted, which in turn will dictate materials and labour requirements, etc.

The last paragraph tells us that the total expected sales for the period are:

45,500/13 = 3,500

The first paragraph states that the ratio in which this will be split between the three products is: 1:2:4, or 1/7:2/7:4/7. So individual sales quantities will be:

A: 1/7 × 3,500 =   500
B: 2/7 × 3,500 =   1,000
C: 4/7 × 3,500 =   2,000

The sales budget can now be prepared, using the price information in the first paragraph. A tabular/columnar format is advisable for all budgets, as it is a clear and efficient layout.

Product	A	B	C	Total
Quantity	500	1,000	2,000	3,500
Price	£215	£250	£300	
Sales value (£)	107,500	250,000	600,000	957,500

(ii) *Production budget*

This is the key budget. All production costs will be based upon the quantities to be produced within the period.

This will follow on from the budgeted sales quantities, but we need to take account of required changes in stock levels of finished goods. For example, if we want more stock at the end of the period than at the beginning, we will need to budget to produce more than we sell. The relationship is described as:

Production $=$ Sales $+$ Closing stock $-$ Opening stock
(finished goods) (finished goods)

Your budget should incorporate this structure for each product. The opening stocks are given to us under 'forecast stocks at current year-end' – here, we are concerned with finished goods stocks (ie. the sub-assemblies). Prior to these figures, we are told that the closing stock requirements are 90% of these levels. The resulting production budget can be drawn up as follows:

Product (units)	A	B	C
Sales [as in (i)]	500	1,000	2,000
Add: Closing stock (90% of opening)	270	630	1,440
Less: Opening stock (given in question)	(300)	(700)	(1,600)
Production	470	930	1,840

Note that in this case production quantities are lower than sales, as stocks are being reduced.

(iii) *Materials usage*

This shows the amounts of each type of material that will be used in the period. This will depend upon the quantities of each product to be produced (as in the production budget) and how much material is used within one unit of each type of product (given near the beginning of the question).

Materials usage $=$ Usage per unit $\times$ Units produced

Again, incorporate this information within your answer to give a clear explanation of where your figures come from:

Product	A	B	C	Total
Production	470	930	1,840	

Frames

Usage per unit	1	1	1	
Total usage	470	930	1,840	3,240

Component D

Usage per unit	5	1	3	
Total usage	2,350	930	5,520	8,800

Component E

Usage per unit	1	7	5	
Total usage	470	6,510	9,200	16,180

Component F

Usage per unit	4	5	1	
Total usage	1,880	4,650	1,840	8,370

(iv)   *Materials purchases*

This shows the amount of each type of material that will be bought in the period, along with the purchase costs.

This is linked with the materials usage budget, but again needs to take stock movements into account – this time, stocks of materials are relevant. Again, as stocks are to be reduced by 10%, the amounts of material purchased in the period will be less than the amounts used. The relationship is as follows:

Materials purchased =

Materials used in production	+	Closing stock (raw materials)	–	Opening stock (raw materials)

The budget will look very similar to that for production, except that it analyses by material type rather than product:

		Components		
Material (units)	*Frame*	*D*	*E*	*F*
Usage [(iii)]	3,240	8,800	16,180	8,370
Add: Closing stock (90% of opening)	900	3,600	9,000	3,600
Less: Opening stock (given)	(1,000)	(4,000)	(10,000)	(4,000)
Purchases (units)	3,140	8,400	15,180	7,970
Purchase cost	£20	£8	£5	£3
Purchases (£)	62,800	67,200	75,900	23,910

Total purchases = £229,810

(iv) *Manpower budget*

This will be based upon the information given concerning operation times. We will start by producing a 'labour utilisation budget' – very similar to the materials usage budget. In some questions, you may in fact be required to produce this budget in its own right.

Once the total hours needed in each department are known, we can use the information about hours per week and weeks per period to determine the number of employees needed.

	A	B	C
Units produced	470	930	1,840
Machining hours required/unit	2	1.5	1.5
∴ Machining hours required	940	1,395	2,760
Assembly hours required/unit	2	2	3
∴ Assembly hours required	940	1,860	5,520

Total machining hours required = 940 + 1,395 + 2,760 = 5,095 hours

This is in respect of a four-week period, in which each employee works 37½ hours, so the number of employees needed in the machining department is:

$$\frac{5,095}{4 \times 37.5} = 34 \text{ people}$$

Similarly, the total assembly hours required are as follows:

$$940 + 1,860 + 5,520 = 8,320 \text{ hours}$$

Number of employees needed in the assembly department is:

$$\frac{8,320}{4 \times 37.5} = 56 \text{ people (rounding up to the nearest person)}$$

(b) **Budgeted profit and loss account**

Most of the information for this can be taken from the budgets previously prepared. The additional information needed is as follows:

- opening and closing stock values (finished goods and raw material)
- labour cost [from the utilisation budget in (iv)]
- variable overhead cost
- production overheads and non-production costs (given in question for a year)

Finished goods valuation – standard cost cards

This requires the production of a 'standard cost card' for each product. We shall assume a marginal costing approach and that opening and closing stocks are valued at the same unit cost.

The information is all taken from the question, with the exception of the closing stock units, which can be taken from the production budget.

	Sub-assembly A £	Sub-assembly B £	Sub-assembly C £
Unit costs			
Frame	20	20	20
Components D (5 × £8, etc.)	40	8	24
Components E (1 × £5, etc.)	5	35	25
Components F (4 × £3, etc.)	12	15	3
Labour			
Skilled (2 × £6, etc.)	12	9	9
Unskilled (2 × £4.50, etc.)	9	9	13.5
Variable overhead	5	4	3.5
Total variable costs	103	100	98

Opening stock

Units	300	700	1,600
Value	£30,900	£70,000	£156,800

Total opening stock = £257,700

Closing stock

Units	270	630	1,440
Value	£27,810	£63,000	£141,120

Total closing stock = £231,930

Raw materials stocks – valuation

This is simply the stock levels (from question and materials purchases budget) multiplied by the buying-in costs (given in question).

		Components		
Material	Frame	D	E	F
Buying-in price	£20	£8	£5	£3

Opening stock

Units	1,000	4,000	10,000	4,000
Value	£20,000	£32,000	£50,000	£12,000

Total opening stock = £114,000

Closing stock

Units	900	3,600	9,000	3,600
Value	£18,000	£28,800	£45,000	£10,800

Total closing stock = £102,600

Labour costs

The utilisation budget in (iv) showed that 5,095 machining hours and 8,320 assembly hours were needed for the period's production.

The cost of these, using the rates given, will be

Machining (skilled):   5,095 × £6   = £30,570
Assembly (unskilled):   8,320 × £4.50 = £37,440

Total cost = £68,010

Variable overhead cost

This is given in the question as a unit cost for each product. The total cost will be the production levels multiplied by these unit costs:

Product	A	B	C	Total
Production	470	930	1,840	
Variable overhead rate	£5	£4	£3.50	
Cost (£)	2,350	3,720	6,440	£12,510

We can now draw up the profit and loss account:

Budgeted profit and loss account for Period 1

	£	£	£
Sales			957,500
Cost of sales			
Opening stocks – raw materials		114,000	
– finished goods		257,700	
		371,700	
Materials purchased		229,810	
Labour		68,010	
Variable overheads		12,510	
		682,030	
Closing stocks – raw materials	102,600		
– finished goods	231,930		
		(334,530)	
			(347,500)
Budgeted contribution			610,000
Fixed overheads			
Production (728,000 × 4/52)		56,000	
Selling and distribution (364,000 × 4/52)		28,000	
Administration (338,000 × 4/52)		26,000	
			(110,000)
Budgeted profit			500,000

Make sure you are quite clear where all the figures come from.

FUNCTIONAL BUDGETS – THE PRACTICAL ASPECTS

Sales budgets

The sales income budget is uniquely difficult to prepare because it involves forecasting the actions of people outside the business (the potential customers).

The extent to which sales forecasting is necessary will depend on the period covered by the outstanding order book and on the consistency of the conversion rate from enquiries to orders. If there is a well-filled order book for some months ahead then less reliance will need to be placed on forecasting techniques.

Forecasts may be made in a variety of ways. The method used will depend on the nature of the business and the amount of information available, but a generalised formal procedure might be as follows:

- Review past years' sales for whatever period is appropriate to the company's business cycle.

- Analyse the time series to identify seasonal, cyclical and random fluctuations.

- Extrapolate from past years' figures, assuming no changes in products or prices.

- Adjust the projection for proposed changes which are controllable by the company, such as price alterations, changes in marketing effort, the introduction of new products, and the discontinuance of existing products (the products' life cycles).

- Adjust for market changes due to external factors, such as government controls, action of competitors or social changes affecting demand. In particular, appropriate adjustments should be made for changing price levels or seasonal trends.

- Check that the resultant quantities are compatible with the quantities that can be purchased or produced.

- Check acceptability of forecast to sectional sales managers. In addition, other personnel who might contribute towards making realistic forecasts of trends should be consulted.

- Check consistency of forecast with long-term corporate plans.

The forecasting method outlined above depends on the existence of a 'time series' of figures from which extrapolation can be made and is mainly applicable to items in continuous demand. For other types of business, the sales forecast will be based on some form of market survey or on subjective estimates by people familiar with the market concerned.

Whichever forecasting method is used, the forecast should take account of significant anticipated changes in circumstances which would affect the validity of any statistically derived calculations.

Budgeting for costs

Budgeting for costs, in the same way as budgeting for sales, begins with physical facts. What physical facts they are will depend on the nature of the business; but every business will employ people, and most businesses will use materials of some kind. A manufacturing business will use tools and probably machinery. Floor space will be needed, also office equipment and perhaps motor vehicles.

All these requirements will be related in some way to the output of the business – its sales and any changes in stocks or work in progress.

In practice there are a wide range of different ways to budget for costs, for example:

- If standards for cost units are available, then there may be computer programs to identify the material and labour standards relative to a given output. It then remains for departmental managers to budget for material wastage or spoilage, labour efficiency and idle time.

- In a business carrying out long-term contracts, cost units (contracts) may be identical with cost centres (each contract having its own controller).

- In some businesses it may be sufficiently accurate for the budget for direct materials cost to be an extrapolation from past total figures, without any attempt at detailed justification or analysis.

Use of standards in budgeting

In Session 4, we looked at the methods of developing technical and cost standards. Budgeting will inevitably make use of these standards, as in the worked example above, and you should ensure you are familiar with the techniques and principles involved in their determination.

However, budgeting will generally extend beyond the simple multiplication of planned production levels by the standard usages and costs for each product for the following reasons:

- Different ranges of output levels will often lead to changes in unit variable costs (eg. materials discounts, learning effects, etc.).

- Some variable costs will not vary neatly with production and will need to be estimated for each particular activity level (eg. wastage, idle time, production set-up costs).

- Fixed costs are independent of production levels, although they may be stepped.

- A large proportion of a business's costs will not be directly involved in the production process (eg. administration, marketing, capital expenditure, etc.).

The following sections describe the common problems encountered in budgeting for the most common cost elements: labour, materials and overheads.

Budgeting for numbers and costs of employees

When budgeting for people to be employed, the starting point must be an assessment of the work to be done by people with various skills and this is equally necessary for manual, clerical and managerial activities.

Having defined what work is to be done, the establishment of budgets for the employment of people falls into two main stages:

- planning the number of people needed; and

- calculating the relevant costs.

In defining the productive workload for the budget year it will be necessary to balance the requirements of the sales budget against the productive capacity available. If there is excess capacity over the year as a whole then a decision will be needed whether to operate below full capacity or to use the excess capacity in building goods for stock or getting ahead with work in progress for the following year.

If the sales budget does not provide a steady workload month by month, then in phasing the budgets it may be decided to keep productive output constant and to balance out the short-term differences by fluctuations in work-in-progress or finished stockholdings.

The degree of precision possible in budgeting for numbers of people employed will depend on the type of work involved and the extent to which work measurement is possible.

Budgeting for the cost of materials

In most businesses a great variety of materials will be used. Considerable effort can be involved in preparing detailed budgets of quantities and purchase prices. Whether this effort is justified will depend on the significance of materials in relation to total costs, and the extent to which effective control can be exercised.

The starting point for materials budgeting is the quantity of material to be used during the budget year, whether in retail sales or in production or for indirect use.

Just as with the budgeting of labour hours, the form of the materials usage budget will depend on the nature of the business. Where repetitive operations are carried out it will be possible, and worth the effort, to set standards for the usage of the various items of material, and these standards can be associated with the production forecast to build up the total material requirements.

The purchase prices to be applied to the usage of the various items may be obtained from stock ledger records or recent purchase invoices, subject to adjustment for forecast price changes.

In budgeting for indirect materials (such as small tools, machine coolants and lubricants, fuel, cleaning materials and office stationery) the common practice is to budget merely for a total cost extrapolated from past experience. It will be important for control purposes, however, that the budget working papers contain as much detail as possible about anticipated usage, even though the individual items may not be evaluated separately.

Budgeting for other expenses

The nature of other expenses will depend on the type of business, but common categories are as follows:

(a)   premises charges;
(b)   costs of plant, motor vehicles and other fixed assets;
(c)   communication expenses;
(d)   travelling and entertaining;
(e)   insurances;
(f)   discretionary costs;
(g)   financial policy costs;
(h)   random costs.

For every type of revenue or cost it is highly desirable that a permanent budget record be prepared, giving the detailed calculations from which the budgeted amount has been derived. In particular, the data relevant to projecting forecasts of income and expenditure must be identified. This will not only impose a discipline on the budget preparation but will also:

●   facilitate the eventual explanation of any differences between budgeted and actual results; and

●   provide a starting point for budget revisions or for the preparation of budgets in future years.

The important features of such a record are:

●   details of the budget calculation;

●   comparison with the actual figures for the previous year; and

●   basis of variability, noting how the amount is related to such factors as levels of output or numbers of people employed.

Capital expenditure budget

The control of capital expenditure projects falls into five stages:

(a)   budgeting;
(b)   project authorisation;
(c)   implementation;
(d)   reporting and review; and
(e)   audit of results achieved.

All short-term operating budgets are in effect abstracts from a continuously developing long-term plan. This, however, is particularly true of the capital expenditure budget because the major items included in it will not be completed within the bounds of any one budget year.

The main purpose of the capital expenditure budget, therefore, is to provide a forecast of the amount of cash likely to be needed for investment projects during the year ahead. It also indicates what items of plant, equipment, vehicles and so on will be needed for the purpose of implementing the profit and loss (or operating) budget; and therefore it must be submitted for approval at an early stage in the budgeting timetable.

Any capital expenditure budget would include:

- a brief descriptive title for the project;
- the total required expenditure;
- an analysis of the costs over various time periods;
- where appropriate, expenditure to date on the project;
- estimates of future benefits from the project;
- investment appraisal calculations including details of assumptions made; and
- intangible benefits from the expenditure.

THE MASTER BUDGET

The master budget for approval by the board will take the form of a budgeted profit and loss account (as seen in the previous example) and a forecast balance sheet as at the year-end. These will be supported by such summaries of the various functional budgets as may be required, and by calculations of the key ratios which indicate conformity with the objectives for the year.

The syllabus for Unit 12 is largely concerned with budgets for income and expenditure and you do not need to be concerned with the detailed preparation of the master budget. The following provides an overview.

The forecast balance sheet

In arriving at the forecast balance sheet, it will be necessary to take account of the following:

- The capital expenditure budget
- Changes in stock levels and work in progress (as calculated in connection with the budgeting of material and labour costs). If work in progress and finished stocks are valued on a 'total cost' basis, then it will be necessary to calculate overhead recovery rates.
- Changes in debtor balances. Subject to any special delays in collection, the closing debtor balances will be calculated by applying the company's normal credit terms to the phased budget of sales.
- Changes in creditor balances. In theory, the closing creditors will be calculated by applying a normal credit period to the phased budgets of material purchases, subcontracted work and any other relevant items. In practice, it may be necessary to review the budgeted cash flow before finalising a decision on the credit to be taken.
- Changes in cash balance. Initially, the closing cash balance may be taken as the balancing figure on the balance sheet, but at some stage this should be validated by building up a cash budget itemised from the other budgets. This is discussed in the following section.

The cash budget

The purposes of the cash budget are as follows:

- To ensure that the various items of income and expenditure budgeted departmentally, and subject to the normal credit policy of the business, will result in cash flows which enable the company to pay its way at all times; in other words, to ensure that there is a practical plan.

- Where the cash flow over the year as a whole is satisfactory but there are intermediate periods of difficulty in financing operations, to give a basis from which the timing of particular items can be replanned.

- Where cash proves inadequate to finance the plan as originally envisaged, to give the financial controller an opportunity to seek sources of additional capital.

  (If the budget cannot be financed as it stands, then a revised budget will have to be prepared.)

- Like any other budget, to provide a basis for control during the forthcoming year.

(**Note:** The preparation of cash budgets is not within the scope of the syllabus for Unit 12.)

BUDGETING FOR CHANGES IN PRICES

Unless frequent budget revisions are to be made, it is essential to take account of anticipated significant changes in prices and costs when establishing budgets. If this is not done, particularly when the costs of the various revenue and capital expenditures are increasing at different rates, then the assumptions on which it is based and accepted may prove to have been completely wrong.

The methods of incorporating price changes into budgets may be considered under three alternative circumstances:

Specific price changes

Where specific changes in costs or in selling prices can be forecast with reasonable certainty, then they should be incorporated into the budget as from the forecast date of implementation, and the phased budget figure should be adjusted accordingly.

Examples in connection with payroll costs are awards payable in accordance with published scales such as 'birthday' increases payable to junior employees.

Uncertain price changes

Where the occurrence of cost changes is reasonably certain but the timing and amount are not, then the best possible estimate should be made and incorporated into the master budget. It may be undesirable, however, to include such estimates in the detailed budgets for departmental or product costs control since they will give rise to uncontrollable variances needing continued explanation.

Examples of changes of this nature are forecast wage claims negotiable with trade unions, and fluctuations in commodity prices.

General inflationary changes

Some of the effects of general price level changes may have been dealt with already as specific changes under the two preceding paragraphs, and no further adjustment would then be necessary.

For items of expenditure not dealt with in this way (particularly the cost of services), an estimated rate of inflationary increase should be prescribed by the budget controller and be included in the detailed budgets of the items concerned.

Probabilistic budgets

The adjustments outlined above result in the normal kind of budget with a particular set of sales, cost, volume and profit targets. Such budgets do not show any indication of the likelihood that the budget will be attained. From a planning perspective, management may wish to try and build into the budget an expression of the probability of certain things occurring, eg. a price change or a level of demand. Probabilistic budgets, as they are usually called, can be developed in three main ways, which vary as regards degree of sophistication:

(a)   Three different budgets are prepared reflecting pessimistic, most likely and optimistic results. The pessimistic budgets will combine together the less favourable assumptions about all the budgeted variables. Although relatively crude, such an approach does make managers consider risk explicitly, and avoids the need to assign definite probabilities to the estimates.

For example, suppose the sales levels and fixed overhead costs for a budget are particularly subject to uncertainty. The three estimates have been made for these and can be combined into the three levels of budget:

		Pessimistic	Most likely	Optimistic
Sales	– Volume (units)	10,000	16,000	20,000
	– Selling price	20	20	20
		£	£	£
	– Value	200,000	320,000	400,000
Variable costs (@ £10 per unit)		(100,000)	(160,000)	(200,000)
Contribution (@ £10 per unit)		100,000	160,000	200,000
Fixed overheads		(120,000)	(100,000)	(90,000)
Profit/(loss)		(20,000)	60,000	110,000

(b)   Alternatively, three estimates of each budget variable (or a single limiting factor if this was felt sufficient), can be made, and definitive probabilities assigned to each estimate. The joint probabilities of different levels of profit can then be calculated. This is obviously a more complex exercise than (a), but perhaps imposes a greater discipline on management thinking. Expected profit can be calculated from the various profits and their probabilities.

Using the example in (a) above, suppose the three sales levels (and thus contributions) and fixed overhead costs are assigned probabilities:

Sales levels (units)	Contribution (£)	Probability	Overheads	Probability
10,000	100,000	0.25	120,000	0.4
16,000	160,000	0.50	100,000	0.5
20,000	200,000	0.25	90,000	0.1

As before, the results will vary between a loss of £20,000 and a profit of £110,000 but these and many other possible results can now be assigned probabilities. The following table shows just some of the figures:

Sales level (units)	Contribution (£)	Overheads (£)	Profit/(loss)	Probability		
10,000	100,000	120,000	(20,000)	0.25 × 0.4	=	0.1
10,000	100,000	100,000	–	0.25 × 0.5	=	0.125
16,000	160,000	100,000	60,000	0.5 × 0.5	=	0.25
16,000	160,000	90,000	70,000	0.5 × 0.1	=	0.05
20,000	200,000	100,000	100,000	0.25 × 0.5	=	0.125
20,000	200,000	90,000	110,000	0.25 × 0.1	=	0.025
						1.000

This analysis can be used to ascertain the probability of profit reaching particular targets. For example, the probability of not exceeding break-even:

$$= \quad \text{Probability of £20,000 loss or £Nil profit}$$
$$= \quad 0.1 + 0.125 = 0.225$$

The expected profit can be obtained by calculating expected contribution and subtracting expected overheads:

		£'000
Expected contribution (£'000)	100 × 0.25 + 160 × 0.5 + 200 × 0.25	155
Expected overheads (£'000)	120 × 0.4 + 100 × 0.5 + 90 × 0.1	(107)
Expected profit		48

(c)   The approach explained in (b) can be applied by developing a computer simulation of the expected budgeted profit. Rather than carrying out the restricted numerical analysis in (b), a random sampling program is employed to facilitate the calculation of profit and associated joint probability. The results are shown as a probability distribution for profit.

QUESTIONS

1   Your organisation   **(AAT CA D94)**

Your organisation is about to commence work on the preparation of the forthcoming year's annual budget.

As assistant management accountant, you have been asked to assist budget-holders and to respond to any queries which they may raise in the course of submitting their budget proposals.

The following notes are extracts taken from your organisation's budget manual:

'The key or principal budget factor in our organisation's budgetary process is sales volume …. The need for co-ordination in the budgetary process is paramount….'

The marketing manager is a budget holder and she has approached you with a number of queries concerning the above extract.

Assessment task

Prepare a memo for the marketing manager, which provides brief answers to the following queries.

(a)   What is meant by the term *key factor* and why is the determination of this factor so important in the budgetary process?

(b)   How can co-ordination be achieved?

2   Master budget

A master budget is created by the integration of many individual budgets.

(a)   Outline what preliminary steps are necessary, before the preparation of budgets is commenced.

(b)   Detail the main budgets you would normally expect to find in a manufacturing business.

(c)   Give reasons why managers may be reluctant to participate in setting budgets.

3   Tiger plc

The managing director of Tiger plc is concerned that his company is not trading efficiently and is therefore losing profits. The company currently has no formal budgeting procedures. The financial accountant and production manager have produced the following information for the first six months of 19X5:

(1)   *Sales*

The company has one product, the CAT. Sales are seasonal with sales in the months of March, April and May being twice the amount sold in other months of the year. Tiger plc expects to sell 45,000 CATs in the first half of 19X5.

The current selling price is £25 per unit; there will be a price increase of 20% in April 19X5.

(2)   *Production*

Each CAT uses 10 kg of raw materials. Tiger plc has a contract with the raw material supplier for monthly deliveries at a fixed price of £60 per 100 kg. This contract expires at the end of April 19X5, when it is expected that the price will be increased by 25%.

Tiger has two categories of labour. Each CAT requires one hour's work by a skilled employee and two hours' work by an unskilled employee. The current wage rates are £5 per hour for skilled workers and £3 per hour for the unskilled.

Production overheads are estimated to be £5 per CAT.

(3)   *Stocks*

To keep the production line running smoothly, it is necessary for Tiger plc to hold enough raw material stocks to meet 80% of the following month's production quota.

To satisfy customer demand, the company holds enough stocks of finished goods to meet 50% of the next month's sales.

Expected stock levels:

	1 January 19X5	*30 June 19X5*
Raw materials	40,000 kg	40,000 kg
Finished goods	2,500 units	2,500 units

Stocks of finished goods are valued at full production cost.

Required

(a)   Prepare the following functional budgets for the six-monthly period to 30 June 19X5 for:

     (i)   material usage (in kg only)

     (ii)   material purchases (in kg and £)

     (iii)   labour utilisation, skilled and unskilled (in hours and £)

(b)   Prepare a budgeted profit and loss account for the six months to 30 June 19X5.

(c)   Write notes for a meeting with the managing director where you will have to explain why Tiger plc should introduce a budgeting system.

SUMMARY

This session contains the detail of how budgets are administered and prepared.

The budget must be prepared in a logical and orderly manner, ensuring co-ordination and co-operation between departments and different levels of management. Final proposals must be fully understood and accepted by all involved via a clear set of instructions and detailed discussions where necessary.

You should be prepared to discuss the types of budgets that may be required for a particular business and how they might be prepared, probably with numerical illustrations.

Budgetary control and responsibility accounting

OBJECTIVES

This session looks at the ways in which budgets may be used to monitor performance of both the business itself and the people who are responsible for its management. It covers the following:

■ use of budgets in controlling the business, by identification and investigation of variances via a management reporting system

■ how budgets and variances are used within a responsibility accounting system

The performance criteria addressed by this session are as follows:

■ Standard cost reports with variances clearly identified are presented in an intelligible form.

■ Variances are clearly identified and reported to management in routine reports.

■ Budget figures are checked and reconciled on an ongoing basis.

■ Significant actual requested or potential over-/under-spends are discussed with managers and assistance given in taking remedial action.

■ Cost estimates are monitored and checked against actual costs incurred and significant discrepancies investigated.

CONTROL AGAINST BUDGETS

Introduction

In order that management control may be exercised, the actual results of the business will be reported period by period to the managers responsible and will be compared with the budgeted allowance. Any discrepancies will be investigated and action will be taken either to modify the budget in line with current conditions or (in most cases more desirable) to adjust future performance so that the discrepancies will be eliminated in the longer run.

These deviations, in money value, between an item and the corresponding budget are variances, the computation of which have been covered in Session 4.

Feedback

The reporting of actual results and of variances from plan is sometimes referred to as the feedback arising from the budgetary control system.

Feedback is the process of continuous self-adjustment of a system. It requires some predetermined standards against which to compare actual results. Any differences between the actual results and standard targets which are outside tolerance limits will indicate the need for action to be taken in an attempt to bring about consistency between actual and target.

Feedback is therefore a fundamental part of any system of control including financial control systems such as budgetary control.

Timing of feedback

Ideally feedback should take place with as little delay as possible from the occurrence of the event it reports. If there is undue delay then, in the intervening period, the underlying position itself may alter; there is then the danger that action correctly taken, given the information contained in the feedback report, will not be the action required by the position then existing.

It is possible that delay in feedback may increase, rather than reduce, deviations from target.

Analysis of variances

The identification of variance from budget is only the first step in exercising control. So that effective action can be taken it will be necessary to identify:

- *who* was responsible for its occurrence – analysis by responsibility;
- *why* the variance has arisen – analysis by cause.

Analysis of variances by responsibility

With a well-designed budgetary control system the analysis of variances by responsibility is simple because the organisation will have been subdivided into budget centres which represent areas of responsibility (hence also known as *responsibility centres*) and separate operating statements will be prepared for each. For this to operate effectively, an integral part of the budgeting process will be to ensure that actual cost and revenue data are correctly coded and allocated to responsibility centres.

The general title for such a system is *responsibility accounting*; that is, a system which recognises various decision centres within a business and traces the results of those decisions to the individual managers who are primarily responsible for making them.

Analysis of variances by cause

In dealing with the analysis of variances by cause (whether sales variances or cost variances) one will be dealing always with two aspects:

- a physical aspect – quantities of products sold, or material used or hours worked, for example; and

- a pricing aspect – the selling price per unit in the case of sales; the cost price per unit in the case of materials, labour and other expenses. (The cost of labour is, of course, the rate of pay.)

In some cases, it may not be possible to identify quantity changes without more effort than would be justified by any improvement in control, but in these cases it must be recognised that this weakness does exist in the control being exercised.

FLEXIBLE BUDGETARY CONTROL

In connection with expense budgeting, the budget working sheets should include some indication of the 'basis of variability' of each item of cost.

The most common general bases of variability of costs are the volume of productive output or of sales. In some systems of budgetary control, therefore, costs are divided between those which tend to vary with the output or sales achieved, and those which tend to remain fixed regardless of the volume of output over an expected range of volumes.

This distinction having been established then, for variable costs, it is possible to establish in any period an allowable level of cost appropriate to the output actually achieved. This new level is known as the *budget allowance* for that volume of output. The total variance from the original budget figure will then be divided into two parts:

- The difference between the *original budget* and the *budget allowance*, assumed to arise from the nature of the business. This is sometimes referred to as an 'activity variance' and may be excluded from sectional control reports.

- The difference between the *budget allowance* and the *actual cost incurred*. This, by definition, should not have occurred and might be thought of as the variance which is 'controllable' by the manager concerned.

A system incorporating budget allowances is referred to as *flexible budgetary control*.

This idea has been seized on by writers of textbooks and setters of examination questions and converted into the concept of 'flexible budgets'; in other words, at the beginning of the year there should be set out in the form of a schedule what the various cost allowances would be at various levels of output. With spreadsheet packages being used to assist budgeting, it is now becoming more common in practice.

Example

The following is typical of an examination question on this topic:

You are the budget officer of Majestic Ltd, which produces a single product. The following forecasts have been prepared from the best information available for the production costs to be incurred at the highest and lowest production levels likely to be encountered in any particular period.

	Production level	
	10,000 units	*20,000 units*
	£	*£*
Direct materials	*2,000*	*4,000*
Direct labour	*15,000*	*30,000*
Warehouse rental	*8,000*	*13,000*
Machine maintenance	*2,400*	*3,000*
Factory rent, rates, etc.	*4,000*	*4,000*
Factory power	*4,500*	*6,300*

Machine maintenance is under contract with the machine supplier. The period cost is based upon the production level and is charged at £15 per 100 units, with a minimum charge payable of £2,400 per period.

Warehouse rent is fixed per warehouse per period. One warehouse is sufficient to cope with the storage demands up to 12,500 units. Should production exceed this level, a further warehouse will need to be rented for the period, at an additional cost of £5,000. This will give sufficient space to cover the highest production level.

All other variable costs and the variable part of semi-variable costs follow constant linear patterns.

Required

Prepare a set of flexible budgets which show the budget allowance for the period for the following activity levels: 10,000 units; 12,500 units; 15,000 units; 17,500 units; 20,000 units.

Solution

The following steps illustrate a good 'exam technique' approach to such a question. You may like to try preparing your own answer as we go through before looking at our solution at the end.

(1) **Draw up a pro forma statement.**

This will have the cost headings listed down the left-hand side and columns headed up with each production level; in this case, five columns will be needed. It is also a good idea to have an additional column next to the cost headings in which to insert references to workings (eg. 'Note 2' etc.).

The statement should also have a heading.

(2) **Insert known figures.**

You have already been given the costs for the lowest and highest production levels, so put these in.

(3) **Deal with the particular costs you have further information about** (in this case, machine maintenance and warehouse rental).

Machine maintenance

This cost will be fixed up to a certain production level (to cover the minimum charge) and will then rise linearly (at £15 per 100 units or £0.15 per unit).

The level up to which the minimum charge is applicable is £2,400/£0.15 = 16,000 units. So the charge for the 12,500 and 15,000 unit levels will also be £2,400.

For 17,500 units the charge will be 17,500 × £0.15 = £2,625 and for 20,000 units it will reach 20,000 × £0.15 = £3,000 (as given)

These can now be inserted in your statement.

Warehouse rental

This is an example of a 'stepped' fixed cost. It will remain at £8,000 for all levels up to (and including) 12,500 units, and will rise to £13,000 for all levels above this.

These can now be inserted in your statement.

(4)   **Deal with remaining costs.**

These will be strictly fixed, strictly variable or semi-variable.

Strictly fixed costs

These will be obvious – here, factory rent and rates must be fixed within the range, as the costs for the lowest and highest production levels are the same.

Insert this fixed cost across all levels on your statement.

Strictly variable costs

Invariably, direct materials and direct labour costs will be strictly variable. You can see here that, as the production level doubles, so does the cost. Use either level to determine the cost per unit:

Direct materials: £2,000/10,000   =   £0.20 per unit
Direct labour: £15,000/10,000 =   £1.50 per unit

Use these to calculate the appropriate cost for the other levels and insert them on the statement.

Semi-variable costs

These costs will not be the same for the two extreme levels, but they will not increase proportionately from one to the other either. If you are not sure, calculate a cost per unit at the two levels; these will not be the same, as they would be if the cost were strictly variable.

In this example, the power cost is semi-variable. It can be split between the fixed and variable elements by the 'high-low' method:

	Production level (units)	Cost (£)
Highest	20,000	6,300
Lowest	10,000	4,500
Change	+10,000	+1,800

Variable cost = £1,800/10,000 = £0.18 per unit

Using the lowest level to determine the fixed cost element:

	£
Total cost	4,500
Less: Variable element (10,000 × £0.18)	(1,800)
Fixed element	2,700

So for each level, the total power cost can be calculated as:

£2,700 + £0.18 × Production level

For example, the cost for 15,000 units will be:

£2,700 + £0.18 × 15,000 = £5,400

The remaining costs can be calculated in this way and the statement completed, as below:

	Production level				
	10,000 units £	*12,500 units £*	*15,000 units £*	*17,500 units £*	*20,000 units £*
Direct materials	2,000	2,500	3,000	3,500	4,000
Direct labour	15,000	18,750	22,500	26,250	30,000
Warehouse rental	8,000	8,000	13,000	13,000	13,000
Machine maintenance	2,400	2,400	2,400	2,625	3,000
Factory rent, rates	4,000	4,000	4,000	4,000	4,000
Factory power	4,500	4,950	5,400	5,850	6,300
Total	35,900	40,600	50,300	55,225	60,300

Budgetary control statement

A typical continuation to the above example would be the requirement to produce a budgetary control statement (or budget report) given some actual data for the period.

Consider the following information:

In period 3, Majestic Ltd produced 17,500 units and incurred the following costs:

	£
Direct materials	3,200
Direct labour	29,750
Warehouse rental	13,000
Machine maintenance	3,150
Factory rent, rates, etc.	3,800
Factory power	4,720

The budgetary control statement will compare these costs with the relevant budget allowances from the flexible budget to highlight variances. In this case, the relevant budget is that for 17,500 units.

	Budget £	Actual £	Variance £
Direct materials	3,500	3,200	300 F
Direct labour	26,250	29,750	3,500 A
Warehouse rental	13,000	13,000	–
Machine maintenance	2,625	3,150	525 A
Factory rent, rates, etc.	4,000	3,800	200 F
Factory power	5,850	4,720	1,130 F
	55,225	57,620	2,395 A

You may then be asked to comment on the variances, suggesting any further investigations or action that might be required.

ZERO-BASED BUDGETING (ZBB)

ZBB is a cost justification technique first developed by Texas Instruments, which is of particular use in controlling the costs of service departments and overheads. It does not simply look at last year's budget and add or subtract a little, but starts 'from scratch' each time a budget is prepared. It is particularly applicable for service cost centres, for non-product costs.

ZBB involves:

- developing **decision packages** for each company activity;

- **evaluating and ranking** theses packages; and

- **allocating resources** to the various activities accordingly.

Decision packages include the following information:

> The function of the activity or department. This sets out the minimum goals that it must achieve.

- The goal of the department. This details the aim of the department – what it would like to achieve.

- The measure of the performance of the department.

- The costs and benefits associated with different ways of organising the department (at different levels of funding).

- The consequence of non-performance of the activity or department.

Advantages of ZBB

- It establishes minimum requirements for service departments; ranks departments; and allocates resources.

- It produces a plan to work to when more resources are available.

- It makes managers think about what they are doing.

- It can be done annually, quarterly, or when crises are envisaged.

Disadvantages of ZBB

- It takes up a good deal of management time and so may not be used every year.

- It generates a great deal of paper, requires education and training, and results may be initially disappointing.

- It is costly.

Most budgets are prepared on an incremental basis. In other words, based on last time's figures plus/minus an incremental amount to cover inflation, etc. However, this technique has the obvious disadvantage of perpetuating poor spending control. As an alternative zero-based or priority-based budgeting may be employed.

USE OF BUDGET INFORMATION TO CONTROL AND MOTIVATE

In addition to asking you to analyse and explain variances, examination questions frequently require a discussion on whether the budgeting procedures used within an organisation are likely to achieve their aims.

These aims, and the methods used to achieve them, can be broadly categorised as follows:

- Efficient management – Management by exception

- Motivation of workforce – Responsibility accounting

Management by exception

The features of this method of reporting are that:

(a)   attention is drawn only to areas where operations are seen to be 'out of control';

(b)   this may be achieved by identifying those variances that are deemed to be 'exceptional';

(c)   only these variances will be investigated and (where possible) corrected; and

(d)   management time and expertise are utilised where it can be most effective in improving the efficiency of future operations.

In order that this method is effective, it is important that:

- exceptional variances are correctly isolated;

- only such variances owing to factors capable of correction be considered for investigation; and

- costs and benefits of investigation are assessed.

Session 5 has covered the investigation of variances in greater depth.

Responsibility accounting

The aim of a responsibility accounting system is to motivate management at all levels to work towards the company's objectives with the minimum of direction.

This involves:

(a)   the use of budgets as 'targets' against which management performance can be measured; and

(b)   the presentation of 'performance reports' relating to particular responsibility centres – these centres fall into three categories:

        (i)   **cost centre** where a manager is held responsible for control of expenditure;

        (ii)   **profit centre** where a manager is held responsible for control of sales revenue and expenditure;

        (iii)   **investment centre** where a manager is held responsible for investment decisions as well as the control of sales revenue and expenditure;

(c)   the requirement that the person deemed responsible for that area give explanations of significant variances shown therein.

Examination questions on this subject tend to concentrate on a practical application of the principles necessary for a system of responsibility accounting to work effectively, and often require the preparation of a draft performance report, or the criticism of such a report. An in-depth theoretical knowledge of the work carried out in this field is not needed; a common-sense approach to a practical problem suffices.

After summarising the main points, the common-sense approach is used to answer a typical examination-type question. You do not need to learn the names of the academics who have contributed to the subject, but it is important that you understand the relevance of what they said about the use of targets and performance reports in practice.

Three main areas need to be examined in relation to the use of budgets in responsibility accounting:

(a)   participation in budget setting;
(b)   budgets as motivational targets; and
(c)   performance evaluation.

The conclusions under each of these headings are largely common sense – you should try to think up practical examples in relation to your own position in study or at work to help you remember them.

Participation

- Most academics agree that worker participation in setting budgets greatly improves commitment to and achievement of targets.

- The extent to which participation enhances the quality of the budgets which are ultimately set, depends upon the market or technological conditions in which the business is working. The more uncertainty involved, the greater the benefit to be obtained from allowing information to flow vertically as well as horizontally.

Research into the effects of participation

Bass and Leavitt demonstrated the importance of involving managers in planning and budgeting. Groups of three managers developed a plan for themselves and then exchanged plans with another group. Each group, therefore, had two plans, one self-developed and the other created for them. In the subsequent implementation of the plans, half of each group operated their own plan first, and half operated their own plan second. The results indicated that managers experienced a greater sense of accomplishment when they were implementing their own plans, and were also more committed to making them work. In addition to this, after formulating the plans they had a greater understanding of their requirements and difficulties, and as a result there were fewer communication problems and fewer consequent errors in following instructions.

Coch and French investigated the effects of workers' participation in the implementation of plans. They studied four groups of workers who underwent comparable changes in their work methods. In one group, the change in work methods was introduced in the normal way: workers were simply informed of the change. The other three groups were given an opportunity to participate in deciding some aspects of the change. In group 1, they were permitted to influence the change through representatives and in groups 2 and 3 they were allowed to influence directly the nature of the change. It was found that groups 2 and 3 gave the best results in terms of productivity.

French, Kay and Meyer found in their research that the usual level of participation was positively related to mutual understanding, acceptance of job objectives, attitude towards the appraisal system and occupational self-fulfilment. In general, an increase in participation resulted in better superior-subordinate relationships. This only appears to work, however, if it is not in conflict with the manager's previous approach. If it does conflict, the change is seen as unauthentic, suspicious and threatening.

Much has been written about the subject of worker participation and its usefulness in a variety of situations.

One aspect to consider is the need for information exchange within the business. A study was undertaken by Lawrence and Lorsch to investigate this, and they found that, where a firm had to deal with uncertainty either in the market place or in the technology underlying the product, the successful firms were structured to allow the flow of information both horizontally and vertically. Lower-level and middle-level managers with the necessary technical insights seemed to have as much influence on decisions as their top-level superiors. In industries where such uncertainties were not a problem, the information required to make decisions was available to senior managers, the successful firms being more hierarchically organised (ie. those having less participation).

Budgets as motivational targets

- In general, it is accepted that corporate objectives are more likely to be met if they are expressed as quantified targets, often in the form of budgets.

- If a target is to have any influence on the performance, the recipient must be aware of its existence and feel committed to achieving it.

- The target must be set at the right level of difficulty to act as a motivator. Both unrealistic and over-generous targets will be demotivational.

- In theory, there may be a need for two budgets to be prepared for the same area that is:

    (i)   a challenging (aspirations) budget to motivate the manager; and

    (ii)   a lower, and more realistic, expectations budget for planning and decision purposes.

    Care should be taken to reward success as well as penalising failure, in order that a benefit is perceived in bettering rather than just achieving the target.

Budgets as targets

Hofstede, in researches carried out in the Netherlands, found that budgets become stronger motivators as they become tighter up to a point, but thereafter motivation declines. The optimal degree of tightness depends on both the situation and the personality of the individuals concerned.

Performance evaluation

- A manager should only be held accountable for items over which they have control.

- Thus a manager of a profit centre may be judged by variances affecting direct contribution (before allocated fixed costs); the performance of the centre itself will be measured by direct controllable contribution (having accounted for costs that are directly attributable to that centre, but not necessarily all controlled by the manager).

- Measures of performance should be devised that promote decisions in line with corporate objectives.

- Hopwood has identified three main styles of management in the use of budget performance reports:

    (i)   the *budget-constrained* style, which lays particular emphasis on results being closely in accordance with the budget plan;

    (ii)   the *profit-conscious* style, which is less concerned with current deviations from budget than with a manager's ability to achieve a trend of results which is acceptable in relation to changing conditions; and

    (iii)   the *non-accounting* style, which tends to disregard accounting reports as a means of measuring management performance and instead looks at factors such as:

    - the number of customer complaints or substandard items produced
    - the staff turnover
    - morale in the department
    - other qualitative measures

    Of the three styles, the middle was felt to be most successful in achieving the company's long-term goals. The first created good cost consciousness but also a great deal of tension between a manager and his subordinates, and manipulation of accounting information. The last promoted general good morale, but managers had a low involvement with costs.

An illustrative example of responsibility accounting

A conference centre has a newly appointed management accountant who has sent the following report to the supervisor of the restaurant. Prior to the receipt of this report, the restaurant supervisor has been congratulating herself on a good start to the year, with a substantial increase in the use of the restaurant.

To: *Restaurant supervisor*
From: *Management accountant*
Subject: *Performance report*   Date: *5 April*

As part of the campaign to improve efficiency within the conference centre, quarterly budgets have been prepared for each department.

I attach a performance report for your department for the three months to the end of March, showing all discrepancies between budgeted and actual expenditure.

'A' indicates an adverse variance and 'F' a favourable variance.

	Budget £	Actual £	Discrepancy £	
Food and other consumables	97,500	111,540	14,040	A
Labour – hourly paid	15,000	16,500	1,500	A
– supervisor	3,750	3,700	50	F
Power	8,500	9,250	750	A
Breakages	1,000	800	200	F
Allocated overheads	21,000	24,000	3,000	A
	146,750	165,790	19,040	A
Number of meals served	32,500	39,000	6,500	F

You have apparently incurred costs which exceed the budget by £19,040. Please explain this to me at the meeting of the management committee on 15 April.

Required

(a)   Discuss the various possible effects on the restaurant supervisor's behaviour caused by receipt of this report.

(b)   Redraft the performance report and supporting memorandum in a way which, in your opinion, would make them more effective management tools.

Suggested solution

Before looking at the answer, have a go for yourself. Jot down the different aspects that need to be considered (headings) and the points that can be made under these headings, including relevant research findings where these are known.

The possible effects on motivation

●   **The way in which the targets were communicated to, and understood by, the supervisor**

If a target is to have any influence on performance, the recipient must be aware of its existence and feel committed to achieving it. From the wording of the memo, it would seem likely that until she received the performance report the restaurant supervisor was unaware of the budget.

Furthermore, the reaction of the supervisor to the memo comparing the department's performance to a previously unheard-of budget is likely to be defensive and rebellious. With no knowledge how the budget was calculated, the supervisor is very likely to devote time and energy to attacking the 'unfair budget'. How can management hope to obtain commitment by issuing budgets 'from on high', with no scope for consultation or explanation with those responsible for fulfilling the budget?

- **Does the supervisor feel able to achieve the target?**

Is she being held responsible for costs which she is unable to control?

Has the budget been properly prepared?

If a target is to act as a motivator the recipients must feel that they are able to reach the target by their own efforts. Clearly the supervisor is not in a position to influence the level of allocated overheads, which is presumably determined by the amount paid for such things as: rent; rates and administrative salaries; and the chosen method of allocation to the departments. Thus the inclusion of such costs in the performance report will demotivate the supervisor.

Also, she can hardly be held responsible for the fact that her own salary differs from the budget. Indeed, becoming aware that she has been paid less than anticipated is likely to alienate her from the senior management.

Finally, the variances have been calculated by comparing the original budget with actual costs. The original budget is based on an anticipated usage of the restaurant of 32,500 meals; in fact, 39,000 meals have been served. If the explanation of variances is to be meaningful it should have been based on a comparison of actual costs with flexed budget. (This has been done in the suggested redraft of the performance report.)

- **Is the supervisor being offered rewards for achieving the target?**

The memo with the report is very brief, concentrating on the fact that costs have been above budget, with no mention of the fact that the restaurant has served more meals than was anticipated. There is no indication that the supervisor is to be rewarded in any way for her efforts to increase the use of the restaurant, and the summons to explain the 'excessive' costs at a formal meeting seems threatening. This is likely to demotivate the supervisor. She will feel that the successful aspects of the restaurant's operation are being ignored while any less successful aspects that there might be are being unfairly highlighted.

- **Is the target of the right degree of difficulty?**

As discussed above, the target costs communicated to the supervisor in the performance report are unrealistic because they have been left at the level of the original budget and have not been flexed to take account of the greater use made of the restaurant. Unrealistic budgets are bound to demotivate. Indeed, rather than working to reach the target, management is likely to expend time and effort criticising the target as unfair.

- **Is the supervisor the sort of person who reacts well to targets?**

As a final consideration it is important to remember that even the most perfect responsibility accounting system will fail if the managers of the responsibility centres are the sort of people who find any target frightening and thus demotivating. Although there are such people, evidence supports the view that most managers are motivated by well-designed, clearly understood targets.

Revised performance report

With all these considerations in mind we can now redraft the performance report and memo in a form which is more likely to have a positive effect on the performance of the restaurant supervisor.

To:	Restaurant supervisor	
From:	Management accountant	
Subject:	Performance report	**Date:** 5 April

I enclose a performance report for your department for the three months to the end of March. The aim of this report is to assist in the efficient use of resources by providing information about which costs differ from their expected level (the original budget figures), and why.

The original budget figures were based on last year's costs; I would like to meet you next Tuesday to discuss whether these figures are sensible targets for this year. I have tried to make the budget more realistic by adjusting the costs upward to reflect the increased use of the restaurant (the flexed budget figures). I have assumed that all controllable costs are entirely variable and have increased the original budget by a factor of 1.2 (39,000 ÷ 32,500). It may be that some of these costs have a fixed element, in which case I have been unduly generous. I would welcome any ideas you have as to:

–   other adjustments that are necessary to the figures in this report; and
–   how the budgets should be established for future periods.

	Original budget	Flexed budget	Actual	Variance flexed budget to actual	
Number of meals served	32,500	39,000	39,000		
Controllable costs					
Food and other consumables	97,500	117,000	111,540	5,460	F
Labour: hourly paid	15,000	18,000	16,500	1,500	F
Power	8,500	10,200	9,250	950	F
Breakages	1,000	1,200	800	400	F
	122,000	146,400	138,090	8,310	
Allocated costs					
Overheads	21,000	21,000	24,000	3,000	A
	143,000	167,400	162,090	5,310	F

F	=	favourable variance
A	=	adverse variance

The restaurant is evidently being well-managed, with many more meals served than in the same period last year, whilst costs have risen by a small proportion. Following our discussion on Tuesday, the performance report, with any agreed amendments, will be reviewed at the meeting of the management committee on 15 April; please ensure you attend to participate in the discussion and explain the reasons for the variances.

BUDGETS AND BUDGETARY CONTROL USING THE COMPUTER

General principles

The mechanics of budget preparation require a good deal of analysis of various items of data. For example sales have to be analysed by product groups, direct costs require to be analysed by areas of responsibility, indirect costs require to be apportioned on some basis between cost centres and finally costs and revenues are generally analysed over control periods. This type of analysis would be done exceedingly laboriously by manual methods. However the advent of microcomputer applications has meant that tools for computation and analysis are readily available through the impact of spreadsheet software.

What is a spreadsheet?

A spreadsheet is the electronic equivalent of the accountant's double pad of columnar analysis paper. It is a matrix of rows and columns. Each set of co-ordinates encloses a **cell**. Each cell can be individually identified and the contents of each cell can be manipulated. This matrix is held within the memory of the machine and is displayed on the VDU screen. Input of the variables to the spreadsheet is done via a keyboard and the results of all the spreadsheet manipulations can be printed out.

	A	B	C	D	E	----	X	Y	Z	AA	AB	AC	AD	AE
01														
02														
03														
04														
05														
06														
07														
08														
09														
10														
11														
12														

Figure 11.1: The concept of the spreadsheet showing the matrix of cells

Use of the spreadsheet

The user of a typical spreadsheet package can generally call upon the following features:

(a) *formulation* – the contents of a cell can be specified in a formula and the inputs of variables in the formula will produce the desired result on the spreadsheet;

(b) *arithmetical operations* – the spreadsheet will sum the contents of cells and store the result in specified locations;

(c) *deletion* – the contents of a cell can be deleted if fresh data is to be input;

(d) *manipulation* – the contents of a cell can be copied or moved to another part of the spreadsheet.

Spreadsheets are particularly useful for analyses, multi-period cash budgets and multi-period trading statements and balance sheets.

The ability to change variables and thus bring about an automatic change in all the cells affected by the calculation enables the cost accountant to reduce the effort involved in preparing complex analyses for management which are free from arithmetical error and which are relatively easy to prepare.

Budgetary control using a computer

It was stated earlier that an important part of good information was the feature of **exception reporting**. The essence of a system of budgetary control lies in its ability to produce various comparisons with the budget and to report the deviations or variations.

Flexible budgets using standard costs have already been discussed. In this section we will turn our attention to ways in which computer systems can be used to aid the process of exception reporting.

(a)   **Sales reports**

A sales report generally makes its greatest impact if it contains the following details by product type:

(i)   sales for the control period;
(ii)   budget for the control period;
(iii)   variance for the control period;
(iv)   sales year to date;
(v)   budget year to date;
(vi)   variance year to date ($\pm$);
(vii)   totals of the above.

In order that such a report can be generated a budget file is created showing the individual budgetary amounts for each product group month by month and in total. Summarised transactions are analysed by product group and accumulated. The program reads the product code, accumulates the sales by product code and computes the variance for the control period. The totals for the control period are then added to the corresponding brought forward figures in order to provide cumulative year to date totals. When the processing is complete the updated budget file is then printed out in order to provide a sales report that might look like Figure 11.2.

(b)   **Reporting on overhead costs**

A similar principle to that described for budget variance may be adopted in processing overhead costs. If budget centres are defined on the basis of responsibility, costs are allocated to these budget centres by coding all source documents with **both** expense type and cost centre identity. A record for each budget centre can be developed; the collection of such can comprise the 'expenses' ledger. When costs are extracted from the purchases invoice process, petty cash process and cash payments routines they are accumulated by type and by cost centre. These accumulated costs are then compared with the month's budgetary allowance and a variance extracted. The current month totals are added to the year to date totals and the individual costs and variances are summed to provide a total cost variance for the month. The details are provided to the manager on a report that is shown in Figure 11.3 and is similar in layout to the sales report discussed earlier.

| | | Month | | | Year to date | | |
Product code	Budget	Actual	Variance	Budget	Actual	Variance
Shirts	XXX	XXX	XXX	XXX	XXX	XXX
Blousons	XXX	XXX	XXX	XXX	XXX	XXX
Jackets	XXX	XXX	XXX	XXX	XXX	XXX
Trousers	XXX	XXX	XXX	XXX	XXX	XXX
Knitwear	XXX	XXX	XXX	XXX	XXX	XXX
Tracksuit	XXX	XXX	XXX	XXX	XXX	XXX
Flying suit	XXX	XXX	XXX	XXX	XXX	XXX
	XXX	XXX	XXX	XXX	XXX	XXX

Page 01

Figure 11.2: Report – Monthly sales budget comparison

| | | Month | | | Year to date | | |
Expense	Budget	Actual	Variance	Budget	Actual	Variance
021 Salaries						
022 Payroll costs						
043 Travel						
046 Entertainment						
047 Recruitment						
049 Training						
067 Dep'n – car						
068 Motor expenses						
074 Leasing charges						
094 Misc. expenses						

Figure 11.3: Monthly budgetary comparison

QUESTIONS

1   Excelsior Manufacturing Company   **(AAT CA Pilot)**

Excelsior Manufacturing Company produces a single product on an assembly line. As budget officer you have prepared the following production budgets from the best information available, to represent the extremes of high and low volume of production likely to be encountered by the company over a three-month period.

	Production of 4,000 units £	*Production of 8,000 units* £
Direct materials	80,000	160,000
Indirect materials	12,000	20,000
Direct labour	50,000	100,000
Power	18,000	24,000
Repairs	20,000	30,000
Supervision	20,000	36,000
Rent, insurance and rates	9,000	9,000

Supervision is a 'step function'. One supervisor is employed for all production levels up to and including 5,000 units. For higher levels of production, an assistant supervisor (£16,000) is also required. For power, a minimum charge is payable on all production up to and including 6,000 units. For production above this level, there is an additional variable charge based on the power consumed.

Other variable and semi-variable costs are incurred evenly over the production range.

Assessment tasks

(a)   Prepare a set of flexible budgets for presentation to the production manager to cover the following levels of production over a period of three months:

    (i)   4,000 units
    (ii)   5,000 units
    (iii)   6,000 units
    (iv)   7,000 units
    (v)   8,000 units

(b)   During the three months July to September (covering most of the summer holiday period) 5,000 units were produced. Costs incurred during the three-month period were as follows:

	£
Direct materials	110,000
Indirect materials	14,000
Direct labour	70,000
Power	18,000
Repairs	30,000
Supervision	20,000
Rent, insurance and rates	8,000

Note that *price variances* have been deducted from the figures for direct and indirect materials and *rate variances* have been deducted from the labour and supervision costs.

Prepare a budget report for presentation to the production manager. For each variance, suggest any further investigations which might be required and any action which might be taken by the production manager.

2   World History Museum   (AAT CA J94)

The World History Museum has an Education Department which specialises in running courses in various subjects. The courses are run on premises which the museum rents for the purpose and they are presented by freelance expert speakers. Each course is of standard type and format and can therefore be treated alike for budgetary control purposes.

The museum currently uses fixed budgets to control expenditure. The following data shows the actual costs of the Education Department for the month of April compared with the budgeted figures.

Education Department – April

	Actual	*Budget*	*Variance*
Number of courses run	5	6	(1)
	£	£	£
Expenditure			
Speakers' fees	2,500	3,180	680
Hire of premises	1,500	1,500	–
Depreciation of equipment	200	180	(20)
Stationery	530	600	70
Catering	1,500	1,750	250
Insurance	700	820	120
Administration	1,650	1,620	(30)
	8,580	9,650	1,070

You have recently started work as the assistant management accountant for the museum. During a discussion with Chris Brooks, the general manager, she expresses to you some doubt about the usefulness of the above statement in providing control information for the Education Department manager.

Chris is interested in the possibility of using flexible budgets to control the activities of the Education Department. You therefore spend some time analysing the behaviour patterns of the costs incurred in the Education Department. Your findings can be summarised as follows:

(1)   Depreciation of equipment is a fixed cost.

(2)   Administration is a fixed cost.

(3)   The budget figures for the catering costs and insurance costs include a fixed element as follows:

    Catering   £250
    Insurance   £100

    The remaining elements of the catering and insurance costs follow linear variable patterns.

(4)   All other costs follow linear variable patterns.

Assessment tasks

(a) Use the above information to produce a budgetary control statement for April, based on a flexible budget for the actual number of courses run.

(b) Calculate the revised variances based on your flexible budget.

(c) Chris Brooks's interest in the control aspects of budgeting has been sparked by her attendance on a course entitled *Budgetary control for managers*. She has shown you the following extract from the course notes she was given:

'A system of participative budgeting involves managers in the process of setting their own budgets. Participative systems are likely to be more successful in planning and controlling the activities of an organisation.'

Write a brief memo to Chris Brooks which explains the advantages and disadvantages of participative budgeting as a part of the budgetary planning and control process.

3 Responsibility accounting

A company manufactures a range of products by passing materials through a number of processes. A number of service departments provide support to the production processes.

(a) Define *responsibility accounting* and comment on the application of responsibility accounting in the context of the above situation.

(b) Explain how responsibility may be shared in respect of the cost of the maintenance department and suggest ways in which the management accounting system may assist in recognising such shared responsibility.

(c) Explain ways in which the provision of more information need not lead to more effective management of a cost centre.

SUMMARY

Variance analysis has been studied in detail in an earlier session; from this session you should be aware of how it relates to:

- management by exception
- responsibility accounting

The main topics are as follows:

- the form and content of a performance report

- how people react to targets and how a system of responsibility accounting should be developed to get the best reaction from managers

Review of Module One

You have now completed your studies for Unit 11 (*Preparing information for cost analysis and control*) and Unit 12 (*Operating a budgetary control system*). The main topics covered have been:

- Standard cost reports and cost variances
- Analysis of accounting information, including ratios and trend analysis
- Cost reduction, quality improvement and value enhancement
- Performance indicators
- Forecasting income and expenditure, including allowance for price changes
- Preparation of budgets and flexible budgeting
- Budgetary control and responsibility accounting systems

Central assessment questions will generally consist of short case studies, assessing the student's ability to apply basic management accounting techniques in simple business situations.

Whilst each task in the assessment can be identified as testing your knowledge of one particular area, several topics and techniques may be covered within one case study. You should be prepared to use knowledge accumulated from earlier tasks in the answering of later ones.

The key technical abilities you must ensure you have developed from your studies so far are as follows:

- Overheads: allocation, apportionment and absorption; the principles of ABC; over- and under-absorption

- Calculation of cost variances for materials, labour and overheads

- Reconciliation of budgeted to actual costs in the form of a budgetary control statement

- Preparation of budgets

- The use of flexible budgets in budgetary control

- Ratio analysis

- Time series analysis

- The use of index numbers in forecasting and trend analysis

These topics cover most of the numerical aspects of the assessment, in which you should be well practised having attempted all the questions set so far.

However, a significant amount of marks will also be allocated to the discursive side of the topics, so you must be prepared to explain the techniques you have learnt – their use in cost and budgetary control, their limitations and the interpretation of your results in the context of the business situation given.

It should be noted that it is an aim of the central assessments to allow sufficient time for students to work through all parts carefully and to achieve a good standard of presentation as well as a high proportion of correct responses. Once you have gained the relevant knowledge, therefore, you should ensure that you practise presenting that knowledge in a structured, concise and professional manner.

Cost information for activity appraisal

OBJECTIVES

Throughout the life of a business, its current activities need to be appraised and potential new areas of activity investigated, to ensure that optimum use is made of the present conditions and future expectations of the environment in which the business is operating.

The cost accountant will be expected to produce cost information about current and proposed activities to assist management in making informed decisions for the short and long term. Such decisions will include pricing policies.

In this session, we shall consider the following:

- the characteristics of business decisions and the role of the management/cost accountant in their determination

- the comparison of absorption costing and marginal costing systems, and the importance of the latter in activity appraisal and decision-making

- the economics of basic pricing policies for existing and future products/services

The performance criteria addressed by this session are as follows:

- Estimates are prepared in an approved form and presented to the appropriate recipient(s) within an agreed timescale.

- Appropriate staff are consulted about technical aspects and any special features of projects.

    Estimates account for the effect of possible variations in capacity on fixed overhead rates.

- Cost estimates are monitored and checked against actual costs incurred and significant discrepancies investigated.

- Recommendations are logically derived and clearly reported.

APPRAISAL OF ACTIVITIES – DECISION-MAKING

Introduction

A decision is a choice among various alternative courses of action for the purpose of achieving some defined goal or objective. Thus a prerequisite of a successful decision is the definition of the objective to be accomplished.

In this session we will discuss the criteria to be used in making operational or tactical decisions that have an impact in the short-term.

A fundamental requirement for good decision-making is that all information, both internal and external, relevant to making the decision is identified and used. In addition, a careful analysis of costs is needed in order to include only those that are relevant to the analysis. Note, however, that it will not always be possible to convert all elements of the decision to quantifiable amounts. In many business situations, it is inevitable that qualitative judgements have to be made. However, it is important that any recommendations which result are logically derived and clearly reported.

In this session we are concerned particularly with quantitative decisions, based on data expressed in monetary values and relating to costs and revenues as measured by the management accountant.

Quantitative decisions

A quantitative decision problem involves four parts:

- **An objective that can be quantified**

  For example our objective may be to maximise profit, or to minimise cost. This is sometimes referred to as the 'choice criterion' or 'objective function'.

- **Constraints**

  In many decision problems there will be one or more 'constraints' on what can be achieved. Therefore it is common to find an objective to, say, maximise profits subject to defined constraints.

- **A range of alternative courses of action under consideration**

  This set of actions should be mutually exclusive and as a whole should exhaust the various possibilities available. In attempting to minimise the costs of a particular manufacturing operation, the available alternatives might be:

  (i)   to continue manufacturing as at present;
  (ii)   to change the manufacturing method;
  (iii)   to sub-contract the work to a third party.

- **Methods** of measuring the effects (outcomes) of the alternative actions and of comparing those outcomes with the objective function

  In measuring the effects of a proposed action it is necessary to identify:

  (i)   the items of information (variables) that are relevant to the action;
  (ii)   the ways in which those variables are interrelated;
  (iii)   the relationship between the variables and the objective function.

Once a decision has been taken, the manager must act to implement it. Thereafter, the results of implementation will be evaluated and reported back. This 'feedback' of information will in some cases lead the manager to review his decision.

The role of the management accountant

The role of the management accountant in this decision-making process is particularly concerned with the following:

- recognising the essential structure of a decision problem and posing the right questions for its solution;

- identifying what information (or data) is relevant to the solution of the problem; and

- providing that information – in particular, all internal and external information relevant in estimating future costs and revenues should be used.

In some cases the management accountant will make decision calculations as well as providing data for them; but it is less likely that he will do so when the computations involve the use of quantitative techniques such as probability theory or linear programming.

These fall within the province of specialists such as the operational researcher or the management scientist. The accountant should, however, have some understanding of these techniques otherwise he will find difficulty in providing appropriate data or in interpreting the results obtained.

Similarly, other appropriate staff should be consulted about the technical aspects or special features of any decision – in terms of project appraisal or evaluation, for example, technical, marketing or other relevant specialists should be consulted.

The objective will be to report recommendations which optimise the long-term benefits to the organisation and which therefore act as a basis for optimal decision-making.

The remainder of this session will be concerned with discussion of the nature of the information which is relevant for the purpose of decision-making. Two general points, however, can be made at this stage:

- As all decisions are concerned with what will happen in the future, costs for decision-making will be estimates of future costs. Historical data will have importance only to the extent that it provides a basis from which the future can be predicted.

  Hence, the preparation of cost estimates will be a key aspect of the decision-making process. Current material, labour and other variable costs must be identified and future trends assessed, whilst the effect of possible variations in capacity on fixed overhead rates must also be taken into account.

  This may involve the use of time series analysis and/or index numbers, as discussed in Session 9.

  Cost estimates should be monitored and checked against actual costs incurred on a regular basis and significant discrepancies investigated to ensure that the basis of estimation is reasonable.

- The decision-maker will be interested only in costs which will change as a result of adopting a particular alternative, in other words, in those costs which could be avoided (and those revenues which would be foregone) if that particular alternative were not adopted.

We shall be dealing, therefore, with the economist's concept of the nature of costs.

ABSORPTION COSTING AND MARGINAL COSTING

Evaluation of all commercial activities is generally based on some sort of profit figure for the activity. Where the production of goods is involved, this profit figure can be significantly affected by the method of costing used. In this section, we shall consider the impact on profit of a marginal costing system compared with an absorption costing system, together with the arguments for the use of marginal costing in activity appraisal and decision-making.

The nature of the two systems

Absorption costing

Absorption costing focuses on the total cost attributable to each unit of product or service. It attempts to identify with the individual unit not only the costs directly involved in its creation (mainly variable costs) but also all the costs of housing and administering the business as a whole (mainly fixed costs).

These general (overhead) costs by their nature cannot be attributed precisely to cost units and any attempt to do so is bound to be imprecise.

In an absorption costing system, therefore, both variable and fixed production costs will be attributed to individual cost units and charged to cost of sales or carried forward in stock as appropriate.

Marginal costing

Marginal cost in the economist's definition is the amount by which, at any given volume of output, aggregate costs are changed if the volume of output is increased or decreased by one unit.

For example:

Output volume	1,000 units	1,001 units
Aggregate costs	£2,500	£2,502

In this instance, the marginal cost of increasing output by one unit from 1,000 units is £2. The units may be measured by quantity, weight, volume or any other way appropriate to the nature of the business activity concerned.

This economic concept is the basis of cost estimation for decision-making. Provided a suitable range of volumes can be defined, it is often possible to achieve a satisfactory approximation to marginal costs by classifying all costs into two categories:

• Those which are fixed regardless of the volume of output.

• Those which will tend to vary in direct proportion to the volume of output.

Once the classification has been made, the variable costs can be treated for most practical purposes as marginal costs.

In accountancy terminology, marginal cost is taken as measuring the variable cost attributable to a cost unit.

In a marginal costing system, therefore, only variable costs will be attributed to cost units, with fixed costs being treated as a 'period costs' and charged in full against the period's profit and loss.

Absorption *vs* marginal costing – effects on profit

The following example sets out the basic profit computations for the two systems.

Example

> *Sally makes dudars. Each dudar has a variable cost of £3 and can be sold for £5.*
>
> *Sally's fixed overheads are expected to amount to £50,000 for the coming year. During this year she expects to make and sell 100,000 dudars.*
>
> *Required*
>
> (a)   *Calculate the total absorption cost of a dudar.*
>
> (b)   *Prepare Sally's budgeted profit and loss account under:*
>
>   (i)   *marginal costing; and*
>   (ii)   *total absorption costing.*

Solution

		£
(a)	Variable cost per unit	3.00
	Fixed cost per unit (W)	0.50
	Total absorption cost per unit	3.50

Working

$$\frac{\text{Total budgeted fixed overhead}}{\text{Total expected production}} = \frac{£50,000}{100,000} = £0.5 \text{ per unit}$$

(b)   The budgeted profit and loss account of Sally for the coming year

   (i)   **Marginal costing**

	Notes	£	£
Sales (100,000 × £5)			500,000
Opening stock	(1)	–	
Production (100,000 × £3)	(2)	300,000	
		300,000	
Closing stock	(1)	–	
Cost of sales			(300,000)
Contribution			200,000
Fixed cost	(3)		(50,000)
Profit			150,000

Notes

(1)   Normally these lines would be omitted as they have a value of nil.
(2)   Production is charged with the marginal cost of the goods produced.
(3)   Fixed costs are charged as a period cost.

Note that sales revenue less the marginal cost of sales is equal to *contribution* not profit. Profit is only obtained when the fixed costs are then taken off the contribution figure.

(ii)   **Total absorption costing**

		£	£
Sales			500,000
Opening stock	(1)	–	
Production (100,000 × £3.50)	(2)	350,000	
Closing stock	(1)	–	
Cost of sales			(350,000)
Profit			150,000

Notes

(1)   Normally these figures will be omitted as they have a value of nil.
(2)   Production is charged with total absorption cost of the goods produced.

Here you will notice that the fixed overhead is charged to production rather than as a period cost. This happens because the total absorption cost includes a proportion of the fixed overhead.

You will probably notice that the profit is the same using either method of costing (although the presentation is different). This is only because there was no change in stock levels. There was no opening stock and no closing stock, so therefore using a different method of valuing stock will not give rise to any difference in the profit figures.

Example continued – The effect of changes in stock

Suppose that in the following year Sally plans to produce 100,000 units but to sell only 90,000 (all other items remaining as before).

[Budgeted profit and loss account of Sally for year 2]

	Notes	TAC £	£	MC £	£
Sales (90,000 × £5)			450,000		450,000
Opening stock		–		–	
Production (as before)		350,000		300,000	
		350,000		300,000	
Closing stock (10,000 × £3.50)	(1)	(35,000)			
(10,000 × £3.00)	(2)			(30,000)	
Cost of sales			(315,000)		(270,000)
			135,000		180,000
Fixed overheads	(3)		–		(50,000)
Profit			135,000		130,000

Notes

(1)   Closing stock valued at total absorption cost.

(2)   Closing stock valued at marginal cost.

(3)   Remember that, in TAC, fixed overheads are included in production costs, whereas in MC they are taken off in total as a period cost.

As you can see there is a difference in profit.

The only difference between the two profit and loss accounts is the value of closing stock.

(Remember: Fixed cost + Cost of production under MC = Cost of production under TAC)

What has happened is that £35,000 of the production cost has been carried forward to the next period under TAC but only £30,000 under MC.

More precisely, under total absorption costing, £5,000 of fixed overheads (10,000 units × £0.50 per unit) have been carried forward while under marginal costing none have.

This leads us to some standard rules.

The relationship between TAC profit and MC profit

If closing stock is greater than opening stock   TAC profit will be greater than MC profit

If closing stock is less than opening stock   TAC profit will be less than MC profit

If closing stock is equal to opening stock   TAC profit will be equal to MC profit

Our two examples have illustrated the first and the third rule. You should be able to illustrate the second for yourself.

The effect of over-/under-absorption

When discussing the treatment of overheads in Session 2, we looked at the problem of over-or-under absorption of fixed costs that might arise in an absorption costing system.

Remember that it is caused by actual production levels being different from those budgeted, which means that the predetermined (standard) absorption rate is, with hindsight, inappropriate.

However, it is important to note that under-/over-absorption of fixed costs does not cause a difference between absorption costing profit and marginal costing profit. This is because an adjustment will be made to compensate for the under-/over-absorption before arriving at the absorption costing profit.

Thus both the marginal and absorption costing profit and loss accounts will include the correct amount of actual overheads incurred (although some of these may be carried forward in stock under absorption costing).

The two costing methods (TAC and MC) compared

TAC and MC adopt fundamentally different attitudes towards the treatment of fixed overheads. Consequently the cost per unit derived under both methods will be quite different. However, each method has a use depending on the circumstances faced by the business and the purpose for which the cost per unit is to be used.

The advantages of one method are the disadvantages of the other and vice versa. These are considered below by focusing on TAC.

Advantages claimed for TAC

Complies with SSAP9

SSAP9 *Stocks and long-term contracts* does not permit marginal costing to be used in the preparation of published financial accounts. For management accountants, this is irrelevant. Management accounts are used for decision-making purposes and should contain information in the form that is most useful to management. If a TAC figure is required for the financial accounts, then it should be calculated separately.

In practice, the use of erroneous financial accounting information for management decisions is most likely in small companies whose staff have limited financial expertise and regard the accounts as something they have to get past the auditor.

Reminds managers of the true cost of production

It is argued that the use of marginal costing will lead managers to believe that products cost less than they actually do. (Remember that stock is valued at marginal cost under a marginal cost system of accounting.)

Others argue that good managers should be aware that this is not so.

Here again, we may have a difference between the theoretical ideal and the practical reality that not every manager has financial training.

Ensures that fixed costs are covered

This is an extension of the above point.

Illustration

The following details apply to a grodget.

	£
Variable cost	700
Fixed cost	3,000
Total cost	3,700

It is argued that if stock is valued at £700 a manager might agree to sell it at £2,000 and believe he has struck a beneficial deal when in fact he has not.

In contrast, if stock is valued at £3,700 the manager will know that he has to achieve this price in order to cover the fixed costs.

This is a very simplistic view that can be challenged on two fronts. The first point will be considered in detail under decision-making.

We shall consider the second point here. Quite simply fixed costs will not be covered by a price of £3,700 unless the required volume is achieved.

Suppose that fixed costs are £30,000; we need to sell ten units at £3,700 to cover our costs. Selling one is not enough, but selling one of £2,000 at least gives a contribution of £1,300 to help cover fixed costs.

Disadvantage of TAC

Unsuitable for one-off decision-making

Using the example set out above, suppose that a one-off order from an overseas customer was received. Suppose further that the order would have no effect on the price obtainable from existing customers.

Under these circumstances it would be worthwhile accepting the order if the price were above £700 because it would make a contribution to profits/fixed costs.

In general, the decision-maker needs to know the costs which will vary as a result of his decision and the costs that will remain unchanged. Absorption costing does not provide a convenient basis for making such calculations. Its main purpose is stock accounting, rather than decision-taking.

PRODUCT LINE PROFITABILITY

The following illustration demonstrates the potential problems with the use of absorption costing when assessing the relative profitability of different product lines (possibly with a view to closure).

Illustration

The following figures relate to a manufacturing company's results for a particular period, using full absorption costing.

		Products		
	Total	A	B	C
	£	£	£	£
Sales	12,300	4,500	3,600	4,200
Direct material	6,092	2,595	2,097	1,400
Direct labour	1,650	450	400	800
Production overhead absorbed	2,850	450	1,000	1,400
Total factory cost	10,592	3,495	3,497	3,600
Gross profit	1,708	1,005	103	600
Add: Over-absorption of production overhead	80	13	28	39
Less: General overheads	(567)	(189)	(189)	(189)
Net profit/(loss)	1,221	829	(58)	450
(% on sales)	9.9%	18.4%	(1.6%)	10.7%

It would appear from this report that product A yields the highest profit per £1 of sales, and that product B involves the company in a loss.

An analysis of indirect expenditure between variable and fixed items, and a representation of the figures on a marginal cost basis, could give a quite different picture, as shown below.

		Products		
	Total	A	B	C
Sales (in units)		2,250	4,800	8,000
	£	£	£	£
Sales revenue	12,300	4,500	3,600	4,200
Direct material	6,092	2,595	2,097	1,400
Direct labour (@ £1 per hour)	1,650	450	400	800
Variable overheads				
Production	1,249	539	130	580
General	49	16	13	20
Marginal cost	9,040	3,600	2,640	2,800
Contribution (sales revenue – marginal costs)	3,260	900	960	1,400
Fixed overheads				
£				
Production 1,521				
General 518	2,039			
Net profit	1,221			

Assuming that the fixed overheads are truly unaffected by product volume or mix, it is now obvious that product B does in fact make a contribution towards those overheads and towards the eventual net profit, and could well be worth retaining.

Contribution [Sales revenue – Marginal (variable) costs] is a key measure in many areas of decision-making and will be discussed more fully in the following session.

Profitability measures

To judge the relative profitability of the three products, the common method is to calculate the ratios of contribution to sales value, which are as follows:

Product A	900/4,500	$\times$ 100	=	20%
Product B	960/3,600	$\times$ 100	=	$26^{2}/_{3}$%
Product C	1,400/4,200	$\times$ 100	=	$33^{1}/_{3}$%

so that it would appear that, other things being equal, the business would be most profitable if it concentrated on sales of product C and that product B is preferable to product A.

The **contribution to sales value ratio (C/S)** is a key feature of marginal costing because it can be used to forecast the effect of volume changes on net profit, and also to assess the relative profitability of different products or activities. The calculation can obviously only be made in relation to individual products or activities. The ratio for the business as a whole will depend on the mix of the various products.

BASIC PRICING POLICIES

One of the most important decisions made by the management accountant is the price that should be charged for a product. If too high a price is charged, customers will be discouraged; if too low a price is charged, insufficient margin may be earned to cover fixed costs and make a profit; alternatively, a low price can deter customers who suspect the quality of a product.

Various methods may be used to establish a price, depending on the objectives of the company. The practical considerations can generally be categorised into three areas: costs, competitors and customers (the three Cs).

Costs

Cost-plus pricing

In the long run, revenues must cover costs, so one, commonly used pricing method is 'cost-plus pricing' – adding a standard mark-up to costs.

The costs used can be full cost (total absorption cost) or marginal cost.

Other linked topics include:

- cost units and cost centres;
- direct and indirect costs;
- allocation, apportionment and absorption of indirect costs; and
- re-apportionment of service department costs.

You may be asked to carry out calculations, explaining and/or criticising the methods you use.

Use of full cost and marginal cost

Both full cost and marginal cost have pros and cons when used in cost-plus pricing.

- Basing a price on *full cost* ensures, to a certain extent, that all costs will be covered. However, it requires future overheads and production levels or hours to be estimated for calculation of the absorption rate per unit. If, as is likely, any of these figures is different from budgeted, the price will be based on an incorrect cost per unit.

- Using *marginal costs* carries the danger of not earning enough revenue to cover costs. However, it represents the true cost of producing each extra unit and is the cost that should always be used in decision making. In fact, when we look at the theoretical aspects of pricing for profit maximisation, we will see that marginal cost, not total absorption cost, should come into the pricing decision.

Competitors

Most firms will have to follow competitors' prices to a certain extent ('going rate' pricing). In some cases, the firm's marketing strategy may lead it to deviate from the average market price.

Price-cutting

Prices may be cut to:

(a)   increase market share (enabling economies of scale to be achieved and cost per unit to be reduced);

(b)   obtain one-off orders;

(c)   promote sales of other products by getting customers interested in a 'loss leader' (for example selling razor blades at a loss and the accompanying razor at a profit);

(d)   launch a new product or break into a market ('penetration pricing');

(e)   sell off old stock; or

(f)   use under-employed production facilities.

Setting a high price

The high quality of a firm's product may enable it to go for the top end of the market and set a high price (*market-skimming*). In fact, some customers may interpret a high price as indicative of higher quality, whether or not this is true. They may buy the product for pure ostentation (*prestige pricing*). A decision has to be made with a product of how it should be 'placed' in a competitive market (at the upper end of the price range or at the bottom).

Competitive bidding (or 'sealed-bid' pricing)

In this case, competitors submit individual bids for particular jobs. The problem for each firm is to estimate what prices its competitors will quote and then to fix its own bid price at a figure sufficiently low to attract the customers away from competitors, but not so low as to risk incurring a loss.

A contract will not always be awarded to the lowest bidder, a reputation for good quality work and reliable completion dates may also be taken into consideration.

In essence, the bidder will attempt to assess the probability of success in obtaining the contract at various bid prices and will then select one of these prices, trying to increase his chances of winning without sacrificing too much profit.

Customers

A company must bear in mind how much customers are willing to pay for the product. In theoretical terms, if the demand curve can be estimated, then a price can be set to maximise profit or revenue. This area of pricing involves mathematical calculations which are beyond the scope of Unit 13, although the general principle of equating marginal costs and revenues is discussed later in this session.

In practice, a company must carry out market research to identify possible price ranges. If the product is already marketed by other firms, then clearly the considerations of competitors' prices will help the company assess the market.

The market research may help the supplier to value the 'non-price variables' in the product. For example, it may be useful to consider the premium a customer might pay for extra reliability, better design, superior after-sales service or a longer guarantee period. This type of pricing, where the supplier tries to estimate the value a customer would put on different qualities of the product, is called 'perceived value' pricing.

Pricing to achieve a specific return on investment

In target pricing, as it is known, a firm attempts to achieve a target rate of return on its capital employed. It requires the determination of:

(a)   the rate of return required;
(b)   the volume of output expected to be achieved;
(c)   the amount of capital required to support that capacity; and
(d)   the estimated total cost at the target level of output.

Illustration

If:

(a)   the required rate of return on capital employed is 20% before tax;
(b)   the expected volume of sales is 10,000 units;
(c)   the amount of capital employed at that volume of output is expected to be £50,000; and
(d)   total costs for 10,000 units are forecast at £70,000.

Then:

(a)   Profit ÷ Capital employed = 20% and Capital employed = £50,000 ∴ Required profit is £10,000.

(b)   With costs £70,000 and profit £10,000, sales value will be £80,000 (£8 per unit).

(c)   Required ratio of profit:sales value = 10,000:80,000 = 12.5%.

(d)   Required mark-up of profit on cost of sales will be 10,000/70,000 = 14.29% (say, 14% approximately).

Problems with target pricing

The method suffers from two theoretical objections:

(a)   Capital employed includes trade debtors, but these cannot be forecast until selling prices are known. In practice, this will not normally have a significant effect on what is already an approximate calculation.

(b)   Where demand is price-sensitive, it is not possible to forecast sales volume without at the same time forecasting a price.

It is for these reasons that the method is used only in certain specialised applications, such as in the nationalised industries, which are required to achieve a specified rate of return on capital employed. In most cases there will be well-documented forecasts of long-term demand, which will often be relatively stable. Capital investment will be predominantly in fixed assets.

Pricing to achieve profit maximisation

The way in which demand for a product is affected by the selling price is explained by means of a demand curve or demand function.

Many products are sold in markets in which demand falls as price rises (and vice versa). An example of such a demand curve is shown below.

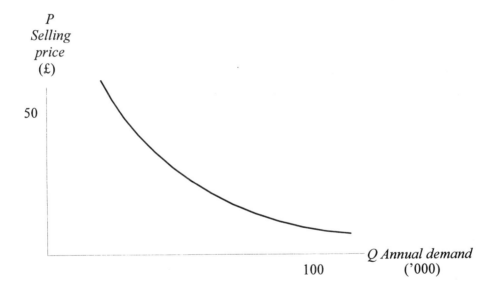

With a downward sloping demand curve, sales volume increases are only achieved by reducing prices. Revenue will only rise if a price cut is more than compensated for by extra sales. There will be a price (and associated quantity) which achieves maximum revenue. To maximise profit, we must also consider costs. Theoretically, the optimum price may be determined by the comparison of marginal cost (MC) with marginal revenue.

Marginal cost (MC) is the extra cost incurred by producing one more unit. If variable cost per unit is constant, this is simply the variable cost. If variable cost per unit increases at high production levels (for example, if overtime costs are incurred), the marginal cost will also increase.

Marginal revenue (MR) is the extra revenue earned by selling one more unit. With a downward sloping demand curve, the sale of one more unit is achieved by lowering the price of all units sold, so the extra revenue earned is not the price of the unit. It is the difference in revenue arising from, for example, moving from sales of 10 units at £100 to 11 units at £99.50 (= £1,000 to £1,094.50, an MR of £94.50).

Consider the effect on profit of making and selling one extra unit:

Provided MR exceeds MC then profits will rise; extra revenue exceeds extra cost, so extra profit is generated.

If more units are produced and sold, MR will generally decrease, whilst MC may remain constant or increase. Thus extra profit will be diminished.

Eventually the production and sale of one extra unit will start to produce a loss for that unit (MC > MR) and profits will fall. The maximum profit will be obtained just before this happens – ie. when MC and MR are just equal. Thus the general result may be stated as:

Profits are maximised where MC = MR

Pricing to achieve revenue maximisation

It is possible that managers may not aim for maximum profit but for an 'acceptable' level of profit and maximum sales revenue. They may do this because high sales, leading to a growth in the organisation and a likely enlargement of the manager's unit, will bring them additional status. It may be decided to adopt this policy to maximise market share. Alternatively, if purchases are made on credit but sales made for cash, this policy will make significant short-term improvements to cash-flows.

To calculate the revenue maximising price, the demand curve must again be considered and resulting revenue from different prices (and corresponding quantities) calculated to determine the optimum position. This can again be found by theoretical calculations which are beyond the scope of Unit 13.

Pricing under inflation

Under conditions of cost inflation, rising costs which are not matched by increases in productivity will reduce profit margins. This will put pressure on management to increase selling prices. Such price increases are often greater than would be justified by the cost increases already experienced. This is done to cover further cost escalation before it arises, and to avoid annoying customers with frequent changes (although a survey of UK pricing methods in the '80s showed that firms were often slow to react to inflationary changes). The problem that any price increase is likely to contribute to further inflation is not one that any business can solve in isolation.

Alternatives to increases in list prices are:

(a)   reducing quantity discounts;

(b)   the imposition of minimum order quantities (quantities below this level being charged at a premium over the normal price);

(c)   reducing product weight or quality;

(d) 'unbundling' products or services, so that a separate charge is made for each element and it is thus less easy to compare a total cost against that of the originally packaged product. One application of this device is to market a new basic product and to offer a range of optional extras; and

(e) putting greater marketing effort into those products which yield the highest marginal contributions.

Particular problems are encountered by companies engaged in long-term contract work where inflation affects the price and profitability of the contract.

Ways of dealing with the problem are to:

(a) write 'escalation clauses' into the contract, enabling specific cost increases to be recovered from the customer;

(b) submit a 'budget quotation' but to delay the negotiation of final price terms as long as possible; and

(c) quote a low price in the knowledge that the customer will subsequently require technical modifications for which high additions to the original price can be negotiated.

Pricing of special orders

Many companies produce one-off or customised products suited to particular tasks. The pricing decision therefore becomes more difficult and will need to be taken locally, often through negotiation. Sales conditions and competition may be erratic, both of which will affect the price that can be quoted.

Buyers are often experts in their field specifying precise requirements and choosing the lowest quotation given that all tenders should meet their requirements. Thus the buyer is in a powerful position. The price quoted will therefore be dependent upon the size of the order, the need for work and the level of likely competitors' bids. Built in to this should be room for negotiation. All input costs will need to be analysed carefully given marginal cost considerations.

Having analysed the various costs, management will need to look at the wider picture. The order may lead to other regular business, current production capability may be idle, the order may bring prestige to the business. Thus a flexible approach must be adopted, often for businesses operating in this manner this is a natural part of trading.

If a product is to have a short sales life, eg. Christmas products, pricing is a vital issue. Expected revenue should yield a contribution quickly. Costs cannot be amortised over long periods; moreover, prices cannot generally be adjusted. They must be right from the outset, it would be far better to underprice and achieve low contribution than overprice and miss the market.

QUESTIONS

1   Bittern (II) Ltd

Bittern Ltd manufactures and sells a single product at a unit selling price of £25. In constant price-level terms its cost structure is as follows.

Variable costs:	Production materials	£10 per unit produced
	Distribution	£1 per unit sold
Semi-variable costs:	Labour	£5,000 per annum, plus
		£2 per unit produced
Fixed costs:	Overheads	£5,000 per annum

For several years, Bittern has operated a system of variable costing for management accounting purposes. It has been decided to review the system and to compare it for management accounting purposes with an absorption costing system.

As part of the review you have been asked to prepare estimates of Bittern's profits in constant price-level terms over a three-year period in two different hypothetical situations, and to compare the two types of system generally for management accounting purposes.

Required

(a)   In each of the following two sets of hypothetical circumstances, calculate Bittern's profit in each of years t1, t2, and t3, and also in total over the three-year period t1 to t3 using, first, a variable costing system, and then a full-cost absorption costing system with fixed cost recovery based on a normal production level of 1,000 units per annum.

(i)   Stable unit levels of production, sales and inventory

	t1	*t2*	*t3*
Opening stock	100	100	100
Production	1,000	1,000	1,000
Sales	1,000	1,000	1,000
Closing stock	100	100	100

(ii)   Stable unit level of sales, but fluctuating unit levels of production and inventory

	t1	*t2*	*t3*
Opening stock	100	600	400
Production	1,500	800	700
Sales	1,000	1,000	1,000
Closing stock	600	400	100

(**Note:** All the data in (i)–(ii) above are volumes, not values.)

(b)   Write a short comparative evaluation of variable and absorption costing systems for management accounting purposes, paying particular attention to profit measurement and using your answer to part (a) to illustrate your arguments if you wish.

2   LMN Ltd   (AAT CA J94)

LMN Ltd manufactures and sells five products. The directors are currently reviewing the latest profit statement for May.

Profit statement for May

	A £	B £	C £	D £	E £	Total £
Sales revenue	18,000	29,700	43,500	14,100	30,940	136,240
Total costs	22,000	24,000	29,000	12,000	26,000	113,000
Profit/(loss)	(4,000)	5,700	14,500	2,100	4,940	23,240

The directors are disappointed with the results and feel that sales of product A should be discontinued because it is making a loss.

Investigation of total costs reveals that 25% of the total costs are fixed and the remainder vary with sales volume. None of the fixed costs is directly attributable to any of the products.

Assessment task

In your role as assistant to the management accountant, you are asked to prepare a report to the directors which covers the following points:

(a)   Your suggestion for an alternative presentation of the statement which would show more clearly the effect on profit of discontinuing product A

(b)   Your recommendations concerning product A

3   JK Company   (AAT CA D94)

You work as assistant accountant for the JK Company which manufactures four products. The results for the latest month, November, are as follows:

Profit statement for November

Product	J £	K £	L £	M £	Total £
Sales revenue	6,400	2,900	2,400	7,600	19,300
Variable costs	3,000	2,400	1,500	5,100	12,000
Contribution	3,400	500	900	2,500	7,300
Fixed costs	(1,280)	(580)	(480)	(1,520)	(3,860)
Profit	2,120	(80)	420	980	3,440

At a recent board meeting, the directors considered the continual poor performance of product K and now wish to evaluate the following proposal from the marketing director.

'Product K should be discontinued. I estimate that sales of the other three products would be affected as follows:

Product J	increase by	5%
Product L	decrease by	15%
Product M	increase by	25%

'I have no idea what this will do to our monthly profitability but I do think that it is worth investigating.'

You have investigated the cost behaviour patterns and have found the following:

(i)   None of the fixed costs is directly attributable to any of the products; they have been arbitrarily apportioned according to sales value.

(ii)   All variable costs vary in direct proportion to the product's sales value.

Assessment tasks

(a)   Prepare a profit statement which shows the effect on monthly profit of the marketing director's proposals.

        State clearly any assumptions which you make.

(b)   On the basis of your profit statement in (a) above, state whether the marketing director's proposals should be accepted.

SUMMARY

This session has considered some of the areas in which the cost accountant will be involved in providing management with cost and other information for the purposes of activity appraisal and decision-making.

Make sure you are confident of the differences between marginal and absorption costing, and the arguments for the use of the latter in activity appraisal.

You only need to be aware of the basic economics of pricing policies – the most relevant areas for Unit 13 will be the provision of cost estimates upon which to base a price, whether it be for a new product, a tender or special order.

The relevant costs to be included in such estimates are examined in more detail in the following session.

Evaluation of operational activities

OBJECTIVES

The principle of the use of marginal costs in activity evaluation and decision-making was discussed in the previous session. This session considers the application of this principle to various types of operational decisions management may face, in particular:

- the use of contribution analysis where a simple cost structure exists, including break-even and sensitivity analysis

- key factor analysis where there are scarce resources to consider

- the use of incremental, relevant or opportunity costs for more complex one-off decisions whose costs do not fit the existing structure

- the application of the above techniques to specific production decisions, including those affecting capacity, and make or buy decisions

The performance criteria addressed by this session are as follows:

Current material, labour and other variable costs are identified and future trends assessed.

- Recommendations are logically derived and clearly reported.

- Internal and external information relevant to making a decision is identified and used.

- Costs relevant to the decision to be made are identified and only those are used in making a recommendation.

- Alternative solutions are assessed and tested using relevant accounting concepts.

- Technical, marketing and other relevant specialists are consulted when conducting an evaluation.

Internal and external information relevant in estimating future costs and revenues are used.

CONTRIBUTION – A VITAL CONCEPT

Throughout this session we will be looking at techniques concerned with decision-making. This may be with regard to the relationship between output and profit, determining our strategy in the light of a restricted resource, evaluation of a one-off contract, or in general terms. What will become apparent is that the concept of contribution is vital in all areas.

Contribution is defined as the difference between selling price and the variable cost of producing and selling that item. This is in contrast to profit per unit, which is the difference between selling price and the total absorption cost of producing and selling that item, which includes an element of fixed cost.

When we are faced with a decision to make, we need to assess which course of action will be most beneficial. We therefore need to consider the revenues and costs under each alternative. Fixed costs, by definition, are unavoidable and do not change with the level of production. Therefore, in any decision which is connected with varying the level of production, fixed costs are not a relevant cost as they do not change regardless of which course of action is taken.

Example

Katie Ltd is currently producing baby rattles. Each rattle sells at £10 each, and has a variable cost of production of £8 per unit. Current production is 900 units per period. Fixed costs are expected to be £900 for the coming period, and therefore are charged at £1 per unit to production.

Katie has been approached to supply a new customer with 100 rattles, but at a discounted price of £8.25 per rattle. Should she accept the order?

Solution

If we look at profit per unit, then the decision would be to reject the order, as we would not sell for £8.25 per unit something which has cost us (£8 + £1) = £9 to produce

However, if we look at total profits generated by the business before and after the acceptance of project, we find:

	Reject £	*Accept* £
Revenue (900 @ £10)	9,000	9,000
(100 @ £8.25)		825
		9,825
Variable costs (900/1,000 @ £8)	(7,200)	(8,000)
Fixed costs	(900)	(900)
Profit	900	925

Therefore we can see that profits are improved by accepting the contract. Whilst revenue is increasing by £825, costs only increase by £800 as **fixed costs do not change**.

We could have derived the same answer by looking at contribution generated by the contract.

Remember contribution is calculated as Selling Price – Variable Cost. On a per unit basis for the contract, this is £8.25 – £8 = £0.25 contribution on each extra unit sold

As we sell 100 units more, this generates a total increase in contribution of £25 (100 × £0.25).

We should accept the project; the use of contribution analysis enables us to determine this quickly.

INTRODUCTION TO BREAK-EVEN ANALYSIS

How many units do we need to sell to make a profit?

By how much will profit fall if price is lowered by £1?

What will happen to our profits if we rent an extra factory but find that we can operate at only half capacity?

All of the above are realistic business questions. One solution would be to set up a model of the business on a computer and feed in the various pieces of information. The development of the microcomputer and associated software packages such as Lotus 1–2–3 and Supercalc mean that this may be a feasible option.

If there is no computer model readily available, break-even analysis provides a quick and often surprisingly accurate alternative.

It is worth noting that another name for break-even analysis is CVP analysis. This stands for cost, volume, profit analysis.

Approach

Costs are assumed to be either fixed or variable, or at least separable into these elements.

Economies or diseconomies of scale are ignored; this ensures that our cost functions are strictly linear.

The effect of changes in volume is determined by looking at the effect that change in volume has on **contribution** (not profit).

Remember, Selling price per unit – Total variable cost per unit = Contribution per unit

BREAK-EVEN POINT

This is the volume of sales at which neither a profit nor a loss is made. It is also the volume of sales at which total contribution (contribution per unit multiplied by number of units sold) is equal to fixed costs. The fixed costs are total fixed costs, ie. fixed production and fixed selling costs.

It can be found using the following formula.

$$\text{Break-even point} = \frac{\text{Fixed cost}}{\text{Contribution / Unit}}$$

This formula can be derived by considering the composition of profit.

For sales of Q units:

	Per unit £	Total £
Sales	P	
Variable costs	(V)	
	——	
Contribution	C × Q =	CQ
Fixed costs		(F)
		——
Profit		P
		——

$$\text{To break even, } P = O$$
$$\Rightarrow CQ = F$$
$$\Rightarrow Q = \frac{F}{C} = \frac{\text{Fixed cost}}{\text{Contribution / Unit}}$$

Example

Rachel's product, the 'Steadyarm' sells for £50. It has a variable cost of £30 per unit. Rachel's fixed costs are £40,000 per annum. What is her break-even point?

Solution

$$\text{Break-even point} = \frac{\text{Fixed cost}}{\text{Contribution unit}} = \frac{£40,000}{£20(W)} = 2,000 \text{ units}$$

Working

	£
Selling price	50
Less: Variable cost	(30)
	——
Contribution	20
	——

We can show that this is the case with a summarised profit and loss account.

	£
Sales (2,000 × £50)	100,000
Variable cost (2,000 × £30)	(60,000)
Fixed cost	(40,000)
	——————
Profit/loss	–
	——————

SALES VOLUME TO ACHIEVE A PARTICULAR PROFIT

A similar approach to the above can be adopted.

$$\text{Sales volume to achieve a particular profit} = \frac{\text{Fixed cost + Required profit}}{\text{Contribution / Unit}}$$

Illustration

Information as above but we now want to know how many units must be sold to make a profit of £100,000.

To achieve a profit of £100,000, we require sufficient contribution to firstly cover the fixed costs (£40,000) and secondly, having covered fixed costs, we require sufficient contribution to give a profit of £100,000. Therefore our required contribution is £140,000.

$$\text{Sales volume to achieve a profit of £100,000} = \frac{\text{Fixed costs} + \text{Required profit}}{\text{Contribution / Unit}}$$

$$= \frac{£40,000 + £100,000}{£20} = 7,000 \text{ units}$$

We can show that this is the case with a summarised profit and loss account.

	£
Sales (7,000 × £50)	350,000
Variable cost (7,000 × £30)	(210,000)
Fixed cost	(40,000)
Profit	100,000

BREAK-EVEN CHARTS

It is possible to show the approach diagramatically.

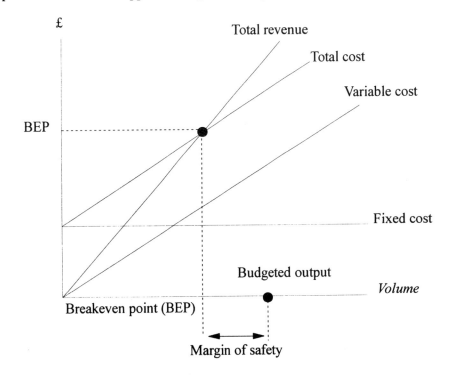

The variable cost and fixed cost line add little to the diagram which is normally shown as:

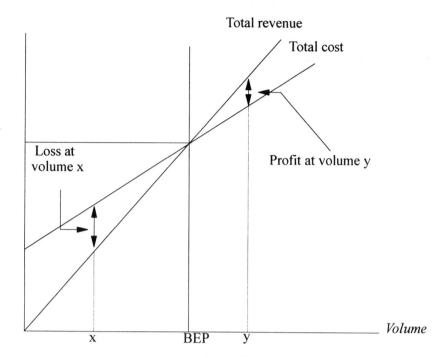

PROFIT-VOLUME (P/V) CHART

This is another way of presenting the information.

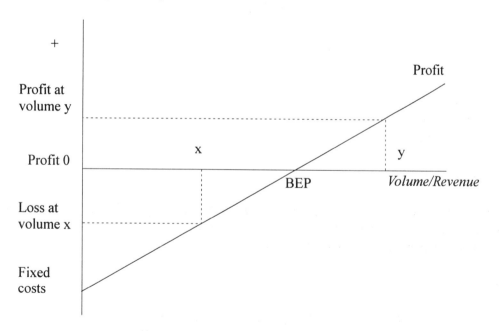

Note that at a sales volume of nil, the total loss will be the same as the business's fixed costs.

P/V RATIO

The P/V ratio is a measure of the rate at which profit (or, strictly, contribution) is generated with sales volume, as measured by revenue. An alternative name which provides a more accurate description is the contribution/sales (C/S) ratio.

$$P/V \text{ ratio} = \frac{\text{Contribution}}{\text{Selling price}}$$

It tells us what proportion of the selling price is contributing to our fixed overhead and profits. It is comparable to the gross profit margin.

If for example the C/S ratio was 40% this would mean that 40% of the selling price was contribution which means therefore that the remaining 60% is variable cost.

It can be used to find the break-even point or the point at which profit is £x in terms of **sales value** (rather than volume).

$$\text{Sales value giving a profit £X} = \frac{\text{Fixed cost} + \text{Profit}}{\text{P / V ratio}}$$

Illustration

As before.

What value of sales will give a profit of £100,000?

$$\text{Sales value giving profit £100,000} = \text{required contribution £140,000}$$

$$= \frac{\text{Fixed cost} + £100,000}{\text{P / V ratio}}$$

$$= \frac{£40,000 + £100,000}{0.4 \text{ (W)}}$$

$$= £350,000$$

Working

$$\text{P/V ratio} = \frac{\text{Contribution}}{\text{Selling price}} = \frac{£20}{£50} = 0.4$$

SENSITIVITY ANALYSIS

A very important aspect of decision-making is concerned with sensitivity analysis, ie. how sensitive is our decision to a change in a particular component? Sensitivity analysis is thus concerned with assessing the point at which our original decision changes.

Illustration

Jonathan plans to manufacture 2,000 units of a product which he can sell for £150 each, the variable cost per unit being £70. Budgeted fixed costs are estimated to be £100,000.

Calculate – Break-even volume
  – Margin of safety
  – Sensitivity of the decision to a change in the fixed costs

- **The break-even point** is as before:

$$\frac{\text{Fixed costs}}{\text{Unit contribution}} = \frac{£100,000}{£150 - £70 = £80} = 1,250 \text{ units}$$

Note: Our budgeted level of output of 2,000 units will therefore result in a budgeted profit of:

	£
Total contribution = 2,000 × £80	160,000
Less: Fixed costs	(100,000)
Budgeted profit	60,000

- The **margin of safety** is the amount by which anticipated sales can fall before the business makes a loss. It can be expressed in units or sales revenue or in relative terms.

Budgeted sales – Break-even sales = Margin of safety

2,000 units – 1,250 units = 750 units

or $\dfrac{\text{Budgeted sales} - \text{Breakeven sales}}{\text{budgeted sales}} \times 100\%$

$= \dfrac{2,000 - 1,250}{2,000} \times 100\% = 37.5\%$

ie. if budgeted sales fall by more than 37.5%, then Jonathan will make a loss, eg. consider a fall of 40% on the original budget.

	£
Revised contribution = 0.6 × 2,000 × 80	96,000
Less: Fixed costs	(100,000)
Budgeted loss	(4,000)

- **Sensitivity of the decision to a change in fixed costs** As we have seen earlier, currently Jonathan has a budgeted profit of £60,000. Thus the original decision will change if fixed costs increase by more than £60,000 and soak up all of the profits we are currently making, ie. an increase of $\dfrac{60,000}{100,000} \times 100\% = 60\%$: fixed costs can increase by up to 60% before Jonathan will make a loss, one could therefore argue fixed costs are fairly insensitive.

ASSUMPTIONS OF BREAK-EVEN ANALYSIS

The approach makes a number of assumptions which are set out below:

- Fixed costs remain fixed throughout the range charted.

- Variable costs fluctuate proportionally with volume.

- Selling prices do not change with volume.

- Efficiency and productivity do not change with volume.

- It is applied to a single product or static mix of products.

- Volume is the only factor affecting cost.

- Linearity is appropriate.

While some of the assumptions may seem unrealistic, over the limited range of activity usually considered, they are often a reasonable approximation to the true position.

We will now consider each of the assumptions in more detail.

Fixed costs remain fixed

If fixed costs are actually stepped fixed costs, it would be possible to have more than one break-even point.

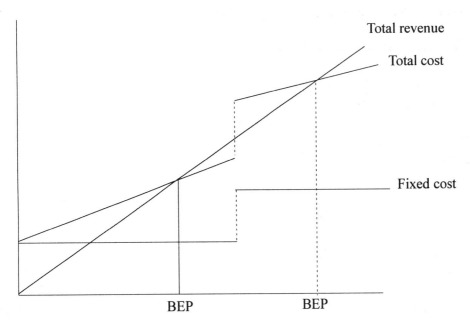

Variable costs change in direct proportion to volume

If this is not the case, then it is invalid to say that a further x units will increase contribution by x multiplied by the existing contribution per unit.

Direct labour is one variable cost that might not change in direct proportion to volume. There might be a learning situation in which case the relationship would be as follows:

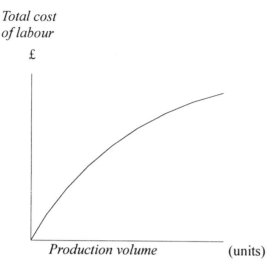

Learning effects are discussed in more detail in Session 4.

Alternatively, there may be no learning effect but overtime is paid at a premium.

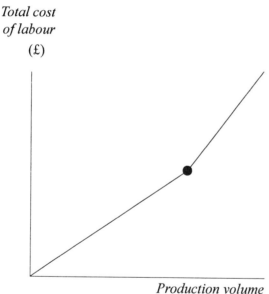

Selling prices, productivity/efficiency do not change

A change in any of these items will require a new break-even chart.

It might be thought likely that to increase volume a reduction in selling price would be necessary, as discussed in the previous session.

Productivity may fall as volume increases and overtime is worked because the workers become tired.

Product mix does not change

If we are performing break-even analysis for a mix of products, then we are working with *average* revenue and *average* variable cost.

Illustration 1

Bob sells X and Y in equal quantities.

	X £	Y £
Selling price	200	180
Variable cost	(100)	(130)
Contribution	100	50

Fixed costs £150,000

$$BEP = \frac{£150,000}{£75 \ (W)} = 2,000 \text{ units}$$

(ie. 1,000 X and 1,000 Y)

Working

Average of £100 and £50, in equal quantities = £75

You may check that does indeed give a break-even situation.

Illustration 2

Suppose now Bob is able to sell three X for every Y.

$$BEP = \frac{£150,000}{£87.50 \ (W)} = 1,715$$

(ie. approximately 429 Y and 1,286 X)

Working

$$\frac{3 \times £100 + 1 \times £50}{4} = £87.50$$

It can be seen then that the change in mix has changed the break-even point from 2,000 units to 1,715 units.

Volume is the only factor affecting cost

It may be the case that government action will affect cost. For example, the government might raise taxes on our inputs and hence raise our total costs. This will of course raise our break-even point.

A similar situation can be conceived as a result of overseas events or even unusual weather conditions.

Linearity is appropriate

In many ways this is a summary of the above assumptions. The economist would argue that the laws of diminishing returns would give us the following break-even chart.

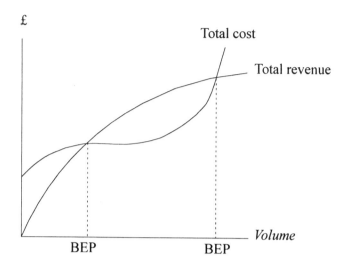

This diagram represents the view that:

● to sell more we have to reduce our price; and

● to buy more raw materials we have to pay more because they are in scarce supply (although we may get the benefits of scale initially).

KEY FACTOR ANALYSIS

Introduction

This is a technique that we can use when we have one resource that is in scarce supply and we can make more than one type of product using that resource. Naturally, we wish to use that resource in the most efficient manner to maximise profits. Key factor analysis will identify that manner.

(If there are two or more resources in restricted supply, we should use the technique of linear programming which is not in the syllabus!)

Approach

● Determine the resource that is in scarce supply.

● Calculate the contribution per unit generated by each type of product we want to make.

● For each product divide its contribution per unit by the number of units of scarce resource needed to make one unit of that product.

● Pick the product with the highest contribution per unit of scarce resource.

Example

Helen makes two products as set out below:

	H £	L £
Selling price	100	30
Material @ £10 per kg	(50)	(10)
Contribution	50	20

Helen can sell all the goods she can make.

Next year she will be able to purchase only 1,000 kg of material.

Required

Find Helen's optimal production plan for next year.

Solution (1)

An unsubtle approach to the problem of how best to use the available material is set out below, this is not the approach we will ultimately adopt.

By inspection, if materials cost £10/kg Hs require 5 kg/unit and Ls £1 kg/unit.

Thus with only 1,000 kg of materials available:

Maximum contribution from making H $\dfrac{1,000}{5} \times £50 = £10,000$

Maximum contribution from making L $\dfrac{1,000}{1} \times £20 = £20,000$

What about some sort of combination?

Every L that is *not* made will:

- reduce contribution by £20; and

- release one kilogram of material.

This one kilogram can be used to produce:

- ¹/₅ of one H; and

- this will give an increased contribution of $\dfrac{£50}{5} = £10$

Therefore it is not worthwhile sacrificing any production of L for H.

Consequently the best option is to use all the material to produce 1,000 Ls.

Solution (2)

We will now rework the calculation adopting the much more efficient key factor approach, ie. identifying the product with the greatest contribution per unit of scarce resource. The scarce resource, which in this case is materials becomes the key factor.

Calculate the contribution per unit of scarce resource as this measures how efficiently the scarce resource is used.

$$H: \frac{\text{Contribution / unit}}{\text{kg material used}}$$

$$= \frac{£50}{5 \text{ kg (W)}} = £10/\text{kg}$$

Working

Total material cost: £50 ÷ £10/kg = 5 kg per unit

$$L: \frac{£20}{1 \text{ kg}} = £20/\text{kg}$$

As L has the higher contribution per unit of scarce resource, Helen should make L. Calculate the total contribution from making either L or H and compare the two to assure yourself this is the case.

In principle, this is all there is to key factor analysis. In exams, the examiner will embellish the question, often in a similar manner to the following example. Try this example before looking at the solution.

Example

Helen's sister Louise is subject to the same restriction of 1,000 kg of material next year.

She makes two products

	L	U
Selling price	*30*	*70*
Material @ £10 per kg	*(10)*	*(20)*
	20	*50*

Louise can sell as much of either product as she can make; however she has signed a contract with William guaranteeing to supply him with 200 L each year.

Required

What is Louise's optimal production plan for next year?

Solution

Again we must calculate contribution per unit of scarce resource.

$$L: \frac{£20}{1} = £20$$

$$U: \frac{£50}{2} = £25$$

This time we do not apply this knowledge immediately. Here Louise is compelled to produce at least 200 L whether it has the highest contribution per scarce resource or not.

After she has produced 200 L she will have 800 kg of material left.

We can determine the use of this 800 kg by key factor analysis. It transpires that it should be used on U which has the higher contribution per unit of scarce resource.

Production plan
200 L
400 U

Example

Louise's husband John is subject to a restriction of £3,200 worth of labour hours in one month. He makes three products.

	A	B	C
Selling price	10	15	20
Labour cost	(3)	(5)	(6)
Other variable costs	(4)	(4)	(5)
Contribution	3	6	9

John must make products B and C in the ratio of two Bs for every one C.

Required

What is John's optimal production plan for the next month?

Solution

Since B and C must be produced in a specified ratio, we cannot treat them as separate products. However, we can link them together and treat them as one product by creating a 'package' of two Bs and one C.

One package:

	Contribution	Labour cost
Two Bs	12	10
One C	9	6
	21	16

We can then compare this package with the alternative production plan, ie. to produce product A.

Contribution per £ of scarce resource:

$$A: \frac{£3}{£3} = £1.00$$

$$\text{Package (2B + 1C):} \quad \frac{£21}{£16} = £1.3125$$

(Note that there is no need to use hours as the unit of measurement – using £s will give the same result.)

Since the package uses labour more efficiently, the package should be produced.

Each package uses £16 worth of hours, therefore we can produce 200 packages with £3,200 worth of hours available.

Produce	400 B	(200 × 2)
	200 C	(200 × 1)

RELEVANT COSTS FOR DECISION-MAKING

Introduction

Although an existing structure of costs, analysed between fixed and activity-variable items, will remain valid over a defined range of existing activities, the purpose of decision-making will normally be to alter some aspect of the business. When this is done, then the pre-existing levels of variable cost per unit or relevant fixed costs will cease to be applicable.

It will therefore become necessary to define for each decision which items of cost or revenue will be changed as a result of taking the decision.

Therefore we are moving away from a formal structure of fixed and variable costs, back to the economist's concept of truly 'marginal' changes.

Relevant costs are only those expected future costs that will differ under alternative courses of action.

The concept of relevant costs will be elaborated in the following paragraphs.

Historical cost

Every decision deals with the future. The function of the decision-maker is to select courses of action for the future and this decision must by its nature be based on predictions. Historical costs in themselves are therefore irrelevant to decisions, though they may be the best available basis for predicting future costs.

Variable costs

Costs which have been classified as variable by convention or on the basis of past experience, may not in fact vary under the circumstances of a particular volume decision. Accepting a special sales order, for example, may not involve incurring additional selling costs.

Fixed costs

Costs which have been classified as fixed by convention or on the basis of past experience may in fact be affected by a particular decision. This may be for two reasons:

- The costs are fixed in relation to the levels of activity previously experienced, but a decision may extend the range of activity and thus cause certain fixed costs to be stepped up to a new level (for example, if a new warehouse needs to be rented).

- The costs are fixed in relation to the normal time horizon for forecasting; but if the time span of an action exceeds the normal period, then fixed costs may change.

Common costs

In considering a range of alternative actions, costs which will be identical for all alternatives are irrelevant and can be ignored for the purpose of decision-making. So, if a manager is paid the same salary whichever project he works on, this cost can be ignored.

Past costs

Costs incurred in the past ('sunk costs') will always be irrelevant. The decision-maker has no opportunity to alter what has already happened. Some specific examples of this are:

- **Obsolete stock** –the cost of stock already held, and now proved to be obsolete, has no relevance to a decision regarding its disposal or other use; even though the decision may result in a book loss being reported.

- **Old equipment** – the cost of new equipment and the disposal value of old equipment are relevant future transactions. The book value of old equipment is irrelevant to any decision-making technique.

OPPORTUNITY COST

This arises when an *existing* resource (labour, stock, fixed asset etc.) is to be used in the project being decided upon. It is the maximum *alternative* benefit that might have been obtained from the use of the resource in question.

In other words we are looking into the future to determine our cost and not back to the original (or historic) cost.

Note this only applies to resources that are 'scarce' – ie. further supplies cannot be bought, or only at an uneconomic cost.

Example

Robin owns some plastic which cost £1,000 two years ago.

He could sell it for £750.

Alternatively, he could use it to produce product X. This would save him purchasing other materials to make X which would have cost £1,250.

What is the relevant cost of using the plastic in a new product Y?

Solution

Having the plastic means that Robin has a choice of:

- receiving £750
- saving £1,250

Clearly he would choose to save £1,250.

The maximum alternative benefit is therefore £1,250.

Therefore, the opportunity cost of using the plastic in product Y is £1,250.

Note how the historic cost is ignored as it has no influence on the future benefits of owning the plastic.

Consider how these principles apply to Louise below before looking at the solution.

Example

Louise owns a barrel of acid which cost £1,700.

She could use it in product A which is a 'one-off' product for an overseas customer.

If she does not use it in product A, it will have to be neutralised at a cost of £500.

What is the machine cost of using the acid in product A?

Solution

Use of the acid gives rise to a *saving*, not a cost at all (saving = £500). Therefore it will be treated as additional revenue from making product A.

Incremental cost

Consider the following.

Example

Kathryn is about to buy machine Q for her factory. It will cost £15,000.

She is offered a contract that will require her to buy a larger machine for £20,000.

What is the machine cost of taking the contract?

Solution

	£
Cost with the contract	20,000
Cost without the contract	(15,000)
Therefore cost to the contract	5,000

Now consider the case of Dick Ltd below.

Example

The component division of Dick Ltd has been offered a contract to supply ten components at a price of £6,000.

The relevant cost of the contract is £3,500.

Head Office charges all contracts with £2,000 to recognise the fact that fixed costs have to be covered. (Head Office costs are unaltered by the acceptance or rejection of this contract.)

Should the contract be accepted?

Solution

If the contract is accepted, the company will be £2,500 better off.

	£
Revenue	6,000
Costs	3,500
	2,500

Therefore the company should accept it.

Note: The Head Office fixed overheads will be the same whether or not the contract is accepted and thus should be ignored.

Another way of putting this is that they are not incremental costs but common costs.

Remember: marginal costs are the *changes* in cash costs that arise as a result of the decision.

A WORKED EXAMPLE

A research project, which to date has cost the company £150,000, is under review. It is anticipated that, should the project be allowed to proceed, it will be completed in approximately one year when the results would be sold to a government agency for £300,000.

Shown below are the additional expenses which the Managing Director estimates will be necessary to complete the work.

Materials – £60,000 original cost

This material, which has just been received and paid for, is extremely toxic and if not used on the project would have to be disposed of by special means, at a cost of £5,000.

Labour – £40,000

The men are highly skilled and very difficult to recruit. They were transferred to the project from a production department and, at a recent board meeting, the Works Director claimed that if the men were returned to him he could earn the company £150,000 extra sales revenue over the next year. The accountant calculated that the prime cost of those sales would be £100,000 (including £40,000 for the cost of the labour) and the overhead absorbed (all fixed) would amount for £20,000.

Research staff – £60,000

This constitutes wages during the research period. A decision has already been taken that this will be the last major piece of research undertaken, and consequently when work on the project ceases the staff involved will be made redundant. Redundancy and severance pay have been estimated at £25,000. If they were to be made redundant now these costs would be only £15,000.

Share of general building services – £35,000

The Managing Director is not very sure what is included in this expense. He knows, however, that the accounts staff charge similar amounts every year to each department.

Required

Assuming the estimates are accurate, advise the Managing Director whether the project should be allowed to proceed. Carefully and clearly explain the reasons for your treatment of each expense item.

Outline other, non-qualifiable factors that may be taken into account in a decision of this kind.

Solution

Differential cash flow

Costs	Note *(see below)*	With project £	Without project £	Difference £
Materials	2	–	(5,000)	5,000
Labour: opportunity cost (gross contribution)	4		90,000	(90,000)
Research staff – wages	3	(60,000)	–	(60,000)
– redundancy		(25,000)	(15,000)	(10,000)
Revenue		300,000	–	300,000
		215,000	(70,000)	145,000

Note: This answer shows relevant costs/revenues only. The same decision would be derived from including all incremental costs and revenues whether relevant or not as they would appear in both columns and the difference column would be unchanged, ie. the difference column shows the incremental costs of proceeding with the project.

Alternative presentation

Evaluation of the costs and benefits of continuing the project

	Note	£
Revenue from the government agency		300,000
Saving of disposal cost	2	5,000
		305,000
Research staff wages		(60,000)
Research staff redundancy costs	3	(10,000)
Labour	4	(90,000)
		145,000

As there is a benefit, the project should continue.

Notes

(1)   *Costs already incurred £150,000*

These will be the same whether or not the project continues. They should therefore be ignored for decision-making purposes.

(2)   *Material saving of £5,000*

The £60,000 purchase price has already been incurred.

It is therefore a sunk cost (ie. will not change with the decision) and should be ignored for decision-making purposes.

The treatment of the saving agrees with the example 'Louise'.

(3)   *Redundancy costs £10,000*

	£
Redundancy costs if the project continues	25,000
Redundancy costs if the project halts	15,000
Cost of continuing the project	10,000

(4)   *Labour £90,000*

Prime cost is the sum of all the direct costs (ie. direct labour, direct material and direct expenses)

Benefit of using labour in existing production department

	£
Extra revenue	150,000
Extra materials and expenses (£100,000–£40,000)	60,000
	90,000

The next best use of labour would earn net revenue of £90,000.

This is therefore the opportunity cost of using the labour for continuing the project.

Note that the labour cost itself and the fixed overhead have been ignored because they will be the same whatever decision is made.

(5)   *General building services*

These costs have been ignored as it seems unlikely that they will change whether the project will continue or not.

Other factors to consider in deciding upon a project

We have examined quantitative aspects which impact on the decision-making process. There are however other factors that must be taken into account which may be of a more qualitative nature. Examples of such items are set out below.

Accuracy of estimates

We may be unwilling to take on a marginal project if it is difficult to estimate costs/revenues accurately.

Time value of money

Money in the future is worth less than money now. This was not taken into account in any of the examples.

Tax

A very important consideration in practice.

Availability of working capital

If money is received later than the date on which costs have to be paid, further working capital will be necessary.

Reliability of suppliers

A failure of supplies may result in a more expensive alternative being used or penalties either of which might have changed the decision had they been known in advance.

Prestige

Association with a particular project may be worthwhile in terms of future work even if the project in question is less than worthwhile.

Prospects of future work

A low initial price may bring profitable business in the future from the same customer.

Alternatively, a particular project may be a means of breaking into a new market.

Retention of skilled staff

It may not be adequate just to pay such people. They may need work to maintain their skills and if they do not receive it they will seek an alternative employer. A borderline project might be useful in retaining such people.

Knowledge of alternatives

Is the company aware of all the opportunities open to it? In evaluating a particular activity, it is important to assess and test the alternatives available.

Creditworthiness of customer

All the analysis in the world will be wasted if the customer is unable to pay.

SPECIFIC PRODUCTION DECISIONS

The concept of relevant costs is not only applicable to decisions regarding new or incremental projects to the business. The following sections consider two decisions concerned with existing operations that will be made by considering the incremental costs and benefits involved.

Capacity decisions

Second shift working to increase capacity

Any decision to increase or decrease capacity will involve some change in the cost structure of the business, ie. there will be incremental changes in fixed costs. This is illustrated in the following problem.

Example

A factory belonging to a manufacturing company operates one shift only for the production of product P.

Annual production is 150,000 units and these are sold at £2.20 each.

The relevant cost information is as follows.

Direct labour	50,000 hours per annum at £1.10 per hour
Direct material costs	£1.25 per unit
Other variable costs	£20,250 per annum
Factory fixed costs	£77,250 per annum

It is decided to consider working a second shift, in order to increase sales to 250,000 units per annum.

Because labour efficiency is expected to be lower than on existing production, it is estimated that 42,000 direct hours will be needed on the second shift. The average rate including shift premium will be £1.50 per hour.

There will be additional fixed costs totalling £17,000 per annum.

Required

(a)   Will the second shift be profitable?

(b)   What profit will be earned by the factory as a whole if the second shift is put into operation?

Solution

(a)   The total additional costs of producing 100,000 units of product P on the second shift will be as follows.

	£
Direct labour – 42,000 hours @ £1.50	63,000
Direct material 100,000 × £1.25	125,000
Other variable costs 100,000/150,000 × £20,250	13,500
Incremental fixed costs	17,000
Total incremental costs	218,500

The incremental cost per unit will thus be £2.185 per unit, which is slightly lower than the selling price of £2.20 per unit, and the second shift is thus profitable.

(b)   The total costs of running the factory will now be as follows.

Costs of original shift

	£
Direct labour – 50,000 hours @ £1.10	55,000
Direct material – 150,000 units @ £1.25	187,500
Variable costs	20,250
Fixed costs	77,250
	340,000
Incremental costs of second shift	218,500
Total costs	558,500

Profit/(loss) statement	Original £	Incremental £	Total £
Sales	330,000	220,000	550,000
Costs	340,000	218,500	558,500
Profit/(loss)	(10,000)	1,500	(8,500)

On 250,000 units these represent an average cost of £2.234 per unit, which is above the selling price per unit. In other words, the original shift was unprofitable.

This is something to look for in all decision problems. The immediate effect of the decision may be beneficial, but if the pre-existing business was not profitable, then a better decision might have been to disengage from that business rather than add profitable patches.

Shut-down of capacity

It is convenient to start with a simple example of a company engaged in engineering jobbing work. This company expanded rapidly, but now finds that market demand has fallen so that it can sell no more than 200,000 hours of work a year, at an average price of £7 per hour. It has incurred a heavy loss in the most recent year and is under pressure from its bankers to restore some measure of profit.

By eliminating a bonus incentive scheme, it can reduce its variable costs to £6.25 per hour. Its fixed costs are currently £250,000 per annum and it asks how far these have to be reduced to achieve a break-even position. Making use of the break-even formula, with X as the symbol for fixed costs, the sustainable level of fixed costs at the current level of output can be calculated as £150,000, thus:

$$\frac{£X}{£7-£6.25} = 200,000$$

$$X = 200,000 \times 0.75 = £150,000$$

Fixed costs must therefore be reduced by £100,000 per annum.

Value of assets

The above example could have led to a decision to shut down the factory. For such decisions there is no question of using a marginal cost approach or investment techniques. The question to be answered is quite simply whether the net proceeds of realising the assets will be sufficient to discharge the liabilities of the company.

In making such calculations one would have to bear in mind many practical considerations, which might include:

(a)   the open market value of specialised buildings in a particular location;

(b)   the saleable value of specialised machines in a second-hand condition; or storage costs pending commencement of a new venture;

(c)   losses due to stocks being obsolete or unsuitable for other purposes;

(d)   redundancy payments to employees;

(e)   liabilities for servicing goods previously sold;

(f)   the cost of completing existing sale contracts;

(g)   costs of terminating outstanding purchase or hire commitments;

(h)   making good any damage or deterioration to rented premises (dilapidations);

(i)   terminal liabilities for taxation including any capital gains;

(j)   temporary staff costs to replace employees who had already left.

The management accountant would be involved in many of these calculations, although clearly his true functions as a management adviser would also be approaching termination.

The 'make or buy' decision

Introduction

Another problem which has a bearing on production planning is the decision whether to make or buy an intermediate product.

Example

A company is at present assembling one of the components needed for a final product. The annual quantity required is 20,000 units, and the annual cost at present is reported as:

	£'000
Direct materials	60
Direct wages	40
Supervision – avoidable if manufacture discontinued	10
Floor space occupancy	7

The assemblies could be purchased for £6.10 each from an outside supplier. If this were done, the floor space vacated could be used for storage purposes, saving warehouse rent and transport costs of £18,000 pa. Should the company continue to assemble the component, or buy it from the outside supplier?

Solution

The cost of floor space occupancy is probably merely an apportioned cost of part of the factory. The whole cost will continue whether or not this particular component is manufactured. It is therefore irrelevant to this decision. The opportunity cost of the alternative use of the floor space is relevant, however, since it is directly affected by the decision taken. The cost of supervision, being avoidable if manufacture is discontinued, is a relevant fixed cost of the decision.

A possible solution, therefore would be as follows.

	£'000
Marginal cost of manufacture	
Direct materials	60
Direct wages	40
Total (= £5 per unit)	100
Relevant fixed cost of supervision	10
Opportunity cost of floor space	18
	128
Cost of outside purchase (20,000 × £6.10)	122

Therefore outside purchase would be preferable as it would save £6,000 pa.

The above is the purely financial solution. Other factors would need to be taken into account, such as the reliability of the outside product, and the ability of the supplier to deliver on time.

If the required volume had been 27,500 units per annum the answer would have been different, because:

Outside purchase would cost more than the variable costs of manufacture by 27,500 units @ £1.10 (£6.10 – £5)	£30,250
Offset by relevant fixed cost savings and opportunity costs of floor space	£28,000
Giving a difference in favour of manufacture	£2,250

Range within which analysis is valid

At any level of production which differed significantly from 20,000 units per annum, whether more or less, the existing analysis of costs might be inapplicable. For example:

(a) The purchase price, whether of materials for assembly or of the sub-contracted work, might be subject to quantity discounts for large quantities or to a fixed minimum charge for small quantities.

(b) The labour costs per unit for own assembly could vary with volume, either because overtime work might be involved or because the efficiency of labour might vary with the length of production run.

(c) Supervision costs would be stepped up or down as the number of direct employees changed. They would not normally, however, be directly variable.

QUESTIONS

1   Roger Morton

Roger makes a single product, the Morton. During 19X9 he plans to make and sell 10,000 Mortons and accordingly has estimated the cost of each to be £50 (see below). Each Morton sells for £75.

	Cost of a Morton £
Material	12
Labour	24
Variable overhead	10
Fixed overhead	4
	—
	50
	—

(a)   Calculate Roger's total fixed overhead.

(b)   Calculate the contribution per unit earned by each Morton.

(c)   What is the total revenue earned if Roger sells 2,000 Mortons?

(d)   Using the information calculated in (a), (b) and (c) above, draw Roger's break-even chart and estimate his break-even point.

(e)   Confirm your estimate of the break-even point by calculating it.

(f)   If Roger makes and sells 1,000 Mortons, how much extra profit will he make?

2 ABC Ltd   (AAT CA Model)

The following information relates to a month's production of ABC Ltd, a small manufacturing company mass producing a single product.

	ABC Ltd
Materials per unit	£4
Labour per unit	£6
Fixed costs per month	£40,000
Production capacity per month	10,000 units
Selling price per unit	£17
Current level of sales per month	7,000 units

Assessment tasks

(a) (i) Using graph paper, prepare a break-even chart for the company.

    (ii) Show clearly the break-even point and the position for the current level of sales per month.

(b) (i) Calculate the break-even point in units using the formula, rather than reading off from the chart.

    (ii) Calculate the current level of profit per month.

(c) DEF Ltd is a competitor with the same production capacity selling a similar product at the same price. DEF Ltd has fixed costs of £60,000 per month and variable costs of £5 per unit.

    (i) Contrast the production methods of ABC Ltd and DEF Ltd from the information given.

    (ii) Which of the two companies will generate profits at a higher rate for levels of production beyond its break-even point? Give reasons for your answer.

(d) The marketing manager of ABC Ltd suggests that the company should increase the selling price to £20 but upgrade the quality of the product by spending an additional £2 per unit on materials. Fixed costs would be increased by £2,000. It is estimated that sales per month would drop to 6,500 units.

    What would be the effect on ABC Ltd's profitability of implementing the above policy?

3 Security services   (AAT CA J94)

The company for which you work provides security services for corporate clients. It currently charges £30 per hour for the service and the cost structure of the service is as follows:

Variable cost per hour	£22
Fixed cost for one month	£18,000

The marketing director has suggested that the company should provide extra benefits to its services. Research conducted amongst current customers suggests that they would be prepared to pay £33 per hour for the improved service. The cost structure would be altered as follows:

Revised variable cost per hour	£20
Revised fixed cost for one month	£39,000

It is not expected that sales levels would alter from the current level of 5,200 hours per month.

Assessment tasks

(a)   Calculate the break-even point in hours per month both in the present situation and with the changes proposed by the marketing director.

(b)   Calculate the monthly profit both in the present situation and with the changes proposed by the marketing director.

(c)   Comment briefly on the way in which the revised cost and selling price structure will affect future profit changes if sales increase or decrease from their current level.

4   Dample Ltd

As cost accountant at Dample Ltd, you produce the following information relating to the department manufacturing concrete blocks for the three month period ended 31 December 19X1:

	£
Sales (217,600 units)	272,000
Direct costs	
Materials	89,200
Labour	63,120
	152,320
Variable overheads	
Production	14,012
Selling	12,100
	26,112
Fixed overheads	
Production	16,000
Selling	10,000
	26,000
Total costs	204,432
Net profit	67,568

You are informed that in the quarter ended 31 March 19X2 direct labour rates are likely to rise by 10%.

Required

(a)   Calculate:

      (i)   the break-even point as revealed by the accounts for the three months ended 31 December 19X1; and

      (ii)   the additional sales required for the three months ended 31 March 19X2 to maintain the same amount of net profit as in the three months ended 31 December 19X1 on the assumption that selling prices will not be raised.

(b)   Demonstrate, with the aid of a graph, the manner in which break-even analysis could be used by Dample Ltd to show the effect of changes in costs and revenues.

(c)   Comment on the limitations of break-even analysis.

5   Robert Motherwell   (AAT CA Model)

Robert Motherwell operates a small workshop which makes two products, a garden seat and a child's swing, which are marketed by an agent who takes all units produced and receives a commission of 20% of the wholesale selling price. He estimates that his current costs per unit of production are as follows:

	Garden seat per unit	Child's swing £ per unit
Raw materials	2	8
Bought-out components	8	1
Labour	3	9
Production overheads (Variable)	1	3
General overheads (Fixed)	4	4
Wholesale selling price	30	40
Current annual production	2,000 units	2,000 units

Robert estimates that production overheads are incurred at the rate of 33$\frac{1}{3}$% of labour costs. General overheads include depreciation, insurance, rates, professional fees and administrative costs. He estimates that these amount to £16,000 in total per annum and, for costing purposes, these costs are apportioned equally between all units of production.

Robert is thinking of making a number of changes in the way in which he runs his business. He asks you as his financial adviser to prepare a memo on each of the following proposals in turn, setting out clearly the probable effects of each proposal on profitability. Give your recommendations, taking into account your calculations and any other factors which you feel might be relevant. Treat each proposal as a separate item.

Proposal 1

Robert is considering making some of the bought-out components for the garden seat in his own workshop. He has sufficient spare capacity to do this. He estimates that he will save 75% of the cost of bought-out components but that raw material costs and labour costs would double.

Proposal 2

Robert believes that the workshop could make more profit by undertaking the marketing of his products himself rather than by employing an agent. He estimates that doing the work himself would cost an additional £5,000 per annum plus £4 per unit sold. Sales would not be affected.

Proposal 3

Robert is considering buying a new machine which it is hoped should speed up production of both items of production. This would involve scrapping much of the existing equipment. Robert has sent you a note in which he says, 'I think that it would be worthwhile to buy the new machine were it not for the depreciation on the old machine which we will still have to show in the accounts because, when we bought it three years ago, we agreed to write it off over five years'. Write a memo in reply to Robert's note.

Proposal 4

Robert wishes to plan for the expansion of his business but does not want to increase his labour costs significantly beyond the £24,000 which he currently spends on the 4000 units which are currently produced per annum. Which of the two products should he market most strongly to achieve a product mix which will give him the most profit? Note that all other costs apart from labour could be increased. Write a brief note to Robert giving reasons for your recommendation.

6   Belfry Ltd

Belfry Ltd manufactures two products, Chome and Drib, from one basic ingredient.

The budgeted costs and selling prices for each product are as follows:

	Chome £	Drib £
Direct material @ £4 per kg	10.00	10.00
Direct labour @ £5 per hour	30.00	50.00
Variable production overheads	14.40	24.00
Fixed production overheads	21.60	36.00
	76.00	120.00
Selling price	85.00	132.00

The company absorbs variable and production overheads by direct labour hours. The figures above are derived from a budget encompassing 120,000 labour hours for a 12-month period to 31 December 19X2. This is the maximum time that the company has available.

In addition to the overheads reflected in the costs for each unit, it is expected that the company will incur £125,000 of distribution and administration overheads.

Historically the company has always produced Chome and Drib in the ratio 5:2 which reflects the maximum demand of 15,000 Chomes and 6,000 Dribs, and the budget has been prepared on that basis. The sales director is confident that all production can be sold. There is no opening stock.

The company's managing director is not sure that the production ratio will lead to the greatest total profit for the year. She has asked you to produce a report for the board setting out the budgeted profit for the year if the original budget is followed and to present a revised plan if you feel that there is any way the company could change its production in order to generate higher profits for the year.

Required

Set out the report outlined above, showing detailed calculations to support your recommendations. Briefly include any reservations you may have.

7   World History Museum   (AAT CA J94)

The World History Museum stages exhibitions using its own premises. You are the assistant management accountant for the museum. The managers are currently deciding whether to stage an exhibition of ancient Australian artefacts.

The exhibition will run for three months and you have collected together the following data, which may or may not be relevant to a decision to proceed with the exhibition.

(1)   Display cabinets will be built and installed at a cost of £1,700. In addition, it will be possible to use cabinets which were originally built for another exhibition at a cost of £500. Repair costs of £150 will be incurred if these extra cabinets are used.

(2)   Extra security staff will be employed at a total cost of £6,500 for the three-month period. In addition, two of the permanent full-time security staff can be redeployed from other areas, without the need to replace them. The salary costs for these two people will be £5,000 for the three-month period.

(3)   The exhibition will utilise 400 square metres of space. The museum's policy is to charge all departments £5 per square metre per month to cover the fixed costs of central administration, rates, etc. The museum owns the premises, therefore no rental costs are incurred.

(4)   If the space is not used for this exhibition, it will be possible to rent it to another organisation as storage space, for a price of £6 per square metre per month.

(5)   Posters and handbills bill be printed to advertise the exhibition. These will cost a total of £750, consisting of £450 for the costs of the posters and handbills (paper, ink and power, etc.), £200 for design and £100 for the apportioned fixed costs of the printing department.

(6)   Other costs to be incurred directly as a result of this exhibition will amount to £1,200.

(7)   It is anticipated that 4,000 people will attend the exhibition, paying an average admission fee of £4 each. In addition, it is expected that each person will spend an average of £2 in the museum's cafeteria after their visit. The museum makes a gross margin of 50% on all cafeteria sales.

Assessment task

Chris Brooks, the general manager of the museum, has asked you to present a statement which shows the financial effect of staging this exhibition. In notes beneath your statement you should indicate the reasons for your treatment of each cost and revenue.

8   JK Co   **(AAT CA D94)**

You work as assistant accountant for the JK Company, a manufacturing company which has recently signed a long-term lease for premises which will be used to house the manufacturing facilities for component P. The component is used in all of the company's products. No other suitable premises are available.

Since signing the lease, JK has been approached by a reputable manufacturer who has offered to supply all of JKs requirements for component P at a very competitive price.

If the manufacturers offer is accepted, the directors are undecided as to whether or not to continue with the lease. Although JK would not need the premises itself, there is a possibility of sub-letting to another company for an annual rent of £3,400.

JK has made an initial down-payment of £1,500 to the leasing company and, additionally, the annual rent under the lease will be £3,000. JK can cancel the lease completely, but it would be unable to recover the down-payment of £1,500.

Information on the internal costs associated with manufacturing component P is as follows:

	£ per annum
Variable costs	25,000
Fixed costs	
Lease payment (as above)	3,000
Other	8,000
	36,000

The 'other fixed costs' of £8,000 are general salaries and other apportioned costs which are unlikely to be saved if the component is not manufactured internally.

Assessment task

You have been asked to collect data which will assist the decision regarding whether or not to accept the manufacturer's offer to supply component P.

(a)   Present a statement of the *relevant* annual cost of manufacturing component P internally. State clearly any assumptions which you make.

(b)   In the context of this decision, explain the meaning of the following costs and give an example of each:

    (i)   a sunk or past cost;
    (ii)   an opportunity cost.

9 R & D Ltd

R & D Ltd are jobbing engineers whom you are advising. The three manufacturing departments comprise the foundry, the machine shop and the fitting shop. A manager is in charge of each department and is responsible to the managing director for the departmental profitability.

Much of the company's turnover is attributable to a single product, a valve, which is cast in the foundry, machined in the machine shop and assembled in the fitting shop. Output of the foundry is transferred to the machine shop at an internal transfer price of £4 per unit, and output of the machine shop is transferred to the fitting shop at an internal transfer price of £11 per unit.

The standard cost of this valve is made up as follows:

	Foundry £	Machine shop £	Fitting shop £	Total £
Raw material – bought in		4.00	11.00	
– bought out	0.50		0.75	1.25
Labour	1.00	2.00	0.75	3.75
Overheads: recovery, based on expected annual sales of each shop, at 200% of labour	2.00	4.00	1.50	7.50
	3.50	10.00	14.00	12.50
Transfer price/selling price	4.00	11.00	14.25	14.25
Profit	0.50	1.00	0.25	1.75

The managing director tells you that he is having difficulty with his managers. The machine shop manager claims that castings for this valve bought from the foundry are too expensive at £4 each and that he can buy a similar casting elsewhere for £3.25. The fitting shop manager in turn says that he can buy machined castings elsewhere for £9.50, as opposed to the internal transfer price of £11. 'Of course,' says the managing director, 'I cannot let them buy out like that because the foundry and the machine shop would soon be short of work. Their suggestions would not be so bad if we could dispose of either shop but, as you know, we cannot do that; in fact, our overheads are fixed for a year or more to come. They do not seem to understand that the company's interest is best served if the whole valve is made on the premises.'

Required

Write a letter to the managing director, stating your opinion on the argument and explaining in words and figures why you hold this opinion. Your figures should include a table comparing the results of the three different methods of manufacture of the valve, namely:

(a)   as at present;
(b)   by purchasing castings;
(c)   by purchasing machined castings.

10   Electronics Ltd

Electronics Ltd produces an ultra-sensitive amplifier, the selling price of which is £50, while the standard cost of £35 is made up as follows:

	£
Direct materials	20
Direct labour	5
Variable overhead	2
Fixed overhead	8

The factory is currently producing 100,000 amplifiers per year; this output represents 100% capacity at single shift working.

Demand for the amplifier is in excess of production and the marketing manager considers that an increase of 50% in the quantity sold could be achieved during the forthcoming year.

A second shift has been proposed. This would increase production capacity to 180,000 amplifiers per annum and would incur additional fixed overheads of £550,000. A shift work premium of 20% would be payable to the direct labour force engaged on the second shift, but if production were to be increased to 150,000 units or more per annum, the whole of the direct materials used would qualify for a 'larger user' discount of 10%.

(a)   Prepare statements showing:

  (i)   whether it would be profitable for Electronics Ltd to add the second shift in order to meet the increased demand; and

  (ii)   the minimum increase in production/sales to justify the addition of the second shift.

(b)   Comment briefly upon any other matters which should receive attention when considering expansion of this kind.

SUMMARY

Throughout this session, we have considered different activity evaluations that might face management.

Although the calculations and techniques adopted in each area vary, there are some fundamental underlying principles:

•   absorption costing is never appropriate to a decision making problem and must be avoided;

•   contribution is of vital importance;

•   incremental and opportunity costs should always be used where appropriate.

Investment appraisal

OBJECTIVES

Part of the management accountant's job will be to contribute towards the appraisal of long-term projects or investments.

After studying this session you should be able to undertake the following:

■ Identify possible investment opportunities.

■ Calculate return on capital employed, payback period, net present values and internal rates of return.

■ Understand the limitations of basic investment appraisal calculations.

The performance criteria addressed by this session are as follows:

■ Estimates are prepared in an approved form and presented to the appropriate recipient(s) within an agreed timescale.

   Appropriate staff are consulted about technical aspects and any special features of projects.

■ Internal and external information relevant to making a decision is identified and used.

   Recommendations which optimise the long-term benefits to the organisation are clearly reported.

   Internal and external information relevant in estimating future costs and revenues are used.

■ Technical, marketing and other relevant specialists are consulted when conducting a project appraisal.

CAPITAL INVESTMENT

In the preceding sessions, we have considered the evaluation of the current activities of a business – break-even levels, dealing with temporary resource shortages, the viability of one-off, incremental projects and other specific short-term production decisions.

In this and the following session, we shall consider the evaluation of longer-term projects that involve significant capital investment.

What is a capital investment project?

The key characteristic of such projects is the tying up of capital for a number of years, in order to earn profits or returns over the period. Although it will generally be possible to pull out of the project earlier than originally intended, this will normally cause the return on investment to be considerably lowered and may even cause a loss.

This differentiates this type of investment from the type more commonly undertaken by individuals, such as the purchasing of shares or depositing money at a building society, where the capital can often be recovered with a reasonable return at any time.

What will the capital be invested in?

The most common investment you will encounter will be in tangible fixed assets, such as the purchase of a new machine, factory or premises from which to operate a new service business.

Other less tangible forms of investment will include research and development, patent rights or goodwill obtained upon the purchase of an existing business.

What form will the returns take?

The purchase of a new fixed asset will often be with the intention of starting a new line of business – be it the manufacturing of a new product, or the provision of a new or extended service. Thus the returns will be the net income generated by the new business.

Alternatively, the investment may be to benefit the existing operations, such that sales are increased (where existing products/services are improved technologically or in quality) or costs are reduced (where production processes are updated or personnel reorganised). In this case, the returns will be measured as the increase in net income or net reduction in costs resulting from the investment.

Authorisation for a capital project

For projects involving a significant amount of capital investment, authorisation for its go-ahead will usually be given by the main board, or a sub-committee formed from the board for this purpose. Smaller projects (such as the replacement of an existing machine) may be within the authorisation limits of the manager of the area of business involved.

The decision will be based upon a project proposal, the main contents of which will be a summary of the costs and benefits arising from the project.

There will also be some form of project appraisal, using methods such as payback, return on capital employed or discounted cash flow. These are discussed in detail later in the session.

Although these appraisal methods will usually give a basis for a recommendation as to whether or not the project should be accepted, they will only be able to take account of monetary costs and benefits. Qualitative factors will also need to be considered when reaching a final decision – such as possible effects on staff morale (for example, if the project involves increased automation or considerable overtime), the environment, customer satisfaction and the business's status/reputation.

Estimation of monetary costs and benefits

Costs of the initial investment and the ongoing, year-by-year operating costs and income relevant to the project will need to be estimated – not only for the initial appraisal decision, but also for budgeting, resource allocation and cost control purposes.

These estimates will consist of both monetary amounts and timings.

The particular problems in estimation of income/costs for capital projects include the following:

(a) *Timescale* – Such projects may extend over tens of years, during which inflation rates (general and specific) and availability of resources can vary considerably. These will in turn affect the prices of resources used.

Markets will be affected by changes in the economy, technology and competition which will affect the level of sales achieved and prices that can be charged.

The project appraisal should incorporate some form of sensitivity analysis to determine the extent to which the most significant of these factors could vary from the original estimates before the project ceases to be viable.

(b) *Unknown territory* – If the project involves a new line of business, the management may have little knowledge of the relevant factors involved. Technical, marketing and other relevant specialists will need to be consulted, often from outside the existing management.

Data relating to other businesses who currently operate in the appropriate sector will need to be gathered, along with general industry and market information.

(c) *Identification of the relevant costs/income* – These may differ, depending upon the appraisal method used and the purpose of the information.

For appraisal purposes, particularly under discounted cash flow techniques, only the 'direct' costs and income of the project should be taken into account.

In this context, 'direct' means costs or items of income that can be attributed *directly* to the project that would not arise if the project were not to be accepted. These include increased fixed overheads (for example, the renting of additional premises or machine hire costs) as well as the more obvious material and labour costs.

Where the new project involves the development of a new product or service that is related to the existing business, it will often be difficult to draw a clear dividing line between direct and indirect costs/income. The launch of the new product or service may well have an affect on the sales of the existing ones, or on the cost structure of the company, and it will be difficult to isolate the relevant costs/income of the project.

For pricing and reporting purposes, the business will normally wish to include a recovery of existing overheads and investment costs already incurred (such as preliminary research) within the costs of the contract. This will often be a standard rate applied to all projects of a similar nature and will vary from industry to industry.

If the project is in the form of a contract (for example, the provision of goods or services to a public sector body) the overhead rate used may mean the difference between winning and losing the contract, and may need to be negotiated to secure it.

INVESTMENT APPRAISAL – INTRODUCTION

It is important to appreciate that there are any number of criteria that could be employed in making investment decisions. It is therefore vital that, before choosing any particular criterion, we should decide what our ultimate objective is. Traditionally we are brought up to believe in the profit motive and that, as a result, the be-all and end-all in any investment decision should be to achieve maximum profit. Of course, this will not be relevant for not-for-profit organisations. Investment appraisal for such bodies will normally take the form of a cost/benefit analysis. This is covered in the next session.

We may well end up deciding that a high profit is indeed desirable, but this still begs the question 'Why?' We shall take as our starting point that the objective of any investor is to maximise his or her wealth, ie. that the greater the increase in the worth of the investment then the better off and hence the 'happier' the investor is, whether the investor be an individual investing a lump sum in a project or a shareholder investing in a share of a company. We shall therefore, in considering the criteria available, discuss their likely effect on the wealth of the investor and hence their applicability to the investment decision. In the following sections we shall consider three criteria:

(a)   return on capital employed;
(b)   payback period;
(c)   discounted cash flow (DCF).

It is important in an examination context that you are aware of the principles involved in each of these techniques and that you are capable of applying them to specific examples. You will not be required to do particularly detailed calculations using the first two criteria. The bulk of the calculations in the examination involve the use of DCF techniques and the remainder of this session will deal with the various problems with which you are likely to be faced and the techniques available for their solution. It is vital you can both perform the calculations and understand the nature of the problem and of the solution.

RETURN ON CAPITAL EMPLOYED (ROCE)

Introduction

The ROCE approach (also known as *return on investment* and *accounting rate of return*) makes the assumption that the main factor in determining the worth of an investment is the level of profitability that is expected to be achieved. Hence, the return on capital employed is simply a measure of the profitability of an investment using financial accounting rules and not an opportunity or relevant cost approach.

The standard definition return on capital employed (ROCE) is as follows:

ROCE is the average annual profit from an investment, after depreciation, expressed as a percentage of the original capital invested.

Which may be expressed as:

$$\text{ROCE} = \frac{\text{Average annual profit after depreciation}}{\text{original capital invested}} \times 100$$

Example

A machine is available for purchase at a cost of £80,000. We expect it to have a life of five years and to have a scrap value of £10,000 at the end of the five-year period. We have estimated that it will generate additional profits over its life as follows:

	£
1st year	20,000
2nd year	40,000
3rd year	30,000
4th year	15,000
5th year	5,000

These estimates are of profits before depreciation.

Required

Calculate the return on capital employed.

Solution

Total profit before depreciation over the life of the machine = £110,000

Therefore average profit pa. (before depreciation) $= \dfrac{£110,000}{5} = £22,000$

Total depreciation over the life of the machine = 80,000 – 10,000 = £70,000

Therefore average depreciation p.a. $= \dfrac{£70,000}{5} = £14,000$

Therefore average annual profit after depreciation = 22,000 – 14,000

Original investment required = £80,000

Therefore ROCE $= \dfrac{8,000}{80,000} \times 100\% = 10\%$

Having calculated a measure of the profitability of the investment, we need a required rate of return for comparison purposes in order to make our decision; if we had a required rate of return of (say) 8%, then our decision would be to accept the project.

This is a very simple measure and may well be considered a somewhat naïve basis for a decision. As a result, one may well choose to amend the approach in practice but in all cases the basic premise remains the same (ie. the ROCE is some measure of the average profitability of the investment). As long as one was consistent in one's approach, it would be a question of what precise definition seemed most appropriate to the circumstances. In an examination context, the definition given above is the one to apply unless you were told specifically to calculate it differently. We will consider one standard variation later in this section.

Merits and demerits

Although the following merits and demerits of ROCE have a relevance in their own right, it is also important to consider them again after discussion of the other approaches to investment appraisal.

Merits

(a) *It is simple to calculate.* This may seem a somewhat fatuous comment since making a correct decision would be of rather more importance than saving time! However, given that we are likely to be dealing with rough estimates of anticipated profitability, there could certainly be occasions where a 'rough and ready' measure would be quite sufficient.

(b) *It is easy to understand.* This again may seem a trifle irrelevant, but at the end of the day it is management who have to make the decision and shareholders who have to be convinced. One cannot expect, however ideal, that all management and shareholders should be skilled in financial management techniques.

(c) If high profits are required, this is certainly a way of achieving them. This may appear a truism, but we have yet to consider whether or not high profits are the object of the exercise. We will discuss this under 'demerits', but if shareholders do require high profits, then whether we consider them to be correct or incorrect it is surely management's function to achieve high profits on their behalf. If this is the case then ROCE is certainly a way of achieving this requirement.

(d) It is consistent with the return-on-investment measure used to compare divisional performance in many companies.

This would perhaps make comparisons easier, enable the information to be more easily collected, and, again, make the criterion more easily understood.

Demerits

(a) *It is an average and hence takes no account of the timing of the profits.* For example, if there were an alternative machine which was identical in all respects except that the expected profits were:

1st year	£100,000
5th year	£10,000

with no profits in the 2nd, 3rd and 4th years, then the ROCE would still be 10% and on that criterion alone we would be indifferent between the two machines. One would, however, expect that most would prefer the second machine because it yielded the bulk of the profits earlier.

(b) *It does not account for differing lives of projects.* If one were offered an alternative project yielding a ROCE of only 9%, but having a life of 10 years, it would not be valid to say that the one with the higher ROCE was necessarily the better.

(c) *It takes no account of the size of the investment.* This again is mainly a problem when one is comparing alternative projects. If project A required an investment of £80,000 and yielded a ROCE of 10%, whereas project B required an investment of only £10,000 but yielded 20%, it would not be possible to say that in all circumstances B was the better. In order to be able to reach a decision we would need to know what return the £70,000 not invested in a machine could be expected to yield.

(d) It is a profit measure and as such is only a worthwhile measure if it is high profits that are the investor's main objective. This brings us back to the earlier discussion and we must now address ourselves to the problem that is central to any discussion of appraisal techniques which is 'Why invest?'

Why invest?

We have implicitly made the assumption in the above calculations that the investor is primarily interested in profit and that, therefore, the higher the profit, the happier the investor is.

Let us now consider an alternative premise, which is that the primary reason for investing is to achieve a high cash return. It is surely all well and good being able to produce profit and loss accounts showing enormous profits, but this is not going to be particularly beneficial if one were never to realise any of the profit in the form of a cash receipt. The amount of that cash that may be distributed by a company in any one year is limited not by the profit figure in the profit and loss account, but by the amount of cash that the company has available (ignoring any legal restrictions).

In the short term, profits and cash certainly need not equate and a high profit does not necessarily mean that the company has generated a large cash surplus. Reasons for profits and cash not equating include the following:

(a)   debtors, creditors, accruals, prepayments;
(b)   increase/decrease in stock levels;
(c)   depreciation;
(d)   provisions (eg. for doubtful debts).

In the long term, profits will equate to cash in that, for example, debtors will be realised; the provision for doubtful debts will either be written back, or cash from the debtors will be lost; the depreciation charge will equate to the total cash expended on the machine.

As a result, in the long term, high profits will of necessity mean high cash surplus and hence the possibility of high dividends. However, the short-term position will be of relevance to the shareholder.

Consider the following.

There are two projects A and B, expecting profits over the next three years of:

A   £100,000 pa
B   £101,000 pa

In which company would you prefer to invest, assuming both require the same initial outlay?

On the face of it, project B would seem preferable since we can expect a larger profit, albeit fairly marginal. However, suppose that project A is operated on a cash basis (and hence profits equate to cash) whereas project B is more of a long-term contract and although we choose to spread its profits over the three years, no cash is received until the end of the period.

The cash flow would therefore be as follows:

	A £	B £
1st year	100,000	–
2nd year	100,000	–
3rd year	100,000	303,000

Our decision now becomes less obvious. Certainly project B will generate more cash, but project A will enable us to receive cash sooner.

Why should this be relevant?

The answer is that there is a cost attached to money in that by selecting project A we could be investing the cash as received and be earning interest. Alternatively, if we were financed by borrowings, we could use the receipts from project A to reduce our borrowings and hence save interest. Either way round there is a hidden cost attached to selecting company B in that we would be losing interest that could have been received/saved by selecting project A. Our decision would depend on the rate of interest. If we could be receiving 10% pa, then the effects of selecting A or B would be as follows:

			£
Project A	*After 1 year*		100,000
	After 2 years		
	Interest @ 10% on £100,000		10,000
			110,000
	Receipt after 2 years		100,000
			210,000
	After 3 years		
	Interest @ 10% on £210,000		21,000
	receipt after 3 years		100,000
	Cash surplus at end of 3 years		331,000
Project B	Cash surplus at end of 3 years		303,000

On this basis, clearly project A is the better option.

In conclusion, it would certainly seem that it is in any investor's interest to pay more attention to the cash flows expected from an investment and to the timing of these cash flows, than to consider solely the level of profit. This is the main argument against the use of a bland profit measure such as the return on capital employed.

Why then is ROCE still such a popular measure in practice? Despite all of the above, it is still a fact that shareholders are to a certain extent indoctrinated with conventional accounting and with profit and loss accounts produced on an accruals basis. They are certainly affected by the level of dividends, but the main criterion by which they tend to judge the health of their company is the profit for the year. If, as a result, shareholders demand high profits, then the directors have no choice but to try to give them high profits. How can high profits be achieved? The answer is, by making decisions using a profit measure, such as ROCE.

PAYBACK PERIOD

Introduction

We will now consider a second appraisal criterion, the payback period, which is essentially a very simple measure indeed. The definition, which is virtually self-explanatory, is as follows:

> *The payback period is the number of years it takes to recoup the original investment.*

This is a cash measure and as such it measures the number of years taken to recoup the investment in cash terms.

Example

A machine would cost £50,000 and would generate net cash receipts each year as follows:

	£
1st year	*15,000*
2nd year	*30,000*
3rd year	*10,000*
4th year	*5,000*
5th year	*2,000*

It will have a life of five years and zero scrap value at the end of its life.

Required

Calculate the payback period.

Solution

After one year we would have recouped a total of	£15,000
After two years we would have recouped a total of	£45,000

We require to recoup an additional £5,000 to achieve a total of £50,000. Since £10,000 is generated in the third year, we can say that the payback period must be 2.5 years.

It is important to appreciate that we can only say 2.5 years on the assumption that the cash in the third year accrues evenly over the year. If this is not the case, then all we can validly say is that it pays for itself within three years.

We would use this criterion for an accept-or-reject decision by fixing a cut-off limit and comparing the payback period with this limit. For example, if we only accept projects that pay for themselves within four years then this project should be accepted. Alternatively we could choose between projects by selecting the one with the shortest payback period.

Merits and demerits

Merits

(a)   It is easy to calculate.

(b)   It is easy to understand.

(c)   It is less affected by uncertainty.

It is this merit that makes the payback period a fairly attractive measure. One limitation of any measure is that almost inevitably we are faced with making a decision based on estimates of revenue into the future. As a result it is quite possible that in retrospect we may have made the wrong decision.

However, in any normal circumstances one would expect to be more confident of the accuracy of the earlier forecasts than the more distant forecasts and payback period is dependent only on the earlier forecasts. Consequently, in the first example of this section, we can perhaps be reasonably confident of our figure of 2.5 years and any subsequent returns are in a sense merely a bonus. Whether the actual return in the fifth year is £2,000 or only £200, at least the project will already have paid for itself.

(d)   It can obviously be very useful in specific circumstances such as when the company has liquidity problems.

Demerits

(a)   *Flows outside the payback period are ignored.* If, for the same example as before, the receipt in the fifth year had been £20,000 instead of £2,000, the payback period would be unaltered at 2.5 years.

(b)   *The timing of flows within the payback period is ignored.* If, again for the same example, the first two years' receipts had been:

1st year	£44,000
2nd year	£1,000

then again the payback period would be unaltered at 2.5 years.

DISCOUNTED CASH FLOW (DCF)

Terminal value

We have already discussed the idea of, and the reasoning behind, basing decisions on the expected cash flows from an investment. We also explained that because of the cost attached to money by way of interest, the timing of the cash flows was of primary importance. There are several ways in which we can account for the interest, one of which was illustrated by the example earlier.

An alternative way of dealing with the same example would be by 'compounding' the interest on each flow individually. Here, instead of calculating interest year by year on a varying balance, we take each flow individually and calculate the interest applicable. The only technique involved is that one way of adding interest at 10% pa to a balance is by multiplying that balance by 1.1:

£100 now will have grown in one year's time with interest at 10% to £100 + 0.1 of £100 or $1.1 \times$ £100;

after a further year (ie. two years in total) the total will grow by another 10% of the total of $(1.1 \times$ £100) to $1.1 \times (1.1 \times$ £100) ie. $(1.1)^2 \times$ £100 and so on.

Applying this idea to Projects A and B in the earlier example, gives the following:

	Cash flows	£
Project A		
1 year	$100,000 \times (1.1)^2$	121,000
2 years	$100,000 \times 1.1$	110,000
3 years	100,000	100,000
		331,000
Project B		
3 years	303,000	303,000

Here we have compounded each flow by adding on interest at 10% pa for the number of years remaining until the end of the life of the projects.

Clearly the calculations have produced the same result but the method used is somewhat neater. We have compounded the flows to produce what is termed the *terminal value* of each flow.

We are certainly in a position to choose between the two projects (remember, they both require the same initial outlay) but we have not as yet considered whether either of them is worthwhile. This depends on the initial outlay required to generate the £331,000 which we would receive by selecting project A. If we end up with a deficit we will reject the project.

Suppose the projects require an outlay immediately of £220,000. Clearly we cannot compare directly since the £331,000 is the worth of the returns at the end of three years, by which time we will have lost three years' interest on the £220,000 invested. As a result we will need again to calculate the terminal value of the initial outlay by adding three years' interest at 10%.

Note: The idea of compounding the outlay for three years at 10% may beg the question as to whether we are assuming that borrowing and lending are both at the same rate of interest. This assumption is not in fact necessary. If we had financed the project from spare cash then there would be no direct interest cost, rather an opportunity cost in that we would be losing interest that we could have otherwise earned at 10% pa.

Alternatively, if we had borrowed the £220,000 at 10% pa then we would have been correct to compound the receipts at 10% since regardless of what interest the receipts could earn, they could be used to reduce the borrowing and hence save interest at 10%.

The full solution to the problem will thus be as follows:

Year	Cash flows	Compound factor	Terminal value £
0	(220,000)	$\times$ $(1.1)^3$	(292,820)
1	100,000	$\times$ $(1.1)^2$	121,000
2	100,000	$\times$ (1.1)	110,000
3	100,000		100,000
			38,180

The net surplus in this case of £38,180 is known as the net terminal value (NTV) and since it is positive, indicating a surplus, the project is worthwhile and should be accepted. Had it been negative, indicating a deficit, we would have rejected the project.

Our third appraisal criterion may therefore be summarised as follows:

An investment should be accepted if it produces a surplus in cash terms after accounting for interest.

One way of accounting for the interest is, as we have just seen, by compounding the flows and calculating the terminal values. To achieve this we have multiplied in each case by the compound factor which in general terms may be written as:

$$(1 + r)^n$$

where *r* is the rate of interest (here 10% or 0.1) and n is the number of years' compounding required.

Tables may be provided in the examination for these factors and it can be checked that the factor for two years at 10% $((1.1)^2)$ is 1.21. This can obviously save time, particularly if many years were involved, but you should appreciate that tables for only limited rates of interest are provided in the examination and you should therefore be able to calculate from first principles.

Present value

One way of accounting for the interest on cash flows is to calculate the terminal values as we have just seen. This approach is certainly valid, but can prove cumbersome and even misleading at times in that (using the same example as before) the surplus of £38,180 will not arise in full until the expiry of three years.

How could we compare project A with say a third project which had a net terminal value of only £35,000 but this time at the expiry of only two years? This would not be too difficult (we would simply need to add one year's interest to the £35,000 to make them comparable), but the more complicated the cash flows, the more cumbersome would be this approach. For this reason a more common way of accounting for the interest (still keeping to the same criterion, ie. is there a surplus or deficit after accounting for interest?) is to look at the *present values* of each flow. To explain the meaning of the term present value consider the following example:

Suppose we were to receive £50,000 in one year's time and the rate of interest was 20% pa. The present value of the flow of £50,000 is the equivalent amount received now, ie. how much received now would have grown to £50,000 if invested at 20% pa? If the equivalent amount now were £Y, then in one year's time we would have £Y together with 20% interest or $Y \times 1.2$.

To have grown to £50,000:

$Y \times 1.2$	$=$	50,000
or Y	$=$	$50,000 \times \dfrac{1}{12}$ (or $50,000 \div 1.2$)
Therefore Y	$=$	£41,667

(**Note:** Do not work in pence in the examination unless the question is in pence.)

Hence the present value of £50,000 in one year with interest at 20% is £41,667. Check that you have understood the above by calculating the present values of the following:

(a) £100,000 in 1 year with interest at 18% pa.
(b) £60,000 in 2 years with interest at 5% pa.
(c) £200,000 in 3 years with interest at 10% pa.

Answers

(a) $Y \times (1.18)$ $=$ 100,000

     $PV = Y$ $=$ $100,000 \times \dfrac{1}{1.18}$

     $=$ £84,746

(b) $Y \times (1.05)^2$ $=$ 60,000

     $PV = Y$ $=$ $60,000 \times \dfrac{1}{(1.05)^2}$

     $=$ £54,422

(c) PV $=$ $200,000 \times \dfrac{1}{(1.1)^3}$

     $=$ £150,263

Let us apply this approach to the original example where the flows were:

Year	Project A
0	(220,000)
1	100,000
2	100,000
3	100,000

and the interest rate was 10% pa.

Calculate the present value of each flow individually and hence the net present value.

Solution

Year	Cash flows		Present value £
0	(220,000)		(220,000)
1	$100,000 \times 1/1.1$	$=$	90,909
2	$100,000 \times 1/(1.1)^2$	$=$	82,645
3	$100,000 \times 1/(1.1)^3$	$=$	75,131
Net present value			28,685

We can therefore state that, with interest at 10% pa, the original flows are equivalent to a single receipt of £28,685 receivable now, ie. time 0. For an accept or reject decision, the criterion is as before – a positive net present value (NPV) indicates a cash surplus after accounting for interest and therefore we should accept; a negative NPV indicates a cash deficit and we should therefore reject. If we were to choose between various investments, we would now simply select the investment with the highest NPV.

The exercise involved in calculating the present value is known as **discounting** and the factors by which we have multiplied the cash flows (ie. $1/1.1$; $1/(1.1)^2$; $1/(1.1)^3$) are known as the discount factors. In general terms, the discount factor is given by the expression:

$$\frac{1}{(1+r)^n}$$

where r is the rate of interest pa, and n is the number of years over which we are discounting.

Although this expression is fundamental to all the DCF calculations that follow, it is better that the expression should be obvious as a result of the work already done rather than be learned by rote.

With calculators, the calculation of any discount factor does not present too much difficulty, but can occasionally be somewhat cumbersome, eg. the discount factor for 20 years at 5% pa is $1/(1.05)^{20}$. As a result you may be provided with tables in the examination which can save time. Although these are usually sufficient for most questions, it is obviously important that you are capable of calculating the factors using first principles. Tables may be found at the beginning of this Study Pack.

Cover up the right-hand columns below and check that you can write down (a) the expression for the discount factor and (b) the actual factor, from the tables, for each of the following:

		Expression	Discount factor from tables
(i)	12 years @ 8%	$1/(1.08)^{12}$	0.397
(ii)	4 years @ 13%	$1/(1.13)^4$	0.613
(iii)	8 years @ 4%	$1/(1.04)^8$	0.731

Now attempt the following questions.

Example

(a) *A machine costs £80,000 now. We expect cash receipts of £20,000 in one year's time, £50,000 in two years' time, £40,000 in three years' time and £10,000 in four years' time. The rate of interest applicable is 15%. Should we accept or reject the machine?*

(b) *Machine A costs £100,000, payable immediately. Machine B costs £120,000, half payable immediately and half payable in one year's time.*

The cash receipts expected are as follows:

	A	B
at the end of 1 year	*20,000*	*–*
at the end of 2 years	*60,000*	*60,000*
at the end of 3 years	*40,000*	*60,000*
at the end of 4 years	*30,000*	*80,000*
at the end of 5 years	*20,000*	*–*

With interest at 5%, which machine should be selected?

(c) We must buy one of three machines: A, B or C. Machine A will cost £100,000 *payable immediately.* Machine B will cost £110,000 payable half immediately and half in one year's time. Machine C will cost £120,000 payable in three equal, annual instalments the first instalment payable immediately.

All three machines will generate £30,000 pa for the next 20 years with the first receipt being in one year's time.

With interest at 22% pa, which machine should be chosen?

Solution

(a)

Year		Cash flows	DF @ 15%	Present value £
0	Cost	(80,000)	1	(80,000)
1	Inflows	20,000	0.870	17,400
2		50,000	0.756	37,800
3		40,000	0.658	26,320
4		10,000	0.572	5,720
				NPV = 7,240

Since the net present value is positive (ie. a cash surplus) we should accept the machine.

(b) Machine A

Year	Cash flows	DF @ 5%	Present value £
0	(100,000)	1	(100,000)
1	20,000	0.952	19,040
2	60,000	0.907	54,420
3	40,000	0.864	34,560
4	30,000	0.823	24,690
5	20,000	0.784	15,680
			NPV = 48,390

Machine B

Year	Cash flows	DF @ 5%	Present value £
0	(60,000)	1	(60,000)
1	(60,000)	0.952	(57,120)
2	60,000	0.907	54,420
3	60,000	0.864	51,840
4	80,000	0.823	65,840
			NPV = 54,980

Since machine B has the higher NPV, our decision should be to select machine B.

(c) Since for each of the three machines, the returns are identical, we can simplify the calculations by considering only the costs in each case. The machine with the lowest present value of cash flows will be the best alternative.

	A				*B*	
Cash flows	*DF*	*PV*		*Cash flows*	*DF*	*PV*
		£				£
0 (100,000)	1	(100,000)		(55,000)	1	(55,000)
1				(55,000)	1/1.22	(45,082)
		(100,000)				(100,082)

	C	
Cash flows	*DF*	*PV*
		£
(40,000)	1	(40,000)
(40,000)	1/1.22	(32,787)
(40,000)	$(1/1.22)^2$	(26,874)
		(99,661)

Since machine C has the least present value of cost flows, we should select machine C.

(**Note:** By ignoring the cash receipts as common to all alternatives, we have ignored the possibility that all three machines may give a negative NPV and hence may not be worthwhile. However, since the question implied that we had to buy a machine, there is no problem since C is certainly the better of the three.)

Let us now continue with two ways of possibly speeding up the calculations where we have **annuities** or **perpetuities**.

Annuities

An annuity describes the situation where we have an equal annual cash flow such as in the following illustration:

Year	Cash flows
0	(50,000)
1	30,000
2	30,000
3	30,000

Interest rate = 10%

Here we have an annuity of £30,000 pa for three years.

We may appraise this investment in the normal way as follows:

		DF @ 10%	PV £
0	(50,000)	1	(50,000)
1	30,000	0.909	27,270
2	30,000	0.826	24,780
3	30,000	0.751	22,530
			NPV = 24,580

NPV is positive, hence **accept** the project.

However, since for all the receipts we are multiplying the discount factor by £30,000 each time, we can simplify the calculation by multiplying £30,000 by the total of the discount factor:

		DF @ 10%	PV £
0	(50,000)	1	(50,000)
1–3	30,000 pa	2.486	74,580
			NPV = 24,580

This would still be somewhat cumbersome were it not for the fact that you will be provided in the examination with tables for the annuity factors if they are needed. You will find from these tables that the three-year annuity factor at 10% is 2.487, slightly higher than the total of the three separate discount factors because of rounding.

Examples

(a)	0		(160,000)
	1–15		30,000 pa
			with interest at 15%, appraise the project.
(b)	0		(200,000)
	6–15	(inclusive)	50,000
			with interest at 12%, appraise the project.
(c)	0		(100,000)
	0–10		15,000 pa
			with interest at 5%, appraise the project.

Solution

(a)

	£	DF @ 15%	PV £
0	(160,000)	1	(160,000)
1–15	30,000	5.847	175,410
			NPV = 15,410

Accept

(b)

	£	DF @ 12%	PV £
0	(200,000)	1	(200,000)
6–15	50,000	3.206 (see below)	160,300
			(39,700)

Reject

Here we cannot look up the annuity factor directly from the tables, but may use one of two approaches.

(i)   From the tables, the total factor for years 1 to 15 inclusive is 6.811. We require the total for 6 to 15 inclusive, and therefore need to remove the total for years 1 to 5 inclusive, which is (from the tables) 3.605.

Hence the required factor for 6 to 15 may be calculated as:

	1–15	6.811
less:	1–5	3.605
leaves:	6–15	3.206

alternatively:

(ii)   Flows for years 6 to 15 inclusive means we are to receive the cash for a total of 10 years. Had the flows been 1 to 10 inclusive, then we could have multiplied by the ten-year annuity factor of 5.650 to arrive at an equivalent lump sum at time zero. However, the flows are in fact 6 to 15 and are hence 'moved forward' by five years and therefore multiplying by the ten-year annuity factor would give us a 'lump sum' at time 5. To get back from time 5 to now (time zero) we would discount for five years using the ordinary five-year discount factor of $(1/1.12)^5$ or (from the tables) 0.567.

Hence the factor for 6–15 = ten-year annual DF × five-year DF

$$= 5.650 \times 0.567$$

$$= 3.204 \text{ (difference due to rounding)}$$

Either of these two approaches may be used in these circumstances.

(c)

	£	DF @ 5%	PV £
0	15,000 – 100,000 = (85,000)	1	(85,000)
1–10	15,000	7.722	115,830
			NPV = 30,830

Accept

Please note that, although the above could have been arrived at in other ways, the tables only provide annuity factors directly for years 1 to any time.

The only remaining problem area with annuities is that, again, the tables provided in the examination only cover a limited range of rates of interest. For rates not covered by the tables one may either discount each flow individually or calculate the annuity factor using the following formula:

Annuity factor for years 1 to n inclusive $= \dfrac{1}{r}\left(1-\left(\dfrac{1}{1+r}\right)^{n}\right)$

where r is the rate of interest pa.

Using this formula to calculate the five-year annuity factor at 10% gives:

$$\text{Ann. DF} = \dfrac{1}{0.1}\left(1-\left(\dfrac{1}{1.1}\right)^{5}\right)$$

$$= \dfrac{1}{0.1}\,(1-0.6209) = 3.7908$$

This formula should be learnt since the examiner may ask you to calculate a factor not available from the tables. The derivation of the formula is not required for the examination.

Perpetuities

A 'perpetuity' (short for 'annuity in perpetuity') refers to an equal annual flow which will continue indefinitely (or for so long as to be effectively for ever – generally more than 50 years).

Example

0	(100,000)
1 – ∞	12,000 pa

Appraise the investment at 10%.

Solution

Here, resorting to first principles is clearly impractical (although $(1/1.1)^{n}$ will get smaller and smaller as the number of years increases, and will ultimately become virtually nil).

The discount factor for a perpetuity is:

$\frac{1}{r}$ where r is the rate of interest

Hence, for the above example,

	£	DF @ 10%	PV £
0	(100,000)	1	(100,000)
$1 - \infty$	12,000 pa	$\dfrac{1}{0.1}$	120,000
			NPV = 20,000

NPV positive therefore **accept.**

The reasoning behind the discount factor being 1/r may be explained in two ways:

(a)   (For those with a mathematical background)

As stated earlier, the formula for the annuity factor is:

$$\frac{1}{r}\left(1 - \frac{1}{(1+r)^n}\right)$$

For a perpetuity, n goes to infinity and as this happens, $1/(1 + r)^n$ goes to zero leaving a factor of 1/r.

(b)   The objective in discounting

$1 - \infty$ 12,000 pa

is to determine the lump sum amount now that is equivalent (at 10%) to receiving £12,000 pa for ever.

Surely if we were to receive £120,000 now we could invest it at 10% and earn £12,000 pa for ever – the two would be identical.

How did we arrive at £120,000?

By dividing the £12,000 by the rate of interest of 10%.

Try the following examples on perpetuities.

Example

(a)	*1 – ∞*	*£15,000 pa*	*@ 16%*
(b)	*4 – ∞*	*£8,000 pa*	*@ 12%*
(c)	*2 – ∞*	*£10,000 pa*	*@ 10.25%*

Solution

			DF	PV £
(a)	1 – ∞	15,000	$\dfrac{1}{0.16}$	93,750
(b)	4 – ∞	8,000	5.931	47,448

This is similar to the earlier examples on annuities. We can calculate the discount factor for 1 – ∞ (1/r), and to arrive at 4 – ∞ we need to deduct the total for 1 – 3 (the 3 year annuity factor at 12%):

1 – ∞	$\dfrac{1}{0.12}$	=	8.333
Less: 1–3	from tables =		2.402
Therefore 4 – ∞		=	5.931

			DF @ 10.25%	PV
(c)	2 – ∞	10,000	8.8491	£88,491

Workings

1 – ∞	$\dfrac{1}{0.1025}$	=	9.7561
Less: 1 year	$\dfrac{1}{1.1025}$	=	0.9070
Leaves 2 – ∞		=	8.8491

Here we have no problem with tables since we can calculate the factor for a perpetuity quite easily on a calculator for any rate of interest.

Setting up the flows

The three calculations dealt with above – individual flows, annuities and perpetuities – are all very straightforward. However, for all 'net present value' questions there are no other calculations necessary. One can obviously make the problem more involved by introducing more and more flows, but this becomes more of a time problem than one of arithmetical difficulty.

As a result any difficulty encountered is more likely to be in actually setting up the flows on which the discounting is to be performed. These difficulties are best dealt with by experience and a series of more demanding examples will follow which, between them, will illustrate most of the problems you are likely to come across. Do make sure that not only do you arrive at the correct answer, but that you arrive at it for the correct reasons!

First, a brief discussion of the main areas where pitfalls are likely to occur.

(a)   *Cash flows*

Never forget that the basis of the DCF criteria is to base the decision purely on cash flows. This has two implications: firstly, any non-cash flows such as depreciation, are irrelevant to the decision; and secondly, we are interested in all cash flows arising from the investment. As far as the latter is concerned any distinction between capital and revenue flows is irrelevant. If purchase of a machine results in cash receipts of £100,000 from trading and £10,000 from ultimately scrapping the machine, then all £110,000 is relevant to the decision.

(b)   *Timing of flows*

It is vital that you appreciate that if we discount for one year, we are eliminating exactly one year's interest, implying that exactly one year had elapsed before the relevant flow occurred.

For example, if we buy a machine on January 19X3, for £100,000 and the first receipt of £20,000 occurs on 31 December 19X3, then one year would have elapsed and we would therefore need to discount the £20,000 for one year. We do not worry about the odd day here and there and hence if the £20,000 had, in fact, been receivable on 1 January 19X4, then again one year's interest would have been received and therefore one year's discounting would be necessary.

Before discussing further, write against each of the following flows how many years discounting would be required (time 0 being 1 January 19X3).

(i)   31 December 19X4
(ii)   1 January 19X6
(iii)   31 December 19X9
(iv)   30 June 19X8

Answers

(i)   2
(ii)   3
(iii)   7
(iv)   5.5

Do not be afraid of using your fingers! Also do not worry about how we would actually discount for 5.5 years, we will deal with this later. Of course, in practice, the above is unlikely in that cash flows do not normally occur at yearly intervals. It would be more practical to consider the following:

We buy a machine for £100,000 on 1 January 19X3 and the first year's receipts are £20,000. Our year-end is 31 December each year.

This time, the implication is that the £20,000 is receivable over the period 1 January to 31 December 19X3. We could cope with this problem by, for instance, calculating the sales per month and discounting each for one month, two months and so on. This is certainly feasible and we will discuss the mechanics of it later, but for the majority of problems we simplify the position by assuming yearly intervals.

The most common assumption in this example would be 'you are to assume all flows arise on the last day of the accounting period'. Hence we would treat the £20,000 as occurring on 31 December 19X3 and discount for one year. It is therefore important to make sure before attempting any problem that you are clear as to the timing assumptions to be made. Also, this clearly is a reservation about the accuracy of our calculations for any subsequent written question.

(c)   *Sunk costs*

A sunk cost is any expenditure that has already been incurred. For instance, we may be considering purchase of a machine for £100,000 and have carried out a market survey last year at a cost of £10,000 as to the likely demand for the product. Using the DCF criterion, the £10,000 spent on the survey would be completely irrelevant since it is 'dead' money in that we will have paid £10,000 whether or not we decide to go ahead with the acquisition of the machine. We are only concerned with future cash flows.

(d)   *Opportunity costs*

These must be distinguished from sunk costs. Suppose we acquired land 10 years ago for £2 million and are now considering building a factory on the land. The £2 million would be ignored quite correctly as a sunk cost. However, if the land currently has a market value of £10 million, then although there would be no 'direct' cash flow relating to the land, we would be losing £10 million by building the factory that could otherwise have been realised by selling the land. In this case the £10 million would be relevant and would be treated as a cost – known as an *opportunity cost*.

(e)   *Fixed overheads*

It is very common in examination questions to be presented with revenue information in the following fashion.

Expected sales	10,000 units pa
Selling price per unit	£10

	£
Costs per unit	
Materials	3
Labour	3
Variable overheads	1
Fixed overheads	2
	9
Budgeted profit per unit	£1

On the face of it, we would therefore expect a net cash inflow of 10,000 × £1 = £10,000 pa. However, unless you are specifically told to the contrary, you must assume that the total fixed overheads for the business as a whole will remain fixed and that the £2 per unit was simply a reallocation of the existing fixed total. As a result the relevant inflow would be 10,000 × £3 = £30,000 pa. Now attempt the following question.

Example

Jenkins plc (whose year-end is 30 September each year) are having second thoughts about the purchase of a machine to manufacture a new product. They have production plans prepared at a cost of £15,000 (payable on 31 December 19X2) but are considering cancelling their purchase agreement for the machine. Cancellation would result in them having to pay a penalty charge of £10,000 on 1 October 19X2. If they decide to continue, the cost of the machine (£100,000) will be payable in two instalments – half on 1 October 19X2 and the other half twelve months later. The machine will last ten years and have a scrap value of £12,000.

The directors estimate that production of the new product would be 5,000 units in the first year and 10,000 units pa for the remainder of the life of the machine.

The following costing has been prepared.

Selling price per unit	£30
	£
Costs per unit	
Materials	8
Labour	10
Variable overheads	6
Fixed overheads	5
	29
Profit	£1

They expect these costs will be maintained for the future with the exception of labour, which will increase to £11 per unit as from 1 October 19X5.

Fixed overheads include a depreciation charge calculated on a straight-line basis.

All cash flows occur at the ends of the years with the exception of materials, which are purchased and paid for at the beginning of each year. Additional working capital of £18,000 will be required at the commencement of the project. Jenkins' discount rate is 15% pa.

Required

Advise the directors of Jenkins as to whether or not to continue with this proposed purchase. (Ignore corporation tax.)

Solution

Time	Narrative	Flow £	Note	DF @ 15%	PV £
0	Cost – 1st instalment	(50,000)		1	(50,000)
0	Working capital	(18,000)	2	1	(18,000)
0	Penalty saved	10,000	3	1	10,000
1	Cost – 2nd instalment	(50,000)		0.870	(43,500)
1	Sales revenue	150,000		0.870	130,500
2–10	Sales revenue	300,000	4	4.149	1,244,700
0	Materials	(40,000)	5	1	(40,000)
1–9	Materials	(80,000)		4.772	(381,760)
1	Labour	(50,000)		0.870	(43,500)
2–3	Labour	(100,000		1.413	(141,300)
4–10	Labour	(110,000)	6	2.736	(300,960)
1	Variable overheads	(30,000)		0.870	(26,100)
2–10	Variable overheads	(60,000)	4	4.149	(248,940)
10	Scrap proceeds	12,000		0.247	2,964
10	Working capital released	18,000	2	0.247	4,446

NPV = 98,550

Since the net present value is positive, the project should be **accepted.**

Notes

(1)   The cost of preparation of plans has been treated as a sunk cost. £15,000 will be payable whether or not Jenkins plc continue with purchase of the machine. Fixed overheads have been ignored because depreciation is not a cash flow and because the balance is assumed to be a reallocation of an existing fixed total.

(2)   Working capital is required of £18,000 at the commencement of the project. This money will be tied up for the life of the project, but, in the absence of information to the contrary, we have assumed it to be released at the end of the life of the machine (time 10).

(3)   The penalty charge will not be payable if the machine is purchased. We have therefore treated the £10,000 as though it was an inflow as far as continuance is concerned.

(4)   The discount factor for 2–10 has been calculated as follows:

	1–10	5.019
less:	1	0.870
leaves:	2–10	4.149

(5)   We are told that materials are purchased at the beginning of each year. Hence the first year's expenditure occurs on 1.10.X2 (time 0). The remaining expenditure occurs in each of the nine following years.

(6)   The labour cost per unit increases as from 1.10.X5. Since payment is at the end of each year, the first cash flow to increase is that on 30.9.X6. With time 0 as 1.10.X2, then 30.9.X6 is time 4.

The discount factor for 4–10 is calculated as follows:

	1–10	5.019
Less:	1–3	2.283
Leaves:	4–10	2.736

Merits and demerits of NPV

As with return on capital employed, any list of this nature is of more relevance when comparing various criteria. You should therefore be able to compare critically the three areas that have been discussed.

Merits

(a)   It is based on the assumption that cash flows and, hence dividends, determine shareholders' wealth.

This is, above all, the important aspect of this criterion. The reasoning has already been discussed but, since it is dividends that a shareholder will receive and not profits, our objective should be to maximise dividends.

(b)   Cash flows are less subjective than profits.

This is perhaps slightly dubious, but a profit measure relies on such things as depreciation policy which are to a certain extent subjective. Cash, being tangible, suffers from no 'definition' problems and hence leads perhaps to a more objective measure of performance.

Demerits

(a)   Additional uncertainty is introduced by the necessity of calculating the cost of money.

In practice, the cost of money, or cost of capital, can be extremely difficult to calculate at any instant, and even harder to forecast. As a result, any decision stands to be even more dependent on the accuracy of our forecasts.

(b)   Are high cash flows what the shareholder desires?

We have already discussed why shareholders should perhaps be interested in cash rather than profits, but if shareholders do require high profits (even if misguidedly) then our objective should be to achieve high profits.

(c)   We are forced to make impractical assumptions or be faced with over-complicated calculations.

In the examples given so far we have assumed flows at yearly intervals, ignored taxation, ignored inflation – to mention just three simplifying assumptions. Although all of these assumptions may be relaxed to present a more practical position there is a danger of ending up with perhaps too complicated a calculation.

(d)   Discounted cash flow as a concept is more difficult for a layman to grasp.

It would clearly be beneficial for the person on whose behalf we are performing the calculation to have a grasp of the basic concept underlying the technique.

INTERNAL RATE OF RETURN (IRR)

Internal rate of return (IRR) calculations are in no sense a 'fourth' criterion for investment appraisal, but simply another way of employing the DCF technique which can be extremely useful in particular circumstances.

Consider the following.

A machine will cost £80,000 immediately, and will generate cash inflows of:

Time	£
1	40,000
2	50,000
3	10,000

If the cost of capital is 10%, should we accept or reject the project?

Time	£	DF @ 10%	PV £
0	(80,000)	1	(80,000)
1	40,000	0.909	36,360
2	50,000	0.826	41,300
3	10,000	0.751	7,510
			NPV = 5,170

Since the net present value is positive, we should **accept** the project.

However, since our calculation is based on forecasts it could easily be the case that in retrospect the NPV is negative and that we should have rejected. One element that could obviously be incorrect is the cost of capital that we have used of 10%. This could affect our decision in two ways:

Firstly, it may not stay at 10% throughout the life of the investment and secondly, the calculation of the current rate being 10% may be suspect. In either case, the NPV would stand to alter and if ever it ended up being negative we would have made the wrong decision. At first glance, the first problem would appear the most important. However, we will assume for the time being that the cost of capital will remain constant over the investment's life.

The second problem is, in practice, a very severe difficulty. For an individual, the cost of borrowing is easy to identify, but a company has several sources of finance – shareholders' funds, debentures, bank borrowing – and the exact cost can be virtually impossible to calculate.

On the basis of the above, we may therefore be in the position where all we can say is that the cost of capital is about 10%. At exactly 10% the NPV is positive and we accept, but what if the cost were actually 10.5% or 11% – would the NPV still be positive, and would we still be correct in accepting? One approach to deal with this problem would be to calculate the NPV at various rates of interest and investigate the results.

For the above example, the NPV at various rates of interest is as follows:

	£
5%	12,070
8%	7,830
10%	5,170
12%	2,690
15%	(820)
20%	(6,190)

These have been calculated in the normal way, and, as one intuitively would expect, the project becomes less worthwhile as the cost of money increases.

If we plot these on a graph:

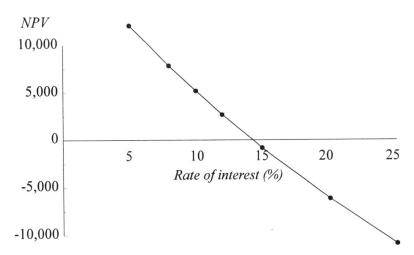

From the graph, we can now identify the ranges of interest for which the NPV will be positive and negative and hence for which we should accept or reject the project.

Since the NPV will be zero for a rate of interest of approximately 14%, we can say that for a cost of capital of up to 14% we should accept the project, whereas if the cost of capital exceeds 14% we should reject the project.

We have now an idea of our margin for error, as a result of this exercise. The break-even rate of 14% is known as the internal rate of return, for which the definition is:

The IRR is the rate of interest that discounts the project flows to a net present value of zero.

Although the above approach is really the only way of finding the exact internal rate of return, it is obviously time-consuming and, as a result, we generally use a quick approach to arrive at an approximation. Very rarely would we need a precise figure for the IRR and normally a reasonable approximation will be quite sufficient.

Interpolation

This approach involves calculating the NPV for two different rates of interest and then interpolating linearly between the two to estimate the rate of interest that gives a net present value of zero. Using the same example as before:

at 10% the net present value is + £5,170

10% is clearly not the IRR and, since the NPV at 10% is positive, the IRR must in fact be greater than 10%.

We therefore make a second guess at a rate higher than 10% – eg. 15%

at 15% the net present value is – £820

We now know that the IRR lies certainly between 10% and 15%. We need to estimate the rate that will yield zero.

Over a range of 5% (ie. from 10% to 15%) the net present value has fallen by £5,990 (ie. from + £5,170 to –£820).

We therefore assume that £5,990 equates to 5% and that there is a £1 fall in NPV for every $\dfrac{5}{5,990}$% change in the rate of interest.

If we take 10% as our starting point – for which the NPV is £5,170 – we need a change of £5,170 to get to a NPV of zero. This will require a change in the rate of interest of:

$$5{,}170 \times \frac{5\%}{5{,}990} \quad \text{or} \quad \frac{5{,}170}{5{,}990} \times 5\%$$

The internal rate of return is therefore:

$$10\% + \left(\frac{5{,}170}{5{,}990} \times 5\% \right) = 14.32\%$$

It is of vital importance to appreciate that this is only an approximation to the IRR since we have assumed that the NPV changes linearly with the rate of interest, which we already know from the earlier graph is not, in fact, the case.

Generally, however, as already stated, we do not require a precise IRR and it is normally quite sufficient to be able to say that it is about 14%. Two further points should be noted about this approach:

(1)   It is rather ludicrous to state that the IRR is approximately 14.32% (to two decimal places). In the examination, normally leave it at 14.32% so that your calculations may be checked, but do make the point that this is only an approximation since we have assumed a linearity that does not exist.

(2)   As a result of the above, a different pair of guesses would yield a different IRR. Again, using the same example.

If we had used guesses of 10% and 20% we would have arrived at the following:

at 10% NPV = + £5,170
at 20% NPV = – £6,190

Therefore over a range of 10% (10% to 20%) the NPV has fallen by £11,360 (+£5,170 to –£6,190).

Therefore IRR $= 10\% + \left(\dfrac{5{,}170}{11{,}360} \times 10\% \right) = 14.55\%$

The closer the two guesses are to the true IRR, the better the approximation will be. Do not, however, worry over this point in the examination since credit will be given for any two guesses provided they are not ludicrous (for instance do not use 0% as a guess!).

The above calculation may be expressed as a formula:

$$IRR = R_1 + \left[\frac{N_1}{N_1 - N_2} \times (R_2 - R_1) \right]$$

where R_1, N_1 and R_2, N_2 are the rate of interest and NPV for the first and second guesses respectively. However, you will not be provided with this formula in the examination and (except in desperation) it would seem rather unnecessary to learn this formula for its own sake.

Example

Before discussing the advantages and disadvantages of this calculation, have a quick attempt at the following exercises. In each case you are given the results of two guesses, and are required to calculate the IRR.

(a)	NPV	@	10%	=	+£4,500
	NPV	@	20%	=	–£6,000
(b)	NPV	@	10%	=	–£3,400
	NPV	@	5%	=	+£1,100
(c)	NPV	@	8%	=	+£6,200
	NPV	@	12%	=	+£2,800
(d)	NPV	@	10%	=	–£5,000
	NPV	@	6%	=	–£1,200

Solution

(a)   Over a range of 10%

NPV has fallen by £10,500

Therefore IRR $= \quad 10\% \quad + \quad \left(\dfrac{4,500}{10,500} \times 10\% \right)$

$= \quad 14.29\%$

(b)   Over a range of –5%

NPV has increased by £4,500

$$\text{Therefore IRR} \quad = \quad 10\% \quad - \quad \left(\frac{3,400}{4,500} \times 5\%\right) \quad = \quad 6.22\%$$

or, alternatively,

$$\text{IRR} \quad = \quad 5\% \quad + \quad \left(\frac{1,100}{4,500} \times 5\%\right) \quad = \quad 6.22\%$$

(c)   Over a range of 4%

NPV has fallen by £3,400

$$\text{Therefore IRR} \quad = \quad 8\% \quad + \quad \left(\frac{6,200}{3,400} \times 4\%\right) \quad = \quad 15.29\%$$

or, alternatively,

$$\text{IRR} \quad = \quad 12\% \quad + \quad \left(\frac{2,800}{3,400} \times 4\%\right) \quad = \quad 15.29\%$$

(d)   Over a range of –4%

NPV has increased by £3,800

$$\text{Therefore IRR} \quad = \quad 10\% \quad - \quad \left(\frac{5,000}{3,800} \times 4\%\right) \quad = \quad 4.74\%$$

or, alternatively,

$$\text{IRR} \quad = \quad 6\% \quad - \quad \left(\frac{1,200}{3,800} \times 4\%\right) \quad = \quad 4.74\%$$

The calculation of IRR has two main uses or advantages, and two main drawbacks.

Advantages

(a)   *The IRR provides a margin for error.* It is this that makes IRR such an important measure in practice. It is all very well calculating an NPV of (say) +£10,000 at a cost of money of 10% and therefore deciding to accept, but this can only be 'guaranteed' to be the correct decision if the cost of money is indeed exactly 10%. If, as is the case in practice, we are unsure as to the exact cost of money and can only say that it is about 10%, then we are faced with a problem. If the cost of capital turns out to be 11%, will the NPV still be positive, or should we have rejected? If we can calculate the IRR at (say) 15%, then we can say with certainty that as long as the cost of money is less than 15% then the NPV will be positive, and we will be correct to accept.

(b)   *The IRR is easier for laymen to understand.* Although the IRR is not truly a rate of return, it does provide a basis for a decision that is more readily acceptable by a layman with no understanding of the net present value concept. To say that a project has a positive NPV at 10% means little to a layman, whereas to say that money is costing 10% and that a project is generating a return of 15% is far more obvious.

Disadvantages

(a)   *An investment may have more than one internal rate of return*, depending on the pattern of cash flows. If there is indeed more than one internal rate of return it becomes more difficult to consider a margin for error, and certainly becomes more confusing for a layman.

(b)   It is not possible to use internal rates of return when choosing between two or more investments.

Let us suppose that we are offered two investments, A and B, which are mutually exclusive. The term 'mutually exclusive' means that we may invest in one or other of the investments, but not in both. In addition, we are told that only one of each of the investments is available. Investment A yields a return of 80% for one year and investment B yields a return of 20% for one year. The cost of borrowing is 10% pa. Which is the preferable investment?

The immediate conclusion would be to select investment A since both give a return in excess of the cost of borrowing, and that from A is substantially higher than that from B. However, suppose that we are told in addition that investment A requires an outlay of only £100 whereas investment B requires an investment of £10,000. It is obvious in this single illustration that a 20% return on an investment of £10,000 is preferable to an 80% return on £100 even after deducting the cost of borrowing of 10%.

		Investment A				*Investment B*	
		DF	PV @ 10%			DF	PV @ 10%
	£		£		£		£
0	(100)	1	(100)	0	(10,000)	1	(10,000)
1	180	1/1.1	164	1	12,000	1/1.1	10,909
		NPV	64			NPV	909

There can be little doubt that investment B is the better option. We have selected the investment giving the higher net present value despite the fact that investment A has by far the greater IRR.

(**Note:** The fact that B requires 100 times the outlay required by A presents no problem. We assume (as always, unless told otherwise) that we may borrow in unlimited amounts at 10% pa. Remember that the NPV is effectively the surplus we are left with after repayment of the borrowing together with interest.)

This example alone serves to illustrate the problem in comparison of IRRs. However, it may seem to be an extreme example, in that most mutually exclusive projects would perhaps require roughly the same initial investment. If this were the case would it not then be valid to compare IRRs?

Unfortunately the answer is still 'No'! Consider the following, mutually exclusive, investments.

Illustration

	Investment A £		Investment B £
0	(20,000)	0	(20,000)
1	4,000	1	20,000
2	24,000	2	6,250

The cost of borrowing is 10% pa.

Here we have two investments that both require the same initial investment. If we calculate the NPV and IRR for each of the two investments we arrive at the following results:

	Investment A	Investment B
IRR	20%	25%
NPV @ 10%	£3,460	£3,343

(Check the above calculations yourself.)

Without doubt, investment A is to be preferred since it generates a greater NPV despite the fact that it has a lower IRR and the same initial outlay.

How may we explain this seemingly anomalous position?

Let us consider the two investments again by plotting a graph of the NPV as against the cost of borrowing for each:

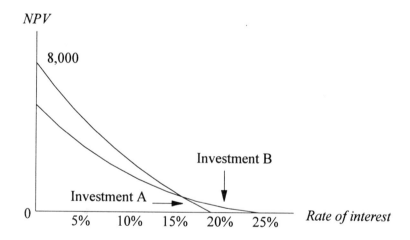

(Note that these graphs are not linear.)

It can be seen from the graphs that although investment B has a greater IRR than investment A, the investment having the greater NPV depends on the discount rate. In our example the cost of borrowing was 10%, and it can be clearly seen from the graph that at 10% A has the higher NPV and is therefore the investment to be selected.

Summary

In conclusion, therefore, although the IRR may be useful in an accept or reject decision, we should not use it as a basis for comparing between investments. It is not valid to compare percentage returns in any context and we should use the NPV. However, there is one problem remaining:

Why is it that (despite the above) the IRR is more commonly used in practice for comparison between investments?

It would be easy to answer that this stems from lack of understanding! However, there is a virtue in selecting (in our example) investment B purely because it has the higher IRR. The reason for this is that in practice we are unlikely to be confident of our estimate of the cost of borrowing. By selecting investments B we have at least a greater margin for error should our cost of borrowing calculation be incorrect. We are therefore more confident of achieving a positive NPV. In our example both investments have a wide margin for error, but in practice this margin is likely to be much narrower, making these comments more significant.

QUESTIONS

1   Clarke Ltd

Clarke Ltd is considering a project requiring an investment of £120,000 in assets having a life of five years and a final scrap value of £20,000. The project will generate the following net cash earnings before tax and depreciation. Also shown are estimates of the scrap value of the assets throughout the life of the project.

Year	1	2	3	4	5
Net cash earnings	£30,000	£40,000	£30,000	£20,000	£10,000
Scrap values	£70,000	£50,000	£35,000	£25,000	£20,000

Required

Calculate:

(a)   return on capital employed;

(b)   payback period.

2   Loamshire County Council   (AAT CA Model)

Loamshire County Council operates a library service.

In order to reduce operating expenses over the next tour or five years, there is a proposal to introduce a major upgrade to the computer system used by the library service.   Two alternative projects are under examination with different initial outlays and different estimated savings over time. The computer manager has prepared the following schedule:

	Project A £	Project B £
Initial outlay	75,000	100,000
Annual cash savings		
1st year	20,000	30,000
2nd year	30,000	45,000
3rd year	30,000	45,000
4th year	25,000	40,000
5th year	20,000	–

Assume that the cash savings occur at the end of the year, even though in practice they would be spread over the year. From a technical point of view, both systems meet the librarian's specification. It is assumed that there will be no further savings after year 5 and it may be necessary to install a new system by that date. The county uses the net present value method for evaluating projects at a 10% discount rate.

Assessment task

Prepare a report to the County Librarian with your recommendations. Include the relevant calculations in your report. She is not familiar with DCF calculations and has asked you to explain why the authority uses a DCF technique in preference to the 'payback' method of appraising capital projects.

Note: Present value of £1 at a discount rate of 10%

Number of years from the present	£
1	0.9091
2	0.8264
3	0.7513
4	0.6830
5	0.6209
6	0.5645

3 Transport company (AAT CA J94)

A transport company is considering purchasing an automatic vehicle-cleansing machine. At present, all vehicles are cleaned by hand.

The machine will cost £80,000 to purchase and install and it will have a useful life of four years with no residual value.

The operating costs of the machine will amount to £8,000 in the first year, increasing by 5% each year in line with the number of vehicles cleaned. Savings in labour costs will be £25,000 each year.

In addition to using the machine for its own vehicles, the company will be able to clean vehicles for other organisations. Revenue from this service will amount to £14,000 each year. Additional direct costs of 10% of revenue will be incurred for every vehicle cleaned on behalf of another organisation.

The company uses a discount rate of 10% to appraise all capital projects.

Assessment task

As assistant management accountant, you are asked to carry out an appraisal of the proposal to purchase the machine and prepare a report to the general manager of the company. Your report should contain the following information:

(1) The net present value of the cash flows from the project
(2) The payback period of the proposal
(3) A recommendation as to whether or not the proposal should be accepted

In your calculations, you should ignore the effects of inflation and assume that all cash flows occur at the end of the year.

Note: The present value of £1 at a discount rate of 10% is as follows:

Number of years from the present	£
1	0.9091
2	0.8264
3	0.7513
4	0.6830

4   Printing company   (AAT CA D94)

Your organisation currently uses a specialist printing company to provide all of its requirements for headed stationery, annual reports, publicity material and so on.

Consideration is now being given to setting up an in-house printing facility and cancelling the contract with the printing company. A single penalty payment of £4,000 would be charged but the annual saving would be £33,000 which is paid to the printing company under the terms of the contract.

Machines costing £12,400 will be purchased. They will last for four years and will have no value at the end of this time.

The operating costs of the new printing department will amount to £27,200 each year. This includes staff salaries, material costs, hire of equipment, administration and so on.

In addition to using the facility for your organisation's own purposes, it will be possible to undertake printing jobs for other organisations, earning incremental revenue of £1,600 each year. Incremental direct costs of this service will amount to 30% of revenue.

Assessment tasks

(a)   Calculate the net present value of the cash flows from the proposal, using a 12% discount rate over four years.

Ignore the effect of taxation and inflation and assume that all cash flows occur at the end of the year.

Note: The present value of £1 at a discount rate of 12% is as follows:

Number of years from the present	£
1	0.89
2	0.80
3	0.71
4	0.64

(b)   Calculate the payback period for the proposal and explain the advantages and disadvantages of using this appraisal method.

---

5   Duggan Ltd

Duggan Ltd has a cost of capital of 7% and wishes to decide between projects with the following cash flows:

	Cash flows @	t_0	t_1	t_2	t_3
Project	A	(£2,210,000)	£1,000,000	£1,000,000	£1,000,000
	B	(£2,210,000)	£545,750	£1,000,000	£1,552,029

Required

(a)   Select one project on the basis of:

      (i)   NPV;

      (ii)   IRR.

(b)   Discuss your results and make an overall recommendation, assuming no capital rationing.

SUMMARY

In this session we have considered the mechanics, the advantages and the disadvantages of various investment appraisal techniques. In the context of an examination question, you must be able to undertake the following:

- Calculate – Return on capital employed (ROCE)
  - – Payback period
  - – Net present value (NPV)
  - – Internal rate of return (IRR)

- Calculate terminal values and present values of annuities and perpetuities.

- Discuss relative merits of the appraisal techniques.

Further aspects of investment appraisal

OBJECTIVES

After studying this session, you should be able to:

- build inflationary effects into DCF computations

- take account of the impact of taxation on the cash flows for appraisal

- appreciate the problems of, and the possible methods of dealing with, uncertainty and risk in investment appraisal

- be aware of the particular concerns of public/non-profit seeking organisations in appraising investments and the use of cost-benefit analysis in this context

The performance criteria addressed by this session are as follows:

- Recommendations which optimise the long-term benefits to the organisation are clearly reported.

  Internal and external information relevant in estimating future costs and revenues are used.

DCF AND INFLATION

In our examples so far we have in each case taken the estimated cash flows for our investments and discounted at the cost of capital. The purpose of the discounting was, and will remain, to account for the time value of money: that is, to account for the interest that would have to be paid on the borrowings or the opportunity cost of interest that would otherwise have been receivable had we not invested. In no sense were we considering the effects of inflation.

What then are the effects of inflation? The first obvious problem relates to our estimate of cash flows from the investment. Having decided that the DCF criterion is perhaps the best approach, our object is to determine the cash flow that will result and to discount them at the cost of capital. In estimating the future cash flows we need to take account of inflation, and therefore need to estimate the rate of inflation expected.

Illustration

Consider the following illustration.

A machine costs £10,000 and is expected to yield the following net cash returns (estimated in current prices):

	£
1	5,000
2	8,000
3	6,000

We expect inflation to be at the rate of 5% per annum and the cost of capital is 15.5% per annum.

Before considering the solution to this problem it is important to be clear about the term 'current prices'. In this context, if we estimate a flow at time 1 to be £5,000 in 'current prices' it means that we would expect a cash receipt of £5,000 in one year's time were there no inflation. It further implies that with inflation at 5%, the actual cash receipt in one year's time will be £5,000 plus one year's inflation, and that, similarly, the 'actual' (or 'money') cash receipt in two years' time will be £8,000 plus two years' inflation, and so on.

Since the object of the exercise is, as always, to discount the actual cash flows at the cost of money (15.5%), there is no point in discounting the flows as they stand as they do not represent our actual cash expectations.

Let us therefore calculate the actual cash flows we expect.

	'Current' prices £			'Actual' cash flows £
0	(10,000)			(10,000)
1	5,000	$\times 1.05$	=	5,250
2	8,000	$\times (1.05)^2$	=	8,820
3	6,000	$\times (1.05)^3$	=	6,946

For each flow we have added inflation at 5% by multiplying by $(1.05)^n$ where n is the number of years inflation.

Having calculated the 'actual' cash flows, we are now in a position to complete the problem by discounting in the usual manner.

	Cash flow £	DF @ 15.5%	PV £
0	(10,000)	1	(10,000)
1	5,250	$\dfrac{1}{1.155}$	4,545
2	8,820	$\left(\dfrac{1}{1.155}\right)^2$	6,612
3	6,946	$\left(\dfrac{1}{1.155}\right)^3$	4,508
		NPV =	5,665

Since the NPV is positive, we should accept the investment.

This illustration may seem over-simplistic and may certainly beg many questions. We will discuss these problems in full shortly and consider the effects of inflation more deeply. However, our answer to the above illustration is correct and the approach used is the easiest approach in most questions.

Effective rates

Using the same example, we will consider an alternative approach that can save time.

Look again at how we arrived at the present value of the cash flow at time 2:

We have taken the flow at current prices, multiplied by $(1.05)^2$ to inflate so as to arrive at the actual cash flow (£8,820), and then multiplied by $\left(\dfrac{1}{1.155}\right)^2$ to discount at 15.5%.

Since it was, ultimately, only the present value in which we were interested, we could have simply taken the flow at current prices and multiplied by:

$$(1.05)^2 \times \left(\frac{1}{1.155}\right)^2$$

Which is equal to $\left(\dfrac{1.05}{1.155}\right)^2 = \left(\dfrac{1}{1.1}\right)^2$

(**Note:** The above arithmetic should be reasonably straightforward to understand, but is certainly nothing to worry about.)

So, inflating for two years at 5% and discounting for two years at 15.5% is equivalent to discounting for two years at 10% the 'effective' discount rate, e.

As a result, we could have arrived at the answer as follows:

	Current prices £			PV £
0	(10,000)	× 1	=	(10,000)
1	5,000	$\times \dfrac{1}{1.1}$	=	4,545
2	8,000	$\times \left(\dfrac{1}{1.1}\right)^2$	=	6,612
3	6,000	$\times \left(\dfrac{1}{1.1}\right)^3$	=	4,508
			NPV =	5,665

It would be too time-consuming to have to calculate e in the fashion used above on each occasion, and therefore the following formula is worthy of committing to memory:

$$1 + e = \frac{1 + m}{1 + i}$$

where e is the effective rate

　　　　m is the 'money rate' (cost of capital)

　　　　i is the rate of inflation.

For this example, m = 15.5%　i = 5%

$$\text{hence } 1 + e = \frac{1.155}{1.05} = 1.10$$

Therefore e = 0.10 or 10%

Example

Now attempt the following example using the effective rate approach.

A machine costs £40,000 payable in two instalments: £10,000 immediately, and the balance in one year's time. We expect to produce and sell 1,000 units per annum over the life of the machine, which is estimated to be six years (production to start immediately). The costs per unit are estimated as follows:

	£
Materials	6
Labour	4
Variable overheads	3
Fixed overheads	3
	16

The selling price per unit has been fixed for the first year at £18 and will be increased in each future year by 10% per annum. The machine is expected to have a scrap value of £5,000 at the end of its life. With the exception of the purchase price and scrap proceeds, all flows are expressed in current prices and are expected to inflate at the following rates:

Materials	4% per annum
Labour	14.4% per annum
Overheads	10% per annum

All flows will occur at the ends of years. The cost of capital is 14.4%.

Should we accept or reject the machine?

Solution

		£	DF	Notes	PV £
0	Purchase cost	(10,000)	1		(10,000)
1	Purchase cost	(30,000)	$\dfrac{1}{1.144}$	(1)	(26,224)
1–6	Materials	(6,000)	4.355	(2)	(26,130)
1–6	Labour	(4,000)	6	(3)	(24,000)
1–6	Variable overheads	(3,000)	5.242	(4)	(15,726)
1–6	Sales revenue	18,000	5.242	(4)	94,356
6	Scrap proceeds	5,000	0.446	(1)	2,230
				NPV	(5,494)

Since the NPV is negative, we should reject the machine.

Notes

(1) Since the purchase price and the scrap proceeds are 'actual' cash estimates, they have been discounted at the cost of capital of 14.4%.

$$= 0.564 \times 0.790 \text{ (from the tables)} = 0.446$$

(2) The effective rate for materials is given by:

$$1 + e = \frac{1.144}{1.04} = 1.1$$

ie. e = 0.1 or 10%

This is the discount rate used in the six-year annuity factor, ie. 4.355.

---

(3) Since labour is inflating at the same rate as the cost of capital, 14.4%, the present value of each flow of £4,000 could be calculated from first principles thus:

Inflation		*Discount*	
$4,000 \times (1.144)^n$	$\times$	$\left(\dfrac{1}{1.144}\right)^n =$	$4,000$

As there are six years of flows and the present value of each is £4,000, then the total present value is $6 \times 4,000 = £24,000$.

Alternatively, the effective rate is given by:

$$1 + e \quad = \quad \frac{1.144}{1.144} = 1$$

Therefore $e \quad = \quad 0\%$

With an effective rate of 0%, £4,000 discounts to £4,000 and the above paragraph applies once more.

(4) The effective rate for variable overheads and sales is given by:

$$1 + e = \frac{1.144}{1.10} = 1.04$$

ie. $e = 0.04$ or 4%

Thus the discount factor used is the six-year annuity factor at 4% (ie. 5.242).

Limitations

Having dealt with the calculations we are now in a position to discuss the limitations of the problem. Let us look once more at the earlier problem.

	Current £		*Actual cash flows* £		*PV* £
0	(10,000)		(10,000)	1	(10,000)
1	$5,000 \times 1.05$	$=$	5,250	$\dfrac{1}{1.155}$	4,545
2	$8,000 \times (1.05)^2$	$=$	8,820	$\left(\dfrac{1}{1.155}\right)^2$	6,612
3	$6,000 \times (1.05)^3$	$=$	6,946	$\left(\dfrac{1}{1.155}\right)^3$	4,508
				NPV	5,665

Inflation was at 5% per annum and the cost of capital was 15.5%. (We have already seen that we could have arrived at the same solution by discounting at the effective rate of 10%.) What reservations would you have as to your decision to accept as a result of the above calculation?

The reservations surely relate to the accuracy of the various estimates used in the calculation. If we were certain as to all the flows and rates used, then our decision to accept would be unquestionable (assuming, of course, that we are satisfied with the use of the DCF criterion in the first place).

In practice, clearly, we are unlikely to be certain as to our estimates. Let us consider each factor in turn.

(1) *The flows at current prices* – These amounts are subject to uncertainty in that they must be dependent on estimated levels of demand which may alter in the future. Also the costings which resulted in the net inflows may be suspect, despite the fact that we are ignoring any inflation in estimating them.

At least by considering the problem in terms of expected flows in the absence of inflation separately from the anticipated levels of inflation we can investigate the uncertainty inherent in both estimates individually and should certainly be able to estimate the flows at current prices with more accuracy than the actual flows.

We could perform sensitivity analysis on the current cost flows in isolation. This would not remove the uncertainty but could give some indication as to the degrees of accuracy necessary.

(2) *The current rate of inflation* – Hopefully, we would normally be in a position to determine the current rate of inflation with a fair degree of accuracy. However, this may prove more of a problem than would perhaps appear as we shall discuss shortly.

(3) *The future rate of inflation* – Even if we are confident that the current rate of inflation is 5%, it is ludicrous in practice, in all but the most restrictive circumstances, to assume that the rate of inflation will remain at 5% throughout the life of the project. We could, certainly, perform the calculation with differing estimates of inflation from year to year but the problems of estimating the rates for each year would be enormous. Normally, we assume for the calculation that the current rate will be maintained which, on the face of it, would present one of the severest limitations of our decision.

(4) *The current cost of capital* – In practice it is extremely difficult to calculate the cost of capital for a company at any point in time with any degree of accuracy. This therefore is a limitation of any net present value calculation.

(5) *The future cost of capital* – As always, we have assumed in the calculation that the current cost of capital will remain constant throughout the life of the project. Again, this would appear rather ludicrous since certainly in practice interest rates do fluctuate from year to year.

DCF AND TAXATION

We have ignored taxation in all the examples considered so far. However, a company would have a potential liability to pay tax on all profits. In addition, allowances for capital expenditure may be given, which will reduce the taxation payable.

Tax is certainly a cash payment and hence any tax flows are relevant to an investment decision using the DCF criterion.

Assumptions

In any question various assumptions will be necessary as to the tax effect. Do make sure that you read each question carefully and identify the particular assumptions that you are told to make. Read through the following list and make sure that you are clear about the effects of the various assumptions that may be made, and about the limitations of each. This is not a taxation examination and the depth of knowledge of tax rules required is covered in the following paragraphs.

Corporation tax rates

A profit-making company will generally have to pay corporation tax on its profits each year.

We will normally assume that the rate of corporation tax will remain constant over the life of a project. We could cope with a future change of rate, but it is extremely unlikely that we would ever be in a position to predict this eventuality in practice. As a result however, this is certainly a reservation we would have in our confidence of having made the correct decision. To save repetition, we will assume a corporation tax rate of 33% throughout this section unless stated otherwise.

The calculation of tax payable

In practice, tax is calculated on the 'adjusted profits'. These are the profits as reported in the financial accounts, adjusted for certain 'disallowable' expenses and other items. Generally, however, we are only given information as to the expected cash flows and must assume that the tax payable is 33% of these cash flows.

For example: a cash inflow of £5,000 will give rise to a cash outflow by way of tax of 33% × £5,000 = £1,650

Tax savings

In the same way that additional receipts will give rise to tax payments, we assume that additional costs will give rise to tax savings.

For example: if a project results in paying for material at the rate of £4,000 (a cash outflow), we assume that our profits will therefore be reduced by £4,000 pa and that our tax liability will be 33%× £4,000 (ie. £1,320 less than it otherwise would have been). An outflow of £4,000 will therefore give rise to a tax saving or (effectively) an inflow of £1,320.

Note that this implicitly assumes that we have sufficient profits either from the particular project or from our other operations to ensure that we get the full benefit of the tax saving.

One of the adjustments made to accounting profits in arriving at taxable profits is to replace the business's own depreciation charges with standard capital allowances. Different categories of fixed assets attract different capital allowances, but the two schemes that you should be familiar with for this examination are as follows:

(a)   100% first year allowances (FYA)
(b)   25% writing down allowances (WDA)

To demonstrate the effect of these two schemes on the cash flows of a business, we will use the following illustration.

Illustration

A business draws up its accounts to 31 December each year. During 19X0, it buys a machine for £100,000; this is expected to have a useful life of five years, with no residual value. The business has a straight-line depreciation policy.

In the accounts, the depreciation charged against profits in respect of this machine would be £100,000/5 = £20,000 per annum for five years. However, this would be added back before computing the taxable profits and replaced by one of the following two types of capital allowance:

(1)   100% first year allowance

This type of capital allowance has in fact been largely phased out of the UK tax system, but the examiner may wish to simplify matters by asking you to use it.

The effect is that, for tax purposes, the business is allowed to set off the entire cost of a purchased fixed asset against the business profits generated in the first year of its ownership.

So the profits for the year ended 31 December 19X0 (before depreciation) would be reduced by £100,000 before calculating the tax payable. The tax saving would thus amount to 33% × £100,000 = £33,000. This would be a one-off saving, for the first year only.

Note that it is assumed that the business will have sufficient profits (not necessarily from the project for which the machine is being used) to take full advantage of all available capital allowances. You will not be expected to deal with tax losses.

(2)   25% writing down allowance

This is far more common in practice and is more likely to be used by the examiner. It is basically the reducing balance system of depreciation, at a standard rate of 25% per annum.

So, in the above example, the effects would be:

19X0   Allowance = 25% × £100,000 = £25,000

              Tax saving = 33% × £25,000 = £8,250

19X1   Tax written down value (WDV) at start of year (= cost less accumulated capital allowances) = £(100,000 – 25,000) = £75,000

              Allowance = 25% × £75,000 = £18,750

              Tax saving = 33% × £18,750 = £6,188

19X2   Tax WDV = £(75,000 – 18,750) = £56,250

              Allowance = 25% × £56,250 = £14,063

              Tax saving = 33% × £14,063 = £4,641

This will continue until the asset is sold or otherwise disposed of when, for the purposes this examination, you should assume that a 'balancing allowance or charge' is made.

The effect of this balancing adjustment is to ensure that the business has been given sufficient (and no more) allowances to cover the actual total cost of using the asset – that is, the difference between the original purchase price and the final sales proceeds (if any). The easiest way to compute the adjustment is to compare the sales proceeds with the tax written down value at the start of the year in which the asset is sold.

For example, suppose in the above example, the machine was sold during 19X3 for £45,000. Thus the 'cost' of using the asset to the business has been £100,000 – £45,000 = £55,000.

If you add up the allowances for 19X0 to 19X2, you should get a total of £57,813. Thus the business has been given excess allowances of £2,813. This can more easily be calculated as follows:

Tax WDV at the start of 19X3 = £(56,250 – 14,063) =	£42,187
Sales proceeds	£45,000
Excess allowances given	£2,813

This balancing charge will be added to the taxable profits (rather than deducted, as an allowance would be) causing an additional tax cost of £2,813 × 33% = £928

Working capital

Working capital cash flows are assumed to have no tax implications whatsoever.

The timing of the tax payments

In practice, a company has to pay its corporation tax nine months after the end of the accounting period to which it relates. So a company that makes up its accounts to 31 December each year would have to pay its tax by 30 September the following year.

However, for investment appraisal purposes, it is usual to assume a one-year time lag, so the tax on the adjusted profits for, say, the year to 31 December 19X0 is assumed to be paid on the 31 December 19X1. This will include the effects of capital allowances on any assets bought during 19X0.

Illustration

A machine costs £10,000 on 1 January 19X4. We expect net revenue of £5,000, £8,000 and £4,000 in each of the first three years. The machine will have a scrap value of £1,000 in three years' time. All flows occur at the ends of years.

(Year-end: 31 December each year; corporation tax 33%; cost of capital 10%.)

Capital allowances

Machine purchased 1.1.X4 (time 0)

First capital allowance will be against profits at 31.12.X4 (Time 1), giving benefit to cash flow one year later (time 2).

Note: If the machine had been purchased one day earlier, on 31.12.X3 (still time 0), the benefit to cash flow would be one *year* earlier as a full year's capital allowance is given in the year of purchase, in this case against the profits to 31.12.X3. The benefit would be felt when the tax was paid, on 31.12.X4.

Tax calculations

Time		Capital allowance		Tax saving		Tax on net revenue	
1	25% × 10,000	= 2,500 ×33%	–		–		
2	25% × (10,000 – 2,500)	= 1,875 ×33%	825	5,000 × 33%	=	(1,650)	
3	Balancing allowance	4,625 ×33%	619	8,000 × 33%	=	(2,640)	
4		– ×33%	1,526	4,000 × 33%	=	(1,320)	

	£
* Disposal on 31.12.X6 for £1,000	
Tax WDV (10,000 – 2,500 – 1,875)	5,625
Proceeds	(1,000)
Balancing allowance	4,625

We can now set out the NPV calculation. Note the alternative 'horizontal' form of presentation shown here, with the times represented by columns across the page and different types of flows listed down the side. This is an efficient method of dealing with sets of uneven cash flows, as it eliminates repeated narrative and means that only one discounting computation needs to be carried out for each time, on the aggregate of all cash flows occurring at that time.

Time	0	1	2	3	4
Capital	(10,000)	–	–	1,000	–
Net revenue	–	5,000	8,000	4,000	–
Tax on net revenue	–	–	(1,650)	(2,640)	(1,320)
Tax saving on capital allowances	–	–	825	619	1,526
	(10,000)	5,000	7,175	2,979	206
10% discount factors	1	0.909	0.826	0.751	0.683
Present value	(10,000)	4,545	5,927	2,237	141

$\therefore$ NPV = £2,850

The project is therefore viable at the current cost of capital, assuming projected cash flows are correct.

Before leaving this section, consider the following example which brings in most of the potential problem areas.

Illustration

D Ltd are considering the purchase of a machine to produce gidgets on 1 July 19X5 at a cost of £230,000. They expect demand for gidgets to be 10,000 units pa over the life of the machine which is expected to be four years.

The following cost card has been prepared:

	£ per unit
Selling price	23
Materials	5
Labour	8
Variable overheads	3
Fixed overheads	2
	18
Profit	5

The machine will have a scrap value of £30,000 at the end of four years.

Additional working capital of £20,000 will be required as from the date of purchase of the machine.

The company has a year-end of 30 June each year and all flows, unless told otherwise, are to be assumed to occur at the ends of years.

Corporation tax at the rate of 33% is payable one year in arrears and a 25% writing-down allowance can be claimed.

M Ltd has a cost of capital of 8%.

Solution

Relevant cash flows

As with all decision-making, we must only include those flows that are incremental to the business. Clearly **sales revenue** and **variable costs** will be relevant, and total annual cash flows will be obtained by multiplying the unit price/cost by 10,000 units. **Fixed overheads** have been absorbed at a rate of £2 per unit but this does not necessarily imply that the business fixed costs as a whole will increase by £20,000 per annum. In fact, it is normal to assume, unless told otherwise, that total fixed costs remain constant and that the absorption rate simply reallocates some of the existing costs to this project. So they can be ignored. The additional **working capital** may represent the purchase of extra stocks or the setting aside of extra cash balances and will normally be considered as relevant. It is also normally assumed that this will be recovered at the end of the project (ie. there will be an equal inflow).

All of the relevant project flows, as identified above, will have associated **tax costs** or **tax savings**, with the exception of the working capital.

Timing of cash flows

The main project flows will take place in times 0–4. However, with a one-year lag on the tax flows, we shall need to take the calculation up to time 5. So project cash flows arising at times 1–4 will have tax effects at times 2–5.

Layout

You can adopt either a horizontal or a vertical layout here; there is not much difference when annuities are involved.

Computations

The main working needed will be that for tax savings on capital allowances. This should be done separately from your main answer and cross-referenced to it. You may also wish to show workings for discount factors where these are not read straight from the tables.

To cut down on the number of separate figures used in the tax and NPV computations, it will also be useful to calculate a cash contribution figure for the product, combining revenue and variable costs.

Your final answer should appear as follows (workings follow):

Time	Cash flow	£	8% DF	PV £
0	Cost of machine	(230,000)	1	(230,000)
	Working capital	(20,000)	1	(20,000)
1–4	Contribution (W1)	70,000	3.312	231,840
4	Working capital	20,000	0.735	14,700
	Scrap proceeds	30,000	0.735	22,050
NPV before tax				18,590
2	Tax savings	18,975	0.857	16,262
3	on capital	14,231	0.794	11,299
4	allowances (W2)	10,674	0.735	7,845
5		22,120	0.681	15,064
2–5	Tax on contribution (W1)	(23,100)	3.067 (W3)	(70,848)
NPV after tax				(1,788)

Note that the NPV before tax has been highlighted and is positive, whereas the effects of tax have been to reverse this position. The project should be rejected.

Why has this reversal occurred when tax flows are basically 33% of the project cash flows? The answer lies in the **timing**. The tax on the contribution is charged in full the following year. However the tax **savings** on the original purchase of the machine are not received the year after the purchase, but spread out over the next four years, with a heavy weighting at the end. This is reflected in a relatively lower time value and ultimately a negative NPV.

Workings

(1) **Contribution**

Contribution per unit	=	Selling price – Variable costs
	=	23 – (5 + 8 + 3)
	=	£7

Contribution per annum = 10,000 × £7 = £70,000 (times 1–4)

Tax on contribution per annum = £70,000 × 33% = £23,100 (times 2–5)

(2) **Tax savings on capital allowances**

Date		Tax WDV/ Capital allowances		Tax savings	Timing (Time 0 = 1.7.X5)
1.7.X5	Purchase	230,000			
30.X.X6	WDA (25%)	(57,500)	× 33%	18,975	Time 2
		172,500			
30.6.X7	WDA (25%)	(43,125)	× 33%	14,231	Time 3
		129,375			
30.6.X8	WDA (25%)	(32,344)	× 33%	10,674	Time 4
		97,031			
30.6.X9	Proceeds	(30,000)			
	BA	67,031	× 33%	22,120	Time 5

(3) **Discount factor for times 2–5**

Cumulative factor times 1–5	3.993
Less: Factor for time 1	(0.926)
	3.067

Implications for management

In our treatment of tax we have made several assumptions to simplify the calculation. In practice these assumptions could certainly be relaxed in order to make the position more accurate. However, despite these assumptions, the examples considered do illustrate the importance to management of tax planning as regards the timing of flows in addition to the obvious desire to reduce the actual bill.

For example, we have seen the potential importance of the determination of the dates on which to purchase and dispose of an asset. If we consider the more practical of the timing assumptions – ie. that tax is payable by reference to the end of the accounting period during which the flow occurred – then there may certainly be scope for improving the viability of an investment. In an earlier example, the machine was purchased at the beginning of an accounting period and hence there was delay for two years before receipt of the saving resulting from the capital allowances. If we had purchased the machine one day earlier, then the transaction would have taken place in the previous accounting period and the delay in benefiting from the capital allowances would have been reduced to only one year. This would have increased the present value of the savings and would, in this example, have resulted in a positive NPV making the investment worthwhile. Similarly, by selling the machine one day later, the flow would have occurred in the following accounting period thus extending the delay in payment of any balancing charge to two years. This would serve to make the investment more worthwhile.

COST-BENEFIT ANALYSIS

For public/non-profit-making organisations seeking to make investment decisions, the concept of NPV may not be regarded as entirely appropriate. That is, the principle of discounting remains valid but, since the objective is no longer simply profit maximisation, what are regarded as the costs and benefits of a project must be re specified. This is the purpose of cost-benefit analysis, which is essentially discounted cash flow analysis for public-sector institutions. For a business assessing a project such as building a road bridge, the criterion for acceptance will be the profit potential of the project in comparison with the other investment opportunities currently available. As such, the only factors which will influence the decision will be those costs and benefits incurred and received privately by the firm. In contrast, from society's point of view, road building has effects in the community which confer both costs and benefits on society as a whole; eg. increased traffic may add to the level of environmental pollution but at the same time may create jobs in the area around the road. The firm building the bridge does not have to pay society for the additional pollution created, nor does it receive payment for the jobs created. There exists, therefore, a difference between the private costs and benefits and the social costs and benefits of the project. It is this difference that cost-benefit analysis seeks to identify and take account of.

The main questions

In seeking to help public organisations/nationalised industries make investment decisions, cost-benefit analysis serves as a means of establishing the factors which need to be taken into account when making the investment choices. The objective function of private concerns is one of profit maximisation. In the public sector, the objective is the maximisation of social welfare.

The procedures involved in cost-benefit analysis can be broken down into a number of stages.

(a)   Identification of those affected by the investment.

(b)   Specification of a method for valuing the costs incurred and benefits received. This is vital as the methodology may be complex because of the intangible nature of some of the costs/benefits (eg. noise).

(c)   Determination of the rate of discount.

(d)   Calculation of a net present value for the project by discounting the future costs and benefits.

We shall now look at each of these stages in more detail.

Identification of those affected

In the case of large-scale investments, the number of people and groups affected is likely to be large and it must be recognised that the effects may be direct or indirect, but for cost-benefit analysis both must be taken into account. Completion of the M25, for example, will have speeded up traffic and reduced accidents on the motorway itself, and these are direct effects; indirectly, feeder roads may suffer more congestion and accidents and the noise and pollution for people living on these roads will have increased. The term given to such effects is **externalities**, ie. the costs and benefits which accrue to bodies other than the one sponsoring the project. An essential difference between cost-benefit analysis and private-sector project appraisal is that the former takes full account of such externalities in establishing a net present value for a project.

Valuation of costs and benefits

This is the stage of the analysis which involves most work. Having identified all the affected parties, the project's influence on their welfare must be expressed in monetary terms, as it would be valued by them. Suppose that building a second Severn road bridge (as has been proposed) a short distance south of the existing one reduces the traffic on the road between the bridges by 20%. As a result, houses in the area become more attractive to buyers and the prices rise by 10%; the average gain per household and the total number of households affected can be calculated. Notice that, in making the calculation, a price has been placed on the benefit of reduced noise and traffic pollution; an item not marketed can still be given a market value.

There are a few costs/benefits which cannot be valued in this way and they remain as separate issues for consideration when the final decisions on the project are made. For example, when the Roskill Commission reported the results of its cost-benefit analysis of the proposed sites for a third London airport, one issue which could not be quantified was the effect of the airport, if sited at Foulness, on the local bird life; rare geese used the area for breeding and they would disappear if the airport was built. It is impossible to put a price on permanent environmental destruction. In the end the relative importance of such matters, as opposed to the quantifiable net gains of an investment, remain a matter for subjective judgement.

One other contentious issue is encountered when placing a value on costs and benefits: whether they can simply be added up without regard for the fact that they affect different groups of people, all of whom will have different levels of welfare. That is, can we say that a £1 loss/gain to a poor man is worth only the same as a £1 loss/gain to a man on an average/above average income? If not, then before the costs and benefits are summed a system of weighting to account for the differing utility of wealth must be devised.

The rate of discount

For a private sector project, the rate of discount is the marginal or weighted average cost of capital for the business. In the public sector, the selected rate of discount must reflect the cost of investment funds to society as a whole, so it is generally referred to as the social rate of discount. This is complex because, in selecting a discount rate, one is effectively placing a value on consumption in the future relative to consumption today. If the government spends £2 billion on constructing new hospitals, that £2 billion will provide better medical care facilities at a future date, but will temporarily deprive society of the sum invested, which could, for example, have been used to reduce the rate of income tax. As a simple way out of the problem, the discount rate could be set at the market rate of interest on long-term risk-free investments such as gilt-edged securities. In practice, the market interest rate does not necessarily reflect the value to society of investment as opposed to consumption, but only the relative value for the average investor. A market interest rate therefore forms the starting point for determining a social rate of discount and this will then be adjusted to a level which ensures an optimal consumption:investment ratio; this optimum is government-determined.

Summary

It is clear that cost-benefit analysis is simply a special form of capital budgeting which is applicable to the public sector. In view of the problems that can be encountered both in determining the value of the costs and benefits and in fixing a social rate of discount it is a method which must be used with great care. Because a number of effects of a project may be unquantifiable, subjective judgment will also be an important part of cost-benefit analysis, but despite these drawbacks it must still be recognised that in standardising procedures for public sector project appraisal, the technique makes a significant contribution towards improved decision-making.

The two principal techniques used for solving capital budgeting problem are NPV and IRR and you should be able to compare these two. Remember that the relevance of this sort of approach to a problem depends on the objective of the organisation, and we have seen that, for the public sector in particular, an alternative may be necessary.

INVESTMENT INCENTIVES

Investment incentives take a variety of forms, including rates relief, rent-free periods for land and buildings, and lump-sum grants towards the costs of an investment project. The incentives may be offered by either central or local government, but the primary purpose which they are intended to serve is to attract investment and, in particular, employment-generating investment, into areas which would otherwise be regarded as unattractive. From the viewpoint of the investing firm, therefore, the effect of such incentives is to change the cash flow pattern of an investment.

The value of such incentives can be seen when one considers that the bulk of the expense associated with an investment occurs in the first few years of the project's life. If the basis of appraisal is discounted cash flow analysis, such payments will be discounted because of their timing. Hence any reduction in cash outflows resulting from investment incentives can serve to convert a negative NPV into a positive one, and of course this is the purpose behind their being offered. Additionally, because the total sum invested is reduced, and consequently the risk, investment incentives may also serve to encourage the acceptance of a more risky profile of investment opportunities than would otherwise be the case.

To illustrate the points made above two examples of the importance of investment incentives to the siting of an investment may be considered.

(a)   Nissan, the Japanese car manufacturer, wished to establish a European assembly plant to reduce its operating costs in the light of expanding European sales. In consequence, because of the employment and general economic benefits which would flow from such a plant, a number of European countries began competing for the site by offering the company investment incentives of varying types. For reasons of market size, the UK was the best potential site, but then even within the UK itself there was scope for some competition amongst local authorities for the site. Ultimately, the North East was chosen, because it offered the best return on the investment. Significant variations in costs (eg. of labour between sites) combined with investment grants can serve to convert a non-viable investment into a viable one.

(b)   Northern Ireland is an area which has suffered significant economic decline in the post-war years because of the civil troubles there. In consequence, there are large grants and incentives available to firms willing to establish businesses in the province. De Lorean was one such business, which aimed to produce a high-class sports car targeted at the top end of the market. In retrospect, the business would not have been viable sited anywhere else in the UK but the special incentives which attracted it to Northern Ireland temporarily gave life to the investment. Ultimately, after only several months of full production, even despite the grants, the business folded, with zero return to the tax-payer.

For examination purposes, the topic of incentives is most likely to arise in the context of assessing the viability of a particular investment. As such it will only be necessary to record the cash flow effects and net effect on the NPV.

QUESTIONS

1   Currie Ltd

Currie Ltd has calculated its cost of capital in money terms to be 15.5%. The company wishes to undertake a project making heavy-duty locks requiring an initial investment of £400,000 payable in two equal annual instalments. It is expected that the project will generate additional revenue of £450,000 per annum in current terms at an additional annual cost of £300,000. This large contribution will not be maintained throughout the 11-year life of the project since whilst revenue will be expected to rise by 5% per annum, costs will rise by 10% annually.

Required

If the first annual receipts of revenue and payment of costs occur at the same time as the second payment of £200,000, find:

(a)   whether the project is worth accepting;

(b)   the contribution in the final year;

(c)   whether it might be advantageous to terminate the project before the 11-year life expires, and is so, when to terminate the project.

2   Dumnonii & Co

Dumnonii & Co are an old firm which bottles and sells Cornish cream. In the past, they have been using earthenware bottles but now they are considering changing to glass bottles. The various costs involved are set out below for the new and old schemes:

Costs per 1,000 bottles (at current prices)	Old Scheme £	New Scheme £
Bottles	20	15
Labelling – Labour	5	4
Labels	3	4
Overheads	2	1
Bottling – Labour	7	6
Overheads	2	5
	£39	£35

The conversion from earthenware to glass will cost £75,000 spread over two years; £50,000 payable on 1 January 19X1 and £25,000 payable on 1 January 19X2. Savings from the annual production of 1.2 million bottles will first come at the end of year 19X2. If Dumnonii expect a return of 13.4% from projects, labour rates are expected to rise by 8% per annum and other costs by 5%, calculate the net present value of the project assuming receipts will continue in perpetuity.

3   Licensing Ltd

You have been asked to advise a company which has recently negotiated a licensing agreement with a US corporation that will enable it to manufacture and sell a new product as an addition to the company's existing product lines. The manager of the new product and his staff have been investigating the problems of manufacturing and selling the product with a view to obtaining board sanction for the necessary capital expenditure.

It is estimated that the product would sell at £6 per unit and the variable costs associated with manufacture and sale would be £3 per unit. The new product would involve the company entering into commitments for additional fixed overheads of £50,000 per year (including £5,000 per annum depreciation). The new plant and machinery will cost £60,000.

The company is situated in the London area and its existing buildings will be adequate to accommodate the new product. The foreseeable life for the product is four years and, at the end of that period, the plant and machinery would have a scrap value of £10,000. The current rate of corporation tax is 35%. Assume that Licensing Ltd can claim a 25% WDA on the reducing balance and that tax is payable 12 months in arrears on the relevant cash flows.

The board requires a minimum rate of return on new investments of 10% after tax.

Required

Advise the company as to whether the project is acceptable:

(a)   on the assumption that the sales volume will be 30,000 units per year and the additional working capital required will be £15,000; and

(b)   on the alternative assumption that the sales volume will be 20,000 units and the additional working capital required will be £12,000.

SUMMARY

In this session, we have considered the advanced aspects of investment appraisal. In the context of an examination question, you must be able to:

- Build inflationary effects into investment appraisal.

- Calculate and understand real, effective and money discounts rates and apply each when appropriate;

- Build taxation effects into investment appraisal; this will include the calculation of capital allowances, the tax flows arising from them and the correct timing of those flows.

- Reflect uncertainty in cash flows via the use of probabilities.

- Perform and interpret the results of sensitivity analysis.

Each of the complications examined in this session can be dealt with relatively easily by adopting the approaches set out above.

Make sure that you have understood:

(a)   how to adjust a discount rate for inflation and how to work in real terms or money terms with project cash flows;

(b)   that corporation tax is assumed to arise on the *cash flows* of a project unless otherwise told;

(c)   that the technique of expected values can be applied to a capital budgeting situation but with certain limitations.

Review of Module Two

Sessions 12 to 15 cover topics specific to Unit 13 (*Preparing information for the appraisal of activities and projects*), although sessions 1 and 2 are also relevant.

The main areas of Unit 13 are as follows:

- Cost estimation and presentation for decision-making, including marginal costing in comparison with absorption costing

- Pricing decisions

- Short-term decision-making techniques employing the marginal costing principles, including break-even and key factor analysis, and the 'make or buy' decision

- Use of relevant and opportunity costs

- Longer-term project appraisal methods, including payback and DCF techniques

Generally speaking, each part of the central assessment for Unit 13 will address one of the above areas. They are all closely connected, however, employing the same basic principle of marginal costing to all types of decision-making.

The identification of relevant, or marginal, costs for a particular decision will rely upon a sound knowledge of costing topics covered in Session 2, particularly cost behaviour and the analysis of semi-variable costs.

The other key technical abilities required for Unit 13 are as follows:

- the presentation of profit statements in both marginal and absorption costing formats, and the reconciliation of the results derived therefrom

- the application of marginal costing principles to product profitability statements

- the calculation of break-even points and margins of safety and the drawing of related charts and graphs

- application of key factor analysis to simple limited resource problems

- the identification of the relevant costs for a particular decision

- the calculation of the net present value, internal rate of return and payback period for a given set of project flows

- the incorporation of inflation and taxation effects into the DCF appraisal methods

- the use of expected monetary return in the context of basic risk analysis

Comments made in the review of your first module of study (for Units 11 and 12) regarding the importance of the discursive side of topics and the presentation of your answer apply equally to Unit 13.

Answers

SESSION 1

Attributes of MI

(a)   **Criteria for management accounting information**

    (i)   **Verifiability**

        Management information to be used in the planning and control of operations should be capable of verification to some reputable source. For example, estimates of future sales figures may be based on past trends which are verifiable.

    (ii)   **Objectivity**

        The information should be objective rather than subjective as far as possible. Estimates of the material cost per unit should be based on a study of procedures and actual experience to measure the quantity required. However, the future price charged by supplier may not be capable of such objective measurement.

    (iii)   **Timeliness**

        For information to be useful, it must be produced in time for actions to be taken if necessary. For example, cost data must be assembled in time for a decision as to the price to offer to a customer.

    (iv)   **Comparability**

        When comparing performance against a budget or against previous performance, the results must have been produced in such a way as to facilitate comparability. For example, a change in the method of valuing work in progress from one period to the next would have to be allowed for in any profit statement comparison.

    (v)   **Reliability**

        Unreliable information should not be used for the planning, control or decision-making of activities. Other actions taken may themselves be unreliable. For example, the amount of raw material used on a job must not be guessed at but rather, taken from a reliable source such as stores requisitions.

    (vi)   **Understandability**

        The information presented must be understandable to the user if he is to act upon it. A variances report where there is no indication of adverse or favourable would make it very difficult for the manager to answer.

(vii)   **Relevance**

Management's time should not be wasted with information which is not relevant to them. They should be allowed to focus on their own specific areas of responsibility. Variance reports should restrict themselves to those variances for which the manager is responsible.

(b)   The need to produce timely information may create pressure which causes some of the other criteria such as reliability or understandability to be compromised. For example, reports may be issued in 'jargon' form to speed things up but people outside a certain department may not fully understand the terms used.

SESSION 2

1   AB Ltd

(a)

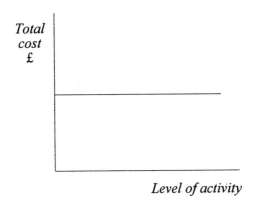

(i)   **Fixed cost**

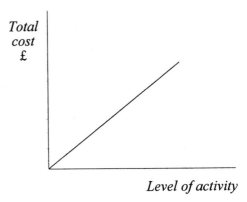

(ii)   **Variable cost**

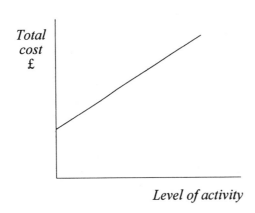

(iii)   **Semi-variable cost**

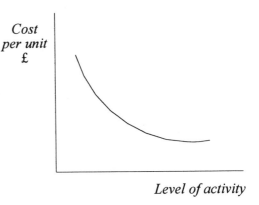

(iv)   **Fixed cost per unit**

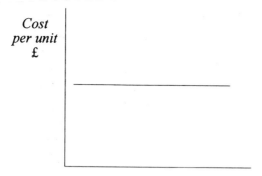

Level of activity

    (v)   **Variable cost per unit**

(b)   (i)   Fixed costs – The graph is a straight horizontal line because the cost remains constant for all levels of activity. Two examples could be office rent and administrative salaries.

    (ii)   Variable costs – The graph slopes upwards because each unit adds a constant amount to the total cost. Two examples could be direct materials and direct labour.

    (iii)   Semi-variable costs – The cost includes a basic amount of fixed cost, therefore the graph starts part-way up the vertical axis. It then slopes upwards because each unit adds a constant amount of variable cost to the total cost. Two examples could be telephone costs and electricity costs.

    (iv)   Fixed cost per unit – The graph slopes downwards because the fixed cost per unit reduces as the constant amount of fixed cost is spread over more units.

    (v)   Variable cost per unit – The graph is a straight horizontal line because the cost per unit remains constant for all levels of activity.

(c)   An understanding of cost behaviour patterns is necessary for effective planning so that managers can predict the effect on cost of proposed changes in activity levels.

It is also necessary for effective control so that realistic targets can be set for the purposes of comparison with the actual cost incurred.

2   Linear costs

(a)   There are many examples which you could choose, including the following three:

    (i)   The relationship between cost and amount of raw material purchased will be linear between limits but at a certain level a quantity discount may be introduced which destroys the linearity.

    (ii)   In agriculture, as rainfall increases, many items of food (eg. grain and fruit) will have better crops, but if there is too much rain the crops will be damaged.

    (iii)   The theory of marginal costing assumes that fixed costs are constant irrespective of the quantities produced, but if sales rise drastically, the total of fixed costs will increase respectively, as extra equipment is acquired.

(b)

x	y	$x - \bar{x}$	$y - \bar{y}$	$(x - \bar{x})(y - \bar{y})$	$(x - \bar{x})^2$
5	11.8	−5	−9.08	45.40	25
7	14.7	−3	−6.18	18.54	9
9	18.5	−1	−2.38	2.38	1
11	24.0	+1	3.12	3.12	1
13	26.2	+3	5.32	15.96	9
15	30.1	+5	9.22	46.10	25
60	125.3			131.50	70

$$\bar{x} = \frac{60}{6} = 10$$

$$\bar{y} = \frac{125.3}{6} = 20.88$$

$$b = \frac{\Sigma(x - \bar{x})(y - \bar{y})}{\Sigma(x - \bar{x})^2} = \frac{131.50}{70} = 1.88$$

$$a = \bar{y} - b\bar{x} = 20.88 - (1.88 \times 10) = 2.08$$

Regression line is:

$$y = 1.88x + 2.08$$

Thus fixed cost = £2,080

and variable cost = £1,880 per 1,000 units

3 Luda Ltd

(a)

	Machine area £	Finishing shop £
Fixed overhead	100,800	94,500
	Hours	*Hours*
Labour hours P 6,000 units × 2, 1.5	12,000	9,000
Q 8,000 units × 1, 1	8,000	8,000
R 2,000 units × 2, 2	4,000	4,000
	24,000	21,000
Overhead absorption rate per labour hour	£4.20	£4.50

		Hours	Hours
Machine hours	P 6,000 × 4, 0.5	24,000	3,000
	Q 8,000 × 1.5, 0.5	12,000	4,000
	R 2,000 × 3, 1	6,000	2,000
		42,000	9,000
Overhead absorption rate per machine hour		£2.40	£10.50

(b)   Product costs

	P £	Q £	R £
Materials	18.50	15.00	22.50
Wages	16.00	9.00	18.00
Prime cost	34.50	24.00	40.50

(i)   **Labour hour rate absorption**

	P £	Q £	R £
Prime costs as above	34.50	24.00	40.50
Fixed overheads			
Machine area £4.20 × 2, 1, 2	8.40	4.20	8.40
Finishing shop £4.50 × 1.5, 1, 2	6.75	4.50	9.00
	49.65	32.70	57.90

(ii)   **Machine hour rate absorption**

	P £	Q £	R £
Prime costs as above	34.50	24.00	40.50
Fixed overheads			
Machine area £2.40 × 4, 1.5, 3	9.60	3.60	7.20
Finishing shop £10.50 × 0.5, 0.5, 1	5.25	5.25	10.50
	49.35	32.85	58.20

(c)   The alternatives shown in (b) above produce very similar results. If a labour hour rate were used in total, the rate to be applied would be (£195,300/45,000) – £4.34 per hour – not greatly different from either of the two rates calculated separately. However the same cannot be said of the machine hour rate which in total would be £195,300/51,000) £3.83 per hour, compared with rates of £2.40 and £10.50 calculated separately.

4   Lorus Ltd

MEMORANDUM

To: Managing Director
           (cc. Production heads – sawing, assembly, finishing, materials handling, maintenance)

From: Management Accountant

Subject: Statement to show allotment of overhead   **Date:**

(a)

	Sawing £	Assembly £	Finishing £	MH £	Maintenance £
Overhead	75,000	50,000	20,000	9,000	20,000
Apportion service department overhead					
(1) Maintenance	6,000	8,000	4,000	2,000	(20,000)
(2) MH	5,500	2,200	3,300	(11,000)	–
Total allotted	86,500	60,200	27,300	–	–

Note: Service department overhead has been apportioned to production departments on the basis of percentage estimates of relative benefit, as specified.

(b)   4,000 cupboards produced with the following costs incurred

	Sawing £	Assembly £	Finishing £	Total £	Unit cost £
Materials	120,000	80,000	20,000	220,000	55.00
Wages	50,000	25,000	40,000	115,000	28.75
Overheads	86,500	60,200	27,300	174,000	43.50
	256,500	165,200	87,300	509,000	127.25

The unit cost of a cupboard is £127.25.

5   Bennick Ltd

Overhead distribution statement period to . . . . . .

	Basis (see below)	Total £'000	A £'000	B £'000	Stores £'000	Maintenance £'000	Tool room £'000
					Cost centres		
Indirect labour		1,837	620	846	149	115	107
Supervision	1	140	30	50	10	20	30
Power	2	160	80	40	4	20	16
Rent	3	280	50	125	55	30	20
Rates	3	112	20	50	22	12	8
Plant insurance	4	40	20	16	–	2	2
Plant depreciation	4	20	10	8	–	1	1
		2,589	830	1,135	240	200	184
Sundry apportionment							
Stores costs	5		75	90	(240)	30	45
Maintenance	6		80	90		(230)	60
Tool room	6		119	170			(289)
		2,589	1,104	1,485			
Machine hours			55,200	99,000			
Absorption rate per machine hour			£20	£15			

Distribution bases

1   Number of employees
2   Kilowatt hours
3   Floor area
4   Plant value
5   Number of material requisitions
6   Hours attributable

6   Costing methods

Cost allocation, apportionment and absorption are methods used in management accounting to charge overhead costs to the units of product passing through the production process. First the business must identify the cost unit to be used; this is a quantitative unit of product or service in relation to which costs are ascertained (for example a ton of coal or a man-hour of service provided). Next the business must identify its cost centres; these are locations, functions or items of equipment in respect of which costs may be ascertained and related to cost units for control purposes.

Cost allocation is defined as the charging of discrete identifiable items of cost to cost centres or cost units. For example if a business has identified factory A as being a cost centre, then the electricity bill for the factory is wholly attributable to that cost centre; the cost of that bill is allocated to factory A. No other cost centres are involved.

Cost apportionment is defined as the division of costs amongst two or more cost centres in proportion to the estimated benefit received. For example, a canteen might serve meals to the employees of two production centres A and B. When the canteen costs for a period come to be attributed to the cost centres, they can be apportioned between centres A and B, perhaps on the basis of the number of employees in each centre. The basis of apportionment has to be chosen in each situation as best reflecting the amount of benefit received by each cost centre.

The costs of the business have now been allocated and apportioned to the production cost centres. The final task is to charge these tasks to the units of product themselves. This is achieved by the process of cost absorption.

Absorption is the process of charging overheads into the costs of specific products or saleable services by means of a predetermined absorption rate. This rate will depend on production volume. It is common to calculate absorption rates as an amount per labour hour, but alternative rates could be per machine hour or per unit of output.

The above has explained the traditional method of attributing costs to products, by a process of allocation, apportionment and then absorption. However, in recent years the traditional method has been subject to heavy attack from detractors who query the relevance, in particular, of fixed overhead absorption. The last 20 years have seen businesses switching from labour-intensive activities to capital-intensive activities, so the absolute amount of fixed overheads has increased while the number of labour hours worked in the business has fallen. In such circumstances the absorption rate for fixed overhead per labour hour has increased very sharply, to a level where its relevance is now being seriously questioned.

Attention has now turned to the method of **activity-based costing** (ABC) rather than the traditional method. Proponents of ABC point out that it is not labour hours that result in overhead cost, but the incidence of so-called cost-drivers, those activities performed in the manufacturing process which lead to costs being incurred. An example cost-driver is the number of production set-ups carried out in a particular period. ABC uses an absorption rate calculated from the number of cost-drivers in the period rather than the number of labour hours worked and in this form ABC can be seen as a refinement of the traditional method of charging costs to product units.

SESSION 3

1 ICI profits

The diagram shown is a component bar chart with a slight difference from those already seen. Each bar shows the trading profit for a different division. For example, the Agriculture division had a trading profit of just under £200 million in 19X3 and approximately £160 million in 19X2. The total height of the bar thus represents the 19X3 figure and the 19X2 figure is included within this. Previous examples would have represented these figures with a bar of height £360 million (200 + 160).

From the diagram the following points can be noted:

(a) The future for ICI looks rosy since a major recovery in profits has taken place.

(b) In 19X3 only the Fibres, Organics and Petrochemicals & Plastics divisions made losses. These were very small and in two of these divisions the losses were significantly lower than the 19X2 losses.

(c)   The Organics division is the only one which made a profit in 19X2 but then a loss in 19X3.

(d)   All other divisions made increased profits in 19X3 (compared with 19X2).

(e)   Total profit made by ICI (approximately):

19X2   £350m
19X3   £630m

This represents an 80% increase in profits, although it is important to remember that these figures are only approximate.

2   Pydec

The following points in the extract from the company report would give the trades union cause for concern.

Profits

(a)   The vertical axis of the graph starts at eight thus distorting the actual change in profits. Profits have in fact fallen from £10 million to just below 8.5 million, ie. approximately 15%. (The report, on the other hand, refers to 'almost 20%'.)

(b)   The vertical scale is presumably profit (labelled 'millions') rather than £ millions.

(c)   Is the picture as bad as that painted? The rate of decrease in profits seems to be getting smaller; perhaps levelling out.

(d)   What does the dotted line mean? Presumably it is a projection but what evidence is it based upon?

(e)   The graph gives only a general indication of the behaviour of profits. More definite conclusions could be drawn if more detailed figures were available.

Production

(a)   The scale of the bar chart is correct this time.

(b)   Production has fallen as stated (by 10,000 sets or 20% overall) but this is confined to the Dundee factory.

(c)   A 20% fall in production that only gives rise to a 15% fall in profits shows strong evidence of successful cost control.

(d)   Are production figures for audio equipment available?

(e)   Report states 'some of our competitors have been doing much better'. Where is the evidence for this?

(f)   Since production probably follows demand, the split between factories is irrelevant; more important are sales by region.

Wages

(a)   The report states 'the average wage of all employees rose by £7.23 per week' and claims this is good. What percentage increase is this? What was the rate of inflation and have *real* wages increased?

(b)   Commentary and data are inconsistent: 'If we compare average wages between 19W5 and 19X0...' but diagrams are for 19W6 and 19X1.

(c)   The pictogram is misleading. In terms of the figures, wages have almost doubled, yet the diagram looks like a four-fold increase took place (twice the height and twice the width).

3   Data presentation

A Gantt chart is the most unlikely method to be used. These are most useful as progress charts, ie. comparing actual performance with target.

4 **Not at all obvious**

(a)

To: Mrs Jenkins

SURVEY REPORT COMPARING THE ABILITY OF TWO TYPES OF DISPLAY STAND TO GENERATE SALES OF CARDS

Introduction

The object of this report is to compare two types of display stand by analysing their ability to generate sales of cards in newsagents.

The first type of card stand is the traditional one. This is five feet wide, made from formica with sloping perspex divisions.

The second type is the revolving metal card stand. This is two feet in diameter.

For the purpose of this report we will call them Traditional and Revolving.

Procedure

The survey was carried out in three cities, Bristol, Aberdeen and Manchester. The results shown in this report are those from Bristol.

Ten newsagents from Bristol were studied over a period of six working days, the 15th to 20th March. Half of these newsagents have the traditional stand to display cards and the other half have the revolving card stand. Details of the names and addresses of all ten shops are in the Appendix. For easier comparison the shops have been allocated letters from A to E.

Findings

The following table shows the number of cards sold over the six days in Bristol:

Traditional			*Revolving*	
Shop	*Card sales*		*Shop*	*Card sales*
A			B	
C			E	435
D			F	475
G	286		H	575
I	275		J	525

The findings were similar in the other two cities chosen for the survey.

Conclusion

The higher numbers of cards sold are all in shops which use the revolving card stands.

(b)

Memorandum

To: Jo Bloggs   **Date:**

From: A Clerk

Report on comparison of display stands and their ability to generate sales

Having read your survey report there are a number of questions that I would like you to answer:

1   How and why were the three cities chosen?

2   How and why were the ten newsagents in Bristol chosen?

3   Only six results are shown out of the ten shops studied. Where are the results from the others?

4   Are the figures for Aberdeen and Manchester available?

5   Have you considered exchanging Traditional for Revolving stands to determine whether the higher level of sales is a function of the type of stand or the size and location of the shop.

SESSION 4

1   Standard revision

The revision of technical standards (material quantities and specification and labour hours and grades) is quite divorced from questions of budget revision. Technical standards are there to be complied with. They must therefore be revised every time there are changes in method, specification or product design. Does this mean that every revision of technical standards must be reflected immediately in the standard costing system? In general the answer is 'no'. Standard costs should be revised when accumulations of changes result in variances becoming excessive in relation to existing standards. Within this context, the revision of cost standards (wage rates and material prices) is conveniently undertaken at the time new budgets are set.

Under a system of rolling budgets this opportunity will occur at each review period. Note, however, that whilst all cost standards may be reviewed, it may not be necessary to revise all of them. Revision may be confined to selected major items. It may be desirable to update all standards once a year.

2   Standards come unstuck?

It cannot be repeated too often that, subject to statutory controls, selling prices should be related to the level of costs which will be experienced during the manufacture (or purchase) of what is to be sold; in order words, selling prices are based on forecast costs, even though it may not be possible due to market pressures to cover those costs completely. A standard costing system can help price-fixing in three ways:

(a)   Once technical standards have been fixed, it is relatively easy to apply alternative cost figures to them. The existence of technical standards thus helps price fixing.

(b)   If forecast cost standards are used they will represent the sort of forecast that is needed for price fixing over the period during which they remain in force.

(c)   Whatever type of cost standards are used, the trend of variances from these standards will often assist the estimator in forecasting future cost trends.

3   WH Ltd

WH Ltd

Memorandum

To: Production Manager   Date: 12 December 19X4

From: Assistant Accountant

Subject: Determining the standard price per kg of material

As requested I detail below the information which would be needed to determine the standard price of material and possible sources of the information.

(a) *The information which is needed*	(b) *Possible sources*
• Type and quality of material	Technical specification
• Quantity and timing of purchases, for determining any bulk discounts	Production and purchasing schedules
• Past trend in prices	Historical records in company Supplier records Government statistics Trade association statistics Movements in price indexes
• Future trend in prices	Discussions/negotiations with suppliers Trade association forecasts Financial press forecasts Government forecasts of key indexes
• Carriage costs to be added	Historical records in company Supplier records
• Type of standard to be set: eg. average for year, or increasing with inflation	Company policy on standard setting

4   Attainable and ideal standard

(a)   An **attainable standard** is a standard which can be attained if a standard unit of work is carried out efficiently, a machine properly operated or material properly used. The standard makes allowances for normal shrinkage, waste and machine breakdowns. It is intended to have a motivational impact on employees.

An **ideal standard** is a standard which can be attained under the most favourable conditions. The standard makes no provision for shrinkage, spoilage or machine breakdowns.

Ideal standards are not widely used in practice because of their adverse effect on employee motivation. Unfavourable variances usually result, making them less useful for planning purposes.

(b)   (i)   **Actual profit for the period**

	£	£
Sales (2,250 units × £15)		33,750
Production costs (2,500 units)		
Direct materials	12,000	
Direct labour	9,000	
	21,000	
Less: Closing stock (250 units at £10 per unit)	2,500	
Cost of sales		18,500
Actual profit		15,250

(ii)   **Standard cost data per unit**

	£
Direct materials (3 kg at £2 per kg)	6.00
Direct labour (2 hours at £2 per hour)	4.00
	10.00

Material price variance

	£
Actual usage (5,000 kg) at actual cost	12,000
Actual usage (5,000 kg) at standard cost (£2 per kg)	10,000
Material price variance	2,000 (A)

Material usage variance

	£
Actual usage (5,000 kg) at standard cost (£2 per kg)	10,000
Standard usage [for actual production (7,500 kg)] at standard cost (£2 per kg)	15,000
Material usage variance	5,000 (F)

Labour rate variance

	£
Actual hours (6,000 hours) at actual rate (£1.50 per hour)	9,000
Actual hours (6,000 hours) at standard rate (£2 per hour)	12,000
Labour rate variance	3,000 (F)

Labour efficiency variance

	£
Actual hours (6,000 hours) at standard rate (£2 per hour)	12,000
Standard hours for actual production (5,000 hours) at standard rate (£2 per hour)	10,000
Labour efficiency variance	2,000 (A)

5 Product XY

(a) Standard product cost sheet for one unit of product XY

	£
Materials – 8 kg at £1.50 per kg	12.00
Labour – 2 hours at £4 per hour	8.00
Variable overhead – 2 hours at £1 per hour	2.00
	22.00

Workings

(1) **Materials**

	kg	£
Actual materials used at actual cost	150,000	210,000
Price variance	–	15,000 (F)
Actual materials used at standard cost ie. £1.50 per kg	150,000	225,000
Usage variance (at £1.50 per kg)	6,000	9,000 (A)
Standard materials at standard cost	144,000	216,000

With a production level of 18,000 units:

Standard material usage $\dfrac{144,000 \text{ kg}}{18,000 \text{ units}}$ = 8 kg per unit

Standard material price $\dfrac{£216,000}{144,000 \text{ kg}}$ = £1.50 per kg

(2) **Labour**

	Hours	£
Actual hours worked at actual rate	32,000	136,000
Rate variance	–	8,000 (A)
Actual hours worked at standard rate ie. £4 per hour	32,000	128,000
Efficiency variance (at £4 per hour)	4,000	16,000 (F)
Standard hours at standard rate	36,000	144,000

With a production level of 18,000 units:

Standard labour efficiency $\dfrac{36,000 \text{ hours}}{18,000 \text{ units}}$ = 2 hours per unit

Standard labour rate $\dfrac{£144,000}{36,000 \text{ hours}}$ = £4 per hour

(3) **Variable production overhead**

	Hours	£
Actual hours worked at actual rate	32,000	38,000
Expenditure variance	–	6,000 (A)
Actual hours worked at standard rate ie. £1 per hour	32,000	32,000
Efficiency variance (at £1 per hour)	4,000	4,000 (F)
Standard hours at standard rate	36,000	36,000

With a production level of 18,000 units:

Standard variable overhead efficiency $\dfrac{36,000 \text{ hours}}{18,000 \text{ units}}$ = 2 hours per unit

Standard variable overhead expenditure $\dfrac{£36,000}{36,000 \text{ hours}}$ = £1 per hour

Notes

(1)   There are a number of ways of approaching the solution to this question. The suggestion here is just one of those methods.

(2)   Common sense and a thorough understanding of the meaning of variances as well as methods of calculation are essential.

(3)   The resulting standards will usually be fairly 'round number' figures. If they are not, it is worth an extra check.

(b)   **Types of standard that can be used for a standard costing system**

The three major types of standard are as follows.

Ideal standard

This is a standard which can only be attained under the most favourable conditions.

This standard therefore makes no allowance for spoilage, machine breakdowns or inefficiency resulting for any reason. It can serve as a reminder that there is scope for improvement, but it is considered unsuitable for motivational purposes as employees may become demoralised if they consistently fail to achieve the standard. Ideal standards are normally too optimistic to be useful for planning purposes and, if used for control purposes, would generally show large adverse variances.

Attainable standard

This is a standard which can be attained if a standard unit of work is carried out efficiently, a machine properly operated or material properly used.

This standard does make allowances for spoilage, machine breakdowns, shrinkage and waste. It usually represents future performance rather than past performance and will be based on a standard which is reasonably attainable.

It is useful for motivating employees, who may achieve a higher level of output simply by attempting to meet the standard required. It is also useful for all aspects of planning including budgeting, production scheduling and cashflow projections. Currently attainable standards can be used for control purposes, although small adverse variances may be accepted as being reasonable.

Basic standard

This is a standard established for use over a long period from which a current standard can be developed.

This standard does not have much use for motivation, planning or control purposes, but can be useful for predicting trends.

6 AB Ltd

(a)

Direct material price variance	=	($8 – £8.50) × 19,500
	=	£9,750 adverse
Direct material usage variance	=	[(4,500 × 4.3kg) – 19,500] × £8
	=	£1,200 adverse
Direct labour rate variance	=	(£4 – £3.90) × 6,740
	=	£674 favourable
Direct labour utilisation variance	=	[(4,500 × 1.5 hours) – 6,740] × £4
	=	£40 favourable

(b) Reconciliation of standard direct cost of production with actual direct cost for June

Actual production = 4,500 units

	£	£
Standard direct cost of production = 4,500 × £40.40		181,800
Direct cost variances		
Direct material price	9,750 A	
Direct material usage	1,200 A	
		10,950 A
Direct labour rate	674 F	
Direct labour utilisation	40 F	
		714 F
Actual direct cost of production		192,036

7 WH Ltd

(a)

(i)	Direct material price variance	=	(£4.90 – £4.60) × 2,100
		=	£630 favourable
(ii)	Direct material usage variance	=	[(400 × 4.5) – 2,100] × £4.90
		=	£1,470 adverse
(iii)	Direct labour rate variance	=	(£3.50 – £4) × 4,000
		=	£2,000 adverse
(iv)	Direct labour utilisation variance	=	[(400 × 10.3) – 4,000] × £3.50
		=	£420 favourable

(b) **Reconciliation of standard direct cost of production with actual direct cost for November**

	£	£
Standard direct cost of production (400 × £58.10)		23,240
Direct cost variances:		
Direct material – price	630 F	
– usage	1,470 A	
		840 A
Direct labour – rate	2,000 A	
– utilisation	420 F	
		1,580 A
Actual direct cost of production		25,660

Note: A = adverse variance; F = favourable variance

SESSION 5

1 AB Ltd

Memorandum

To: A N Other

From: Assistant Accountant

Date: June 19X4

Subject: Explanations for overhead variances

___

As you requested, I outline below possible explanations for each of the overhead variances which you have calculated.

Overhead price variance

The adverse variance would have been caused by production overhead expenditure being higher than budgeted. This could have resulted from the expenditure on any item of fixed production overhead being higher than budgeted. One possible reason was that the factory rent was higher than had been budgeted.

Overhead efficiency variance

The efficiency variance is favourable and this is directly related to the favourable labour utilisation variance. We know from the calculation of the direct labour utilisation variance that the labour force took less time than the standard hours expected for 4,500 units. Therefore the overhead efficiency variance could have been caused by any factor which enabled time to be saved against the standard allowance. One possible reason could be that the standard time allowance was set too high.

Overhead volume variance

The volume variance is favourable, indicating that more use was made of available capacity than was originally budgeted (ie. more hours were worked in total). One possible reason for this could be that there were more employees than had been budgeted.

2 Revamp Furniture Ltd

(a) **Reconciliation for Period 1**

Working		Favourable £	Adverse £	£
(1)	Flexed budgeted cost			41,080
Cost variances				
(2)	Materials			
	price	270		
	usage		400	
(3)	Labour			
	rate of pay		1,412	
	efficiency	512		
(4)	Variable overhead			
	expenditure		102	
	efficiency	192		
(5)	Fixed overhead			
	expenditure		50	
	efficiency	80		
	capacity	20		
		1,074	1,964	890
(6)	Actual cost			41,970

(b) (i) Although standard costing has, as one of its purposes, the allocation of responsibility for cost variances, it is often found in practice that the analysis of variances is merely the beginning of a further task of investigation before ultimate responsibility can be equitably assigned.

On the operating statement submitted for part (a) of this question there is disclosed a favourable material price variance and an adverse usage variance. Theoretically this should indicate that the buyer is operating efficiently and the production manager inefficiently. This need not necessarily be true, however. The buyer could have taken advantage of a special offer of material at less than standard price, not appreciating that the material was slightly below standard quality. It is very likely that the inferior material would give rise to production problems of machining, handling and possibly others which could well result in excess usage; hence the adverse usage variance.

(ii)   As regards labour, the payment of higher than standard rates (suggested by the adverse rate of pay variance in the operating statement) may well have had the effect of providing greater motivation, and hence speedier work, which is reflected in the favourable efficiency variance.

There may well be interdependence between the material and labour cost variances; for instance, the speedier work suggested by the favourable labour efficiency variance may have been accomplished by disregarding material usage standards.

From the foregoing it will be seen that not only is there possible interdependence between the variances of each element of cost, but also cross-interdependence between the elements of cost.

Workings

(1)   Standard cost per unit

		£
Materials		3.00
Labour		3.20
Variable overhead		1.20
Fixed overhead $\dfrac{£30,000}{120,00}$ = 25p per hr × 2 hrs		0.50
		7.90

Flexed budgeted cost 5,200 × 7.90	£41,080

(2)   Materials

(i)   Price variance

	£
Actual cost of 32,000 lb	15,730
Standard cost	16,000
	270 (F)

(ii)   Usage variance

	lb
Expected usage for 5,200 chairs	31,200
Actual usage	32,000
Excessive usage	800

@ 50p per lb	£400 (A)

(3) Labour

    (i)   Rate of pay

	£
Actual cost of 10,080 hrs	17,540
Standard cost	16,128
	1,412 (A)

    (ii)   Efficiency

	Hrs
Standard time for 5,200 chairs	10,400
Actual time taken	10,080
Hours gained through efficiency	320
@ 160p per hour	512 (F)

(4) Variable overhead

    (i)   Expenditure variance

	£
Actual cost of 10,080 hours	6,150
Standard cost	6,048
	102 (A)

    (ii)   Efficiency variance

320 hours @ 60p	192 (F)

(5) Fixed overhead

    (i)   Expenditure variance

	£
Budgeted cost	2,500
Actual cost	2,550
	50 (A)

    (ii)   Efficiency variance

320 hours @ 25p	80 (F)

(The absorption rate is calculated by dividing the budgeted cost by the budgeted number of hours to be worked: £30,000 / (60,000 × 2 hrs) = 25p)

(iii)	Volume variance	
		£
	Actual hours worked	10,080
	Budgeted 20/240 × 120,000	10,000
		80
	@ 25p per hour	20 (F)

(6)   Actual cost statement

	£
Materials	15,730
Labour	17,540
Variable overhead	6,150
Fixed overhead	2,550
	41,970

3   XYZ Manufacturing Company

Key points in the report

–   Although the total variance is only 1.57% of the total, this disguises significant individual variances which require investigation.

–   The favourable variances are entirely price variances and therefore largely outside management control. The controllable variances are all adverse.

–   Investigation of materials wastage, labour utilisation and usage of overhead facilities required. The relevant adverse valances are 5.5%, 3.75% and 2.6% of actual cost.

–   Adverse volume variance due to operating below planned capacity. Not substantial but efforts should be made to increase capacity.

4   WH Ltd

WH Ltd

Memorandum

To: Production Manager   Date: 12 December 19X4

From: Assistant Accountant

Subject: Direct cost variances for November

As you requested, I detail below explanations of the direct cost variances and possible suggestions as to their cause in November.

(a)   **The meaning of the variances**

Direct material price variance

This variance shows the saving or over-spending which resulted from paying a lower or higher price than standard for the direct material used in the period. The favourable variance indicates that a lower than standard price was paid.

Direct material usage variance

This variance shows the saving or over-spending, at standard prices, which resulted from using less or more material than standard to manufacture the production for the period. The adverse variance indicates that more material was used than standard.

Direct labour rate variance

This variance shows the saving or over-spending which resulted from paying a lower or higher hourly rate than standard for the hours worked in the period. The adverse variance indicates that a higher than standard hourly rate was paid.

Direct labour utilisation variance

This variance shows the saving or overspending, at standard rates, which resulted from working less or more hours than standard to manufacture the production for the period. The favourable variance indicates that less hours were worked than standard.

(b)   **Possible causes of the variances**

Favourable direct material price variance

Bulk discounts were received which were not allowed for in the standard.
The standard price of material was set too high.
A lower quality material was purchased, at a lower price than standard.
Effective negotiations by the buyer secured a price lower than the standard.

Adverse direct material usage variance

Material wastage was higher than allowed in the standard.
The standard usage was set too low.
There was a higher than standard level of rejects.
Theft of material.

Adverse direct labour rate variance

High levels of overtime were paid for compared with the standard allowance.
The standard wage rate was set too low.
A higher grade of labour was used.
Bonus payments were higher than standard.

Favourable direct labour utilisation variance

Employees were working faster than standard.
More skilled employees were used.
There were savings through the learning effect.
The standard labour time was set too high.
The material was easy to process, leading to savings against the standard time.

(c)   Two examples of interdependence, where one variance can be related to others, could include the following:

The savings made on material price (favourable material price variance) may indicate that poor quality material was purchased, leading to high wastage, rejects and an adverse usage variance.

Bulk discounts may have resulted in the saving on material price. However, the consequent excessive stocks may have led to deterioration and write-offs, hence the adverse usage variance.

Direct workers may have been of a higher grade than standard, resulting in higher hourly rates and the adverse rate variance. However, the higher skill level may have led to time savings and the favourable utilisation variance.

Higher than standard bonus payments may have caused the adverse labour rate variance, but the bonuses may have resulted from faster working and hence the favourable utilisation variance.

Faster working resulted in the favourable utilisation variance, but less care may have been taken over weighing and handling the material, hence the adverse material usage variance.

SESSION 6

1   Retail ratios

–   Rate of stock turnover = Total sales/Average stock

The higher the better. Reduces the risk of obsolescence. Makes best use of working capital.

–   Gross profit margin = (Sales – Purchases) as % of sales (or as % of purchases. Trading profitability. Preferably as high as possible but the company might have a policy of low margins with high turnover.

–   Creditors settlement period = 12 divided by (Annual purchases/Average creditors) months. Could also be expressed in weeks or days. How quickly is the company settling its debts?. The higher the period, the better use being made of working capital but, if too high it could lead to lack of goodwill with creditors.

–   ROCE: overall profitability of the company's investment in the business.

2   WH Ltd

WH Ltd

Report

To:	Senior Management Committee	Date: 12 December 19X4
From:	Assistant Accountant	
Subject:	Profitability and asset turnover ratios	

We have received the Trade Association results for year 4 and this report looks in detail at the profitability and asset turnover ratios.

(a)   **What each ratio is designed to show**

(i)   *Return on capital employed (ROCE)*

This ratio shows the percentage rate of profit which has been earned on the capital invested in the business, (ie. the return on the resources controlled by management). The expected return would vary depending on the type of business and it is usually calculated as follows:

$$\text{Return on capital employed} = \frac{\text{Profit before interest and tax}}{\text{Capital employed}} \times 100\%$$

Other profit figures can be used, as well as various definitions of capital employed.

(ii)   *Net operating profit margin*

This ratio shows the operating profit as a percentage of sales. The operating profit is calculated before interest and tax and it is the profit over which operational managers can exercise day to day control. It is the amount left out of sales value after all direct costs and overheads have been deducted.

$$\text{Net operating profit margin} = \frac{\text{Operating profit}}{\text{Sales value}} \times 100\%$$

(iii)   *Asset turnover*

This ratio shows how effectively the assets of a business are being used to generate sales:

$$\text{Asset turnover} = \frac{\text{Sales}}{\text{Capital employed}}$$

If the same figure for capital employed is used as in ROCE, then ratios (i) to (iii) can be related together as follows.

(i)   ROCE = (ii) Net operating profit margin × (iii) Asset turnover

(iv)   *Gross margin*

This ratio measures the profitability of sales:

$$\text{Gross margin} = \frac{\text{Gross profit}}{\text{Sales value}} \times 100\%$$

The gross profit is calculated as the sales value less the cost of goods sold and this ratio therefore focuses on the company's manufacturing and trading activities.

(b)   **WH Ltd's profitability and asset turnover**

WH Ltd's ROCE is lower than the trade association average, possibly indicating that the assets are not being used as profitably in this company as the average for the industry.

WH Ltd's operating profit margin is higher than the trade association average, despite a lower than average gross profit margin. This suggests that overheads are lower relative to sales value in WH Ltd.

WH Ltd's asset turnover ratio is lower than the trade association average. This may mean that assets are not being used as effectively in our company and it is the cause of the lower than average ROCE.

WH Ltd's gross profit margin is lower than the trade association average. This suggests either that WH's direct costs are higher than average, or that selling prices are lower.

(c)   **Limitations of the ratios and of inter-company comparisons**

There are a number of limitations of which management should be aware before drawing any firm conclusions from a comparison of these ratios:

(i)   The ratios are merely averages, based on year-end balance sheet data, which may not be representative.

(ii)   One particular factor which could affect these ratios is if there has been any new investment towards the end of the financial year. This investment would increase the value of the assets or capital employed, but the profits from the investment would not yet have accumulated in the profit and loss account.

Generally, newer assets tend to depress the asset turnover and hence the ROCE in the short term. It is possible that this is the cause of our company's lower asset turnover and ROCE.

(iii) Although the trade association probably makes some attempt to standardise the data, different member companies may be using different accounting policies, for example in calculating depreciation and valuing stock.

(iv) Our company's analyst may have used a different formula for calculating any of the ratios. For example, as noted above, there is a variety of ways of calculating capital employed. However, it is likely that the trade association would provide information on the basis of calculation of the ratios.

(v) The member companies will have some activities in common, hence their membership of the trade association. However, some may have a diversified range of activities, which will distort the ratios and make direct comparison difficult.

3   XY Builders plc

Report prepared for Board discussion

To: Managing Director

From: Management Consultant

Date: XX/XX/XX

Subject: Interim report on strategic issues

Some comments on overall group performance

Profitability

(a)   Gross profit on sales shows a yield of 42.8% for group as a whole. This is not uniform amongst the different grade of shops which show:

C grade	=	44.5%
B grade	=	41.8%
A grade	=	38.8%

The reasons for their difference need to be investigated. It may be due to mix of products sold, or certain high profit lines stocked only in the largest stores, or advantageous bulk purchasing. Investigation should show whether it is possible to transfer the benefit enjoyed by C grade into smaller stores.

(b)   Net profit on sales shows greater divergence.

C grade	=	15.4%
B grade	=	13.3%
A grade	=	(10.8% loss)

With an overall group performance of 11.2%.

The relative level of A's direct operating costs is more than twice that of B grade and more than three times that of C grade. These high costs of A may be a function of their small size and currently A is failing to make any contribution to group overheads. There is an implied case for harvesting A grade shops by selling on or closure, though further investigation will be needed to check whether some A units are performing efficiently as individuals. Also, the effect of shared overheads borne by C and B grade stores only would need to be appraised.

Profitability by individual store is essential information and should be expressed in terms that allow comparison, for example contribution per square foot or return per product category.

(c)   *Overheads*

Group administration costs of £959,000 represent 5.4% of total sales. This should be reviewed to see if some operations could be decentralised to individual stores or discontinued.

Management of working capital

(a)   *Stock levels* – Based on the year-end figures, stock represents 76 days' sales. Given that normal shelf replenishment orders would be satisfied in less than seven days, the conclusion would seem to be that there is overstocking and/or a high proportion of slow-moving lines. Between the different grades of stores it is noticeable that the smallest stores carry proportionately the highest stock holdings.

(b)   *Debtor/creditor balance* – The overall debtor position represents 4.3 months' trading. Although a high proportion of trade would be on a credit basis, this should be limited to one month from the end of the month in which goods were delivered, ie. average six weeks. It would be helpful to ascertain debtor balances by individual store and also an ageing balance. Given that builders, as an occupation group, usually figure in the top three positions of the bankruptcy league, the likelihood of bad debts is inescapable. A tighter credit control system is required.

Trade creditors represent more than nine weeks' sales; it is unlikely that this could be extended significantly.

If XY is able to maintain its creditor position and reduce debtors to six weeks then some £4.3 million would become available to the company, virtually erasing the overdraft. A prompt payment discount scheme or factoring should be considered as part of a stricter debtor policy.

Property

The values stated in the balance sheet for freehold and leasehold properties should be checked and brought into line with current values. This would be an essential prerequisite for all the strategic issues under discussion.

Financial structure

The long-term debenture of £1.5 million is due for repayment in the coming year. Although this could be met from the raising of further finance, this would affect borrowing levels and may inhibit certain strategy options. It would be better practice to reduce working capital and so release the funds for repayment. In addition to the £4.3m debtor excess, there may be £500,000 available from better stock management.

C grade shops operate on 115 days' trading held as stock

B grade shops operate on 146 days' trading held as stock

A grade shops operate on 173 days' trading held as stock

If 115 days became the overall practice, then £516,000 would be released.

SESSION 7

1   Product design

Product design is a fertile source of cost reduction opportunities. Simply by evaluating existing designs against the findings of market research, the designer may find prospects for cost reduction in improved design or in a reduction of the product range and the number of variants from basic models.

Improved design when coupled with improved production methods, may result in considerable cost savings. Improvements of this kind may:

(a)   reduce wastage of material and scrapped work in progress or finished products;

(b)   reduce total production time for increased productivity – this will reduce labour costs and overheads giving reduced costs per unit of output.

Product range and variety has to be examined in relation to:

(a)   the scope of simplification and standardisation of both products and their component parts;

(b)   knowledge of the products market and the customer and/or consumer opinion; the simplification and standardisation of products and their component parts, which may result in a smaller number of products containing fewer components, can bring savings of many kinds: lower production set up costs; reduced material and labour costs; lower overheads of all kinds – including servicing and repair costs.

The market for products may be so complex and competitive that variety of product and relatively broad product range is justified by the additional value of sales that they generate. Motor car manufacturers used to believe this to be the case for their industry, but since the late sixties and early seventies they have aimed for a small number of basic models with largely external variations.

Good or improved design should, of course, affect the behaviour and attitudes of the people who make the products and those who manage both these people and the processes in which they are employed. Good design addresses the question of quality control and should tend to reduce inspection time; increasingly it leads to ways of improving motivation and increasing the interest of those who produce to the design specification; in both of these tendencies lie prospects for further cost reduction.

2 Control v Reduction

The purpose of cost control is to contain the cost of a product or service, with some predetermined target or budget, or according to some preset standard. By contrast, the aim of cost reduction is to reduce the cost of a product or service without affecting its function, quality or saleable value, and implies a challenging of existing cost standards. Both activities are concerned with the efficient and effective use of resources and both employ the same techniques of cost analysis. However, clearly, the one is different from the other as a more detailed consideration will show.

(a) *Cost control* is a general term used to define all methods of controlling the cost of manufacturing or processing products or services through all the various stages. The main methods used by management accountants are:

    (i)   standard costing;
    (ii)   budgetary control.

These both entail targets or standards together with feedback on performance against standards and the correction of deviations or variances. The application of these methods relates to some predetermined time period at the end of which targets or standards are reviewed and set for a subsequent period.

(b) Cost reduction actively seeks to make real reductions in the cost of a product or a service by lowering the cost of any item that contributes to the total cost, without impairing the suitability of the products for their intended use.

Broad methods of reducing costs are:

    (i)   unit cost reduction by expenditure reduction or greater volume of output;

    (ii)   unit cost reduction by an increase in productivity, ie. an increase in output yield or rate of output for a given amount of expenditure. Unlike cost control which is a relatively stable activity, cost reduction activity is dynamic because it includes a continuous search for opportunities to change the current standards or targets.

3 Value analysis

Value analysis has been defined as: 'the analysis of the utilitarian or marketing function of a product or procedure in an organised way with the aim of identifying any alternative ways of achieving the required end and in choosing the least cost method of doing this from the alternatives found'.

Briefly, value analysis is a means of eliminating costs by a systematic search for ways of achieving the same, or a better, performance for an existing manufactured product at a lower cost without reducing the quality. Quite obviously, value analysis is a technique of cost reduction.

Value analysis proceeds by an analysis of the function of a product or of its component parts. Function is the criterion for determining the value of an item; one with a high value is one that satisfies exactly the function which makes the item work or sell at the lowest cost. Value analysis may result in the substitution of materials, or modifications to the design in order to make the best use of materials, or cheaper marketing methods and so forth.

Value analysis should be contrasted with method study, with which it is sometimes confused. Method study accepts products as they are shown on drawings and concentrates on how they are made in the workshop. Value analysis concentrates on the drawings themselves and attempts to find ways of altering the drawings in order to achieve savings. The main thrust of value analysis is towards savings on material costs which may result in savings on labour costs. Method study's main concern is the saving of labour costs.

4   Quality circles

Quality circles were invented by the American IBM Company, during the late 1950s, but are associated more with the operation of Japanese organisations. Quality circles comprise small groups of either staff or operatives who meet regularly to discuss problems of quality control in their work area. They advance possible solutions and ideas to resolve the problems, and possibly on how to improve the quality of output.

Supervisors obviously play a big role in operating the circles since they do the training and lead the groups. In the Western world this creates a problem, since the responsibility for operational planning and the essential tooling standards and control is the province of a staff technician, rather than the operatives. Consequently, for effective implementation in the Western world, attitudes need to change about the employment of operatives in a consultative session. Worse still, the functional experts may resent their potential loss of status if they are not put in charge of the circles, or if they are made to relate with the operatives. As a result of this, quality circles have been less than successful in traditional Western industrial environment of computer engineering.

A further failing in the West has been that the participants were expected to give of their own time to attend the meetings, rather than go in the firm's time. By contrast, in Japan, where the success has been considerable, the employees attend in the company time, encouraged to volunteer to serve on the quality circles which are often seen as a means of being noticed for promotion.

SESSION 8

1   Transport company

Performance ratios

Cost control ratios

Cost per mile
Cost per tonne carried   } each of these ratios could be calculated for fixed and variable
Cost per journey   costs separately
Cost per tonne/mile

Fixed cost per available day

Fixed cost per working day

Usage ratios

Tonne/miles per period
Days available as a percentage of total working days
Days used as a percentage of available days
Tonnes carried per available day
Journeys made per available day
Tonnes/miles per journey

2   Loamshire County Council (1)

(a)

	A	B	C	D	E
		Policy		Inflation	
	Budget	variations	A+B	allowance	Budget
	1992/93	1993/94		1993/94	1993/94
	£'000	£'000	£'000	£'000	£'000
Employees					
Professional	1,200	24	1,224	24	1,248
Clerical	2,100	42	2,142	43	2,185
Other	305	6	311	6	317
Premises	550	–	550	16	566
Supplies and services					
Book fund	1,700	–150	1,550	62	1,612
Cassettes and CDs	160	–20	140	6	146
Other	70	–	70	2	72
Transport	120	–10	110	3	113
Establishment expenses	210	–	210	6	216
Debt charges	550	20	570	–	570
	6,965	–88	6,877	168	7,045
Income from fees, charges and trading	400	80	480	–	480
Cash allocated to the Library Service	6,565	–168	6,397	168	6,565

(b)   Book fund reduced by £150,000 at 1992/93 price.

$$\% \text{ reduction} = \frac{150}{1,700} \times 100 = 8.8\%$$

(c)   –   Measures of efficiency in routine tasks: issues per clerical employee or accessions per clerical employee.

–   Level of service measures: library users as percentage of county population. Issues per user.

–   Measure of income generation: income as percentage of total budget.

–   Quality of the stock: average cost per item (books, cassettes, CDs). Stock analysed by age of accession. Number of accessions in the current year (or other period) as percentage of total stock.

3 **Armstrong**

Allocation and apportionment in the NHS

Possible purposes for these measures

(1)   Justifying price rises – to see if certain medical services are so costly that charges should be levied or to form a basis for charging for all medical services.

(2)   Alternative support services – to compare the cost of an NHS organised catering service, say, with outside costs for such services with a view to using such private support.

(3)   Other reasons:

–   comparing with cost of private medicine

–   putting onus on primary cost centres to justify their use and control the cost of support services (though hardly a sensible plan and one not achieved in his **way**).

Methods used

(1)   Though an attempt has been made to apportion costs on a fair basis allocating directly to primary cost centres where appropriate, no attempt seems to have been made to distinguish between **variable** and **fixed costs** and **avoidable** and **unavoidable** (direct or indirect) fixed costs which would be necessary for purpose (2) above.

(2)   Using catering as an example, the **method** of apportionment used seems to imply that employees of primary cost centres do not eat (no attempt being made to spread indirect support services over primary cost centres), that the canteen doesn't get cleaned nor domestic staff eat (no attempt being made to spread indirect support services between other support services). It is fair to assume that direct support service costs need not be spread over indirect support cost centres. The benefit from such additional work on apportionment may well be exceeded by the additional effort required in obtaining the appropriate information.

(3)   The **bases** used, though perhaps reasonable, could be improved. For instance the effort and time spent by domestic staff in various departments may not just depend on floor area but the extent to which that floor area is cluttered by furniture and equipment or cleaned by other staff. Certain types of patients may put greater demands on the 'CSSD' than others.

SESSION 9

1   **Time series example**

The quarterly sales of alcoholic drinks in off-licences and supermarkets in the UK is an example of a time series.

The trend would probably be a gradual but steady increase due to increased standards of living.

Seasonal variations would appear as a dramatic increase in sales just before Christmas.

Cyclical variations would not be apparent over a short period of time but if the figures could be scrutinised over many years there should be some evidence that the sales of alcohol were linked with the economic situation. In a period of economic depression people do not have as much money to spend on luxuries such as alcohol.

Random variations could occur because of a budget decision to raise the duty on alcoholic drinks sharply.

2 Distribution data

(a) The first thing you need to do when using a moving averages approach is to decide upon the appropriate *order*, ie. how many values to amalgamate within each average value. In this case, as the data is given by quarters, it will be reasonable to assume that order 4 should be used. As this is an even order, it will be necessary to 'centre' the moving average.

The following steps should therefore be taken:

(1) List out the time series (TS) in chronological order (leave a space between each value to make centring easier).

(2) Create a four-quarter moving total column as follows:

Add together the first four numbers and put the total in the next column, aligned between the second and third TS values.

Now move down one value in the TS and add together the next four figures – so that you are adding the second, third, fourth and fifth values in the TS.

The easiest way to do this is to take your first total, subtract the first TS value and add the fifth TS value.

Enter this total under the first, aligned between the third and fourth TS values.

Continue with this process until you have totalled the last four TS values (with the total between the second and third from last TS values).

(3) Before averaging, you now need to centre the data, by creating an eight-quarter moving total column. (As mentioned in the example in the text, TS Ltd, you could average and then centre, but this in fact involves two lots of averaging, which can be time-consuming.)

This is done by adding successive pairs of the four-quarter moving totals – the first + second, second + third etc. – and putting the result in a new column, aligned between the two values you have added. These totals will now align with values in the original TS.

(4) Finally, you average the eight-quarter moving totals by dividing by eight to get the trend. (Remember, you have added two four-quarter totals, thus including eight values in total.)

These steps are illustrated for the data in the question in the table below:

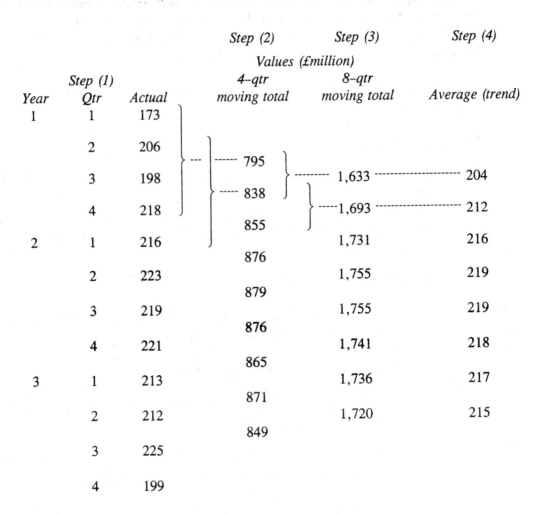

			Step (2)	Step (3)	Step (4)
			Values (£million)		
	Step (1)		*4–qtr*	*8–qtr*	
Year	*Qtr*	*Actual*	*moving total*	*moving total*	*Average (trend)*
1	1	173			
	2	206			
			795		
	3	198		1,633	204
			838		
	4	218		1,693	212
			855		
2	1	216		1,731	216
			876		
	2	223		1,755	219
			879		
	3	219		1,755	219
			876		
	4	221		1,741	218
			865		
3	1	213		1,736	217
			871		
	2	212		1,720	215
			849		
	3	225			
	4	199			

Expenditure by distributive trades

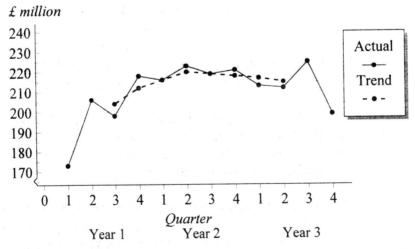

(b) The method of least squares would be used in preference to the method of moving averages only in cases where the trend follows a regular increasing or decreasing path which appears on the graph as almost a straight line. In the present case the trend path is a curved line in the graph; therefore the method of moving averages will produce a more useful trend line.

3 Ships in time

(a) Step 1

The seasonal variations are obtained by comparison of the time series (TS) with a calculated set of trend figures. The trend must therefore first be calculated, using centred moving averages, order 4, as in the previous question.

Step 2

The seasonal variations can then be obtained by subtracting the trend value from the corresponding TS value.

These two steps are illustrated below:

Year	Qtr	Value	*4–qtr moving total*	*8–qtr moving total*	*Step (1) Centred average (trend)*	*Step (2) Seasonal variations*
19X7	1	134				
	2	153				
			601			
	3	163		1,203	150.4	+12.6
			602			
	4	151		1,205	150.6	+0.4
			603			
19X8	1	135		1,202	150.3	−15.3
			599			
	2	154		1,202	150.3	+3.7
			603			
	3	159		1,203	150.4	+8.6
			600			
	4	155		1,205	150.6	+4.4
			605			
19X9	1	132		1,228	153.5	−21.5
			623			
	2	159		1,250	156.3	+2.7
			627			
	3	177				
	4	159				

Step 3

The seasonal variations for corresponding quarters now need to be averaged. This is most easily done by constructing a table with a column for each quarter (in fact in the same format as the data was given in the question), entering the seasonal variations as calculated above and averaging the figures in each quarter column:

	Qtr 1	*Qtr 2*	*Qtr 3*	*Qtr 4*
19X7			+12.6	+0.4
19X8	–15.3	+3.7	+8.6	+4.4
19X9	–21.5	+2.7		
Sum	–36.8	+6.4	+21.2	+4.8
Average	–18.4	+3.2	+10.6	+2.4

Step 4

The deseasonalised data is obtained by eliminating the effect of the appropriate average seasonal variation from each value of the TS. Thus, for example, each quarter 1 TS value is being *reduced* by a *negative* average seasonal variation of 18.4. Thus the effect of this can be eliminated by *adding 18.4* back to the TS value.

Conversely, quarters 2, 3 and 4 TS values will be adjusted by *subtracting* the appropriate positive seasonal variation value:

Deseasonalisation

Year	*Qtr*	*Value*	*Variations*	*Deseasonalised data*
19X7	1	134	–18.4	152.4
	2	153	+3.2	149.8
	3	163	+10.6	152.4
	4	151	+2.4	148.6
19X8	1	135	–18.4	153.4
	2	154	+3.2	150.8
	3	159	+10.6	148.4
	4	155	+2.4	152.6
19X9	1	132	–18.4	150.4
	2	159	+3.2	155.8
	3	177	+10.6	166.4
	4	159	+2.4	156.6

(b)   The method used for extending the trend will vary according to the pattern, or lack of it, in the trend data available. Unless it follows an obvious progression (eg. linear) the choice of method will be subjective and various approaches will be acceptable.

Looking at the trend figures obtained in part (a), Step 1, the first six values are reasonably steady at around 150.3. However, the last two show an upward trend, with an increase of around three per quarter.

Two possible approaches to predicting the trend for later times would be as follows:

(i)   Use 150.3, on the basis that the majority of the values centre around this and the last two values may be exhibiting abnormal variations that are unlikely to be continued.

(ii)   Assume that the later data is more likely to be indicative of future values and adopt an average increment of (say) three per quarter.

You could use the average of the last two increments, 2.9 (150.6 to 153.5) and 2.8 (153.5 to 156.3), which would be 2.85. Considering the rather arbitrary nature of the forecasting process, this could be viewed as spurious accuracy.

The two trend values thus obtained for Quarter 3, 19Y0 would be

(i)   150.3

(ii)   156.3   + 5×3 =   171.3

      (X9, Q2)   (X9, Q3, 4 + Y0, Q1–3)

These now need to be adjusted to include the appropriate seasonal variation, which for quarter 3 is an increase of 10.6.

The projections under the two methods would thus be:

(i)   150.3 + 10.6 = 160.9 (say 161)
(ii)   171.3 + 10.6 = 181.9 (say 182)

In practice, a lot more data would be used to get a clearer picture of the trend before the forecast would be made.

4   Your organisation

(a)   (i)   Seasonal variations are regular patterns of fluctuations which occur over the year. For example, the seasonal variation for quarter 1 is minus 50 units. This indicates that the sales volume for quarter 1 is on average 50 units below the general trend in sales. Similarly, the sales volume for quarter 2 is generally 22 units above the general trend.

(ii)   A trend line is the underlying direction in which a time series of data is moving. The trend is determined by removing the effect of seasonal variations, usually by using the technique of moving averages.

In the data provided, the monthly sales volume appears to be increasing by an average of 45 units in each quarter, after eliminating the seasonal variations. This is the underlying trend in the data, which the analyst suggests should be used to project the sales data into the future. This is known as *extrapolating the trend* (ie. continuing its general direction as a basis for the sales forecast).

(b)   **Sales volume forecasts**

Working: calculating the average quarterly increase in the trend

Year	Quarter	Trend (units)	Increase in trend (units)
3	4	3,407	
4	1	3,452	45
	2	3,496	44
	3	3,541	45
	4	3,587	46
			180 Average = 180/4 = 45 units

Sales volume forecast for year 5

Quarter	1 units	2 units	3 units	4 units
Trend	3,632	3,677	3,722	3,767
Seasonal adjustment	−50	+22	+60	−32
Forecast	3,582	3,699	3,782	3,735

5 Transport Company

Fuel costs expressed in terms of year 4 prices

Year	Expenditure £	Adjust for movement in fuel price index £	Expenditure at year 4 prices £
1	18,000	× 128/100	23,040
2	19,292	× 128/106	23,296
3	21,468	× 128/120	22,899
4	23,010		23,010

The increases in expenditure on fuel are mainly the result of increases in fuel prices. When expenditure is adjusted to year 4 prices, it is possible to see that expenditure has not varied significantly in real terms.

SESSION 10

1 Your organisation

Memorandum

To: Marketing Manager	Date: 12 December 19X4
From: Assistant Management Accountant	
Subject: Budgetary planning process	

As requested, I provide below answers to your queries about the budgetary planning process.

(a) The key factor

Otherwise known as the *principal budget factor* or *limiting factor*, the key factor is the factor which limits the activity of an organisation. In our organisation it is sales volume, since there is a limit to how much we can sell. However, it is possible for other factors to be key factors, especially in the short term. Examples could be cash, machine capacity or skilled labour.

The determination of the key factor is important in the budgetary process because this is the budget which must be prepared first. Then all other budgets can be co-ordinated to this budget.

For example, once the sales budget has been determined, this will provide the basis for the production budget and for other budgets such as the purchasing budget and the cash budget.

(b)   A number of steps can be taken to achieve co-ordination in the budgetary planning process, including the following:

    (i)   Set up a budget committee which consists of representatives from all parts of the organisation. Regular meetings of this committee should ensure that each part of the organisation is aware of what all other parts are doing.

    (ii)   Give one person the overall responsibility for ensuring that budgets are prepared on time and that they take into account all relevant factors. This person is often called the *budget officer* and will usually chair the budget committee.

    (iii)   Provide a timetable to all those involved in the budgetary process, detailing who is responsible for preparing each budget and when it must be prepared. This should reduce the risk of bottlenecks in the budgetary process and will co-ordinate the order of budget preparation.

    (iv)   Provide a budget manual to all those involved in the budgetary process. The contents of the budget manual would include the budget timetable mentioned above, instructions on completing the budget planning forms, details on key assumptions to be made in the planning process (such as the inflation rate and exchange rate), and so on.

    (v)   Provide regular feedback on the progress of budget preparation.

The key to co-ordinated budget preparation is communication.

2   Master budget

(a)   The necessary preliminary steps before commencing to prepare budgets would include the following:

    (i)   Consideration of the longer-term plans for the business and setting goals for such aspects as market share, profit and capital investment.

    (ii)   Confirmation of the organisation structure of the business, including profit, cost and investment centres.

    (iii)   Issue of budget instructions.

    (iv)   Preparation of forecasts of the relevant exogeneous conditions for the budget period (and possibly for some additional period). This might be regarded either as preliminary work or as the first step in budget development.

(b)   The main budgets to be found in a manufacturing business are likely to be:

    (i)   Sales budget, by areas of responsibility, consistent with assumptions and forecasts above and within production and inventory capacity (subject to policy on buying-in), and based on estimates of demand schedules.

(ii)   Production budget, based on sales budget, allowing for controlled inventory policy and incorporating specific plans for resource acquisition and disposition (materials, labour, energy, overheads).

(iii)   Resource budgets within production centres, by area and level of responsibility.

(iv)   Budgets of marketing, selling and distribution expense.

(v)   Budgets of general administrative expense.

(vi)   Budgets for R&D, including product development.

(vii)   Profit budgets by areas of profit responsibility (product group, geographical area, etc.).

(viii) Capital expenditure budget.

(ix)   Working capital budgets, including inventory, debt management, cash management, borrowing capacity.

(x)   Master budget, with suitably analysed P/L a/c, B/S and funds statement.

(c)   Managers may be reluctant to participate in setting budgets, because 'participation' may not be on an acceptable basis. According to the management style of a business the term may cover almost any degree or lack of consultation.

At one extreme minimal discussion may be used as the basis for an authoritarian, imposed budget. At the other extreme a laissez-faire management style may lead to a lack of interest by or incentive for managers to set budgets which provide real targets for improvement. For participation in budgeting to be successful it must stem from full and frank discussion between managers at all levels. It must be based on accepted areas of responsibility and full knowledge of the objectives to be achieved and of the interaction of one department's activities with those of others. Managers must also be capable of understanding the financial and accounting implications of their actions, and may need to be given training in these subjects.

Finally any budget will be based on forecasts of future circumstances, and these will often be imperfect. In exercising control against budgets, therefore, it is necessary to judge whether managers' achievement has been satisfactory in relation to the actual circumstances then prevailing. This is not to say that the ultimate profit objective should be abandoned, but that 'participation' shall be a continuous activity in modifying detailed targets where necessary in order to approach the achievement of the required profit in a different way.

3 Tiger plc

(a) Although it is not specifically required by the question, a production budget is essential for material and labour budgets.

Information relating to production levels is therefore the first thing you must look for.

In this question, you are not given this information directly. You are, however, given information about sales quantities and stock levels, which can be used to derive production levels as follows:

Production = Sales + Closing stock – Opening stock
(finished goods) (finished goods)

The monthly sales need a little computation, so this will be your first working. Note that you only need *units* for the production budget, but part (b) requires a profit and loss, so you will also need *revenue*, which you may as well incorporate into this working.

Your second working will then be the production budget, using the results from your sales working and the stock level requirements given in the question.

These and other workings should be done on a separate sheet of paper, to be included at the end of your answer, cross-referenced as appropriate.

These first two workings should enable you to complete the three parts of part (a).

Note that, although it is not a necessary requirement of (a), it will be useful to calculate total production quantity and total costs for materials purchases and labour for (b).

(i) **Materials utilisation**

	Jan	Feb	Mar	Apr	May	June	Total
Production quantity (W2) @ 10 kg/unit	5,000	7,500	10,000	10,000	7,500	5,000	45,000
Materials used	50,000	75,000	100,000	100,000	75,000	50,000	450,000

(ii) **Purchases**

Remember the link between materials usage and purchases quantities:

Purchases = Usage + Closing stock – Opening stock
(raw materials) (raw materials)

Usage is taken from your answer to (i) and stock information from the question – 'stocks to meet 80% of the following month's production quota' simply means 80% of the following month's usage.

	Jan	Feb	Mar	Apr	May	June	Total
Materials used (i)	50,000	75,000	100,000	100,000	75,000	50,000	450,000
Less: Opening stock	(40,000)	(60,000)	(80,000)	(80,000)	(60,000)	(40,000)	(40,000)
	10,000	15,000	20,000	20,000	15,000	10,000	410,000
Add: Closing stock	60,000	80,000	80,000	60,000	40,000	40,000	40,000
Purchases (kg)	70,000	95,000	100,000	80,000	55,000	50,000	450,000
@	60p	60p	60p	60p	75p	75p	
Purchases (£)	42,000	57,000	60,000	48,000	41,250	37,500	285,750

(iii) **Skilled labour**

	Jan	Feb	Mar	Apr	May	June	Total
Units produced (W2)	5,000	7,500	10,000	10,000	7,500	5,000	45,000
Skilled labour cost (£5 per unit)	£25,000	£37,500	£50,000	£50,000	£37,500	£25,000	£225,000

Unskilled labour

	Jan	Feb	Mar	Apr	May	June	Total
Units produced (W2)	5,000	7,500	10,000	10,000	7,500	5,000	45,000
Unskilled labour cost (£6 per unit)	£30,000	£45,000	£60,000	£60,000	£45,000	£30,000	£270,000

(b)   Most of the figures for the profit and loss can be taken from the answers/workings to part (a). Additional workings will be required for valuation of stocks of raw materials and finished goods.

The former can be easily calculated by multiplying the opening/closing stock quantities (in your purchases budget) by the opening/closing prices (60p/75p); this can be indicated on the face of the profit and loss itself.

The valuation of stocks of finished goods involves the calculation of unit costs – not forgetting the change of materials cost over the period. This is shown in working 3 at the end of the answer.

Finally, do not forget overheads – easy to calculate (£5 × total production) but also easy to miss!

Budgeted profit and loss account for six months to 30 June 19X5

		£	£
Sales (W1)			1,250,000
Cost of sales			
Opening stock:	Raw materials (60p)	24,000	
	Finished goods (W3)	55,000	
		79,000	
Materials purchased		285,750	
Skilled labour		225,000	
Unskilled labour		270,000	
Production overheads (45,000 × £5)		225,000	
		1,084,750	
Closing stock:	Raw materials (75p)	(30,000)	
	Finished goods (W3)	(58,750)	
			(996,000)
Gross profit			254,000

(c) **Objectives of budgetary control**

The objectives of budgetary control are to:

(i) plan and control income and expenditure in order to achieve maximum profitability;

(ii) ensure that sufficient working capital is available for the efficient operation of the company;

(iii) direct capital expenditure in the most profitable direction;

(iv) centralise control;

(v) decentralise responsibility;

(vi) provide a yardstick against which actual results may be compared;

(vii) show management when action is needed to remedy a situation;

(viii) aid management in decision-making when unforeseen conditions affect the budget.

Workings

(1) *Sales by month*

The easiest way to calculate these is to assign weights to each month – an 'ordinary' month having a weighting of 1, with the 'seasonal' months having twice this weighting. Thus, over the six-month period, there will be the equivalent of 3 × 1 plus 3 × 2 = 9 'ordinary' months worth of sales. As total sales are expected to be 45,000, this implies an 'ordinary' month's sales of 45,000/9 = 5,000 units.

	Jan	Feb	Mar	Apr	May	June	Total
Weighting	1	1	2	2	2	1	9
Sales quantity	5,000	5,000	10,000	10,000	10,000	5,000	45,000
Selling price	£25	£25	£25	£30	£30	£30	
Sales revenue	£125,000	£125,000	£250,000	£300,000	£300,000	£150,000	£1,250,000

(2) *Production budget (units)*

The opening and closing stocks for the period are given in the question (2,500 units). In between, the closing stock for each month (and the opening stock for the following month) represents 50% of the following month's sales units.

	Jan	Feb	Mar	Apr	May	June
Sales	5,000	5,000	10,000	10,000	10,000	5,000
Less: Opening stock	(2,500)	(2,500)	(5,000)	(5,000)	(5,000)	(2,500)
	2,500	2,500	5,000	5,000	5,000	2,500
Add: Closing stock	2,500	5,000	5,000	5,000	2,500	2,500
Production	5,000	7,500	10,000	10,000	7,500	5,000

Total production = 45,000 units

(3) *Cost per unit*

	To April £	From May £
Raw materials (10 kg)	6.00	7.50
Labour: Skilled	5.00	5.00
Semi-skilled	6.00	6.00
Production overheads	5.00	5.00
	22.00	23.50

Stocks of finished goods	– opening 2,500 units @ £22	£55,000
	– closing 2,500 units @ £23.50	£58,750

SESSION 11

1 Excelsior Manufacturing Company

(a)

	4,000 £	5,000 £	6,000 £	7,000 £	8,000 £
Direct materials	80,000	100,000	120,000	140,000	160,000
Indirect materials	12,000	14,000	16,000	18,000	20,000
Direct labour	50,000	62,500	75,000	87,500	100,000
Power	18,000	18,000	18,000	21,000	24,000
Repairs	20,000	22,500	25,000	27,500	30,000
Supervision	20,000	20,000	36,000	36,000	36,000
Rent, insurance and rates	9,000	9,000	9,000	9,000	9,000
	209,000	246,000	299,000	339,000	379,000

(b)

	Budget (5,000) £	Actual £	Variance £
Direct materiais	100,000	110,000	10,000
Indirect materials	14,000	14,000	–
Direct labour	62,500	70,000	7,500
Power	18,000	18,000	–
Repairs	22,500	30,000	7,500
Supervision	20,000	20,000	–
Rent, insurance and rates	9,000	8,000	+1,000
	246,000	270,000	24,000

Comments on variances

– Direct materials: Waste in production, poor quality materials, operatives need more training. Is a particular department or machine at fault?

– Direct labour: Supervision? Excessive overtime (should not be needed at a low level of production)?

- Repairs: Needs investigation. Possible exceptional item. Do some pieces of capital equipment need replacing?

- Rent, insurance and rates: This is probably a price variance. Is this an exceptional item or does the budget need to be altered in future?

2   World History Museum

(a)   **Analysis of budgeted costs:**

	Fixed cost £	Variable cost £	Variable cost per course £
Speakers' fees	–	3,180	530
Hire of premises	–	1,500	250
Depreciation of equipment	180	–	–
Stationery	–	600	100
Catering	250	1,500	250
Insurance	100	720	120
Administration	1,620	–	–

(b)   **Flexible budget control statement for April**

Expenditure	Fixed cost allowance £	Variable cost allowance £	Total cost allowance £	Actual cost £	Variance £
Speakers' fees	–	2,650	2,650	2,500	150
Hire of premises	–	1,250	1,250	1,500	(250)
Depreciation of equipment	180	–	180	200	(20)
Stationery	–	500	500	530	(30)
Catering	250	1,250	1,500	1,500	–
Insurance	100	600	700	700	–
Administration	1,620	–	1,620	1,650	(30)
	2,150	6,250	8,400	8,580	(180)

(c)   **Memorandum**

To: Chris Brooks   Date: Monday 13 June 19X4

From: Assistant Management Accountant

Subject: Participative budgeting

___

As requested, I enclose brief explanations of the advantages and disadvantages of participative budgeting.

Advantages

(i)   Managers are likely to be demotivated if budgets are imposed on them without any prior consultation. If they are consulted, they are more likely to accept the budgets as realistic targets.

(ii)   If managers are consulted, then the budgets are more likely to take account of their own aspiration levels. Aspiration levels are personal targets which individuals or departments set for themselves. If budget targets exceed aspiration levels, then the budgets can have a negative motivational impact because they will be perceived as unachievable. However, if the targets fall too far below aspiration levels, then the performance of the individuals or departments may be lower than might otherwise have been achieved.

(iii)   Managers who are consulted may be motivated by the feeling that their views are valuable to senior management.

(iv)   Managers who are closely involved with the day to day running of operations may be able to give very valuable input to the forecasting and planning process.

Disadvantages

(i)   If too many people are involved in budgetary planning, it can make the process very slow and difficult to manage.

(ii)   Senior managers may need to overrule decisions made by local managers. This can be demotivating if it is not dealt with correctly.

(iii)   The participative process may not be genuine. Managers must feel that their participation is really valued by senior management. A false attempt to appear to be interested in their views can be even more demotivating than a system of imposed budgets.

(iv)   Managers may attempt to include excess expenditure in their budgets, due to 'empire-building' or to a desire to guard against unforeseen circumstances.

3   Responsibility accounting

(a)   *Responsibility accounting* has been defined as 'a system of accounting that segregates revenues and costs into areas of personal responsibility in order to assess the performance attained by persons to whom authority has been assigned'.

The idea derives from the need simultaneously to motivate divisional managers whilst at the same time evaluating their financial performance. For example, if a manager is held responsible for a decision over which he had only partial control then he will be demotivated. Similarly he should be rewarded personally for excellent results arising from areas for which he was responsible.

One main problem in practice arises from the need to define the scope of each manager's responsibility (ie. the boundaries of the division to be controlled and the nature of the responsibility). The situation given in the question tells of a range of products, a number of processes and a number of service departments.

Each separate process may already have a manager responsible for the process. If each process is given the status of a cost centre, then the costs for each process will be separately recorded and monitored, and management will be held responsible for the reporting of costs and explanation of variances from budgeted figures. Production costs which are incurred by several processes and which are apportioned among those processes for reporting purposes may be excluded from the costs for which process managers are responsible, since no individual process manager will feel responsible for the apportioned cost; a more senior manager responsible for the suite of processes may instead be held responsible for the apportioned costs.

The costs of the service departments should be charged to the production departments on the basis of service used in the period. It will be helpful if predetermined rates can be set for each service activity as part of the budgeting process before the start of each year. That way, if a service department is inefficient in providing its service, an adverse variance arises in the service department for which the service manager is answerable, rather than the production manager feeling aggrieved that he is going to have to pay for someone else's inefficiency. The converse is also the case, so that the service manager is not aggrieved when his team has to stand idle for a period of time before they are allowed to start supplying their service, the delay arising from incompetence in the production department; in such a situation, the production manager should be held responsible for the adverse variance arising.

(b)   The maintenance department is likely to carry out work throughout the business operations, ranging from repairing broken down machines to carrying out regular preventative maintenance on the process plant and working for other service departments. The departmental staff should be trained to keep detailed documentation concerning their activities, including timesheets and material requisitions and returns.

Once it is clear what work has been carried out, the next step is to ensure that the responsible manager is charged for the cost of operations under his ambit. Cost incurred in mending a broken down machine, for example, could have arisen because the purchasing department had bought inappropriate raw materials, or the training department had wrongly advised the operator on proper procedures, or the machine had been improperly installed in the first place. The chief engineer should ensure that the responsibility accounting principle is applied to charge the manager for costs for which he is responsible.

The management accounting system can assist in recognising the managers responsible for costs incurred by insisting on the detailed record-keeping described above, by anticipating problems at the time of the budgetary process, and by analysing variances according to their causes. In particular a system of planning and operational variances will help to identify the manager responsible for each variance arising.

(c)   The provision of more information need not automatically lead to more effective management of a cost centre for the following reasons.

(i)   **Information overload** – If a manager is faced with more information than he thinks he can cope with, then he will just give up and apply 'seat of the pants' management rather than try to take any sort of rigorous approach to his decision-making responsibilities.

(ii)   **Good quality information** – Quality is more important than quantity in the area of information provision. Modern information technology has enabled vast volumes of information to be produced quickly, but management needs the important points to be highlighted, so that for example information should be provided on an exception basis, clearly pointing out major deviations from standard to be investigated.

(iii) **Lack of goal congruence** – A manager may be given all the information that he needs to carry out his objective, but that objective might not be in the best interests of the company as a whole. For example, the manager might be seeking to build up a personal empire or to maximise sales revenue or to maximise his own departmental profits rather than thinking of optimising overall company performance.

SESSION 12

1   Bittern (II) Ltd

(a) (i) **Variable costing**

	t1 £'000		t2 £'000	t3 £'000		Total £'000
Sales		25	25	25		75
Variable cost of sales (W1)		(12)	(12)	(12)		(36)
		13	13	13		39
Distribution costs		(1)	(1)	(1)		(3)
		12	12	12		36
Fixed costs						
Labour	5		5	5	15	
Fixed overheads	5		5	5	15	
		(10)	(10)	(10)		(30)
Profit		2	2	2		6

Full cost absorption

	t1 £'000	t2 £'000	t3 £'000	Total £'000
Sales	25	25	25	75
Full cost of sales (W2)	(22)	(22)	(22)	(66)
	3	3	3	9
Distribution costs	(1)	(1)	(1)	(3)
Profit	2	2	2	6

(ii) **Variable costing**

		t1 £'000		t2 £'000		t3 £'000		Total £'000
Sales		25		25		25		75
Opening stock	1.2		7.2		4.8		1.2	
Cost of production	18		9.6		8.4		36	
Closing stock	(7.2)		(4.8)		(12)		(12)	
Variable cost of sales		(12)		(12)		(12)		(36)
		13		13		13		39
Distribution costs		(1)		(1)		(1)		(3)
Contribution		12		12		12		36
Fixed costs								
Labour	5		5		5			
Overheads	5		5		5			
		(10)		(10)		(10)		(30)
Profit		2		2		2		6

Full cost absorption

		t1 £'000		t2 £'000		t3 £'000		Total £'000
Sales		25		25		25		75
Opening stock	2.2		13.2		8.8		2.2	
Cost of production	33		17.6		15.4		6.6	
Closing stock	(13.2)		(8.8)		(2.2)		(2.2)	
Absorption cost of sales		22		22		22		66
		3		3		3		9
(Under-)/over-absorption of fixed costs								
500 × £10		5						
200 × £10				(2)				
300 × £10						(3)		–
		8		1		–		9
Distribution costs		(1)		(1)		(1)		(3)
Profit/(loss)		7		–		(1)		6

Workings

(1)　　Stock valuation – variable costs

		£
Production materials		10
Labour		2
		12

(2)　　Stock valuation – full cost absorption with fixed cost recovery based on a normal production level of 1,000 units per annum.

		£
Production materials		10
Labour (variable)		2
Fixed labour and overheads		10
		22

Fixed overhead absorption rate

	£
Labour	5,000
Overheads	5,000
	10,000

£10,000/1,000 units = £10 per unit

(b)　**Absorption costing**

This is defined as 'a principle whereby fixed as well as variable costs are allotted to cost units. The term may be applied where (a) production costs only or (b) costs of all functions are so allotted'.

This principle or concept derives from many years of practice in determining the total unit cost of a product so that a selling price might be found by the addition of a percentage for profit. So long as planned output and sales levels are achieved, this practice has probably been effective for the purpose.

If stocks are valued at cost, then under absorption costing 'cost' includes full production overhead, a practice recommended in SSAP9. However, full production overhead includes fixed production overhead which has to be related to units of output in some way. The apportionment and absorption of fixed overhead into units of output can only be approximate, so that the resulting unit costs are to some extent unreliable.

Variable or marginal costing

This is defined as 'a principle whereby marginal costs of cost units are ascertained. Only variable costs are charged to cost units, the fixed costs attributable to a relevant period being written off in full against the contribution for that period'.

Only by separating variable and fixed costs can advantage be taken of the important contribution concept. Because fixed costs tend to remain unaffected by fluctuations in volume of output, attention can be concentrated on sales value and variable costs which tend to move together with volume changes. Sales values minus the variable cost is the contribution which provides a fund to meet the fixed costs and profit of the undertaking.

The benefits of marginal costing relate to profit planning and decision-making, and so absorption costing alone denies the management great advantages.

Under variable costing no fixed cost can be included in stock valuation. All fixed costs are charged against revenue for the period on the basis that fixed costs are 'period' costs, that is, they accrue in relation to the passage of time.

SSAP9 states 'where management accounts are prepared on a marginal cost basis, it will be necessary to add to the figure of stock so arrived at the appropriate proportion of the production overhead not already included in the marginal cost'.

The inclusion of fixed overhead in stock valuation for published accounts does not, however, prevent the use of marginal costing for internal management purposes.

The effect on profit of absorption and variable costing

Stock valuation under absorption costing is always higher than under variable costing because the former figure also includes some fixed costs. Where opening and closing stock units are unchanged, reported profit for the period will be the same under both systems because of unchanged stock values (as can be seen in part (a)(i) with stable levels of inventory).

If production exceeds sales in a period, then because some fixed costs will be included in the closing stock valuation and not all charged against sales revenue, the absorption costing system will report the higher profit (as illustrated by part (a)(ii) during the year t1).

When sales exceed production in a period the opposite will result with the variable costing system reporting the higher profit (as illustrated by part (a)(ii) during years t2 and t3). In this situation under absorption costing, high fixed costs are charged against sales; not only the fixed costs for the period, but also some fixed costs brought forward from the previous period and included in opening stock.

Thus it can be seen that variable costing highlights the importance of making sales, whereas absorption costing applies the accruals concept to fixed costs.

2   LMN Ltd

Report

To: Company Directors   Date: June 19X4

From: Assistant to the Management Accountant

Subject: The profit statement for May

The statement would be more useful if it were prepared in a marginal costing format.

An alternative presentation would be as follows:

Profit statement for May

	£	£	£	£	£	£
Sales revenue	18,000	29,700	43,500	14,100	30,940	136,240
Variable costs	16,500	18,000	21,750	9,000	19,500	84,750
Contribution	1,500	11,700	21,750	5,100	11,440	51,490
Fixed costs						28,250
Profit						23,240

This statement shows more clearly the effect of discontinuing product A. The contribution of £1,500 would be lost and profit would reduce by this amount. Therefore product A should not be discontinued unless its sales can be replaced by a product which would earn a contribution of more than £1,500.

3   JK Company

(a)   **Assumptions**

(1)   November is a representative month which can be used for forecast projections.

(2)   Fixed costs will remain unaltered despite the change in output volume and product mix.

(3)   Other cost and revenue patterns remain similarly unaltered.

Profit statement for one month with proposed changes to product mix

Product	J £	L £	M £	Total £
Sales revenue	6,720	2,040	9,500	18,260
Variable costs	3,150	1,275	6,375	10,800
Contribution	3,570	765	3,125	7,460
Fixed costs				3,860
Profit				3,600

(b)   On the basis of the profit statement in part (a), the marketeting director's proposals should be accepted and product K should be discontinued. Monthly profit increases to £3,600. The extra contribution from the increase in sales of the other products is sufficient to compensate for the loss of the contribution currently being earned by product K.

SESSION 13

1   Roger Morton

(a)   To obtain a cost per unit for fixed overhead Roger divided his fixed overhead by the number of units he expected to produce, ie.

$$\frac{\text{Fixed overhead}}{10,000} = £4$$

In other words his fixed overheads were £40,000.

Note that we are *not* saying that for every unit produced fixed overheads will go up by £4; they cannot (fixed overheads are fixed).

(b)

	£	£
Selling price		75
Variable cost		
Material	12	
Labour	24	
Variable overhead	10	
		(46)
Contribution		29

(c)   2,000 × £75 = £150,000

(d)

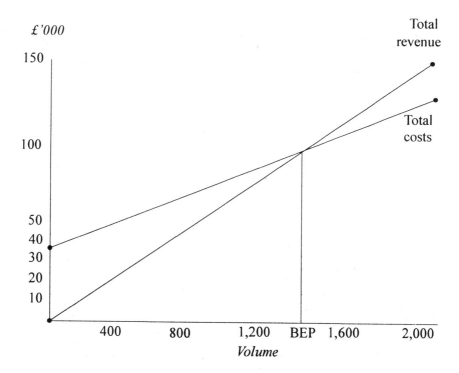

£'000

Total revenue

Total costs

Volume

Estimated BEP = 1,400 units

(e) $BEP = \dfrac{\text{Fixed cost}}{\text{Contribution / unit}} = \dfrac{£40,000}{£29} = 1,379 \text{ units}$

(f)   However many extra units Roger makes, his fixed costs will remain constant. The only items that will change are his revenue (total) and variable costs (total).

Accordingly the extra can be found by multiplying the increase in sales by the contribution per unit.

$1,000 \times £29 = £29,000$

2 ABC Ltd

(a)   **Handwork Ltd – breakeven chart**

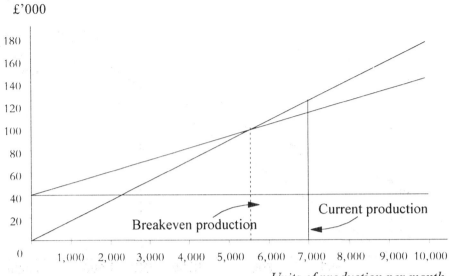

£'000

Units of production per month

(b)   (i)   Breakeven point: 5,714 units
       (ii)   Profit at 7,000 units: £9,000

(c)   (i)   DEF Ltd is likely to use a more capital intensive method of production than ABC Ltd. Higher fixed costs but with lower variable labour costs per unit.

       (ii)   DEF Ltd generates a higher rate of profit after the breakeven point than ABC Ltd (wider angle of incidence).

(d)   Profit under the revised policy: £10,000 per month

3 Security services

(a)   Breakeven point:

Present situation $\dfrac{£18,000}{£(30-22)}$ =   2,250 hours

Proposed situation $\dfrac{£39,000}{£(33-20)}$ =   3,000 hours

(b)   Monthly profit:

Present situation   Sales   =   5,200 hours
                     Breakeven   =   2,250 hours
                     Margin of safety   =   2,950 hours
                                            × £8 per hour contribution

                     Monthly profit   £23,600

Proposed situation

Sales	=	5,200 hours
Breakeven	=	3,000 hours
Margin of safety	=	2,200 hours
		× £13 per hour contribution
Monthly profit		£28,600

(c)   The changes will result in higher fixed costs and a higher contribution per hour. This means that, if sales increase, then profits will grow more quickly because more contribution is earned per hour.

However, it also means that profits will reduce more rapidly if sales start to fall in the future. This is reflected by the higher breakeven point and means that the proposed situation is riskier than at present.

4   Dample Ltd

(a)   (i)   *Breakeven point (BEP)*

$$\text{In units, BEP} = \frac{\text{Fixed costs}}{\text{Contribution}/\text{unit}}$$

$$\text{Contribution per unit} = \frac{272,000 - 152,320 - 26,112}{217,600}$$

$$= £0.43$$

$$\text{So BEP} = \frac{26,000}{0.43}$$

$$= 60,465$$

$$\text{In sales value, BEP} = \frac{\text{Fixed costs}}{\text{C}/\text{S ratio}}$$

$$\text{Selling price per unit} = \frac{272,000}{217,600}$$

$$= £1.25$$

$$\text{C/S ratio} = \frac{0.43}{1.25}$$

$$\text{So BEP} = \frac{26,000 \times 1.25}{0.43}$$

$$= £75,581$$

(ii)   *Additional sales*

$$\text{New contribution per unit} = \frac{£93,568 - £6,312}{217,600} = £0.401$$

For a profit of £67,568 or a contribution of £93,568:

$$\text{Sales must rise to } \frac{£93,568}{0.401} = 233,337$$

This represents additional sales of 15,737 units.

(b) **Breakeven charts**

The type of graph which might be used by Dample Ltd to show the effects of changes in costs and revenues (or perhaps more appropriately changes in unit costs and selling prices as in (a)(ii) above) is a breakeven chart (though a PV graph would have the same effect). Here a series of cost or revenue lines could be shown corresponding to various unit costs or selling prices. The chart below illustrates the type of problem suggested in (a) above but using a 50% increase in labour rates.

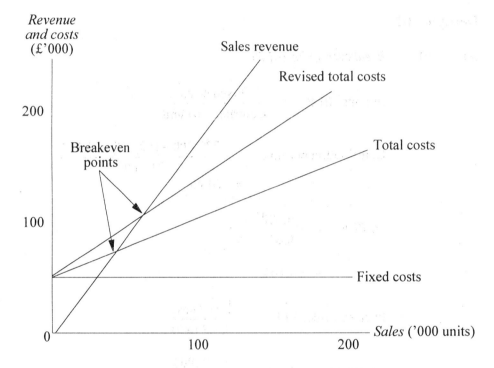

The graph shows that the breakeven point moves when the variable cost rises. Any alteration in selling price, variable cost or fixed overheads can be catered for by plotting the new cost or revenue line on the graph. At existing prices the revenue, costs and profit at any level of activity can be read from the graph.

(c) **The limitations of breakeven analysis**

The use of simple breakeven analysis assumes that all costs can be split into fixed and variable components, and furthermore that one 'activity base' (eg. units produced, units sold, hours worked) will be suitable for describing all variable costs and revenues.

Linear relationships are assumed. This means that fixed costs are assumed to be fixed at all levels of activity, and that variable cost per unit and sales price per unit are constants and independent of the level of activity.

In practice, fixed costs will only be constant over the 'relevant range'. Over a larger range most fixed costs are stepped. If necessary this can be adjusted for on the breakeven chart.

It is more difficult to show how variable cost will behave at various activity levels, but the cost accountant's linear model is bound to be incorrect over a wide range. For example, as activity increases variable costs may fall because it is possible to buy raw materials cheaper in bulk, or because of increases in worker efficiency. On the other hand, scarcity of resources at high levels of activity may lead to higher variable costs.

The linear relationship used for revenue totally ignores the sales price/demand relationship for the product. The market may not be perfect and, in order to increase sales of the product, it may be necessary to reduce its price.

Simple breakeven analysis also assumes that there is a constant sales mix, or that sales of only one product are being considered. Furthermore it assumes that there are no changes in stock levels (ie. that units produced equals units sold). This last point will not matter if stock is valued at variable cost, but if an absorption costing system is in use it becomes more difficult to predict profits at different levels of activity if stock levels are changing.

Simple breakeven analysis is therefore most useful when predictions are made within range of company's normal activity levels and when there is no significant building up or running down of stocks.

5   Robert Motherwell

Proposal 1

–   Variable costs at present: £14 per unit

–   Variable cost if components made in the factory:

4 (mat) + 2 (components) + 6 (labour) + 2 (prod. 0/H) = £14 per unit

–   No cost difference. Probably better to continue buying the components from outside: less effort, fewer problems, more flexibility

Proposal 2

–   Current profit per unit (80% of 30) – 18 = 6 (Seats)
                              (80% of 40) – 25 = 7 (Swing)

Total profit = (6 × 2,000) + (7 × 2,000) = 26,000

–   Profit if marketing done by Robert:

26,000 (Current Profit) + (2,000 × 6) + (2,000 × 8) (Commission saved) – 5,000 – (4 × 4,000) (Marketing costs) = £33,000

Therefore significantly better for Robert to do the marketing.

Proposal 3

Key point to make in the memo: cost of existing machinery is a 'sunk' cost. It should therefore be ignored in making a decision about future capital expenditure.

Proposal 4

Key point to make in the memo: labour is the 'limiting factor'. Marketing should concentrate on increasing sales of the garden seat as this requires only £3 of labour per unit compared with £9 labour per unit for the swing. Reduce production of the swing to maximise the contribution to profit from the limiting factor.

6 Belfry Ltd

To:	Board of Directors
From:	Management Accountant
Subject:	Budgeted Production Plan **Date:** 8 October 19X1

Historically the Company has always produced its two products, the Chome and Drib, in the ratio of 5:2 based on maximum demand considerations.

If this policy is continued for the forthcoming year, when labour hours are restricted to 120,000 hours then the budgeted profit will be £40,600 (Appendix 1).

By considering each product's contribution in respect of the amount of labour hours required to make it (Appendix 2), it becomes apparent that it is better to concentrate the scarce resource, ie. labour hours, in making Chomes as this gives a higher contribution.

If this policy of maximising the contribution in respect of labour hours is followed the result is that the budgeted profit will increase by £5,400 to £46,000. In order to achieve this the production plan for the forthcoming year should be to produce 15,000 Chomes (maximum demand) and 3,000 Dribs (Appendix 3).

As the basis of the revised production plan has been the calculation of each unit's contribution per labour hour, a change in a unit's contribution, or a change in the number of hours required to make a unit, might well have an effect upon the revised plan. It is further possible that if labour hours were to be increased and a different production factor was to become limited then again this would have an effect on the revised plan.

Appendix 1

Existing budgeted production:

			Hours
Maximum demand:	Chomes	15,000 × 6 hrs	90,000
	Dribs	6,000 × 10 hrs	60,000
			150,000

To produce maximum no of each product requires 150,000 labour hours.

Have only 120,000 hours available therefore will reduce production by 20%.

			Units
Budgeted production:	Chome	15,000 × 80%	12,000
	Dribs	6,000 × 80%	4,800

			£
Budgeted profit:	Chomes	12,000 × (£85 – £76)	108,000
	Dribs	4,800 × (£132 – £120)	57,600
			165,600
Less: Distribution and administration overheads			(125,000)
			40,600

Appendix 2

	Chomes £	*Dribs* £
Direct material	10.00	10.00
Direct labour	30.00	50.00
Variable production overheads	14.40	24.00
	54.40	84.00
Selling price	85.00	132.00
Contribution	30.60	48.00

Contribution per labour hour	$\dfrac{£30.60}{6}$	$\dfrac{£48.00}{10}$
	£5.10	£4.80
Preference	1st	2nd

Appendix 3

Optimal production plan:

		Hours
Chomes (maximum demand)	15,000 × 6 hrs	90,000
Dribs (balance)	3,000 × 10 hrs	30,000
		120,000

Budgeted profit from above plan:

			£	£
Contribution:	Chomes	15,000 × £30.60		459,000
	Dribs	3,000 × £48.00		144,000
				603,000
Less: (i)	Fixed production overheads:			
	Chomes	12,000 × £21.60	259,200	
	Dribs	4,800 × £36.00	172,800	
			432,000	
(ii)	Distribution and administration		125,000	
				(557,000)
				46,000

7   WH Museum

The financial effect of staging the exhibition

Notes

			£	£
(1)	Display cabinets			1,700
(2)	Repair costs			150
(3)	Security staff			6,500
(4)	Rental income forgone			7,200
(5)	Posters and handbills			650
(6)	Other costs			1,200
				17,400
(7)	Revenue from visitors		16,000	
(8)	Gross margin on cafeteria sales		4,000	
				20,000
	Net gain from the exhibition			2,600

Notes

(1)   This is an incremental cost and is therefore relevant to the decision.

(2)   The original cost of the cabinets is sunk and not relevant.

(3)   The salaries of the redeployed security staff would be incurred anyway and are not relevant.

(4)   The central administration costs would be incurred anyway and are not relevant. The opportunity cost of the rental income foregone is relevant and should be included.

(5)   Only the incremental costs of printing are relevant. The fixed costs would be incurred anyway.

(6)   These are incremental costs and are therefore relevant.

(7)   This is the incremental revenue which will be earned from visitors.

(8)   An average gross margin of £1 per person will be earned.

8   JK Co

(a)   **Relevant annual cost of internal manufacture**

	£
Variable costs	25,000
Premises: Forgone rent	3,400
	28,400

Assumptions

(1)   'Other fixed costs' would be incurred anyway.

(2)   Variable costs are all incremental costs which would be saved if the manufacturer's offer was accepted.

(3)   The premises would be sub-let if not used for manufacturing.

(b)   (i)   A sunk cost is a cost which has already been incurred and which cannot now be recovered. In this situation, the down payment of £1,500 is a sunk cost. It cannot be recovered and is not a relevant cost of the decision to continue internal manufacture.

        (ii)   An opportunity cost is a benefit forgone as the result of selecting one course of action in preference to another. If JK decides to manufacture the component internally, they will lose the opportunity to sub-let the premises for £3,400. The relevant cost of using the premises for internal manufacture is therefore the full opportunity cost of £3,400.

9   R & D Ltd

Reginald Casting Esq   RL Tellue
Managing Director   Wisdom Street
R & D Ltd   Nottingham
Nottingham   26 November 19X1

Dear Mr Casting

Valve production

With regard to the matter of purchasing your requirements of machined or unmachined valve castings, instead of producing them in your factory, I have studied the figures you gave me at our last meeting and would advise you that I am strongly against the proposal to purchase the component.

You have stated that your company's overhead is fixed for a year or more to come. In consequence, 60% of your total costs would still be incurred even if the complete valve were to be purchased. The following statement summarises the position in terms of standard costs per valve.

	Producing internally £		*Purchasing unmachined castings* £		*Purchasing machined castings* £
Material	1.25	(3.25 + 0.75)	4.00	(9.50 + 0.75)	10.25
Labour	3.75	(2.00 + 0.75)	2.75		0.75
Overhead	7.50		7.50		7.50
	12.50		14.25		18.50
Profit/(Loss)	1.75		–		(4.25)
Selling price	14.25		14.25		14.25

It is clear that the maximum profit is gained by the present policy of producing the valve entirely in your own works.

I have, of course, had to assume that the standard costs correspond reasonably closely with the actual costs incurred, and it would be advisable for you to check this point with your cost department. At the same time, I would suggest you obtain a list of the overhead costs associated with the foundry and machine shop, and confirm for yourself that the overhead would still be incurred even if the departments were closed down.

In discussions with your managers you should point out that the internal transfer price is irrelevant. It is worth stressing that, if the company is able to obtain more orders for the valves, only the variable costs will be incurred (ie. a total of £5), whereas if they were buying unmachined or machined castings, the cost would be £6.75 or £11 respectively. With regard to the internal transfer price, it is perhaps better to pay a little extra than the market price to safeguard delivery and quality.

If outside suppliers are used, control of supply will pass out of the company, and there is no guarantee that the original prices quoted are not subsequently raised. Your company could investigate the possibility of entering the market for unmachined and machined castings, provided there is sufficient capacity in the foundry and machine shop, and that the additional costs of marketing and administration would still enable the company to compete.

In the long term, however, if the savings of fixed overhead resulting from the closure of the foundry and/or machine shop were greater than the difference between the outside purchase value and the marginal costs of internal manufacture, the company should consider closure of one or both departments.

I hope the above will prove helpful in your talks with managers – it merely confirms what you already thought, but please contact me again if your investigations into actual costs and overhead costs indicate that the figures we have both been using are suspect.

Yours sincerely

RL Tellue

10   Electronics Ltd

(a)   (i)

		£
Revenue from additional production		
50,000 amplifiers at £50		2,500,000
Large user discount		
100,000 amplifiers at (10% of £20 = £2)		200,000
Increase in revenue		2,700,000

Cost of additional production:	£	£
Direct materials (£20 less 10%)	18	
Direct labour (£5 + 20%)	6	
Variable overhead	2	
	26 × 50,000	1,300,000
Additional fixed overhead		550,000
Increase in costs		1,850,000
Profit from additional production		850,000

(ii)   Additional fixed overhead of second shift   550,000

Unit contribution of second shift production
£50 – £(20* + 6 + 2)   22

Minimum annual increase in production to justify the addition of the second shift:

$$\frac{£550,000}{£22} = 25,000 \text{ amplifiers}$$

*(**Note:** Since additional profit is made when production is increased by 50,000, it follows that the breakeven additional production is less than 50,000; ie. less than the quantity which necessitates the purchase of materials at a level which qualifies for the 'larger user' discount.)

(b)   Other matters which should receive attention include:

(i)   confidence in marketing manager's forecast;

(ii)   availability of materials, personnel, plant, space for production, and storage; and

(iii)   availability of the necessary additional capital to finance stock holdings and facilities. The cost of that capital would have to be taken into account and this would involve calculating the marginal rate of return on that capital.

SESSION 14

1   Clarke Ltd

(a) $\text{ROCE} = \dfrac{E - D}{I} \times 100$

where:	E	=	Earnings $1/5 \times £130,000$	=	£26,000
	D	=	Depreciation $1/5 \times £100,000$	=	£20,000
	I	=	Investment	=	£120,000

$$\text{ROCE} = \frac{26 - 20}{120} \times 100 = 5\%$$

(b)   £120,000 recouped after 4 years

P = 4 years

2   Loamshire County Council

	Discounted cash flows @ 10%	
	Project A £	Project B £
Initial Outlay	−75,000	−100,000
Annual cash savings		
1st year	+18,182	+27,273
2nd year	+24,792	+37,188
3rd year	+22,539	+33,808
4th year	+17,075	+27,320
5th year	+12,418	–
	+20,006	+25,589

Key points in the report: Project B recommended (higher discounted cashflow). Payback is a cruder method of allowing for future cashflows. No account taken of flows after the payback period and equal weight given to flows within the payback period.

3   Transport Co

To: General Manager
From: Assistant management accountant
Date: Monday 13 June 19X4

Report on proposal to purchase vehicle cleansing machine

(a)   *The results of the investment appraisal*

I have carried out an appraisal of this proposal using the net present value method and the payback method. The results of my calculations are shown in the Appendix.

The cashflows from the project are forecast to pay back the initial outlay in approximately 2.7 years, which is a long payback period for a project with a life of only four years.

However, the project generates a positive net present value of £12,018. This means that the wealth of the company would be increased by this amount if the project is undertaken (ignoring risk and inflation).

(b)   *A recommendation concerning the proposal*

Since the proposal is forecast to result in a positive net present value, I recommend that it should be accepted.

If I can be of any further assistance in this matter, please do not hesitate to contact me.

Appendix: Appraisal calculations

The net present value of the cashflows from the project

Year	Initial purchase £	Operating costs £	Labour savings £	Other contn. £	Total cashflow £	Discount factor £	Present value £
0	(80,000)				(80,000)	1.0000	(80,000)
1		(8,000)	25,000	12,600	29,600	0.9091	26,909
2		(8,400)	25,000	12,600	29,200	0.8264	24,131
3		(8,820)	25,000	12,600	28,780	0.7513	21,622
4		(9,261)	25,000	12,600	28,339	0.6830	19,356
Net present value							12,018

Payback period

Year	Cumulative cashflow £
0	(80,000)
1	(50,400)
2	(21,200)
3	7,580

Payback period = 2 years + (21,200/28,780) = 2.7 years approx., assuming even cashflows.

4 Printing Co

(a) Initial cash outflow:

	£
Penalty payment	4,000
Machines purchased	12,400
	16,400

Annual net cash inflow:

	£
Annual saving	33,000
Operating costs	(27,200)
Net incremental income (£1,600 × 70%)	1,120
	6,920

Net present value:

		£
Present value of cash inflows for our years:		
£6,920 × 3.04		21,037
Initial outflow		16,400
		———
Net present value		4,637
		———

(b)   Payback period $\dfrac{£16,400}{£6,920}$ = 2.4 years, assuming even cashflows

The advantages of the payback method include the following:

(1)   It is simple to calculate and understand.

(2)   It helps to preserve an organisation's liquidity, by focusing on early cashflows.

(3)   It helps to reduce risk, since it places less emphasis on later cashflows, which can be difficult to forecast with any certainty.

The disadvantages include the following:

(1)   It ignores cashflows after the payback period. These may be substantial and potentially large profits may be forgone.

(2)   It does not help to distinguish between proposals which have the same or similar payback periods.

(3)   It does not quantify the time value of money, ie. the fact that cash received earlier can be reinvested by the organisation.

5   Duggan Ltd

(a)   (i)

		Project A		*Project B*	
Year	*7% factor*	*Cashflow*	*Present value*	*Cashflow*	*Present value*
		£	£	£	£
0	1	(2,210,000)	(2,210,000)	(2,210,000)	(2,210,000)
1	1/1.07	1,000,000	934,579	545,750	510,047
2	1/1.07^2	1,000,000	873,439	1,000,000	873,439
3	1/107^3	1,000,000	816,298	1,552,029	1,266,918
			———		———
Net present values			414,316		440,404
			———		———

On the above calculations, one would select project B.

(ii)   *Project A:* Cum factor at IRR = 2.21; IRR = 17%

       Project B

Year	Cashflow £	15% factor	Present value £	16% factor	Present value £
0	(2,210,000)	1	(2,210,000)	1	(2,210,000)
1	545,750	$\dfrac{1}{1.15}$	474,565	$\dfrac{1}{1.16}$	470,474
2	1,000,000	$\dfrac{1}{1.15^2}$	756,144	$\dfrac{1}{1.16^2}$	743,163
3	1,552,029	$\dfrac{1}{1.15^3}$	1,020,484	$\dfrac{1}{1.16^3}$	994,319
			41,193		(2,044)

    IRR = between 15% and 16%

    On the above calculations, one would select project A.

(b)   The results in part (a) appear to be in conflict with each other. However, where there is no capital rationing, the net present value approach should be used to choose between projects and thus project B should be undertaken in preference to A. This assumes that they are mutually exclusive; otherwise, both should be accepted, as both have a positive NPV at the cost of capital.

    The IRR simply shows the cost of capital at which each project will show a zero NPV. The fact that project B has a higher NPV than A at 7%, but a lower IRR indicates that it is more sensitive to increases in the discount rate; that is, its NPV will fall at a faster rate. This is not relevant when choosing between projects at a specified rate.

SESSION 15

1   Currie Ltd

Cost of capital   = 15.5%
Revenue: Inflation rate   =   5%   Effective discount rate = 10%
Costs: Inflation rate   = 10%   Effective discount rate = 5%

(a)

Year		Current cash £	Effective discount factor 5% or 10%	Present value £
0	Investment	(200,000)	1	(200,000)
1	Investment	(200,000)	$\dfrac{1}{1.155}$	(173,160)
1–11	Revenue	450,000	6.495	2,922,750
1–11	Costs	(300,000)	8.306	(2,491,800)
				57,790

In view of the above positive net present value, the project should be accepted.

(b)   *In the final year*

Revenue   = £450,000 × 1.05^{11} = £450,000 × $\dfrac{1}{0.584679}$

Costs   = £300,000 × 1.10^{11} = £300,000 × $\dfrac{1}{0.350494}$

Contribution = £769,653 – £855,935 = £(86,282)

In the final year, the project is producing a loss.

(c)   In the light of the calculation in (b) above, it would clearly be advantageous to terminate the project early. Just reducing the life by one year would increase the project's NPV by

$$\dfrac{£86,282}{1.155^{11}} = £17,681$$

Tabulating annual revenue and costs:

Year	5% Discount factor (a)	10% Discount factor (b)	Actual revenue 450 ÷ a £'000	Actual costs 300 ÷ b £'000
10	0.614	0.386	733	777
9	0.645	0.424	698	708
8	0.677	0.467	665	642

Beyond eight years, the differential inflation rates act to produce greater annual costs than revenue. The project should therefore be terminated after the eighth year.

2   Dumnonii

Labour savings are £2 per 1,000 bottles. Other savings are also £2 per 1,000 bottles.

With an annual production of 1.2 million bottles:

Labour savings per annum = £2,400
Other savings per annum   = £2,400

	Time	Cashflow £	5% factor	8% factor	13.4% factor	Present value £
Capital	0	(50,000)	–	–	1	(50,000)
Capital	1	(25,000)	–	–	0.88	(22,000)
Labour	1–∞	2,400	$\dfrac{1}{0.05}$	–	–	48,000
Others	1–∞	2,400	–	$\dfrac{1}{0.08}$	–	30,000
Labour	1	(2,400)	0.95	–	–	(2,280)
Others	1	(2,400)	–	0.93	–	(2,232)
Net present value						1,488

3   Licensing Ltd

(a)   *NPV calculations at 30,000 units per annum*

Time	0 £	1 £	2 £	3 £	4 £	5 £
Plant	(60,000)					
Working capital	(15,000)					
Net income (W2)		45,000	45,000	45,000	45,000	
Tax on income			(15,750)	(15,750)	(15,750)	(15,750)
Capital allowances (W1)		5,250	3,938	2,953	2,215	3,144
Scrap proceeds					10,000	
Working capital					15,000	
Net cashflow	(75,000)	50,250	33,188	32,203	56,465	(12,606)
Discount factor @ 10%	1	0.91	0.83	0.75	0.68	0.62
Present value	(75,000)	45,728	27,546	24,152	38,396	(7,816)

Net present value = £53,006

Conclusion

With sales volume of 30,000 units per annum and working capital of £15,000 at time 0, the project has a positive NPV irrespective of whether working capital can be recovered or not.

(The NPV of the working capital being £15,000 × 0.68 = £10,200)

(b)   *NPV calculations at 20,000 units per annum*

Time	0	1	2	3	4	5
	£	£	£	£	£	£
Plant	(60,000)					
Working capital	(12,000)					
Net income (W3)		15,000	15,000	15,000	15,000	
Tax on income			(5,250)	(5,250)	(5,250)	(5,250)
Capital allowances (W1)		5,250	3,938	2,953	2,215	3,144
Scrap proceeds					10,000	
Working capital					12,000	
Net cashflow	(72,000)	20,250	13,688	12,703	33,965	(2,106)
Discount factor @ 10%	1	0.91	0.83	0.75	0.68	0.62
Present value	(72,000)	18,428	11,361	9,527	23,096	(1,306)

Net present value = £(10,894)

Conclusion

Under the revised conditions, the project has a negative net present value and so should be rejected.

Workings

(1) Capital allowances

Time		£		Cash saved £	Time
0	Cost	60,000			
	WDA (25%)	15,000	× 35%	5,250	1
		45,000			
1	WDA (25%)	11,250	× 35%	3,938	2
		33,750			
2	WDA (25%)	8,438	× 35%	2,953	3
		25,312			
3	WDA (25%)	6,328	× 35%	2,215	4
		18,984			
4	Sale proceeds	(10,000)			
	Balancing allowance	8,984	× 35%	3,144	5

(2) Net income at 30,000 units per annum

		£
Revenue	= 30,000 × 6	180,000
Variable costs	= 30,000 × 3	(90,000)
Fixed costs	= (50,000 – 5,000)	(45,000)
Net annual income		45,000

(3) Net income at 20,000 units per annum

		£
Revenue	= 20,000 × 6	120,000
Variable costs	= 20,000 × 3	(60,000)
Fixed costs	= 50,000 – 5,000	(45,000)
Net annual income		15,000

Practice Central Assessment 1: Units 11 and 12

Time allowed – **3 hours**

This practice central assessment tests topics from Units 11 and 12. It consists of four sections; you should complete all tasks in each section.

SECTION 1

Data

You are the assistant management accountant for Trendy Products Ltd. The company operates with three production departments, each of which is, for costing purposes, regarded as a cost centre. For the four-week period ended 31 December 19X4, production overhead was as follows:

		£
Building services:	rates and insurance	840
	building depreciation	180
	electric light	360
	building repairs	450
	heating	900
Equipment services:	electric power	840
	depreciation on plant	210
	plant repairs	670
Production services:	supervision salaries	3,600
Material services:	central stores	720
	stock insurance	90
Personnel services:	salaries	756
	canteen	480
	welfare	480
	employers' liability insurance	72
		10,648

Other information for the same period is:

	Dept A	Dept B	Dept C	Total
Total wages	£3,000	£6,000	£3,000	£12,000
Number of personnel	60	90	30	180
Floor area (square metres)	6,000	12,000	9,000	27,000
Cubic capacity (cubic metres)	90,000	120,000	150,000	360,000
Plant written-down value	£12,000	£6,000	£24,000	£42,000
Average stock held	£9,000	£6,000	£3,000	£18,000
Material consumed	£15,000	£3,000	£6,000	£24,000
Total horsepower of plant	12	15	3	30

Plant depreciation is calculated on the reducing balance method.

Rates and insurance includes the appropriate charge for a special risk in Dept B, where the annual premium is £3,900.

Canteen includes £120 being the cost of the separate canteen operated by Dept C.

Plant repairs includes £40 for special plant repairs applicable to Dept A.

TASK 1

(a)   Using the above information, prepare a cost allocation statement for the period, allocating the costs over the three departments and stating the basis of allocation.

(b)   Discuss the validity of the arguments which support the view that the costs of service departments in a firm should be charged eventually to the production departments which use the services.

TASK 2

Your managing director has asked you for information on three management accounting analysis techniques:

(1)   value analysis;
(2)   SWOT (strengths, weaknesses, opportunities, threats) analysis;
(3)   time series analysis.

Write short notes for the benefit of the managing director, explaining the following for each of the three techniques:

(a)   what the technique is;
(b)   a situation in which the technique can be used.

SECTION 2

Data

NC Ltd uses flexible budgets and standard costing for its single product P which it makes and sells.

Three kg of material, having a standard cost of £4.40 per kg, are required for each unit of P. Actual material purchased and used in April cost £336,000 with the actual purchase price being £4.20 per kg. Each unit of P requires 30 minutes of direct labour time and the standard wages rate per hour is £5. The actual wages rate in April was £5.40 per hour. Sufficient direct labour time was utilised to produce 28,000 units of P, although actual production in April was 25,000 units.

The company has a normal operating capacity of 15,000 hours per month and flexible overhead budgets are:

Hours of operation	12,500	14,000	15,000
	£	£	£
Variable production overhead	150,000	168,000	180,000
Fixed production overhead	270,000	270,000	270,000
	420,000	438,000	450,000

Actual overhead incurred in April was £430,000 of which £270,000 was fixed.

TASK 1

(a)   **Calculate the appropriate variances for material, labour and overhead.**

(b)   **Show the variances in a statement suitable for presentation to management, reconciling the standard cost with the actual cost of production.**

TASK 2

The managing director of NC Ltd has received a copy of your variance analysis statement and is not convinced of its value to management.

As assistant accountant, you are required to produce a memo to the managing director, in which you discuss the ways in which variance analysis helps management to control a business.

SECTION 3

Data

One of your organisation's subsidiaries produces a single product and uses flexible budgets to control expenditure. The following forecasts have been prepared for the production costs to be incurred at the highest and lowest activity levels likely to be experienced in any particular period.

	Production level 5,000 units £	15,000 units £
Direct material	25,000	75,000
Direct labour	10,000	30,000
Indirect material	8,000	18,000
Indirect labour	12,000	22,000
Machine rental	4,000	8,000
Rent, rates, etc.	6,000	6,000

Indirect labour costs are fixed for activity levels up to and including 10,000 units. For all units produced in excess of 10,000 per period, a bonus payment of £2 per unit is paid, in addition to the fixed costs.

All other variable costs and the variable part of semi-variable costs follow constant linear patterns.

Machine rental costs are stepped fixed costs. For activity levels up to and including 12,000 units, one machine is needed at a rental cost of £4,000 per period. Above 12,000 units, two machines are needed.

TASK 1

Prepare a set of flexible budgets which show the production cost allowances for the period for the following activity levels:

5,000 units; 10,000 units; 12,000 units; 15,000 units

TASK 2

During the latest period ended 30 November, the company was operating at full capacity in order to build up stocks in anticipation of a sales drive. The actual costs incurred were as follows.

Production output   15,000 units

Production costs incurred:

	£
Direct material	69,400
Direct labour	37,700
Indirect material	18,250
Indirect labour	28,780
Machine rental	8,000
Rent, rates, etc.	5,800

Present this data as a budgetary control statement for the period. Beneath your statement, write brief notes commenting on the significant variances, suggesting what further management action might be necessary.

SECTION 4

Data

You are employed by a medium-sized London-based company in the construction industry which builds low cost houses for sale mainly to 'first time buyers'. The business has been suffering badly during the recession and the Directors of the company are very anxious about future trends in the industry. They have asked you to collect as much relevant information as you can from published statistics and other sources as a first step towards undertaking an appraisal of the company's 'external environment'. So far, you have been able to locate the following:

– Official statistics relating to employment, unemployment and labour rates.

– Information on 'new housing starts'

– Retail and wholesale price indices

– Information published by building societies on the price of houses of different types in different parts of the country and the value of mortgages granted

– Population statistics

– Figures of average costs of firms in the industry published by the trade association

– Special surveys of the industry in the financial press

TASK 1

Write a report to the managing director explaining how information from **any four** of these sources might be of value in assessing future trends for the company. Remember that you need to bear in mind the particular situation of the company when analysing the detailed information. Comment on the relevance, reliability and timeliness of the information.

TASK 2

The managing director has been reading a statistical report on general trends in the construction industry published **by** the trade association. He has highlighted certain phrases in the report as follows:

'It is difficult to <u>extrapolate</u> a trend line because the industry is subject to pronounced <u>cyclical fluctuations</u>.............. The wide <u>seasonal variations</u> which are experienced in the industry can be eliminated by using <u>moving averages</u>....... Experience has shown that expenditure on capital equipment by the industry is a fairly weak <u>leading indicator</u> for trends in the industry as a whole.'

Briefly explain each of the highlighted phrases in non-technical language.

Practice Central Assessment 2: Unit 13

Time allowed – **2 hours**

This practice central assessment tests topics from Units 13. It consists of three sections; you should complete all tasks in each section.

SECTION 1

Data

You work as the assistant management accountant for Jets Ltd, a company which specialises in warehousing and packing other companies' goods on a contract basis.

Your company has been approached by Sykes Ltd, who have offered Jets Ltd the contract to pack their product. Sykes will deliver the unpacked units and will collect the packed product on a regular basis. There will be no need to provide warehousing facilities.

You have carried out some preliminary costings and the results of your investigations are as follows:

Sykes contract

Estimated number of units to be packed each week = 200
Contract price per unit packed = £27

Cost to be incurred at this activity level:

Packing materials	£15 per unit packed
Packing labour	Salaries: £568 per week Bonuses: £0.80 per unit packed
Loading labour	Salaries: £350 per week Bonuses: £0.50 per unit loaded
Hire of packing machine	£100 per week
Administration and other costs	£480 per week

Assume that all units packed are loaded in the same week.

The costs stated above relate solely to this contract. For example, the labour will be employed full-time on this contract work.

TASK 1

Prepare a cost and profit statement for one week of this contract, which shows the following:

(a)   variable costs in total and per unit;
(b)   fixed costs in total and per unit;
(c)   profit in total and per unit.

TASK 2

(a)   Calculate the following for the contract:

(i)   the break-even point in units per week;
(ii)   the margin of safety for an activity level of 200 units per week;
(iii)   the profit which would be earned if activity increased by 20% to 240 units per week.

(b)   Prepare a memorandum to the managing director which contains the following:

(i)   brief comments on the forecast results for this contract;

(ii)   an explanation of the problems involved in using the data supplied to forecast the profit result for an activity level of 240 units per week.

SECTION 2

Data

You are the assistant accountant of PC Ltd which manufactures two products.

At a recent conference 'Cost Control in a Period of Reduction in Demand', your managing director was impressed by the remarks of one of the speakers who advocated a marginal costing system of management reporting.

The managing director has now asked you to compare the present absorption costing system with an alternative marginal costing system.

You have obtained the following information:

	Product A £	Product B £
Direct materials		
Units required	20	5
Price per unit	£0.50	£1.00
Direct labour		
Hours allowed	5	10
Rate per hour	£2.00	£1.50

Budgeted data for the year is as follows:

Direct labour hours	55,000
Production overhead	£220,000

	Product A	Product B
Sales in £'000	375	300
Profit as a percentage of selling price	20%	10%

Overhead absorption:

Production overhead is absorbed by a direct labour hour rate.

Administration overhead is absorbed on a basis of 20% of production cost.

Selling and distribution overhead is absorbed on a basis of 30% of production cost.

For the purpose of this presentation it has been decided that in order to facilitate the preparation of the marginal cost statement, it can be assumed that, using the overhead absorption cost per unit as a base, 20% of the production overhead can be regarded as variable and 33% of the selling and distribution overhead can be regarded as variable.

TASK 1

(a)   Set out the merits of:

     (i)   a marginal costing system; and
     (ii)   an absorption costing system.

(b)   Prepare for presentation to your board of directors two statements showing the budgeted results for the year in:

     (i)   an absorption costing form;
     (ii)   a marginal costing form.

TASK 2

Present ratios with each statement to show the relative profitability of each product and comment briefly on these ratios.

SECTION 3

Data

Your organisation has made widgets for many years. It is now considering a new product, the wotsit. The following information is available:

(1)   Wotsits would be made on a new machine, to be bought on hire purchase. Under the hire purchase agreement, a deposit of £10,000 would be paid on delivery of the machine, and six annual instalments of £15,000 would be paid, starting one year after payment of the deposit.

(2)   The company's current annual fixed costs are £80,000. If both widgets and wotsits were produced, this would rise to £180,000, but it would revert to £80,000 when production of wotsits ceased.

(3)   Each wotsit would sell for £2 and 500,000 wotsits could be sold in each of the first three years, but after that 700,000 wotsits could be sold each year.

(4)   The government wishes to encourage production of wotsits, and will pay a subsidy of 10% of gross sales revenue, payment to be made every three years in arrears.

(5)   The normal variable cost of production of wotsits is £1.20 per wotsit, including 50p for materials. However, materials for producing the first 500,000 wotsits have already been bought, at a cost of £200,000. If not used to produce wotsits, these materials could be sold immediately for £210,000.

(6)   The market rate of interest is 8% and all cash flows accruing over a year are deemed to arise at the end of that year.

(7)   The directors are concerned that a general election, due four years from now, might be followed by the abolition of government subsidies (so that none would be received after the third year of production).

TASK 1

Calculate the net present value of the cash flows from the production of wotsits for six years using an 8% discount rate.

Note: The present value of £1 at a discount rate of 8% is as follows:

Number of years from the present	£
1	0.926
2	0.857
3	0.794
4	0.735
5	0.681
6	0.630

TASK 2

Write a report to the directors on the production of wotsits, including:

(a)   a recommendation for action, based upon your calculations in Task 1;

(b)   a non-technical explanation of net present value computations;

(c)   a comment upon the effect of your evaluation of each of the following circumstances (considered independently):

      (i)   the general election

      (ii)   the government deciding to impose a fixed annual levy of £5,000 on all companies, starting immediately.

Index

Publications Questionnaire

At Financial Training we are interested in knowing your views of our products. We would appreciate your assistance in helping us to maintain our high standards by completing this simple questionnaire.

1   Title of publication _____

2   Content

For each question, tick the box which most closely reflects your view.

	Excellent	Good	Satisfactory	Poor
Did the content cover the syllabus thoroughly?	☐	☐	☐	☐
Was the writing style clear and easy to understand?	☐	☐	☐	☐
Were the worked examples useful and relevant?	☐	☐	☐	☐
Were there sufficient diagrams, graphs and tables?	☐	☐	☐	☐
Were the exam style questions beneficial?	☐	☐	☐	☐
Were the answers to questions comprehensive?	☐	☐	☐	☐
Were the style and layout clear?	☐	☐	☐	☐

3   General

Please suggest any improvements that you feel would be beneficial:

_____

_____

_____

Have you noticed any errors in this publication? If so, please specify:

Page   **Error**

_____   _____

_____   _____

_____   _____

4   Further Information

If you would like to receive information on other Financial Training products and courses, please supply your name and address:

_____

_____

Thank you for your co-operation.

Please return your completed questionnaire to: AAT Department
Financial Training
10-14 White Lion Street, London N1 9PE